AFTER MUSSOLINI

Praise for the Italian edition, *Ritrovare se stessi. Gli ebrei nell'Italia postfascista*:

Schwarz's book offers a rich set of suggestions and new insight, combining new research on some key issues (particularly on the politics of memory implemented by the Italian-Jewish leadership and the difficult transition from Fascism to the Republic) to the reconstruction of a complex historiographic debate, of which we had until now only a partial understanding.

Bruno Maida (University of Turin), in *Il Mestiere di Storico. Annale della Società Italiana per lo Studio della Storia Contemporanea*', 2005

With a patient weaving of archival sources, extracts from the press and the memoirs, Guri Schwarz traces the 'internal war' that shook the Jewish minority since 1945. [This book] is a chronicle of the doubts and disappointments, but also the pragmatic choices that allowed the Italian Jews to overcome this new and terrible ford in their history. From racial persecution, the Jews came prostrate. It was a physical devastation, and a fracture in the sense of identity. According to Schwarz, the representative communities, and the Jews who had a public voice, chose the path of reconciliation. The guilt for the persecution was blamed almost exclusively on the Germans, while for Italians the focus was on remembering solidarity and not anti-Semitism ... Thus began, even on the Jewish side, the development of the myth of the 'good Italian', which for decades has clouded a true historical recollection of what had happened.

Giulio Busi (Freie Universitaet of Berlin), in *Il Sole 24 Ore*, 24 October 2004

About memory as consciousness of our present, here is the beautiful book by Guri Schwarz, a young scholar at the University of Pisa ... It is a study of the Italian Jewish Community in the aftermath of the Holocaust, which represents a valuable contribution to the rediscovery of the 'real' Jews, not always convergent to the images that are widespread in the public opinion. Schwarz tells us how in our country the Fascist persecution of Italian Jews – now just little more than thirty thousand souls – did not lead to the radical abandonment of the identity models that emerged with the *Risorgimento* and emancipation. In other words, after the horrific Nazi-Fascist storm, the community turned back on the footsteps of the path of integration with an ever stronger confidence in the future, although most troubled by the recent past. With two points of reference: the State of Israel, which has reshaped the mental and emotional landscape of Judaism, and the memory of the past to be seen both as an identity marker and bridge for a possible dialogue with others.

Elena Lowenthal, in *La Stampa*, 27 November 2004

AFTER MUSSOLINI

Jewish Life and Jewish Memories in Post-Fascist Italy

Guri Schwarz

Translated from Italian by
Giovanni Noor Mazhar

VALLENTINE MITCHELL
LONDON • CHICAGO

First published in paper in 2021 by Vallentine Mitchell

Catalyst House
720 Centennial Court, Centennial Park
Elstree WD6 3SY, UK

814 N. Franklin Street
Chicago
IL 60610 USA

www.vmbooks.com

Originally published in Italian by Gius. Laterza & Figli as
Ritrovare se stessi. Gli ebrei nell'Italia postfascista

First published in cloth in 2012

British Library Cataloguing in Publication Data
An entry can be found on request

ISBN 978 0 85303 855 9 (cloth)
ISBN 978 1 912676 90 3 (paper)

Library of Congress Cataloging-in-Publication Data
An entry can be found on request

Contents

Preface to the English Edition

In 1922, in a Vienna where anti-Jewish sentiments were intense and exploited by various political movements, the Austrian-Jewish writer Hugo Bettauer provocatively chose to publish a short novel representing the expulsion of the Jews from the city. With a vivacious and bitterly ironic style he describes the ejection and its consequences: the sciences and the arts withered, trade and commerce shrank to unseen lows, and even parties and mundane life appeared gloomy and deprived of the joyfulness of earlier times. The emptied capital city had lost its soul. Thus, in his fictitious narration, its citizens soon realized the mistake they had made and determined to call back the Jews, merrily celebrating their return with a grandiose salutation.[1] As we know, not many years later Bettauer's amusing satire was turned into a much darker and more tragic reality.

Once the Second World War was over, the surviving remnant of European Jewry attempting to return to their homes wasn't of course greeted with an affectionate embrace, as in Bettauer's fiction. To comprehend the post-war situation, we must remember that the anti-Jewish sentiments that had offered fertile ground for racial persecutions could not disappear all of a sudden. Furthermore the economic situation was dire all over the continent, and everywhere intense political struggles characterized the post-war situation. All Europeans were, in different ways, survivors. Traumatized by the war, divided by ideological and political clashes, all had dramatic issues to elaborate, and there was little or no sensibility for the specific Jewish plight.

While more research is still to be done, it must be noted that in recent years the history of European Jewry in the aftermath of racial persecutions has been the object of several studies. The post-war situation has been studied – with a main focus on the German case – from various perspectives, ranging from the persistence of anti-Semitism, to the economic consequences and the problems connected to restitutions and reparations, the issues of memory, the new distribution of Jewish presences across the continent, the life in Displaced Persons' Camps, the migrations to Palestine and later the State of Israel, the reorganization of community life.[2] The aim of this book is to offer a reconstruction of the consequences of fascist anti-Semitic policies, analysing the rebirth of Jewish life in post-war Italy, concentrating on the process of social and cultural reintegration, the reorganization of community life, as well as the transformations of the minority's identity.

Since 1945, in Italy as elsewhere in the West, the small Jewish minority has played the delicate role of cultural intermediary both as regards the memory of the Shoah and the Middle Eastern conflict, a role which has partly been imposed by events and the post-war cultural climate, and which, to a certain extent, individual Jews and Jewish institutions have voluntarily taken up. Certainly, Judaism, Jewish culture and life, cannot only be confined to remembrance of Nazi mass murders or to the relationship, which in any case can vary greatly, with the Zionist dream and its realization. Nevertheless – in an extensively secularized society, which has lost touch with traditional culture – these are undoubtedly two of the most visible and prominent aspects in which contemporary Jewish identity publicly manifests itself. Therefore, piecing together the history of the Jews in Republican Italy requires a reconstruction of the processes that have led to the assigning of that role of testimony and mediation, as well as considering the meaning and repercussions of that historical process.

While taking into account this range of questions and problems, this work is not, however, restricted to examining the role of the Jew in the post-1945 Italian collective imagination. In fact, I felt that it was appropriate to contribute to a rediscovery of the *real Jews*, and thus did not limit this study to the analysis of the role and nature of the *imaginary Jew*. I therefore chose to carry out the research from an internal vantage point, aiming first of all at portraying the dynamics of the Italian-Jewish community itself rather than dealing with the attitudes of friendship, hostility or indifference of the surrounding world. It is however implicit that there is no intention of isolating the Jewish community from the wider context; the interest in studying the Jews in the post-war period also arises from the fact that it offers a particular point of view from which to interpret the Italian Republic's social, cultural and political history. A reflection on the Jewish condition in post-fascist Italy touches, in particular, on the problem of the continuity between Fascism and the post-war period, as it entails evaluating the long-term effects of the racial persecution. Perhaps it is only in considering the post-1945 events that it is possible to understand fully the vast range of social, cultural and psychological changes triggered by the racist policies. Recognizing this can help to overcome the temptation – which emerges periodically – of minimizing the relevance and the impact of those events.

Traditionally, fascist anti-Semitism has not merited much consideration in either the Italian or foreign historiography. Italy is often described as an exceptional nation, virtually free of the modern anti-Jewish hatred that thrived on the rest of the continent. The Italian debate on the subject was quite limited until the end of the 1980s. After the important pioneering research of Meir Michaelis and Renzo De Felice, who demonstrated definitively that Fascist racist policies were not imposed by Hitler on Mussolini, a general stagnation persisted for several years in this field of study.[3] However, those two very important works did not deal with several salient questions: what were the cultural roots of Mussolini's racist shift? How autonomous were the fascist racial ideology and practice in Italy? How were the racist laws implemented? What long-term effect did they have on Italian society (and on the local Jews in particular)? Such crucial questions were set aside for a long time, as the consensus was that the racist policies in the country had little or no roots and had been implemented with a certain degree of mildness.

Since the fiftieth anniversary of the Fascist regime's racist twist, which was marked in 1988, a new period of systematic in-depth research and lively debate unfolded in Italy. New scholarly works soon set out to re-examine the traditional interpretations: the cultural origins of the phenomenon were actually revealed to be deeply rooted in Italian culture; and the implementation of the racist laws was shown to be both systematic and merciless. While fascist anti-Semitism did not lead to exterminationist policies, it was the fruit of the peculiar Italian cultural development since the late nineteenth century. Therefore, it must be read considering its autonomous and peculiar history, and not merely in comparison to Nazi ideology.[4]

These steps forward soon raised a new problem: if we accept the results of recent research, then how is it possible that a set of representations tending to absolve Italian culture took form and gained a practically hegemonic grasp on post-fascist public opinion? Such a collective absolution was directly connected and intertwined with the formation of the anti-fascist national identity that was nurtured after the war, becoming one of the foundations of the Italian Republic. The 'myth of the good Italian',[5] as this self-representation was defined, has marked for decades the way Italians perceived themselves, easily obscuring the many atrocities committed during the fascist regime and the war years (from the civilian massacres in the Balkans and in Greece, to the use of nerve gas in Ethiopia, up to the anti-Semitic campaign).

I believe that the study of post-war Italian Jewry is of fundamental importance to fully grasp how such a myth came to be, and how it rapidly gained consensus both in Italy and abroad. In fact we can assert that without the support of Italian-Jewish intellectuals and institutions, such a simplistic depiction of fascist racism, its origins and consequences, could not have imposed itself so strongly on public opinion as well as on the scholarly community. This work will illustrate how Italian-Jewish institutions, as well as single individuals, contributed to create and legitimate that cultural representation, offering insight on its function within the framework of the minority's processes of socio-cultural reintegration.

The limited amount of scholarship available and the extreme dispersion of the documentary material, stored in several Italian archives (often awaiting appropriate cataloguing), but also in Israel and the United States, do not, today, permit the drawing up of a complete, systematic and exhaustive account of all aspects of Jewish life in post-fascist Italy. What is here proposed is, rather, an initial analysis of some crucial, problematic points, which could shed a critical light on issues that – as we shall see – were closely related: the reorganization of the Italian-Jewish community, the remembrance of the Shoah, the relationship with Zionism and the State of Israel.

The account which follows tackles these problems starting from research on archive sources and printed matter, which systematically covered the period 1943–61 (from the arrival of the Allied armies in Italy to the trial of Eichmann); due to the inaccessibility of consistent documentary material, only brief mention is made of the subsequent period, without claiming to provide a thorough treatment. Considerable space and attention have been dedicated to the delicate transitional period of 1943–48, because of the significance of the political and cultural processes which, having emerged clearly in that first phase, have had a lasting effect on the development of Jewish life in Republican Italy.

The book is divided into two parts: the first part elucidates the changes in the organization of the life of the community and the structuring of the minority's collective identity, while the second part is concerned with the Jewish memory of the fascist persecution, its relationship with the general cultural climate and its influence on the development of the memory of the persecution and of the early historiography.

Finally, I feel that I should point out that the nature of the available documentation has led me to favour an institutional perspective, paying attention to the life of the community as it emerges from the documents of organizations and associations or from reports of the Jewish press. This does not mean that I am not fully cognisant of how Jewish life, in Italy as elsewhere, unfolds, more often than not, far from or in fact outside the institutional framework: there are many ways of being and of feeling Jewish. This issue is undoubtedly of very great interest for the historian and, however difficult it may be to grasp what is firmly enclosed in people's hearts, I have tried to confront with this delicate question, turning to literary sources and memoirs in undertaking the exploration of those 'mental nebulae'[6] which constitute the individual and collective identity of Italian Jews.

As a last remark I wish to clarify that the present English language edition is a revised version of the earlier Italian publication. While the overall structure and the main thesis of the book have not changed, I have made some modifications to the text, and particularly enriched the endnotes and bibliography, in order to take into due account the scholarly works that have appeared in the eight years that passed since this work was first published.

NOTES

1. H. Bettauer, *The City without Jews* (New York: Bloch Publishing Company, 1926 [1922]).
2. Among the few attempts at a comparative, Continent-wide analysis see: B. Wasserstein, *Vanishing Diaspora: The Jews in Europe since 1945* (Cambridge, MA: Harvard University Press, 1996); D. Bankier (ed.), *The Jews are Coming Back: The Return of the Jews to their Countries of Origin after*

WWII (New York and Jerusalem: Berghahn Books/Yad Vashem, 2005); L. Brazzo and G. Schwarz (eds), 'Jews in Europe after the Shoah: Studies and Research Perspectives', *Quest. Issues in Contemporary History*, 1 (April 2010), available at http://www.quest-cdecjournal.it/. Concerning the issue of property restitution in various countries, see M. Dean, C. Goshler and P. Ther (eds), *Robbery and Restitution: The Conflict over Jewish Property in Europe* (New York: Berghahn Books, 2007). As stated above, scholarly research on post-war European Jewery has concentrated mainly on the German case; a focal point attracting the attention of researchers has been the life of the survivors in the Displaced Persons' Camps. On this, see M. Meyers Feinstein, *Holocaust Survivors in Post-War Germany (1945–1957)*, (Cambridge: Cambridge University Press, 2009); Z.W. Mankowitz, *Life between Memory and Hope: The Survivors of the Holocaust in Occupied Germany* (Cambridge: Cambridge University Press, 2002); A. Königseder, J. Wetzel, *Waiting for Hope: Jewish Displaced Persons in Post-World War II Germany* (Evanston, IL: Northwestern University Press, 2001); A. Patt and M. Berkowitz (eds), *We Are Here: New Approaches to Jewish Displaced Persons in Post-War Germany* (Detroit, MI: Wayne State University Press, 2010); A. Grossmann, *Jews, German, Allies: Close Encounters in Occupied Germany* (Princeton, NJ: Princeton University Press, 2009); H. Lavsky, *New Beginnings: Holocaust Survivors in Bergen Belsen and the British Zone in Germany 1945–1950* (Detroit, MI: Wayne State University Press, 2002). For a wider approach and the study of the reconstruction of Jewish community life in post-war Germany, see instead: M. Brenner, *After the Holocaust: Rebuilding Jewish Lives in Post-War Germany* (Princeton, NJ: Princeton University Press, 1997 [1995]); Y.M. Bodeman (ed.), *Jews, Germans, Memory: The Reconstruction of Jewish Life in Germany* (Ann Arbor, MI: University of Michigan Press, 1996); E. Kolinsky, *After the Holocaust: Jewish Survivors in Germany after 1945* (London: Pimlico, 2004); J.H. Geller, *Jews in Post-Holocaust Germany 1945–1953* (Cambridge: Cambridge University Press, 2005); A.D. Kauders, *Unmögliche Heimat: Eine deutsch-jüdische Geschichte der Bundesrepublik* (Munich: Deutsche Verlags-Anstalt, 2007).

3. Meir Michaelis, *Mussolini and the Jews: German–Italian Relations and the Jewish Question in Italy, 1922–1945* (London: Clarendon Press, 1978); Renzo De Felice, *Gli ebrei in Italia sotto il fascismo* (Turin: Einaudi, 1961); revised editions appeared in 1974, 1988 and 1993; English edition: *The Jews in Fascist Italy: A History* (New York: Enigma Books, 2001).
4. Among the most relevant contributions that appeared in this new phase, see (for a general reconstruction of the phenomenon), M. Sarfatti, *Mussolini contro gli ebrei. Cronaca dell'elaborazione delle leggi razziali* (Turin: Zamorani, 1993); M. Sarfatti, *Gli ebrei nell'Italia fascista. Vicende, identità, persecuzione* (Turin: Einaudi, 2000); English edition: *The Jews in Mussolini's Italy: From Equality to Persecution* (Madison, WI: University of Wisconsin Press, 2006). See also M.-A. Matard-Bonucci, *L'Italia fascista e la persecuzione degli ebrei* (Bologna: Il Mulino, 2008). For the implementation of the racist norms, see: Fabio Levi (ed.), *L'ebreo in oggetto. L'applicazione della normativa antiebraica a Torino, 1938–1943* (Turin: Zamorani, 1991); Fabio Levi (ed.), *Le case e le cose. Persecuzione degli ebrei torinesi nelle carte dell'EGELI, 1938–1945* (Turin: Compagnia di San Paolo, 1998); Enzo Collotti (ed.), *Razza e fascism. La persecuzione contro gli ebrei in Toscana, 1938–1943* (Rome: Carocci, 1999), vol. I. For the impact on the cultural and academic world, see: Annalisa Capristo, *L'espulsione degli ebrei dalle accademie italiane* (Turin: Zamorani, 2002); Roberto Finzi, *Le leggi razziali e l'università italiana* (Rome: Editori Riuniti, 2003); Giorgio Fabre, *L'elenco. Censura fascista, editoria e autori ebrei* (Turin: Zamorani, 1998). For the origins and development of Italian racist theories: Roberto Maiocchi, *Scienza italiana e razzismo fascista* (Florence: La Nuova Italia, 1999); Roberto Maiocchi, *Scienza e fascismo* (Rome: Carocci, 2004); Giorgio Israel and Pietro Nastasi, *Scienza e razza nell'Italia fascista* (Bologna: Il Mulino, 1998); Anna Treves, *Le nascite e la politica nell'Italia del Novecento* (Milan: LED, 2001); F. Cassata, *Molti sani e forti. L'eugentica in Italia* (Turin: Bollati Boringhieri, 2006); A. Gillette, *Racial Theories in Fascist Italy* (London and New York: Routledge, 2002); C. Mantovani, *Rigenerare la società: L'eugenetica in Italia dalle origini ottocentesche agli anni Trenta* (Catanzaro: Rubettino, 2004); G. Israel, *Il fascismo e la razza. La scienza italiana e le politiche razziali del regime* (Bologna: Il Mulino, 2010).
5. D. Bidussa, *Il mito del bravo italiano* (Milan: Il Saggiatore, 1994).
6. J. Le Goff, 'Les mentalités. Une histoire ambiguë', in J. Le Goff and P. Nora (eds), *Faire de l'histoire* (Paris: Gallimard, 1974), vol. III, p.92.

Acknowledgements

This book has had a long incubation: the embryo of the project was conceived in 1995, thanks to Michele Luzzati, who directed me towards the conquest of a research area still, to a great extent, unexplored. I am glad to be able, here, to thank him for all his encouragement through the years.

In conducting my research, I have had the opportunity of meeting different researchers, to all of whom I would like to convey my sincere gratitude. I want to mention in particular Adrian Lyttelton, who especially enriched my first phase of study and reflection; David Bidussa, Simon Levis Sullam and Barbara Armani, whose willingness to discuss has been very important to me; Alberto Cavaglion, who read an earlier draft of this work and who helped me very much in reflecting on it and improving it; Michele Sarfatti, who has followed the development of this book and with whom, in the final years, I had an intense exchange of information and views, which has been of great benefit for this work.

David Cesarani's support has been of fundamental importance for the realization of this English edition of my research. I also wish to express my gratitude to the Fondazione Maimonide of Milan whose grant covered the expenses of the translation from the original Italian text into this revised English edition.

I am also grateful to the friends and colleagues of the History seminar of the Scuola Normale – Carlotta Ferrara degli Uberti, Ilaria Pavan and Marco Mondini – who, in various ways, participated in the slow gestation of this work.

I owe special thanks to Michele Battini, who has patiently and attentively followed my studies in these years and has kept a close eye on the drafting of this book. Without his encouragement this work would not have come into being.

Most of all I wish to thank my parents and my wife for their affectionate support during all these years.

As is customary, I take full responsibility for this text and any errors it may contain.

Guri Schwarz
Pisa, January 2012

Abbreviations

ACDEC	Archivio Centro di Documentazione Ebraica Contemporanea, Milano (Archives of the Center for Contemporary Jewish Documentation, Milan)
ACS	Archivio Centrale di Stato (Central State Archives)
AHJP	Archives for the History of the Jewish People, Jerusalem
ASMAE	Archivio Storico Ministero Affari Esteri (Foreign Ministry Historical Archives)
AUCII	Archivio Unione delle Comunità Israelitiche Italiane (Archives of the Union of Italian-Jewish Communities)
BARM	Biblioteca Archivio Renato Maestro, Venezia (Renato Maestro Library Archives, Venice)
BCIM	*Bollettino della Comunità Israelitica di Milano* (Bulletin of the Milan Jewish Community)
CZA	Central Zionist Archives, Jerusalem
DGPS	Direzione Generale Pubblica Sicurezza (General Direction Public Security)
FSI	Federazione Sionistica Italian (Italian Zionist Federation)
Min. Int.	Ministero degli Interni (Ministry of the Interior)
PCM	Presidenza del Consiglio dei Ministri (Presidency of the Council of Ministers)
RMI	*Rassegna Mensile di Israele* (*Israeli Monthly Review*)
UCII	Unione delle Comunità Israelitiche Italiane (Union of Italian-Jewish Communities)
Verb. Cons.	Verbali del Consiglio dell'Unione delle Comunità Israelitiche Italiane (Minutes of the Council of the Union of Italian-Jewish Communities)
Verb. Giunta	Verbali della Giunta dell'Unione delle Comunità Israelitiche Italiane (Minutes of the Committee of the Union of Italian-Jewish Communities)
WJC	World Jewish Congress
WZO	World Zionist Organization

Part 1

THE REORGANIZATION OF JEWISH LIFE

1

Echoes of the Catastrophe

NUMBERS

In order to reconstruct the history of the Jews in Italy after 1945, it is impossible not to take as a starting point the most dramatic and obvious consequences of the persecution. There were approximately 47,000 Jews in Italy before the persecution, while after 1945 there were fewer than 30,000 and the Jewish population in Republican Italy stabilized around this figure in the following decades. In just seven years, Italian Judaism lost 40 per cent of its members, but during and after the war it took in others, from abroad, 5,000 of whom would settle permanently in Italy. Such a transformation can be ascribed to a variety of causes; it is necessary to take into account about 4,000 abjurations, which occurred after 1938 and of which only a small number were retracted after the war, the emigration of about 11,000 foreign Jews and of almost 6,000 Italian Jews, as well as over 8,000 dead (both foreign and Italian Jews) due to the persecution and the war.[1]

These demographic changes led to an overall geographic redistribution of Italian Jewry. As a result of the persecution, the migration of the Jewish population from the villages and small cities to the major urban areas, already in force since the 1800s, gathered pace; while there were eighty-seven Jewish communities registered in Italy in 1840, after 1945 there were little more than twenty. The Jewish population gravitated more and more towards the main cities and so many of the smaller and peripheral communities, which had often been active centres of Italian-Jewish life, irremediably lost their vitality.[2] The larger communities grew and those which became the main centres, in terms of size and importance, were the one in Rome – which always remained the most numerous and the seat of the most important Jewish institutions – and that of Milan. A clear picture is supplied by the numbers given in the paper presented by the outgoing Council at the V Congress of the Union of the Italian Jewish Communities (June 1956): two communities exceeded 6,000 people (Rome and Milan), six had over 1,000 (Florence, Genoa, Livorno, Turin, Trieste, Venice), two had more than 500 (Naples and Pisa), nine had over 100 (Alessandria, Ancona, Bologna, Modena, Ferrara, Mantua, Padua, Vercelli, Verona) and finally there were four other communities with fewer than 100 people. A distressing scenario; only Rome (12,000) maintained levels similar to the pre-war ones and Milan grew slightly; in the following decades, the population of the former would increase above all due to natural growth, while the latter would increase very noticeably, in a short time, mainly thanks to its ability to attract Jewish groups arriving from abroad.[3]

These data constitute an indispensable starting point for this study, but of course the whole issue of the consequences of fascist racism cannot be reduced to a matter of numbers; in order to arrive at a full understanding of the phenomenon, apart from the most immediate and evident effects of the persecution, there are others which need to be considered. There were significant changes in the self-image of the persecuted which the above-mentioned data can sometimes suggest, but not fully explain. For the vast majority of Italian Jews fascist ostracism constituted a very deep trauma and the years following 1938 were exceptionally distressing, inasmuch as every decision heralded painful internal wounds. The tragedy is conveyed in all its intensity in the words of Renzo Segre:

> We were worn out, tired ever since 15 July 1938, when, for the first time, after a long, insidious campaign, we were officially told that we were no longer considered Italian citizens; since November when we were peremptorily sacked; worn out by our attempts to defend ourselves from all the injustices we had borne, almost daily, like an endless stream, for six years....
>
> We are dead inside. The terrible anguish we have suffered – and which still assails us when we think of our many dear ones whom we will certainly never see again – has changed us, to such an extent, physically and mentally, that it has made us different people.[4]

The campaign overturned the lives of thousands of citizens; even those who had escaped deportation and death suffered irreversible harm. When the war ended, still weighed down by suffering and sadness, the survivors had to face an uncertain course towards social, economic, civil reintegration.

THE CHALLENGES OF REINTEGRATION

For all Italians, the first post-war phase was characterized by the evacuees, the military and the deportees returning home, families being reunited, the mournful counting of the fallen. The search for friends and relations, of whom there was no longer any trace, was also undertaken by the organizations of the Roman Jewish community, who, as early as 1944, had set up a Committee for the Search of Deported Jews (Comitato Ricerche Deportati Ebrei – CRDE). Not without a certain naivety, the promoters of the Committee intended to assist the deportees, seized by the Germans – also thanks to the collaboration of the Italian authorities – during the incursion in the Roman Ghetto of 16 October 1943: 'old people, women and children, without the necessary clothing, [who] found themselves, for almost a year, including the entire winter, in the German concentration camps, and one supposes that they were in a terrible condition, both physical and in terms of morale'.[5] One cannot help being struck by these words, which bear witness to the inability to grasp the scale and nature of the events which had occurred. It took some time for everyone to accept what had been the fate of those who had been deported eastward. The first years of freedom were marked by long and heart-rending periods of waiting, in most cases without a happy outcome: of over 7,000 Italian-Jewish deportees only 831 would return home.[6]

The survivors had to face a process of reintegration which was anything but immediate and painless. After the fall of Mussolini on 25 July 1943 and the creation of the first Badoglio government (27 July 1943 – 10 December 1944), the Italian authorities did not show much interest in revising the racial laws. In an encounter with Father Pietro Tacchi Venturi, a Jesuit who served as unofficial liaison between the Italian government and the Vatican before and after the fall of the fascist regime, the new Prime Minister Pietro Badoglio inquired on the position of the Holy See concerning the anti-Semitic legislation. He was told on that occasion that the persecutory measures did not lack elements 'deserving confirmation'.[7] It was the Allies that pressured the Italian authorities to act in order to abrogate the racial laws, imposing such a condition in art. n.31 of the 'long armistice' signed in Malta on 29 September 1943. After a lengthy process that was concluded only in 1947, this led to the unequivocal abolition of the racist laws and the full restitution of civil and political rights to those who had been persecuted.[8]

The rescinding of the discriminatory laws did not, however, exonerate the corrupt spirits of the regime's propaganda. Fascist anti-Semitism had not only affected the persecuted minority and the rapacious vultures who had taken advantage of its fragility, but had involved the rewriting of the statutes of citizenship and the formulation – also through the representation of a negative, antithetical stereotype – of a different conception of national identity, which acquired a prescriptive character. Only a few people realized this and came to terms with all the implications of the fascist plan. Among the rare signs of an insightful approach, reference has to be made to an important article which appeared in September 1944 in *La Nazione del Popolo*, the organ of the Tuscan Committee of National Liberation:

> In the fascist era, there was a great deal of discussion, in the press, magazines and on walls, of the so-called problem of race, and those words were accompanied by actions which were so ferocious and offensive to the Italians' standards of civilization, that the sudden silence regarding this subject is generally welcomed with relief … If the racial laws and persecutions had constituted an occasional episode in the long history of fascist misdeeds, the silence would be justified. If the harm done by these laws had only concerned those who were its victims, we would only have to abolish these laws, trying to remedy, as far as possible, with a spirit of

> fraternal solidarity, the harm and grief suffered by the persecuted … But the racial policy was not an occasional episode and its present injuries have overturned not only the persecuted, but the whole life of the Nation … We will not be able to call ourselves truly free from the evil shadow of Fascism until we will have eliminated from our souls and our customs the last trace of the racial distinction. The problem involves all our civilization, and should not, today, be left unspoken, nor reduced to a simple issue of justice and the claiming of one's rights.[9]

That appeal was not answered and this is all the more significant if one considers that the opportunities to do so were not lacking. Not only because of the slow return of the survivors of the death camps – which only attracted the attention of a few people[10] – nor with regard to the very meagre debate about the reintegrative legislation, but also because post-war Italy was directly involved in the plight of approximately 30,000 foreign Jews who, fleeing from the inhospitable territories of Eastern Europe, reached the peninsula between 1945 and 1948. The majority of those refugees tried to violate the English naval blockade and to reach Palestine/Israel; nevertheless, for months, sometimes years, many thousands stayed in Italy, finding temporary asylum in specific refugee camps in various regions. It has rightly been noted that the press, the politicians and, in more general terms, the public opinion of the time were not able to reflect critically and in-depth on these developments, and in general on the delicate process which led to the birth of the State of Israel.[11]

Inevitably, in the absence of an adequate critical reflection, the echoes and repercussions of the tragedy which had occurred in Europe had long-term effects not only on the state of mind of the persecuted, but also on that of the persecutors or of the bystanders. For many years following the end of the war, at least until the 1960s, nowhere in Europe was there an in-depth, balanced attempt to come to terms with the significance and nature of the extermination of the Jews. In Eastern Europe – particularly in Poland, the geographical heart of the Shoah – after 1947, the specifically racial and anti-Semitic nature of the persecution was denied and hidden, the exterminated Jews being included in the total figures of the citizens who had been victims of the Nazi war. It was thus, until very recent times, that the true nature of that tragedy was prevented from being analysed, casting a veil over the responsibilities of the local population in having supported the Nazis in their plan of extermination. The camp of Auschwitz was turned into a monument, becoming the site of an ideologized remembrance which denied the identity of the victims and, highlighting their anonymity, extolled the Poles as victims of a generic fascism, considered the degenerate fruit of capitalism.[12] In the West, there was a different climate, and yet this did not lead to a full awareness, at least not in the first decades of the post-war period; the tragedy was not concealed, as was happening in Eastern Europe, but neither did it receive the critical attention it deserved. Thus, it happened that the mark of the Nazi racist classification continued to weigh on the West in the post-war years: the survivors of the concentration camps, having come under Allied protection, were still identified, in accordance with the racial hetero-classification imposed by the persecutors, as 'Jews', rather than Poles, Italians, Germans, French, Hungarians, etc., also in the documents provided by the new authorities.[13] Once having insinuated itself in people's minds, like red tape, the idea of dividing mankind into 'races' proved difficult to eradicate. The viscosity of the racist categories enabled them to resist anti-fascist cleansing; thus it could happen that, in Italy in 1946, a magistrate, in referring to the victims of a massacre carried out two years earlier, distinguished between 'Jews' and 'Aryans';[14] again in 1946, a border guard inquired about the 'race' of a citizen who was re-entering the country;[15] in 1948, arrest warrants, issued in 1944 on racial grounds by the authorities of the Italian Social Republic, were acted upon;[16] or, as late as the early 1950s, there was still the practice of indicating 'race' on the personal data certificates issued by the Rome City Council.[17] There are only a few examples, out of the many which could be cited, yet they offer clear indication of how difficult it was to eradicate social practices and world views which had become customary.

Even though the racist laws had been eliminated and the manifestations of actual anti-Semitism in post-war Italy were, until the 1960s, a 'residual and secondary expression of neo-Fascism and Catholic traditionalism',[18] periodic outbreaks of traditional anti-Semitism or new forms of anti-Jewish hatred, tied to the unfolding of the Middle Eastern crisis, punctuated the post-war Italian scene, as, after all, has happened elsewhere in Western Europe. The tendency to separate the Jews from the rest of society has appeared on various occasions in post-war Europe;[19] this fact should not be over-emphasized, nevertheless, pointing it out enables us to refute the widespread idea that, once the regimes responsible for the persecution had been overthrown, Western Jews were able to reintegrate effortlessly, as if, from one day to the next, the effects of years of indoctrination and concrete racist practices could simply be eliminated from the minds of individuals.

Recent historiographical developments regarding this subject permit the outlining of a situation characterized by many grey areas: the reintegration of the victims of persecution was often slow, painful and difficult; it was marked by the opposition of some limited sectors of society, the lack of understanding of the majority, great indifference and disregard which only rarely appeared as open hostility. The survivors, who had escaped the manhunt, were not welcomed back warmly, but were often regarded with suspicion and treated with impatience, almost as if they were illegitimate usurpers in claiming the homes or property of which they had been deprived, the jobs they had lost, the rights and the dignity which had been wrested from them.

A spine-chilling case in point is provided by the writings, drawn up between December 1945 and January 1946, by a prominent figure in the anti-fascist political-cultural scenario, Cesare Merzagora. He knew too well what had been the effects of racial persecution as his career in Pirelli had been boosted by the sacking, on racial grounds, of the Central Administrative Director, Ugo Tagliacozzo. After 8 September, Merzagora had joined the Resistance, becoming a member of the National Liberation Committee of Northern Italy. Thus, he launched himself on a brilliant political career, in the Liberal Party, which brought him to the Presidency of the Senate of the Republic (1963–67). Following the Liberation, he intervened in the difficult issue of the reintegration of the persecuted: expressing himself in a communicative vein typical of a certain rhetoric resulting in anti-Semitism, he began by pointing out that 'almost all' of his 'dearest friends' were Jewish, and then harshly attacked the victims of persecution, giving them a disquieting decalogue of suggestions. The first point was that those who were returning from exile should 'not complain too much'. The third point maintained that 'those who are returning to their commercial practices have to understand that if they want to contribute to the hoped-for national unity they must not take up their old ways as a consequence of which whoever entered a shop or office belonging to a Jew could have difficulty in finding non-Jews there, apart from the errand boy'. His criticisms became more and more bitter, in an intimidating crescendo: 'It is necessary', states the fifth point, 'that the Jews who return should control themselves. Italy has changed in many ways. They must get used to sitting around the table, neither above nor below it, as is, to a certain extent, their wont'. The tenth point invites those who had been baptized not to change their minds. Finally, he did not fail to remind the persecuted of 'their atavistic defects', whose existence, according to him, is undeniable, otherwise 'how could one explain the persecutions they have borne for two thousand years?' This intervention originally appeared – accompanied by the editorial office's critical note, which distanced itself from the article – in the liberal newspaper *La Libertà*, but it would later be reprinted in a bigger pamphlet entitled *I Pavidi* (The Cowards), which could boast a controversial preface by Benedetto Croce.[20]

The Neapolitan intellectual, who during the persecution had maintained an undeniably noble attitude, now invited the Jews 'to fuse more and more with the other Italians; ensuring the elimination of that distinction and division in which they have persisted through the centuries and which, just as it has given the opportunity and the pretext for persecutions, in the past, it is to be feared that it could do the same in future'. The solution to the 'Jewish problem' could only coincide – for Croce – with the complete assimilation of and the definitive loss of identity by the minority. A stand which, naturally, did not fail to provoke heated, but equally ineffectual, reactions on the part of Jewish institutions,[21] and which – even more than Merzagora's aggressive and vulgar statements – prepares us very well for an understanding of the delicate climate in which the heredity of the racial persecution came to be weighed up. Arnaldo Momigliano, an admirer of Croce, ascribed such an attitude to the 'lack of any contact with Jewish culture', linking his stand with a more general lacuna in Italian culture, or rather with the 'surprising inability of non-Jewish intellectuals to acknowledge the Hebrew tradition, which has been a component of Italian culture since the beginning of Christianity'.[22] Large sectors of Italian culture in the post-war period – liberals, marxists, Catholics were transversely involved – showed themselves to be unable, or unwilling, to tackle the problems posed by Judaism and by the Jewish condition in the West. At stake, after the Second World War, was the reformulation of the minority's condition within the national State. Failing to recognize – in the style of Sartre – how modern anti-Semitism should be interpreted in relation to the needs and the autonomous cultural processes of who observes, identifies and persecutes the 'Jew', Italian culture – while condemning the phenomenon – proved to be incapable of opposing it. Attributing anti-Semitism to presumed historical characteristics or to behaviours on the part of the minority, the object of hatred, resulted in denying the Jews the right to preserve their particular identity. It is a question of serious structural flaws, which meant that the Republic was unable to reintegrate the Jews without – at the same time – rejecting them.[23]

It is also in relation to this cultural climate that all the incidents and difficulties, which shattered many of the expectations of those who had to be reintegrated, should be interpreted. The reparatory legislation undoubtedly sanctioned the return to sacrosanct principles of equality, but the application of those laws was anything but simple and immediate. The studies conducted in the last few years on the world of the university have effectively brought to light the difficulties and inconsistencies which marked the complicated practices to reinstate those who had been sacked in 1938. In the post-war period, the victims of persecution often found themselves in a condition of inferiority with respect to the colleagues who had taken their places, encountering scant solidarity and all too little understanding on the part of an institution which, after all like the rest of the country, cast an embarrassed veil over the past racist misdeeds.[24] Even if with due caution, this scenario could be extended beyond the confines of the academic world: those who had had the racist laws enacted or had profited from them generally continued their activities undisturbed, while, because of scarce interest or scant sensitivity, the lives of those who wanted to reintegrate themselves was often more wretched than a mere reading of the laws passed in their favour would suggest. The very sullen atmosphere which marked the social reintegration of the Jews has been very effectively described by the jurist Andrea Tabet, who has indicated how in many administrative offices 'public or private', following the dismissal of citizens of 'Jewish race', expedient replacements had been carried out so that:

> it was neither easy nor convenient to reinstate that ghostly figure, who had escaped deportation by chance, and presented himself after seven

> years to claim a post which was his due. Therefore the bosses would hire him, then fire him again and pay him off. It was a behaviour which was as brutal as it was logical for the person who proposed it. The citizen who wanted to reintegrate himself left disappointed, with a small severance package which would soon be nullified by devaluation. Other bodies resisted even more harshly, forcing the postulant to long, expensive, uncertain legal proceedings.[25]

Even in the absence of bad intentions on the part of employers, the socio-economic condition of the persecuted had objectively worsened and reinstatement, far from representing an opportunity for recovering their initial condition, ended up sanctioning the harm done, the regression suffered amidst general indifference. Thus, the moment of reinstatement in the post, which had been lost and for a long time nostalgically missed, could represent an umpteenth humiliation, as can be seen from the testimony of Lia Levi, who thus remembers her father's professional reinstatement:

> In his reserved shyness, [my father] feared that he would encounter a kind of official reception, such as speeches or ostentatious handshakes. 'I hope they don't say anything …', he grumbled pacing up and down the room. 'I hope that they have, at least, the decency to keep quiet …'.
>
> And my mother calmed him down: 'But of course, you'll see that they won't say anything…'. But she looked at us as if to say that she was only saying that not to upset father.
>
> In fact, they didn't say anything to him. One can say that they didn't even look at him …. That no one had greeted him was the first thing he told us, but then he said that they had given him the same place and rank of six years earlier, namely when they had dismissed him … those who were of the same age were all office supervisors or managers or something else, and certainly they looked at him condescendingly ….
>
> In his former work, today once again his, father never felt at ease.[26]

Demographic research indicates that the traumas induced by the persecution and the uncertain reintegration led to long-term changes in the minority's socio-professional set-up; there was a sharp drop in the number of Jews in public employment or in the ranks of the military, there was also a slight drop in the number of Jews in the liberal professions, while there was a considerable increase in the number of Jewish citizens engaged in commercial activities. The latter had constituted a kind of refuge for the victims of the racial legislation and, once having fallen back on such activities, large sections of the Jewish population remained in them even after the end of the war.[27] Andrea Tabet commented,

> Having seen their fathers ignominiously sacked from the posts they had so legitimately attained the sons did not feel like facing the struggles of

> open competitions, training and studies to reinstate themselves, as in the past, in state organizations. In fact, the robes, the uniforms, the academic insignia had not prevented their fathers from suffering the ultimate outrage of deportation, torture, death.[28]

The growing sense of diffidence towards the public apparatus, compromised with the regime and directly involved in the application of the racial laws, could have influenced the attitude of the Jewish minority,[29] but perhaps other factors should also be taken into account, including the weakening of the structure of the secular State and the increasing power of the Catholic party which, in a short time, reached 'a formidable level of fusion' with the State apparatus.[30]

Manifest difficulties, in resuming work, were also encountered by merchants, tradesmen and entrepreneurs, who had lost control of their activities due to the persecution. The attempts to regain possession of what had been confiscated or ceded under duress led to exhausting, long-running legal battles in the post-war period. Numerous disputed cases had come into being as a result of agreements of convenience, mainly drawn up in a desperate attempt to preserve the entrepreneurial activities which had to be confiscated in accordance with the persecutory law: the agreements, drawn up in moments of emergency and extreme weakness, were not always respected. An already extremely tangled situation was further complicated by reparatory laws, issued by governments of the anti-fascist coalition, sometimes couched in terms which were too vague and generic. This greatly complicated the implementation of those laws by various State and private bodies, as well as by the judiciary which, in respecting the letter of the law, often ended up betraying its authentic spirit.[31] There was a lack of consensus among the intellectuals regarding the ways in which the thorny question of the reintegration of those who had been persecuted on racial grounds should be tackled – as has already been seen – and among both the judiciary – who often proposed contrasting interpretations of the same laws – and among the members of the governing coalition who had drawn up those laws. In this context, it is interesting to consider the discussion held in the Council of Ministers on 4 April 1945: the debate centred on the delicate issue of T.E.C.O.E.L. PLC, a textile firm originally owned by a citizen considered of 'Jewish race', which, after 1938, had been taken over and run by the workers, on a cooperative basis. Prime Minister Ivanoe Bonomi presented to the Council of Ministers the request formulated by the workers, who asked that 'in the cases in which firms belonging to victims of the racial laws [had been] taken over by the workers, the restitution of these firms, to the owners or those who had been expropriated, should not be accepted'. While the ministers Manlio Brosio, Mario Cevolotto, Luigi Gasparotto, Giulio Rodinò and Meuccio Ruini declared their opposition to the proposal, the Finance Minister Pesenti – a leading figure of the Italian Communist Party – expressed his approval. Like Merzagora, who intervened a few months later, the communist leader maintained that the institutions were 'exaggerating in the welfare measures for the Jews'.[32] The very singular episode of T.E.C.O.E.L. PLC illustrates very well the extensive and intricate nature of the misunderstandings which marked public opinion about the delicate question. In that chaotic context, it was difficult for a consistent and, above all, just policy to come into being. In this regard it is important to note that the legislation of Republican Italy, in stark contrast with what was happening in the rest of Europe, tended to sanction the full legitimacy of the sale contracts of property and firms drawn up by the victims of racial persecution after 1938, in circumstances which were, at the very least, suspect.[33]

What has so far been considered concerns, in particular, the economic enterprises confiscated, in various ways, since 1938. In more general terms, as regards the confiscation of property, effected in 1938 and 1943, it has been ascertained that what was confiscated and then entrusted to the EGELI (Ente Gestione e Liquidazione Immobiliare, the Organization for the Management and Sale of Property) was returned, not without costs and loss of time, in almost its entirety.[34] Yet for an accurate assessment of the economic and material damages borne by the persecuted it would be necessary to take into consideration the property destroyed by the war or subject to theft – effected by the fascists, the occupying German forces or by ordinary citizens – and which had very little likelihood of being recovered, as well as what was spent for board and lodging and protection between 1943 and 1945, in the dark years of the manhunt.

The overall picture appears varied and multifaceted, being, at times, confused and so difficult to decipher in its entirety. Many variables were involved, if for some the harm, in terms of friends and relations who had been lost, psychological traumas and, finally, also economic losses, could be limited, for others it was enormous and irreparable. The objective data and each person's subjective reactions to the events varied greatly. All this makes it very difficult to give a synthetic outline of the nature and outcomes of the process of reintegration. Almost ten years after the Liberation, the evaluation on the part of those directly involved, or more precisely of the representatives of the Italian Jews, was not wholly positive; in an internal document of 1954 Giorgio Zevi, the President of the Union of Italian Jewish Communities, noted: 'for a long time the legislative measures to redress, even if only partially, the wrongs suffered by the Jews following the racial laws, were requested, but the measures issued have been few and inadequate as regards effectively righting those wrongs'.[35] Having noted the disappointment of the leaders of the Jewish communities, the bureaucratic delays and various obstacles encountered by the persecuted in their reintegration, it should, however, be remembered that it was an extremely difficult time for the whole nation, wounded, humiliated and impoverished by the dictatorship and the war-time defeat. The period of reconstruction was very hard for all Italians and perhaps this helps to explain why there was little attention for, and understanding of, the particular sufferings borne by the Jewish population.[36] The process of reintegration was neither simple nor straightforward, nevertheless in Italy conditions were much better than in many other parts of Europe; in the Eastern regions, reintegration was often impossible and tens of thousands of Jews continued to flee from those territories until the end of the 1940s.[37] On the whole, in the newly born Italian Republic conditions permitted the majority of Italian Jews to feel that they could take up their lives again, forcing themselves, insofar as it was possible, to forget the injustices they had suffered and to try to resume what had, under duress, been interrupted in 1938.

The choices of individuals and families who strongly wanted to remain in the peninsula were not only influenced by the practical problems, to which we have already referred, but also – and perhaps above all – by cultural and spiritual considerations. Reintegration was possible because of the ability of so many Italian Jews to identify with the prevalent cultural system in post-war Italy. It was not, nor on the other hand could it be, a simple return to the pre-1938 reality. State racism had provoked a real *identity crisis* and the post-war period was the moment when the crisis was faced, leading to the re-definition of one's true role, of one's place, in the midst of the national community. The year 1938 ushered in a new season, which, with its burden of questions and disquiet, carried on well into the long post-war period: 'in fact, each of us – as is stated in one of the most interesting Jewish memoirs – continued an agonizing struggle which the cessation of military hostilities did not bring to an end'.[38] In order to take into account the lingering echoes of the racist campaign it is, therefore, necessary to study the Republican post-war period, considering how both the equilibrium within the Jewish community and its relationship with the wider world changed, the attitude of the Jewish minority towards the idea of nation and what form their Jewishness took; how, in other words, did the life of the Jews in Italy change as regards their own self-image as well as in relation to the general social, political and institutional set-up.

NOTES

1. See E.I. Sabatello, 'Le conseguenze sociali ed economiche delle persecuzioni sugli ebrei in Italia', in *La legislazione antiebraica in Italia e in Europa* (Rome: Edizioni della Camera dei Deputati, 1989), p.80. Regarding the abjurations, see D. Lattes, 'Coloro che son partiti', *RMI*, 8–9, XXVI (1960), pp.347–50; D. Lattes, 'Problemi e polemiche', *RMI*, 2, XXVII (1961), pp.51–6. For information regarding the deportations and the killings, see L. Picciotto Fargion, *Il libro della memoria. Gli ebrei deportati dall'Italia 1943–45* (Milan: Mursia, 2002), p.27.
2. Regarding the state of neglect and inertia which characterized, several years after the Liberation, the smallest centres, see the report, dated 4 September 1952, drawn up by Settimio Sorani for the UCII (in AUCII, bb.30–4, f.34).
3. See *Israel*, 38, 7 June 1956. Data organized differently have been proposed by Attilio Milano, who stated that about a decade after the end of the war there were 12,000 Jews in Rome, 6,000 in Milan, 3,000 in Turin, 1,500 in Trieste, 1,400 in Florence and 1,100 in Venice. Instead, according to

Milano, the Jews residing in Genoa and Livorno were 800, 500 in Naples and Pisa, 400 in Ancona and Bologna, about 200 in Padua, Ferrara, Modena and Mantua, while there were about a thousand scattered among the various minor centres: A. Milano, *Storia degli ebri in Italia* (Turin: Einaudi, 1992), pp.410–11. Regarding the socio-demographic dynamics, see S. Della Pergola, *Anatomia dell'ebraismo italiano* (Assisi: Carucci, 1976), pp.59ff.; S. Della Pergola, 'Precursori, convergenti, emarginati. Trasformazioni demografiche degli ebrei in Italia 1870–1945', in AA.VV., *Gli ebrei nell'Italia (1870–1945)*, IV Convegno Italia Judaica (Rome: Ministero per i Beni e le Attività Culturali, 1993), pp.48–69, in particular pp.65–7.

4. R. Segre, *Venti mesi*, preface by N. Tranfaglia (Palermo: Sellerio 1995), pp.51, 37.
5. Quoted in L. Picciotto Fargion, 'La liberazione dai campi di concentramento', in M. Sarfatti (ed.), *Il ritorno alla vita. Vicende e diritti degli ebrei in Italia dopo la seconda guerra mondiale* (Florence: La Giuntina, 1998), p.19.
6. See L. Picciotto Fargion, *Il libro della memoria*, p.27.
7. The quotation is from the report, dated 29 August 1943, by Padre Tacchi Venturi to Cardinal Maglione, the Vatican Secretary of State, in *Actes et documents du Saint Siège relatives à la Seconde Guerre Mondiale*, vol. IX, *Le Saint Siègeet les victimes de la guerre* (Vatican City, 1975), p.459 for the quotation, but see pp.458–62.
8. M. Toscano (ed.), *L'abrogazione delle leggi razziali in Italia (1943–1987)*, preface by G. Spadolini (Rome: Servizio Studi del Senato, 1988).
9. 18–19 September 1944. M. Sarfatti referred to the text and its importance: 'Nota introduttiva', in M. Sarfatti (ed.), *Il ritorno alla vita*, pp.8–9.
10. For some indications about the attitude of the main newspapers, see S. Fantini, *Notizie dalla Shoah. La stampa italiana nel 1945* (Bologna: Pendragon, 2005); M. Matard-Bonucci, 'La libération des camps de concentration et le retour des déportés à travers la presse quotidienne italienne', in A. Wievorka and C. Mouchard (eds), *La Shoah: témoignages, saviors, oeuvres* (Orléans: Cercil/PUV, 1999), pp.101–14.
11. M. Toscano, *La 'porta di Sion'. L'Italia e l'immigrazione clandestina ebraica in Palestina (1945–1948)* (Bologna: Il Mulino, 1990), pp.318ff.
12. C. Tonini, 'The Jews in Poland after the Second World War: Most Recent Contributions of Polish Historiography', *Quest. Issues in Contemporary History*, 1 (April 2010), available at http://www.quest-cdecjournal.it/focus.php?issue=1&id=211; J.T. Gross, *Fear: Anti-Semitism in Poland after Auschwitz: An Essay in Historical Interpretation* (New York: Random House, 2006).
13. P. Lagrou, *The Legacy of Nazi Occupation: Patriotic Memory and National Recovery in Western Europe (1945–1965)* (Cambridge: Cambridge University Press, 2000), p.255.
14. C. Forti, *Il caso Pardo Roques. Un eccidio del 1944 tra memoria e oblio* (Turin: Einaudi, 1998), p.176.
15. See the testimony of A. Luzzatto, 'Autocoscienza e identità ebraica', in C. Vivanti (ed.), *Gli ebrei in Italia. Storia d'Italia, Annali*, vol. XI/2 (Turin: Einaudi, 1997), p.1869.
16. It happened in Florence, upsetting a couple's honeymoon plans. See AUCII, b.85g, f. 'Manifestazione di antisemitismo e stampa', in particular see the letter of protest sent by the Vice President of the Union to the Minister of the Interior, 17 June 1948.
17. See Protests by the Union reported in UCII, V *Congresso delle Comunità (1956–1957): Relazione del Consiglio* (Rome: 1956), p.14.
18. M. Toscano, 'L'antisemitismo nell'Italia contemporanea: note, ipotesi e problemi di ricerca', in *Zakhor*, VI (2003), p.31. For a first concise study of anti-Semitism in Republican history, see A. Goldstaub, *L'antisemitismo in Italia*, in L. Poliakov (ed.), *Storia dell'antisemitismo 1945–1993* (Florence: La Nuova Italia, 1996), pp.425–71; see also A.M. Di Nola, *Antisemitismo in Italia 1962/1972* (Florence: Vallechi, 1973). On Catholic anti-Semitism in the post-war period, see E. Mazzini, 'Aspetti dell'antisemitismo cattolico dopo l'Olocausto', in M. Flores, S. Levis Sullam, M.-A. Matard-Bonucci and E. Traverso (eds), *Storia della Shoah in Italia. Vicende, memorie, rappresentazioni*, vol. II (Turin: UTET, 2010), pp.320–35.
19. Goldstaub, *Storia dell'antisemitismo 1945–1993*, pp.425–71.
20. C. Merzagora, 'Un problema attuale', *La Libertà*, 19 December 1945 and C. Merzagora, 'Ancora sul problema attuale', *La Libertà*, 3 January 1946; in C. Merzagora, *I Pavidi: dalla cospirazione alla Costituente*, preface by B. Croce (Milan: Istituto Editoriale Galileo, 1946), pp.43–55.
21. Dante Lattes intervened regarding the controversy, see F. Pardo, *L'ebraismo secondo B. Croce e la filosofia crociana* (Florence: La Giuntina, 1948). Croce's observations are also in F. Pardo, *Scritti e discorsi politici*, vol. II (Bari: Laterza, 1963).

22. A. Momigliano, *Essays on Ancient and Modern Judaism*, edited by S. Berti (Chicago, IL: University of Chicago Press, 1994), p.139. For a documented analysis of Croce's reflection on the Jewish problem see G. Sasso, *Per invigilare me stesso. I taccuini di lavoro di B. Croce* (Bologna: Il Mulino, 1989), pp.170ff.
23. R. Finzi, *L'università italiana e le leggi antiebraiche* [2nd ed., reviewed and enlarged] (Rome: Editori Riuniti, 2003), pp.135–44.
24. Regarding this, see G. Turi, *Lo stato educatore: politica e intellettuali nell'Italia fascista* (Bari: Laterza, 2002), pp.121–45, in particular about the post-war period pp.141ff.; F. Pelini, 'Appunti per una storia della reintegrazione dei professori perseguitati per motivi razziali', in I. Pavan and G. Schwarz (eds), *Gli ebrei in Italia tra persecuzione fascista e reintegrazione postbellica* (Florence: La Giuntina, 2001) pp.113–39; R. Finzi, *L'università italiana e le leggi antiebraiche*, pp.109ff; V. Galimi and G. Procacci (eds), *Per la difesa della razza: l'applicazione delle leggi antiebraiche nelle universita italiane* (Milan: Unicopli, 2009); I. Pavan and F. Pelini, *La doppia epurazione: l'Universita di Pisa e le leggi razziali tra guerra e dopoguerra* (Bologna: Il Mulino, 2009).
25. A. Tabet, 'Venticinque anni di libertà costituzionale', *RMI*, 6, XXXVI (1970), pp.293–4.
26. L. Levi, *Se va via il re* (Rome: e/o, 1996), pp.26–7.
27. See E.I. Sabatello, 'Le conseguenze sociali ed economiche delle persecuzioni sugli ebrei in Italia', pp.80ff.
28. A. Tabet, 'Venticinque anni di libertà costituzionale', p.293.
29. According to Sabatello ('Le conseguenze sociali ed economiche delle persecuzioni sugli ebrei in Italia', p.87) this feeling was, to a certain extent, passed on to the following generations, thus contributing to a lasting change in the socio-professional characteristics of the Jewish minority.
30. See P. Ginsborg, *Storia d'Italia dal dopoguerra ad oggi. Società e politica 1943–1988* (Turin: Einaudi, 1989), p.204.
31. I. Pavan, 'Gli incerti percorsi della reintegrazione. Note sugli atteggiamenti della magistratura repubblicana 1945–1964', in I. Pavan and G. Schwarz (eds), *Gli ebrei in Italia tra persecuzione fascista e reintegrazione postbellica*, pp.85–107. A.G. Ricci (ed.), *Verbali del Consiglio dei Ministri (1943–1948)*, vol. III (Rome: Presidenza del Consiglio dei Ministri, 1995), pp.529–41.
32. A.G. Ricci (ed.), *Verbali del Consiglio dei Ministri*, pp.529–41.
33. For an in-depth analysis of the problem of confiscation and the difficulties in restitution in the post-war period, which compares the Italian regulations with those of Europe, see I. Pavan, *Tra indifferenza e oblio. Le conseguenze economiche delle leggi razziali in Italia (1938–1970)* (Florence: Le Monnier, 2004). See also G. D'Amico, *Quando l'eccezione diventa norma: la reintegrazione degli ebrei nell'Italia postfascista* (Turin: Bollati Boringhieri, 2006); P. Bertilotti, 'Riconoscimento, reintegrazione e risarcimento. Le vittime della persecuzione antisemita in Italia 1944–1965', in *Italia Contemporanea*, 254 (2008), pp.115–37. To place the Italian situation in a comparative perspective see also M. Dean, C. Goshler and P. Ther (eds), *Robbery and Restitution: The Conflict over Jewish Property in Europe* (New York: Berghahn Books, 2007). For a Europe-wide reconstruction of the properties taken from the persecuted Jews, see M. Dean, *Robbing the Jews: The Confiscation of Jewish Property in the Holocaust 1933–1945* (Cambridge: Cambridge University Press, 2010).
34. See Commissione per la ricostruzione delle vicende che hanno caratterizzato le attività di acquisizione dei beni ebraici da parte di organismi pubblici e privati (Commission for the examination of the acquisition of Jewish property by public and private bodies), *Rapporto Generale* (Rome: Presidenza del Consiglio dei Ministri, Dipartimento per l'informazione e l'editoria, 2001); for an on-line version (available also in English) see: http://www.governo.it/Presidenza/DICA/beni_ebraici/index.html. See also M. Sarfatti, *Gli ebrei nell'Italia fascista. Vicende, identità, persecuzione* (Turin: Einaudi, 2000), pp.189–94. For a local study see F. Levi (ed.), *Le case e le cose. La persecuzione degli ebrei torinesinelle carte dell'EGELI 1938–1945* (Turin: Compagnia San Paolo, 1998).
35. G. Zevi, 'Promemoria', dated 28 November 1954, in AUCII, b.65a. I would like to thank Ilaria Pavan for having brought this document to my attention. Among the measures which had gone unheeded by Republican governments, Zevi included the unpaid cheques for the period spent far from work because of the anti-Jewish laws, the refusal to raise the age limits for retirement, the non-acknowledgement of points, in public open competitions, for the period of enforced absence from service.
36. For an effective overall picture, see E. Di Nolfo, *Le paure e le speranze degli italiani 1943–1945* (Milan: Mondadori, 1986).
37. For a concise vue d'ensemble of the conditions for reintegration in Europe, see B. Wasserstein,

Vanishing Diaspora: The Jews in Europe since 1945 (Cambridge, MA: Harvard University Press, 1996), respectively pp.58–83 and 36–56. See also D. Bankier (ed.), *The Jews are Coming Back: The Return of the Jews to their Countries of Origin after WWII* (New York and Jerusalem: Berghahn Books/Yad Vashem, 2005); L. Brazzo and G. Schwarz (eds), 'Jews in Europe after the Shoah: Studies and Research Perspectives', monographic section of the online journal, *Quest. Issues in Contemporary History*, 1 (April 2010), available at http://www.quest-cdecjournal.it/.

38. A. Segre, *Memorie di vita ebraica*, preface by R. De Felice (Rome: Bonacci, 1979), p.372.

2

A 'New' Leadership

Like all Italians, or perhaps even more than the others, the victims of racial persecution had suffered, apart from enormous economic losses, the devastation of those 'immaterial goods' which constitute the essence of identity. Once peace and freedom had been regained, among the first and most energetic entities who knew how to help individuals and groups in their search for a source which could satisfy their thirst for answers and future possibilities, to come to terms with their recent drama and face the dangers of a very uncertain future, were the political parties, formidable generators of identity. Naturally very active, and capable of extending its embrace to reassure very large sectors of the population, was the Catholic Church.[1] Apart from these entities there was also a myriad of associations which – to make up for the void left by the State, incapable of adequately meeting the needs of the national community – provided assistance for the citizens, paying attention to their symbolic needs (commemorations, honouring the fallen, etc.), as well as their tangible and concrete ones (food, housing, etc.).[2]

The burning desire for solace and answers on the part of the persecuted minority, which faced freedom with an air of confusion and suffering, could be satisfied – not only by the developing political parties – but also by some peculiar sources: a rich network of institutions and associations, including foreign ones, was ready to help and assist Italian Jews, providing them with vital support in order to rouse themselves, leaving the hiding places and refuges, in order to resume their participation in the life of the country.

The first help came from the Allied armed forces, among whose ranks there were also Jewish soldiers; a notable contribution to the moral rebirth and to the material reconstruction of Jewish life in Italy came from Jewish military chaplains, not more than twenty, in the American Army. They did not only carry out an essential role of cultural mediation between the persecuted and the Allied Authorities but, especially in the very first months following the start of the Italian Campaign, they collaborated with some American charitable organizations, laying the foundations for the establishment of a network of assistance for their kin in Italy.[3]

The Anglo-American Army, like any army involved in military operations, was certainly not pleased to see the intrusion of civilians in the war zones, nevertheless, it very soon allowed access to the liberated territories to some

American and English charitable organizations: in April 1944 permission to operate in Italy was given to the representatives of the American Friends' Service Committee and the Friends' Ambulance Unit, representing, respectively, the American and British Quakers, as well as the American Joint Distribution Committee (AJDC, usually called Joint), representing Jewish-American associations. The task of such organizations was to collaborate with the military institutions in offering assistance to the thousands of refugees uprooted from their homelands and scattered throughout the continent.[4] From the time of the liberation of Rome in June 1944, the Joint officially extended its own sphere of action, not only taking care of the foreign Jews in the peninsula but also of the Italian-Jewish community, collaborating in the reorganization of its social and religious life.[5]

Born as an apolitical association in 1914, with the aim of carrying out charitable work for, and offering assistance to, Jews in need, the Joint represented a group of Jews of German extraction, very well integrated in the American social fabric, far from the world of religious orthodoxy and suspicious of, even if not exactly hostile towards, the Zionist message. With the approach of the end of the Second World War and the spread of terrible news about the fate of European Jews, the Joint had undergone a slow and important transformation: it had found itself administering ever larger sums of money since the fundraising among American Jews was enjoying increasing success and, above all, had begun to develop a different approach towards the Zionist Movement, which was acquiring an exceptional strength and appeal. Dedicating itself, in the first place, to helping the tens of thousands of refugees who had escaped the 'final solution' and were dispersed throughout Europe, attending first to their most primary needs – from food to clothing, and education – the Joint could not help being affected by the spread, among those very populations, of an increasing attraction towards Zionism, just as it could not help noticing that for many Jewish refugees – bereft of a homeland – the realization of the Zionist dream had become a dramatic and compelling necessity.[6]

The needs of the Western Jewish communities were different from those of the refugees who, in the post-war period, travelled across Europe fleeing from the prejudice and violence which continued even after the fall of Nazism. In Italy and France, the Jewish communities had borne lesser persecutions – in terms of gravity and duration – compared to those which had occurred in Germany and Eastern Europe, nevertheless also for the Western communities the Joint's contribution, which actively sustained their rebirth, was vitally important. The commitment of such a charitable association to the European Jews was strong and multifaceted and lasted for some decades, profoundly affecting Jewish life in liberated Europe and providing the Jewish institutions of the Old Continent with an essential organizational contribution and indispensable economic support.[7]

A greater and much more important influence, than that which could be exerted by a few military chaplains attached to the American troops, and different from that of the Joint – to which we will return in due course – came from tens of thousands of volunteers from the Jewish settlements in Palestine, enrolled in the British Army.[8] They took on a specific mission, which went beyond the war against the Axis forces: in fact, they committed themselves, in order to help the persecuted, to developing in the latter a Zionist consciousness, trying to propel them towards Palestine, doing their utmost to overrun the blockade against Jewish immigration imposed by Great Britain.[9]

These activities developed fully after the complete liberation of Italy and Europe, but the revival of the Italian-Jewish community had begun about two years earlier, at the same time as the Anglo-American invasion of the peninsula. During the last five centuries, in the Southern regions, the Jewish presence had been virtually non-existent, but recent events had led to the birth of a series of dynamic, if ephemeral, communities. Among the very first groups to meet the Palestinian troops and the other liberators were, in fact, several thousand foreign Jews interned by the fascist regime since 1939 in special camps in Southern Italy,[10] as well as some evacuees who had gone to the south and so encountered the Allies and salvation, and small groups of Yugoslav Jews who, fleeing from the German Army, between the summer and autumn of 1943 had crossed the Otranto Channel arriving in Puglia.[11] With the active support of the Palestinian soldiers, these groups gave rise – first in the internment camps themselves, and then in Bari, Naples and other minor centers – to small but active Jewish communities.[12] In those environments, there would soon have spread, like an unstoppable contagion, the Zionist ideal, to which the propagandist zeal of the Palestinian units would certainly have contributed. Their efforts, however, took root in soil which had been prepared by recent events and in which could grow and develop a new feeling towards that cause: many began to consider the possibility of emigrating to Palestine and so various Zionist groups arose in Southern Italy, small but active, which soon united with the older but scattered groups of Italian Zionism.[13]

The foreign Jewish refugees, together with the representatives of American Judaism and the soldiers from the Palestinian settlements, collaborated, in significant ways, with Italian Judaism, above all from the time of the liberation of the capital, which had occurred following the entry into the city of the troops of General Clark, on 4 June 1944: there was then a meeting of distant Jewish worlds, differentiated by history, mentality, culture.[14] For the Italian-Jewish minority, although the meeting was not always easy, it was stimulating and intense; the impact of the Palestinian soldiers on Italian Judaism was particularly evident, while the contacts between Italian Jews and foreign refugees (estimated at between 15,000 and 20,000 in the period 1943–45) was less marked but by no means irrelevant. In order to avoid triggering anti-Semitic outbursts, the representatives of the Joint tried to keep the foreign refugees far from the cities, directing them to reception centres and collective farms where they were trained to work in the fields in view of their emigration to what was to become the State of Israel.[15] The introduction of new and stimulating environments did not fail to bear fruit in the Italian-Jewish minority: it was also thanks to these contacts that Italian Judaism left the condition of relative isolation in which it had lived for a long time, making itself 'more open and receptive to transalpine and overseas influences'.[16]

The meeting with the representatives of the Yishuv was exciting and unexpected: 'it really seemed as if one were dreaming', wrote the rabbi Elio Toaff in his memoirs.[17] The relevance of that meeting depended upon the fact that their Jewishness was not a simple 'residue', as it was for many Western Jews; they were the standard bearers of an ambitious project of national and spiritual regeneration which did not fail to fascinate many Italian Jews. The mere presence of soldiers who had the Star of David on their epaulettes seemed to open new horizons, inspire hopes of renewal and rebirth. The Palestinian-Jewish soldiers, many of whom were grouped together in November 1944 in a single unit, a specific Jewish Brigade, actively operated to revive the exhausted Jewish groups present in Italy; with this aim in mind, in a meeting held in Fiuggi on 29 October 1944 together with representatives of the Joint, a Centre for the Diaspora (Merkaz Lagolah) was created. Its task was to coordinate the activities of the Palestinian soldiers present in various units of the British Army, with the explicit aim of bringing comfort to both the foreign refugees in the peninsula and Italian Jews and to conduct, among them, educational and propaganda activities. But there was also a hidden agenda, which consisted of acting as the Italian operational branch of the Jewish Agency – the government apparatus *in pectore* of Jewish Palestinian society – promoting with every means illegal immigration to Palestine.[18] The creation of such a centre, which brought together soldiers from different units to help civilians (and all this without the authorization of their superiors), was a singular, exceptional occurrence, which revealed the spirit and true objectives of that contingent. The coordination, thus acquired, enabled the Palestinian soldiers, thanks also to the determining financial collaboration, although not enthusiastically forthcoming, of the Joint, to rationalize their efforts and to make a deep impact on the Jewish worlds with which they came into contact.[19]

The Jews in the liberated regions of Italy approached the Zionist soldiers of the Palestinian units, if for nothing else, because 'they were distributing white bread'; however, that was often the beginning of further contacts, of repeated social and culturally rich exchanges.[20] For example, only a few weeks after the triumphal entry of the Allies in Rome, a youth centre was set up – at the old synagogue of Via Balbo – which became an important venue for meetings and discussions:

> The centre of Via Balbo attracted many young people, many of whom had

> not participated in any Jewish activity. The period of the occupation and its tragic consequences had made even the most lukewarm reflect on their ties with Judaism ... Via Balbo became something more than just a meeting place or centre. Here, we created a real centre where we used to spend our days (we also used to have our meals together benefiting from the military rations made available by the soldiers). ... we used to study, particularly Hebrew, and we used to carry out organizational and cultural activities to revive the life of the Community, which was reorganizing itself after a long period of stagnation.[21]

Tens of young people were influenced by the enthusiasm of the Palestinians, who organized proper seminars on the history of Judaism, Zionism and the Jewish Socialist Movement. Starting from those experiences, some of the more highly motivated young men were then guided towards the *aliyà* (as the 'ascent' towards the land of Israel is called in Hebrew), passing through a period of preparation at a *hackshara* (a collective farm where they were trained to work in the fields), set up on 15 July just outside Rome, at Ponte Nona, on the Via Prenestina. That group of young pioneers was joined by some families who intended emigrating: as early as 1945 a first group of about 200 people was able to leave, heading for Palestinian territory;[22] between 1944 and 1945, a total of 627 people left Italy for Palestine, of which 387 were Italian citizens.[23]

Due to the impetus provided by the Palestinian soldiers – some of whom were exempted from military activities to dedicate themselves full time to helping both Italian Jews and foreign Jewish refugees – the Roman Jewish school resumed its activities. From about sixty pupils at the beginning of June 1944, when the other schools of the capital were still closed, there were soon approximately 500 students, who were exposed to a wind of change: six 'soldier-teachers', for example, imposed, on the pre-existing teaching staff, that Saturday should be a holiday, instead of Sunday, and many hours were given over to teaching Hebrew.[24] These were initiatives which reflected a national conception of Judaism, which took up, for its own ends, traditional symbols and laws, without this implying a return to religious orthodoxy.

That ideological stand and, in general, all the activism of the envoys from Palestine gave rise to an embarrassed disquiet in the Italian-Jewish establishment, which saw its own policy and culture being challenged.

JEWS BY LAW

Like all the country's institutions, Jewish bodies had also been subject to the regime. With the Royal Decree n.1731 of 30 October 1930, the Union of Italian-Jewish Communities (UCII: Unione delle Comunità Israelitiche Italiane) had been created: it represented the single Jewish communities and, in general, Italian Judaism in its relations with State authorities.

This institutional set-up survived until 1987, characterizing the life of Italian Judaism. Among the reasons for its longevity is that the Jewish establishment, both in the 1930s and in the post-war period, recognized the Royal Decree n.1731 as being essential to counteract a process of assimilation which it saw as a threat. It is well to remember that such a decree was the result of a reform desired and promoted by the Committee of Jewish Communities, which in 1929 had submitted to the government a bill autonomously prepared and drafted by the jurist Mario Falco.[25] From the encounter between the State and the Committee's representatives there emerged a decree of a clearly jurisdictional nature, which established a body (the UCII) firmly subject to the government's surveillance and tutelage: the government had the power to dissolve the Council and to approve the nomination of its president. The apparatus thus created not only enabled the regime to exercise increasing control over the Italian-Jewish minority, but it was also useful in attaining the objectives of fascist expansion in the Mediterranean.[26]

There were, however, important compensations for the Jewish establishment. With that decree, appurtenance to Italian Judaism was defined in strict terms, giving a certain power to the ruling groups charged with regulating the ways of entering and leaving the community. Article 4 of the decree in fact laid down that 'all the Jews residing in the territory of the Community belong to it by right'. A right which has almost become compulsory, or which in any case has been removed from the sphere of free choice, because the law soon sanctioned the right of the communities to include among its own 'members the son of a Jewish mother, who does not communicate to the community his baptism nor does he declare that he does not want to be considered Jewish in accordance with art. 3 of the Royal Decree of 30 October 1930, n.1731'.[27] In fact, there was no room for those who wished to express their 'Jewishness' outside the enclosure wanted and erected by the Jewish establishment in agreement with the government. The plan prepared by Mario Falco in the name of the Committee imposed a complete correspondence between belonging to the congregation of the faithful – or rather the system of the communities as outlined in the plan itself – and the faith, the religious feeling of individuals. Consequently, the recognition of each person's 'Jewishness' was subordinated to membership of a community.[28] Belonging to Judaism was thus regulated by law, explicitly renouncing the model of freedom of association as well as the elementary liberal principles inherent in respect for people's consciences and their personal views. From that moment onwards there was only room for one Judaism, the official one; the idea that belonging to the Jewish culture and community could express itself in a multifaceted variety of forms was stifled by a very rigid law.[29]

In evaluating the final result, the representatives of Italian Judaism during the fascist era, like their successors in the post-war period, had to bear in mind that, while the communities became an organ of the State, they received discrete powers, including the mandatory nature of the tribute due to the communities on the part of individuals, as well as the recognition of the pre-eminence of the Union – with respect to the individual communities – which was strengthened, while the most representative bodies, such as the Congress of the Communities and the Council of the Union, were weakened in favour of the executive organs, such as the Committee and the Presidency. The considerable strengthening of the controlling and strategic organs clearly reinforced the Jewish elite and facilitated the carrying out of its tasks.[30]

This explains the Jewish establishment's favourable attitude towards those laws and the strong opposition expressed by all the active sectors of Jewish life when, between the spring and summer of 1944, the Allied Control Commission mooted the hypothesis that the law of 1930 should be repealed, indicating how the laws regulating the life of Italian Judaism needed to be 'adapted to the principles of freedom'.[31] On the whole, that was a minor issue compared to the many and more dramatic questions which the anti-fascist leaders and the Allies had to deal with at the time. This fact, together with the opposition of the active and organized groups of the Jewish minority,[32] led to the shelving of the problem which would only be finally tackled and resolved in the 1980s, following a judgment by the Constitutional Court (13 July 1984, n.239) which ruled on the unconstitutionality of the laws regarding appurtenance to the community. That decision gave an added impetus to the view that had been circulating for some time within the community, strengthening the position of those who for decades had been striving for a revision of the law of 1930. Consequently, after a few years, there was a new understanding between the State and the Jewish communities, agreed to on 27 February 1987: it arose within the context of the policy of the agreements with the different religious confessions promoted in those years by the government.[33]

Thus the Jewish establishment came to reconsider its own statute, which it had strenuously defended for years because it had seen it as an exceptional means with which to promote its own policy.[34] In fact, until the 1980s the only concrete commitment to modernizing the system of the communities, aiming at coming into line with the principles of democratic equality upon which the Republic was based, concerned giving women the right to representation: in the first years of the post-war period, an appropriate request for an exception was forwarded to the Ministry of the Interior in order to be able to proceed with the active participation of women in the Council of the UCII. On the basis of the exception granted by the authorities, Marta Navarra Bernstein, the President of the Association of Jewish Women in Italy (ADEI: Associazione Donne Ebree in Italia), was asked to join the Council of the Union.[35] The first woman elected to the Council was, however, Tullia Zevi in 1951.[36]

Furthermore, because of the Royal Decree n.1731, those who in the post-war years governed the life of the community not only regulated the ways of entering and leaving Italian Judaism (or at least the communities on the basis of the law), but they could also legitimately intervene publicly in the name of an Italian Judaism which they, in fact, did not represent, if not to a very small degree. Actually, for many decades, the articles which restricted electoral participation, on the basis of the census, reduced the number of those having a right to vote to about a third of those who, instead, were called upon to pay a tribute. This, together with the gratuitousness of the community appointments, led to a class exclusiveness which, combined with a majority electoral system, inevitably stifled any attempt to organize internal dissent. It was also for this reason that, throughout the post-war period, it only rarely happened that the number of those voting in the elections for the community councils exceeded 20 per cent of those eligible to vote.[37] This led to an evident dyscrasia between *legal* Judaism, embodied in the organizations structured according to the decree of 1930, and *real* Judaism, which was more numerous and had a greater variety of plans and aspirations than would appear simply from the actions and statements of those who, *de iure*, could call themselves the representatives of the Italian Jews.[38]

The law of 1930 considerably complicated the rotation of the ruling groups: in the very first years of the post-war period, following the (partial) substitution of the ruling class of the fascist era, a new group – mainly in accord, pro-Zionist and without strong opposition – consolidated its position: in its ranks, rotation occurred almost exclusively, for many years, by co-option.

THE HANDOVER

The Jewish establishment of the fascist era soon found itself in difficulties once the process of liberation had started: as early as the summer of 1944, the signs of a profound change within the Jewish institutions were clearly visible.

With the end of the German occupation, the largest Jewish community in the peninsula, that of Rome, revived itself, facing an unprecedented reality in which, despite the memory of the dark months of the Nazi oppression, ideas and plans for renewal could take shape. As has already been seen, the Palestinian units had a strong impact in various ways: reviving the exhausted ranks of Roman Judaism, spreading new ideals, encouraging dynamic activism which strengthened the links of appurtenance to the community, favouring the spread of the Zionist message. There were occasional clashes between the Palestinians and Italian Zionists and there was not always total agreement,[39] also owing to the particular nature of Italian Zionism which had arisen as a movement aiming at the rediscovery of the religious tradition and did not have the deep-seated intolerance towards the passiveness of the religious which had characterized Zionist ideology in other parts of Europe.[40] In any case, the initiatives taken by the Palestinian contingent could not but find favour among the few Italian Zionists present in the newly liberated capital. On 27 June 1944, a Zionist group, under the direction of Carlo Alberto Viterbo,[41] a figure of historical importance in Italian Zionism, was revived in Rome. It devoted itself to promoting meetings and cultural activities, including resuming the publication of Jewish periodical press which had been forcibly interrupted in 1938.[42] The *Bollettino Ebraico d'Informazioni* (*Jewish Information Bulletin*) was started; seventeen issues were printed between 13 July and 23 November 1944, when publication ceased, because the Zionist weekly *Israel*, a historic masthead of Italian Judaism, was able to restart.[43]

From the pages of the bulletin, Roman Zionists intervened resolutely in the life of the local Jewish community, which clearly showed the marks of the serious crises in its institutional apparatus. On 7 July 1944, Colonel Charles Poletti, the Allied Governor of Rome, dissolved the Council of the Community and replaced the President, Ugo Foà, with a temporary commissioner, the lawyer Silvio Ottolenghi: many remembered his fascist past, as well as his militancy in the ranks of the nationalist and anti-Zionist Jews.[44] Challenged by the Zionists, who were preparing the ground for the next Council elections, he did what he could to elicit government help for the community which – as he wrote to the Prime Minister, Ivanoe Bonomi – had 'emerged from the nightmare', but was still encountering enormous obstacles in its attempt to resume a dignified life.[45]

Shortly afterwards, other appointments imposed by the new authorities provoked a serious commotion in Roman Judaism. On 21 September, on the order of the Minister of the Interior, the learned Galician scholar Israel Zolli (originally named Zoller, he had changed his last name to attest his support for the Italian national cause during the First World War) – whom the Community Council removed from his post following the Liberation, because he had been accused of having abandoned the faithful in their hour of need – was reinstated in the Chair of Chief Rabbi of Rome. Zolli had been originally called to take up that position in 1938, following the emigration of Rabbi David Prato who had left Italy for Palestine also because of the attacks launched against him by nationalist Jewish circles on account of his Zionist sympathies.[46] Following 8 September 1943 and the beginning of German occupation, Zolli – worried by the possible tragic consequences of the German occupation – clashed with President Foà and other Community leaders, justly asking that the religious functions in the synagogue should be suspended, that the list of the members should be burnt and that all the co-religionists should be urged to find safety in hiding. His words being unheeded, he decided to flee, finding refuge in the Vatican. Following the Minister's decision, he was reinstated, but his relationship with the Community had been marred: the recent dramatic events must have particularly troubled him, so much so that, after months of friction, on 1 February 1945 he resigned and ten days later his conversion to Catholicism was made known.[47] It was a sensational fact, as serious as it was unexpected, which forcibly struck various observers, even foreign ones, fearful that this could be the start of a proselytizing campaign by the Catholic Church.[48] The newly appointed President of the Community, Vitale Milano, who took office following the elections held on 18 February, recalled David Prato, who returned from Palestine to take up that vacant office until his death in 1951, when Elio Toaff was appointed to the Rabbinical Chair of the capital.[49]

The ‘Zolli case’ and the other changes in the Roman Community took place in a climate of uncertainty and tension, when the process of repealing the racial laws had only just begun and in the North the manhunt for the ‘Jew’ continued; in that climate, exacerbated by the conflicts and made febrile by the increasing number of initiatives and insistent requests, the result was the resignation of the President of the Union. On 1 October 1944, the former Prefect Dante Almansi, who had directed the UCII in the dark years of the persecution, resigned asking for the appointment of an external commissioner of that body because, as he himself stated in his letter of resignation to the Minister of the Interior, ‘the majority of the members of the Council have taken refuge abroad or find themselves in the non-liberated territories … It is not possible to continue with temporary regulations, while it is necessary to see to the drawing up of the budget and of the tasks to be carried’.[50] Apart from these technical factors, there were other reasons which led to that decision: in those months, the absolute impotence of the ruling group had emerged, incapable of directing Jewish life, unable to control the group of Italian Zionists and even less able to influence the choices of the soldiers of the Jewish Brigade. A Memorandum of the Prime Minister’s Office in the summer of 1944 can help us to reconstruct the climate of the Roman Jewish circles:

> Zionist propaganda in Italy – noted an anonymous but acute observer – has assumed a very lively pace since the arrival in Rome of the Palestinian Legion. … although almost all the Italian citizens belonging to the Jewish religion are not at all Zionist and very many of them are decidedly hostile to such a movement, nevertheless it should be noted that the present propaganda, conducted after the recent racial persecutions, could have a certain effect, especially among the young. It should also be pointed out that the financial means employed, particularly with the aim of offering assistance, are considerable.
>
> Zionist propaganda tries to express itself within the Jewish communities, so as to give the movement an official air and make it appear much more widespread than is in fact the case.[51]

The problem for the UCII leadership posed by the frenetic activities of the Zionists and the Palestinians in every sector of Jewish life is particularly evident in the minutes of the meetings held in newly liberated Rome and attended by those few members of the Council of the Union who could be found. The body in charge of Jewish affairs felt in a way challenged and harassed, as one of the councillors, the engineer Segrè, noted in a meeting on 27 August 1944: '…some Jewish elements and groups put themselves forward and in some fields try and replace, or even overwhelm the Union, especially in the educational field'.[52] The same concerns surfaced in the following meeting, held on 6 September, with 'the continuous emergence of Jewish associations and organizations having the most varied names and aims, some being in tune with the Union, while others were at odds with it, to the obvious detriment of its prestige'.[53]

Those who expressed themselves in this way were men who had attained the leadership of the most important Jewish body at the beginning of the campaign of persecution, when it had seemed that a sort of momentary truce was in view between the opposing fronts of the Zionists and the anti-Zionists, who, particularly since 1934, had vigorously fought for control of the community institutions.[54] In line with its mandate, the UCII continued to keep its distance from the Zionists, as is clear from the tone of the reply, on 6 September 1944, to Carlo Alberto Viterbo, who had requested the UCII's support to obtain the necessary authorization to resume publishing the Zionist weekly *Israel*: 'The councillors are of the opinion that the newspaper *Israel* being well known as the publication of an organization having political aims and being in fact the official organ of Zionism in Italy, the Union, although not being in any way opposed to its re-emergence, cannot intervene in favour of the said action'.[55] An act of that kind had very little bearing on real life and did not reflect the concrete reality of the conflict which was looming on the horizon: by then, the situation had become very different from the one in which that group of councillors had established itself. Once the group that had governed Jewish institutions in the fascist era recognized the impossibility of pursuing its own agenda, it could only remit its mandate to the authorities.

Following those resignations, on 17 November 1944, the Minister of the Interior appointed as temporary Commissioner of the UCII Giuseppe Nathan, the son of the better known Ernesto who had been Mayor of Rome from 1907 to 1913. He was probably chosen more because of his excellent relations with the Allies than the prestige he enjoyed within the Jewish minority.[56] Despite the fact that the Zionists were undoubtedly the most active and alert group, the government and the Allied Control Commission had turned to other spheres in choosing commissioners or reinstating rabbis; one can therefore understand why Zionist circles saw the appointment of Nathan as a threat and a provocation, reacting forcibly with a polemical attitude. They very clearly expressed their resentment in the pages of *Israel*: on 7 December 1944, Carlo Alberto Viterbo in fact wrote that 'the choice of the Commissioner is a real surprise for the Jewish establishment in Italy which was not consulted on this matter', and a few days later (*Israel*, 12 February 1944) returned to the attack asking that there should not be any interference resulting in 'the appointment of unsuitable commissioners, the absence of normalizing elections, delays for necessary regulations or the threat of administrative reforms'. The Zionists openly claimed an executive role,[57] which they would actually attain within a short time.

The fears of the Zionist minority, which disputed Nathan's appointment as commissioner, soon showed themselves to be unjustified. The new UCII's administration energetically involved itself on several fronts: from searches for deportees to putting pressure on the authorities to obtain a rapid abrogation of the racist laws and a speedy reintegration of the persecuted.[58] In carrying out his duties, Nathan tried in every way to get the collaboration of the then most active group in a Jewish context, precisely the Zionist one, and he did not fail to show his support for that cause.[59] Nathan's direction ended with the Congress of the Union of 27–28 March 1946, following which Raffaele Cantoni was elected President.[60] He was chosen, from among those who were motivated and capable of holding that office, because he was perhaps the only one who had strong links with both the anti-fascist circles, who were then establishing themselves in running the country, and various foreign Jewish organizations, whose support Italian Judaism could not have done without. Cantoni was President of the Union of the Communities from 1946 to 1951: but he continued to influence its policies throughout the 1950s, directing the process of reorganization of Italian-Jewish life.

Born in Venice in 1896, Raffaele Cantoni had enlisted as a volunteer in the Great War, distinguishing himself for his courage and leadership qualities. At the end of the conflict, he had maintained strong ties with the pro-war circles, going so far as to participate, with D'Annunzio, in the take-over of the town of Fiume. These experiences, and perhaps also his links with free-masonry, brought him close to the early fascist movement, from which, however, he soon distanced himself, becoming an active supporter of the movement 'Italia Libera' (Free Italy) and later taking part in the anti-fascist conspiracy in the circles of the Milanese Justice and Liberty movement. As a result of such political activism he was deferred to the Special Tribunal in 1930 together with renowned anti-fascist militants such as, among others, Riccardo Bauer and Ferruccio Parri. A few years later he stood out as the prime mover of the Jewish assistance organizations which began to form in 1933 with the aim of helping the refugees fleeing from Germany: he played a crucial role in the life of the Milanese body called COMASEBIT (Comitato Assistenza Ebrei in Italia – the Jewish Assistance Committee in Italy) and, after the start of the fascist racial campaign, he continued to follow its activities. In the meantime, this body had also begun to help Italian Jews, subsequently collaborating – after the enforced closure of COMASEBIT – with DELASEM (Delegazione Assistenza Emigrati – the Emigrants' Assistance Committee), a body set up by the UCII in 1939 in agreement with the Italian government with the aim of promoting Jewish emigration.[61] During this period, Cantoni established important relationships with various foreign Jewish organizations such as the American Joint Distribution Committee and the World Jewish Congress, but he also ended up attracting the attention of the regime's repressive forces: when the war broke out he was sent, together with Viterbo and other key figures of Italian Judaism, to the internment camp of Urbisaglia, and from there he was later interned in the Tremiti isles. Having managed to escape, after 8 September 1943 he took up the struggle once again in the DELASEM, in order to save as many co-religionists as possible. He was, in turn, captured and only managed to save himself by jumping off a moving train headed for Auschwitz. Having taken refuge in Switzerland, he established relations with Italian anti-fascists and consolidated his earlier ties with the representatives of important foreign Jewish organizations. He was soon picked out by Commissioner Nathan as one of those who would assist him in his difficult task.[62] Having returned to Milan following the national insurrection of 25 April 1945, he collaborated with the CLNAI (Comitato di Liberazione Nazionale Alta Italia – National Liberation Committee for Northern Italy), as a member of the Central Finance Commission, of which he would become President on 6 June. At the same time, on 29 April, Riccardo Lombardi appointed him temporary Commissioner for the Milan Jewish Community, of which, through free elections, he would become President on 18 November 1945. In this role, he gave strong support to the refugees who were beginning to arrive from Eastern Europe, doing his best, furthermore, for the re-opening of the Jewish School and the setting up of the *Bollettino della Comunità Israelitica di Milano* (*Bulletin of the Milan Jewish Community*), which was, from the outset, pro-Zionist.[63] He would consistently follow that path, including when called upon to direct all Italian Judaism.

The Congress of the Union of Italian Jewish Communities of March 1946 determined a partial, but important, change in the Jewish ruling class. The renewal was natural: deaths and emigration had deprived the minority of numerous important figures, furthermore there were figures of the old ruling group who were now unacceptable, because they had had close ties with the fascist regime.[64] Nevertheless, the radical nature of this change should not be overemphasized: the new ruling group was not made up of outsiders but of people who had already had an important role in the direction of Jewish affairs under fascism. In the early decades of the post-war period, the Council of the Union was made up of prominent figures of Italian Judaism like Viterbo, soon to be joined by Dante Lattes, recalled to Italy in 1946, as well as numerous figures who had distinguished themselves in the Jewish self-help organizations, such as COMASEBIT and DELASEM. These included Cantoni himself, but also Raffaele Jona, Renzo Levi and Lelio Vittorio Valobra. The latter was also the most important link with the direction during the fascist era: he was the only one who had already been a member of the two preceding councils, as well as Vice-President of the UCII under the leadership of Almansi, when he was, above all, responsible for the creation of DELASEM, whose activities he had directed until 1943.[65] The men of the nationalist, anti-Zionist and, at times, openly fascist wing of the Jewish ruling class had ceded ground to a 'new' UCII, led by a small, coherent group of men who were not afraid to show clearly their pro-Zionist sentiment. So much so that the Zionist weekly *Israel*, still viewed with a certain diffidence and suspicion by President Almansi and his Council, could however be designated, by a circular sent to all the communities in April 1946, as the 'official organ of Italian Judaism';[66] and, in effect, this periodical was from that time actively supported and financed by the UCII.[67]

THE UCII AND ITALIAN POLITICS

We will return, in the next chapter, to the issue of Zionism, its significance and weight in the politics of the Jewish establishment in the post-war period. It was certainly not the only element in the political-cultural scenario with which the UCII soon had to come to terms. After the fall of Mussolini, Italian politics quickly became lively and animated, at stake were the reformulation of the concept of citizenship, with the drawing up of the Republican Constitution, and the country's place in the context of the new international political scene.

Naturally, the first great issue on which the UCII had to take a stand was the institutional referendum concerning the fate of the monarchy: the weekly *Israel* – which, as we have seen, the Union defined as its official organ – intervened several times on this topic. Through various articles the editor of the weekly, Carlo Alberto Viterbo, showed himself to be clearly in favour of the Republican option when the nation was called upon to decide whether Italy was to be a Republic or a Monarchy. He recalled, among other things, the cowardice of Victor Emanuel III, contrasting the latter's adhesion to the persecutory policy with the different attitude adopted by the Danish monarch, who had shown solidarity towards the persecuted. The Zionist weekly was, however, much more cautious in expressing its views about the elections to the Constituent Assembly: 'Individual Jews', wrote Viterbo, 'can and have the duty to participate in Italian politics, whereas the attitude of the Jews, as a community, should be as neutral as possible'.[68]

There was a more decisive intervention on the part of the UCII, in a political context, regarding the debate about the confirmation of the Lateran Pacts in the Republican Constitution, when the President of the UCII Cantoni, in conjunction with the representatives of the Waldensian community, took the opportunity to express the unease of the religious minorities. After long discussions with the members of the Council, many of whom felt that it was more prudent and advisable to maintain a discrete distance from the political battle, thereby avoiding a clash with the Church and the Catholic world, Cantoni decided to confirm his already expressed disagreement, and the Council decided to send to the Constituent assembly a telegram in which the representatives of the Italian Jews 'reasserted their previously formulated requests … for the equality of all religions before the law'. A clear stand, which was followed by precautionary wording: '[The Italian Jews] decidedly refute any tendentious insinuation which would wish to make their attitude appear a disturbing element with regard to religious peace in Italy, on the contrary, restating the gratitude of the Jews towards the Head of the Catholic Church for his human solidarity during the period of the recent tragic persecutions'.[69] As is known, the Pacts were confirmed and a privileged status was acknowledged for the Catholic Church: the complaints of Jews and Protestants could do little to change the balance of political power.[70]

The battle over the relationship between the Catholic Church and the State – art. n.7 of the Constitution – was only one aspect of the attempts made by the leadership of the Union to try to protect fully the rights of Italian Jews in the new Republic. With this aim in mind, some proposals were directly addressed to the Constituent Assembly, through the publication of a booklet, edited by the UCII: *Ai deputati dell'Assemblea Costituente. Rilievi e proposte presentate dalla Unione delle Comunità Israelitiche Italiane sul progetto di Costituzione della Repubblica Italiana formulato dalla Commissione per la Costituzione*[71] (To the Deputies of the Constituent Assembly: Important considerations and proposals from the Union of Italian-Jewish Communities regarding the planned Constitution of the Italian Republic formulated by the Constitutional Commission). Among the main points there was the 'subdued request to substitute the word "stripe" (extraction) for "razza" (race), leaving the latter for dogs and horses', advanced in relation to the article regarding the equality of all citizens; the knotty problem of the indissolubility of marriage; the problem of the equality of all religions. The first request, as is known, was not accepted, while the second contributed to the omission of the theme of the indissolubility of marriage from the definitive text (even if the problem of the right to divorce would have been the issue of a longer and harder battle).[72]

Finally, the third point represented the most complex and delicate issue. In the Republican Constitution, the fascist wording about 'accepted religions' was superseded and art. n.19 sanctioned 'the right to profess freely one's own religious faith'. Thus, the freedom to practise, also in public, a faith different from the Catholic religion ceased to be an exception, reserved for the *accepted religions*, and became the rule.[73] Furthermore, art. n.8 of the Republican Constitution ruled that: 'All the religious faiths are equally free before the law. The religions different from Catholicism have the right to organize themselves according to their own statutes inasmuch as they do not clash with the Italian juridical system. Their relations with the State are regulated, by law, on the basis of agreements with the respective representatives.'

The formula sanctioning 'equal freedom' for each religion before the law was considered to be a limit imposed on minority religions by Catholicism and there was a call for a principle of all the religions being on an equal footing in relation to each other: the Union explicitly and officially considered the decision of the

Constituent Assembly in negative terms and maintained that the overall arrangement of the relations between the religions and the State had dealt a serious blow to liberal principles and a political humiliation to the religious minorities.[74] In time, that formulation would have guaranteed adequate safeguards for the peculiarities of each religion, nevertheless those developments were still far off in 1947, just as the problem of the right to diversity was then alien to the sensibility of Italian culture and politics. In that field, as in many others, the Constitution has to be considered a plan which needed a long time for its full realization: the principle of religious 'equal freedom' would have permitted, through the policy of agreements only begun in the 1980s, movement beyond the simple right to equality of individuals and soliciting of a right to diversity, on a collective basis, within the State.[75]

The proposals addressed to the Constituent Assembly were, for a very long time, the Union's last direct intervention in the country's political life. The desire to not get involved, to remain as far as possible above the political mêlée, emerged clearly at the time of the 1948 elections, when the editor of *Israel* explicitly warned against voting for the extreme Right, but did not make any other recommendations, thus bearing witness to the difficult effort made by the leadership of Italian Judaism to maintain a balanced approach, equidistant from all the various political forces.[76]

The UCII's policy of neutrality was put to the test, a few years later, by the climate of widespread participation, which was also an opportunity for a democratic apprenticeship, created in Italy by the debate on the possibility of German rearmament, in the context of the build-up of the opposing blocks in Europe. The birth of a strong and independent Federal German Republic constituted a central element in De Gasperi's political-diplomatic strategy: from the end of the 1940s, and even more at the beginning of the 1950s, Italian diplomacy directed its efforts towards German rearmament as the necessary step for the definition of a new and more favourable international equilibrium – counterbalancing the influence of France and Great Britain – as well as an antidote to the Russian take-over of Europe. The European left-wing parties, and in particular the Italian Left, were opposed to this option. The unfortunate political episode of the European Defence Community – which came into being in 1951 and faded in 1954 – provoked intense controversy and a committed and effective mobilization of the forces of the Left, which evoked German responsibilities for the horrors of the Second World War.[77] The very heated debate that inflamed passions in parliament and in the city squares throughout the first half of the 1950s, with dead and wounded victims in the repeated clashes,[78] deeply influenced the recollection of the war and of fascism. All this could not but involve Italian Jews, as well, who were considered, and considered themselves, the legitimate custodians of the memory of one of Germany's worst crimes.[79]

From 1951 the Union found itself increasingly embarrassed: its aim of political neutrality often clashed with the unease of so many of the persecuted, and also with many community leaders, regarding the hypothesis of the rebirth of German military power in the heart of Europe. The Union was therefore forced to express its opinion on this issue: on 8 February 1951, Cantoni sent a circular to all the communities, imploring them not to take part in any demonstrations or political initiatives. In that text, if, on the one hand, there was a recognition of the moral duty to take a stand on the problem of peace and the question of German rearmament, on the other hand, it was noted how the realization of the desire for peace, in precise choices, inevitably embroiled the communities in the political maelstrom. Reference was therefore made to 'the impossibility for the Union of taking a stand against the present political directives followed by the Italian Government'.[80]

That action would not, however, have sufficed to close the question definitively. Germany's future was one of the controversial issues at the Congress of the Communities held on 25 and 26 March 1951. Three of the six approved motions concerned, directly or indirectly, the German question. While the hypothesis of an agreement between the Federal Republic and the State of Israel – concerning reparations offered by Germany as a testimony of its own remorse – was taking shape, the Congress of the UCII expressed its opposition to the readmission of Germany to the community of civilized nations prior to its having shown 'tangibly, its commitment to make moral and material reparation for the harm it had caused'. Furthermore it declared its decided opposition to the reconstitution of the German army and lamented the fact that too many war criminals had not been punished.[81]

Cantoni's decision, in the above-mentioned circular, was undoubtedly a difficult one, and left many feeling discontented; nevertheless, the first serious crisis in the UCII occurred in May of the same year for very different reasons. The victory in the elections of the Council of the Rome Community of a grouping which opposed Cantoni's centralized policy and active intervention in the life of the community, above all for the costs involved, led the President of the UCII – whose grouping was defeated – to resign from the office whose tenure had been confirmed by the recent Congress. He was soon followed, in this decision, by the Vice-President Renzo Levi, who had also just been reappointed.[82] Following the resignations of Cantoni and Levi, who nevertheless kept their places in the Council, there was a period of uncertainty which lasted several months until the autumn with the appointment of Renzo Bonfiglioli, from Ferrara, as President and Dante Lattes as Vice-President.[83] About a year later, in October 1952, it was Bonfiglioli, a former President of the Community of Ferrara, a Zionist, anti-fascist and with links to the socialist Left, who resigned, both as President and as an ordinary councillor.[84]

And this time the source of the clash was precisely the burning issue of Germany. The cause of the rift was the mounting disagreement within the Committee of the UCII as to how to reply to the query posed by some of the communities regarding the advisability of complying with the heart-felt appeal launched by the left-wing parties and the Committees for Peace for a mobilization against war, or rather against German rearmament and the creation of an anti-Soviet Western military alliance. Bonfiglioli, who had already, in a personal capacity, complied with some of these appeals, clashed with the councillors Valobra and Ottolenghi who proposed issuing an appropriate circular to oppose firmly any question of getting involved in the ongoing political battle.[85] The clash resulted in Bonfiglioli's resignation both as President and as a councillor; following that decision, the Union went through a long crisis: because of the impossibility of replacing him through co-optation, and not wishing to hold new elections, the UCII was provisionally governed for almost two years by the Vice-President Dante Lattes. In the autumn of 1953, Cantoni attempted to find a way out of the impasse by trying to call, to the Council and the presidency, the noted scholar and rector of Ca' Foscari, Gino Luzzato, but the plan did not work out.[86] It was only in February 1954, when Lattes' health worsened, that, as proposed by Raffaele Cantoni, Giorgio Zevi was appointed to the Council by co-optation and elected President. He had been in charge of a Jewish charitable organization operating among the poor in the former Roman ghetto.[87] He played a purely administrative role, while the activities of the UCII proceeded along the path established in 1946, also because of the active presence in the Council of Raffaele Cantoni and Renzo Levi, firm guarantors of continuity.

These changes, based on co-optation and without congressional scrutiny, provoked harsh criticism from young, progressive groups, who protested against the lack of democracy and openness which characterized the activity of the leadership.[88] The latter probably wanted to avoid going to a Congress after the Bonfiglioli crisis – at a time when passions were inflamed by opposing and irreconcilable views – in an attempt to avert further serious rifts in the community. The situation would only have stabilized at the time of the V Congress, held in Rome on 20 and 21 May 1956. On 17 June, the new Council, to which, for the first time in the post-war period, Cantoni had not been elected (though he was later called to sit on the Committee) elected Sergio Piperno Beer to the presidency and, once again, Renzo Levi as Vice-President.[89]

In the following five years, and then above all in the 1960s, the leadership group, which had guided the UCII since the end of the war, began to renew itself and, also because of many deaths, new figures were slowly able to establish themselves. From that time onwards, subdued conflicts began to re-surface and others started germinating, also because there was a growing politicization of important sectors of young Jewish associations, whose attitudes and plans would not always have been reconcilable with those of communities' official representatives. As early as the V Congress of the Communities in 1956, and with growing insistence in the following decades, the members of the Federazione Giovanile Ebraica d'Italia (the Italian Jewish Youth Federation) fought for a renewal of the leadership groups, as well as a revision of the law of 1930 which had instituted the UCII. Also with respect to the changes in the overall picture, the tensions which had emerged during the 1950s burst forth in the 1960s, when it was the youth circles which presented themselves as the only real organized opposition to the ruling class of the communities.

That turbulent period was firmly managed by the President, Sergio Piperno; after a first term (1956–61) he was returned as President on 11 June 1961 by the Council elected in the Congress of 1 and 2 May, while he was partnered – after Renzo Levi's resignation – by Ruggero Disegni as Vice-President.[90] Piperno held that office until 1970, governing the most important Jewish body in Italy in a period full of changes, from the trial of Eichmann to the Six Day War, and including the Second Vatican Council.

In that period, the memory of the persecution – a theme to which, as we will see, the UCII of Piperno gave a lot of attention – acquired an ever-more central role in the minority's collective identity, while the evolution of the Catholic Church's attitude towards the Jews cast a ray of hope for the future.[91] On the other hand, the resolute stand of the PCI (Italian Communist Party) against the State of Israel following the 1967 war[92] caused the eruption of latent conflicts and tensions, giving rise to rifts within the community and marring the relationship of many Jews with the Left. Some were able to find momentary refuge in the PSI (Italian Socialist Party), which still maintained, for a certain time, a traditional sympathy for Israel's cause; in any case, the forces set in motion in the 1960s and 1970s not only gave rise to a progressive shift in public opinion towards an anti-Israeli stance, as well as some important changes in the perception of the Jew, but have further complicated the overall context in which the UCII and, in general, all Italian Judaism, were searching for ways of combining the attachment to Israel with the political cultures of the Republic.[93]

THE UCII'S RELATIONSHIP WITH THE JOINT AND THE WJC

In order to conclude this synthetic reconstruction of the sequence of events in the institutional life of Italian Judaism it is necessary to touch on the decided strengthening of the UCII's ties with various foreign or international Jewish bodies, among which special mention should be made of the American Joint Distribution Committee (Joint), which gave the Italian-Jewish ruling class fundamental financial support, and the World Jewish Congress, which provided political support and an ideological stance.[94]

We have already briefly referred to the first body and its history. After the war, the Joint took it upon itself, in the first place, to assist tens of thousands of refugees, or 'displaced persons' according to the United Nations' definition. In particular, it took care of the Jews, without a homeland to which they could return, scattered throughout Europe following the cessation of hostilities; but it also took it upon itself to deal with the re-establishment of community institutions and Jewish social and cultural life in all the European countries.

At the end of the 1940s, after the first years of adjustment and reconstruction, the problem of the 'displaced persons' seemed to be moving towards a natural solution (with the emigration of many and the social integration of others); there was, instead, growing concern for the worsening condition of the life of Jewish communities in North Africa and, at the same time, the emergency having been overcome, the donations from Jewish Americans decreased causing a reduction in the available funds. These factors led the leadership of the Joint to move towards a gradual disengagement from Europe: the ever scarcer resources had to be diverted to the Jewish communities in Arab countries. By all prospects the situation for European Jewry seemed grim, yet new resources became available unexpectedly as a result of German reparations: the American Joint Distribution Committee found itself administering a very substantial part (about 80 per cent) of the funds that the German Federal Republic destined for the victims of national socialism. Thus, instead of being scaled down, the financial and organizational contribution to Western European Judaism could be increased.

In fact, it should be remembered that at the beginning of the 1950s, the German Prime Minister, Konrad Adenauer, developed a policy aimed at freeing the German Federal Republic from the burden of the past: in a famous speech at the Bundestag on 27 September 1951 he brought to light negotiations underway for some time, explicitly asking for the start of negotiations between, on the one hand, his government and, on the other hand, the 'representatives of Judaism and of the State of Israel'. It was therefore necessary for the many Jewish organizations, divided by their different attitudes, culture and objectives, to set up a sort of coordinating body which could sit, next to the State of Israel, at the negotiating table to enter into discussions with the German government. Thus, there arose the Conference on Jewish Material Claims against Germany (known as the Claims Conference), an umbrella organization which included twenty-two distinct Jewish bodies and at the heart of which the Jewish American associations gained a pre-eminent role for themselves. On 10 September 1952 an agreement was reached: the first section dealt with the political and economic accord reached by the Federal German Republic and the State of Israel, while the second, entered into by the Federal German Republic and the Claims Conference, foresaw the payment to the latter of 450 million marks. Through the Joint, which was the only body in a position to administer the distribution of such a sum, the Claims Conference utilized those funds for the re-organization of European Judaism.[95]

Thus, starting from 1953, and then throughout the 1950s and the 1960s, from that source new funds were destined for the Joint, with the obligation to reserve those resources for the persecuted and their heirs. Hence, the Joint could continue to influence the development of Jewish life in Europe, safeguarding the communities from the threat of assimilation. The available resources changed the character of European Jewish institutions making this possible, especially for those communities which, like the Italian one, were for a long time hardly able to finance themselves, the activation of programmes and the carrying out of activities otherwise out of the question:[96] if between 1944 and 1947 the funds distributed by the Joint overcame the paralysis affecting the UCII's activities, in the following period such resources, which from 1953 and for over a decade constituted about 50 per cent of the total funds available to the Union for each year, permitted the development of detailed plans, especially in the cultural and educational fields.[97]

The collaboration with the Joint favoured the centralization of power within the Italian-Jewish community, speeding up the process, which had already been in motion for some time, of strengthening the Union at the expense of the single communities. Analogous processes can also be found in other European countries, even if very different, as in France and Germany. In post-war Europe, the most marked sense of unity provoked by the massacres and by racially inspired injustices and, then, the necessity of dealing with the pressing need for assistance of their co-religionists, exhausted by the persecution, led to the establishment of central institutions which supervised community organization, planned reconstruction and saw to the needs of Jewish citizens and of the many refugees in transit. In France this role was taken up by the Conseil Représantatif des Juifs de France. The post-war birth and establishment of such a body symbolically marked a turning point in the history of French Judaism: for the first time it was implicitly accepted that there could be an organization which could represent French Judaism not only in a purely religious sense, but also politically. That body became – together with the Fonds Social Juif Unifié, founded in 1949 – one of the Joint's main reference points, which dedicated a large part of its resources to the French community, the largest in Western Europe.[98] In Western Germany, a central representative and coordinating organization would also, if more slowly, have arisen: in a first phase, various single communities came into being, about a hundred in 1948, most of them having fewer than fifty members, divided by their different provenance (German or Eastern European Jews) and by their different cultures. In 1946, a type of coordination developed between the communities of the French, English and American zones of occupation, and in 1947 this association was officially recognized, Arbeitsgemeinschaft Jüdischer Gemeinden in Deutschland, and was finally followed by the establishment, in July 1950, of a central body, the Zentralrat der Juden in Deutschland.[99]

From the beginning of the post-war period, the pre-eminence of the central bodies on the peripheral ones was encouraged everywhere by the Joint,[100] an objective pursued with growing determination from when the problem of efficiently planning the distribution of the funds made available by the Federal

German Republic arose.[101] In Western Europe, because of these and other factors, new bodies came into being, or older institutions enlarged their spheres of action, influencing, more incisively and directly, the life of the communities they were governing, going well beyond their traditional tasks, which generally concerned charitable works and religious organization, becoming active promoters of the consolidation and re-orientation of the Jewish population's collective identity.

A role in encouraging these changes, even though indirect and much less incisive than that of the American Joint Distribution Committee, was also played by the World Jewish Congress, an organization which came into being in 1936 with the aim of establishing a collaborative relationship between various Jewish institutions, also from a defensive point of view, bearing in mind the spread, in Europe, of racism and anti-Semitism.[102] The UCII had already been in contact with the WJC in the 1930s, but deeper ties of collaboration were developed above all by Cantoni, as the prime mover of COMASEBIT and DELASEM.[103] Those ties grew as the persecution increased and they were further strengthened after the war, always due to the efforts of Cantoni.[104] Italian Judaism was certainly not at the top of the WJC's list of priorities – committed to following the reintegration policies of the Jews throughout Europe, monitoring carefully the manifestations of anti-Semitism – nevertheless the exchange of information about the condition of the Jews and the methods adopted by the different European States to resolve the problem of the reintegration of the persecuted would also have been of benefit to Italian Judaism.[105] The WJC was above all concerned with gathering, organizing and transmitting information about the condition of Jews in the Old Continent, even though not intervening in the internal affairs of Jewish bodies and institutions, it encouraged comparisons and a constant exchange of ideas on various themes: from educational policy to the attitudes to be adopted vis-à-vis difficult problems like German rearmament and the fate of war criminals. The support of such an organization perhaps favoured and reinforced the Union in its relations with the Italian political authorities, but above all it provided the Italian-Jewish leadership with better cultural instruments with which to face the problems and challenges of the post-war period.

These relationships, the unprecedented freedom of action deriving from the virtual absence of organized opposition and the strong convictions of the new leadership led to a notable strengthening of the Union, which could intervene with growing energy in the life of the communities, guiding and directing their development, from a position of authority, as had never happened before. Having said that, it should not be thought that the wishes of the central organization would automatically be realized by the peripheral bodies, also because the renewal of the central leadership was not matched by changes in the leadership of the single communities.[106] In spite of everything, the UCII continued to encounter various obstacles and difficulties in its relationship with the single local communities,[107] but in general terms the central body's prestige, influence and ability to act grew considerably in relation to the past.

All this changed the nature of the life of Italian Jews, as Giorgio Romano perceptively noted in analysing the changes undergone by the Italian-Jewish minority in the first decade of the post-war period:

> It was undoubtedly Zionism which brought a breath of fresh air to the Jewish minority; over the last few decades, a transformation of institutions, schools, bodies and of life itself has been under way, which creates new problems. In some ways, the central body has become the regulator of the peripheral ones rather than their representative in some limited sectors, characterizing itself more and more as the centre of Italian-Jewish life, leaving little scope for initiatives on the part of the peripheral bodies.[108]

He clearly grasped Zionism's influence in revitalizing the Jewish minority. In fact it was in line with a precise political and cultural plan, which drew strength from Zionism itself, that the Jewish ruling class of the post-war period acted to reform the life of the community.

NOTES

1. A. Ventrone, *La cittadinanza repubblicana. Forma-partito e identità nazionale alle origini della democrazia italiana (1943–1948)* (Bologna: Il Mulino, 1996), pp.149–52.
2. The inadequacy of the State institutions in effectively dealing with bereavement, memory and the need for an identity after the Second World War concerns the whole of the Western world and not only Italy. See J. Winter and E. Sivan, 'Setting the Framework', in J. Winter and E. Sivan (eds), *War and Remembrance in the Twentieth Century* (Cambridge: Cambridge University Press, 1999), pp.6ff.; P. Lagrou, *The Legacy of Nazi Occupation: Patriotic Memory and National Recovery in Western Europe (1945–1965)* (Cambridge: Cambridge University Press, 2000), pp.302ff. For a specific analysis of the Italian case, see G. Schwarz, *Tu mi devi seppellir. Riti funebri e culto nazionale alle origini della Repubblica* (Turin: UTET, 2010).
3. See A. Grobman, *Rekindling the Flame: American Jewish Chaplains and the Survivors of European Jewry 1944–1948* (Detroit, IL: Wayne State University Press, 1993), pp.16ff.
4. See M. Wyman, *DPs: Europe's Displaced Persons 1945–1951* (London and Toronto: Associated University Presses, 1989); regarding the specific problems of Jewish refugees, see pp.129–55.
5. See K. Voigt, *Il rifugio precario. Gli esuli in Italia dal 1933 al 1945*, vol. II (Florence: La Nuva Italia, 1996), pp.530–1. See also Y. Bauer, *Out of Ashes: The Impact of American Jews on Post-Holocaust European Jewry* (Oxford: Pergamon Press, 1989), pp.22–6.
6. See M. Wyman, *DPs: Europe's Displaced Persons*, pp.137–8; M. Brenner, *After the Holocaust: Rebuilding Jewish Lives in Postwar Germany* (Princeton, NJ: Princeton University Press, 1997), pp.40–1; M. Meyers Feinstein, *Holocaust Survivors in Post-War Germany (1945–1957)* (Cambridge: Cambridge University Press, 2009), pp.275ff.; Z.W. Mankowitz, *Life between Memory and Hope: The Survivors of the Holocaust in Occupied Germany* (Cambridge: Cambridge University Press, 2002), pp.69ff.; A. Königseder and J. Wetzel, *Waiting for Hope: Jewish Displaced Persons in Post-World War II Germany* (Evanston, IL: Northwestern University Press, 2001), pp.143ff. For the particular sentiment towards Zionism nurtured by the younger generation of survivors, see A.J.

Patt, *Finding Home and Homeland: Jewish Youth and Zionism in the Aftermath of the Holocaust* (Detroit, IL: Wayne State University Press, 2009).

7. On the work of the Joint in Europe until the beginning of the 1950s, see Y. Bauer, *Out of Ashes*; as regards Italy and especially the assistance given to the refugees in the peninsula, see pp.245–51. For a more detailed account of the Joint's work in Italy until 1948, see S. Menici, 'L'opera del Joint in Italia. Un "piano Marshall" ebraico per la ricostruzione', *RMI*, a special issue edited by L. Picciotto Fargion, *Saggi sull'ebraismo italiano del Novecento in onore di Luisella Mortasa Ottolenghi*, 1, LXIX (2003), pp.593–618.
8. M. Tagliacozzo, 'Attività dei soldati di Eretz Israel in Italia (1943-1946). Il corpo ausiliario dei soldati palestinesi nell'armata di liberazione inglese', *RMI*, special issue edited by L. Picciotto Fargion, *Saggi sull'ebraismo italiano*, pp.575–86.
9. Y. Bauer, *Flight and Rescue: Bricah* (New York: Random House, 1970). For a post-Zionist stance on the issue, see I. Zerthal, *From Catastrophe to Power: Holocaust Survivors and the Emergence of Israel* (Los Angeles and Berkeley, CA: University of California Press, 1998).
10. The main internment camp for foreign Jews was set up at Ferramonti, in Calabria. See C.S. Capogreco, *Ferramonti. La vita e gli uomini del più grande campo d'internamento fascista, 1940–1945*, preface by L. Picciotto Fargion, introduction by V. Cappelli (Florence: La Giuntina, 1987).
11. V.A. Leuzzi, 'Occupazioni, ex internati e profughi stranieri in Puglia', in V.A. Lezzi and G. Esposito (eds), *Terra di frontiera. Profughi ed ex internati in Puglia 1943–1945* (Bari: Progedit, 2000), pp.8–9.
12. Cf. the account by the military rabbi of the Palestinian units, E. E. Urbach, 'The Beginning of the Assistance to the Refugees on the Part of the Palestinan-Jewish Units in Southern Italy and Rome' [in Hebrew], in D. Carpi, A. Milano and U. Nahon (eds), *Scritti in memoria di Enzo Sereni* (Milan and Jerusalem: Fondazione Sally Mayer, 1970), pp.231–313; F. Terzulli, *La comunità ebraica di Bari (1944–1950)*, in V.A. Lezzi and G. Esposito (eds), *Terra di frontiera*, pp.73–96.
13. According to Voigt in 1944 over half of all the foreign Jews in liberated Italy wanted to emigrate to Palestine, while very few wanted to remain in the peninsula. See K. Voigt, *Il rifugio precario*, vol. II, pp.546–7 and 549ff.
14. See D. Porat, 'One Side of a Jewish Triangle in Italy: The Encounter of Italian Jews with Holocaust Survivors and with Hebrew Soldiers and Zionist Representatives in Italy (1944–1946), in *Gli ebrei nell'Italia unita 1870–1945* (Rome: Ufficio Centrale per i Beni Archivistici, 1993), pp.487–513.
15. See the report forwarded by L.A. Kubowitzky to the board of governors of the WJC dated 14 December 1945, in A.J. Peck (ed.), *American Jewish Archives, Cincinnati. The papers of the World Jewish Congress 1945–1950: Liberation and the Saving Remnant* (New York and London: Garland, 1990), p.148. See also the minutes of the meeting of 27 January 1946 of the advisory committee of the DELASEM, in the appendix of S. Sorani, *L'assistenza ai profughi ebrei in Italia (1933–1947). Contributo alla storia della 'Delasem'* (Rome: Carucci, 1983), p.319.
16. G.J. Piperno, 'Fermenti di vita giovanile ebraica a Roma durante il periodo delle leggi razziali e dopo la liberazione della città', in D. Carpi, A. Milano and U. Nahon (eds), *Scritti in memoria di Enzo Sereni* (Jerusalem: Sally Mayer Foundation, 1970), p.309.
17. See, for example, E. Toaff, *Perfidi giudei fratelli maggiori* (Milan: Mondadori, 1986), p.128.
18. See Y. Bauer, *Flight and Rescue*, pp.63–4. The representatives of the Joint were Arthur Greenleigh and Max Perlman. A few days later, Greenleigh was transferred to France and was replaced, in Italy, by Reuben B. Reznik, who, from December, was partnered by Gaynor I. Jacobson, who played a fundamental role in maintaining contact with the Palestinian soldiers and the American military authorities. See Y. Bauer, *Out of Ashes*, pp.25–6.
19. The points of view of the Jewish Agency, led by Ben Gurion who was also in charge of the Centre of the Diaspora, and of the American Joint Distribution Committee were quite different. The former claimed the right of the Jews to go to Palestine, while the Joint prioritized their right to live in peace in the land in which they were born and had grown up. It was only in February 1946 that an agreement of full cooperation, regarding the Italian scene, was reached between the representatives of the Joint and the Centre for the Diaspora: that choice reflected the transformations wrought by the emergency in a traditionalist and, until then, non-Zionist, if not exactly anti-Zionist, body like the Joint. Only a year later, relations were strained by the unease felt within the Joint by the increasing politicization of the issue: the clandestine emigration was not leading the Jews to Palestine – since the English blockade was rather effective and only 3,000 out of 70,000 of those who set out were able to disembark – but rather it focused the attention and solidarity of the international press on the Zionist cause. Nevertheless, a precarious relationship of collaboration continued and at the end, taking into account all the activities as a whole, it turns out that the Joint covered over half the

expenses for the policy of clandestine immigration to Palestine. See I. Zerthal, *From Catastrophe to Power*, pp.183–211.

20. See F. Della Seta, *L'incendio del Tevere* (Udine: Gaspari, 1996), p.132; see also D. Carpi (in the section edited by him with S. Della Seta), 'Il movimento sionistico', in C. Vivanti (ed.), *Gli ebrei in Italia. Storia d'Italia, Annali*, vol. XI/2 (Turin: Einaudi, 1997), pp.1354–5.
21. G.J. Piperno, 'Fermenti di vita giovanile ebraica a Roma', p.307.
22. See M. Taglacozzo, 'Attività dei soldati di Eretz Israel in Italia (1943–1946). Il corpo ausiliario dei soldati palestinesi nell'armata di liberazione inglese', in L. Picciotto Fargion, *Saggi sull'ebraismo italiano del Novecento in onore di Luisella Mortasa Ottolenghi,* 1, LXIX (2003), pp.583–4; F. Del Canuto, 'La ripresa delle attività sionistiche e delle organizzazioni ebraiche alla Liberazione (1944–1945)', *RMI*, 1–3, XLVII (1981), p.193. A. Fano, 'L'alijàh dall'Italia dal 1928 al 1955', *RMI*, 7, XXI (1955), pp.268–9.
23. See S. Della Pergola and A. Tagliacozzo, *Gli italiani in Israele. Risultati di un'indagine socio-demografica* (Rome: La Rassegna Mensile di Israel and the Federazione sionistica Italiana editori, 1978), p.33.
24. See G.J. Piperno, 'I soldati di Eretz Israel e la riapertura della scuola di Roma', *RMI*, 7–9, XXXVI (1970), pp.327ff.
25. See S. Dazzetti, 'Gli ebrei italiani e il fascismo: la formazione della legge del 1930 sulle comunità israelitiche', in S. Mazzacane (ed.), *Diritto economia e istituzioni nell'Italia fascista* (Baden: Nomos Verlagsgesellschaft, 2002), pp.219–54; G. Fubini, *La condizione giuridica dell'ebraismo italiano*, introduction by A.C. Jemolo (Turin: Rosenberg & Sellier, 1998), pp.51ff.
26. In fact, the Union had been the instrument for bringing the Jewish communities of the Mediterranean area closer to fascism: see S. Della Seta, 'Gli ebrei nel Mediterraneo nella strategia politica fascista sino al 1938: il caso di Rodi', *Storia Contemporanea*, 6, XVII (1986), pp.997–1032.
27. Judgment of the Rome Tribunal, of 19 June 1939, in G. Fubini, *La condizione giuridica*, pp.57–8.
28. Art. 5 states that 'whoever changes religion or declares that he no longer wishes to be considered Jewish *in accordance with the conditions of the present decree* ceases to be part of the [Jewish] community'. The final part, indicated here, for convenience, in italics, was put in by the Minister of Justice Rocco in order to mitigate the tone of the law. Regarding the encounter between the Association of the Communities and Minister Rocco see S. Dazzetti, 'Gli ebrei italiani e il fascismo', pp.238–41.
29. See the thoughts of A. Cavaglion, *Ebrei senza saperlo* (Naples: L'Ancora del Mediterraneo, 2001), pp.103ff. The articles which regulated appurtenance had given rise to criticism and controversies since the 1930s; the standpoints of the following should be remembered: Lodovico Mortara, Arturo Carlo Jemolo, as well as Falco's teacher, Francesco Ruffini. Stefania Dazzetti has brought to light the interesting correspondence between Falco and Ruffini on this thorny issue, although strangely enough this documentation was omitted in the published version of the correspondence edited by M. Vismara Missiroli, 'Caro Falco. Lettere di Francesco Ruffini a Mario Falco (1906–1932)', *Quaderni di diritto e politica ecclesiastica*, 1 (1993), pp.229–90. See S. Dazzetti, 'Gli ebrei italiani e il fascismo', pp.244ff.; this scholar has duly included the letters in question in an appendix (pp.253–4).
30. For a critical contextualization of that law, see G. Fubini, *La condizione giuridica*, pp.60–1.
31. ACS, PCM 1944–1947, cat.3.2.2, f.13680 'Modifica legge vigente sulle Comunità' ('Modify the existing law on the Communities'), the quotation is taken from a note of the Office of Studies and Legislation dated 25 September 1944.
32. Cf. Verb. Giunta, meetings of 27 August 1944 and 6 September 1944; as well as *Israel*, 24 February 1944.
33. See the supplement to n.69 of the Gazzetta Ufficiale of 23.3 89 attached to law 8.3.89 n.101. Regarding the court case which led to the agreement, see G. Fubini, *La condizione giuridica*, pp.134ff.; S. Dazzetti, 'Un percorso di libertà. Il dibattito e le scelte dell'ebraismo italiano preliminary all'Intesa con lo Stato (1977–1987)', in *Diritto Ecclesiastico*, 2 (1998), pp.242–64.
34. The community leaders on numerous occasions took a stand in favour of the preservation of the 1930 law. See, for example, the Verb. Giunta of 20 January 1947 and of 20 October 1950; see also UCII, *V Congresso delle Comunità Israelitiche Italiane (1956–1957): Relazione del Consiglio* (Rome, 1956), p.9.
35. See UCII, *IV Congresso delle Comunità: Relazione del Consiglio* (Rome, 1951), p.28. Regarding the activities of the ADEI after the war see M. Miniati, '"Non dimenticare": il ruolo formativo e culturale dell'ADEI (Associazione Donne Ebree d'Italia) dal dopoguerra ad oggi', in A.M. Piussi (ed.), *Presto apprendere, tardi dimenticare. L'educazione ebraica nell'Italia contemporanea* (Milan: Angeli, 1998), pp.162–93.

36. Tullia Zevi (Milan, 1919–Rome, 2011) was born in a bougeouse and anti-fascist family. When the fascist racial campaign began she was in Switzerland with her family. Afterwards she moved to Paris, to continue her studies in philosophy, and with the coming of the war she went to New York where she was in contact with anti-fascist circles and began a career as a journalist. After the war she returned to Italy, continuing her journalistic activity – she collaborated with several journals among which were the *Jewish Chronicle* and the Israeli newspaper *Maariv* – and participating actively in Italian-Jewish life. She became Vice-President of the Union of Italian Jewish Communities in 1978 and later President in 1983, being repeatedly confirmed in that position until 1998. She wrote the following autobiography: *Ti racconto la mia storia. Dialogo tra nonna e nipote sull'ebraismo* (Milan: Rizzoli, 2007).
37. G. Fubini, *La condizione giuridica*, pp.130–1.
38. I have, here, taken up the reflection of Alberto Cavaglion. See A. Cavaglion, *Ebrei senza saperlo*, p.132.
39. For further information see A. Luzzato, 'Autocoscienza e identità ebraica', in C. Vivanti (ed.), *Gli ebrei in Italia*, pp.1864–5.
40. Regarding the peculiarities of Italian Zionism see the incisive study by A. Cavaglion, 'Tendenze nazionali e albori sionistici', in C. Vivanti (ed.), *Gli ebrei in Italia*, pp.1293ff; see also E. Schächter, *The Jews of Italy 1848–1915: Between Tradition and Transformation* (London and Portland, OR: Vallentine Mitchell, 2010), pp.152–94.
41. Carlo Alberto Viterbo (1889–1974) came from an assimilated bourgeouse family of Florence. He was one of the young Florentine Jews who were deeply influenced by the teaching of the Galitian Shmuel-Zvi Margulies, who – as Chief Rabbi in Florence from 1890 to 1922 – stirred a Jewish and pro-Zionist awakening. Viterbo became President of the Italian Zionist Federation in 1921, and was to take that position again from 1931 to 1933. In 1936 he was sent by the Italian government to study and report about Jews in Ethiopia. In 1940 he was interned for being anti-fascist and a Zionist. He was able to remain in Italy during German occupation and to avoid deportation; after the war he resumed the role of President of the Zionist Federation and also took up the direction of the weekly magazine *Israel*, which he held until 1974. His diaries of the Ethiopian expedition have been published: see C.A. Viterbo, *Ebrei in Etiopia. Due diari*, edited by A. Cohen (Florence: La Giuntina, 1993). Information on Viterbo and – more generally on the dynamics internal to Italian Zionism – can be found in S. Della Seta and D. Carpi, 'Il movimento sionistico', in C. Vivanti (ed.), *Gli ebrei in Italia*, pp.1322–68. On Margulies and the cultural climate of Jewish Florence, see S. Della Seta, 'Identità religiosa e identità nazionale nell'ebraismo italiano del Novecento', in *Italia Judaica IV: Gli ebrei nell'Italia unita* (Rome: Ministero per i beni culturali e archivistici, 1993), pp.263–72; E. Schächter, *The Jews of Italy*, pp.174–6.
42. See M. Sarfatti, 'L'antisemitismo fascista e l'interruzione della stampa ebraica italiana nel 1938', *Bailamme*, 11–12 (1992), pp.165–213.
43. See F. Del Canuto, 'La ripresa delle attività sionistiche', pp.185–90 and 213–16; D. Carpi, 'Il movimento sionista', pp.1357–8. For an anlysis of the weekly in the period just prior to its closure see V. Piattelli, 'Israel e il sionismo in Toscana negli anni Trenta', in E. Collotti (ed.), *Razza e fascismo. La persecuzione contro gli ebrei in Toscana (1938–1943)*, vol. I (Rome: Carocci, 1999), pp.35–72.
44. F. Del Regno, 'Tendenze politiche, religiose e culturali nella Comunità ebraica di Roma tra il 1936 e il 1941', in *Zakhor. Rivista di storia degli ebrei d'Italia*, V (2002), pp.87–108.
45. Ottolenghi's letter of 19 October 1944 to Prime Minister Bonomi, in ACS, PCM 1948–50, cat.32.2, f.12573, sf.1. For a preliminary contextualization of the difficulties encountered by Roman Jews in reintegrating themselves in society, see F. Barozzi, 'L'uscita degli ebrei di Roma dalla clandestinità', in M. Sarfatti (ed.), *Il ritorno alla vita. Vicende e diritti degli ebrei in Italia dopo la seconda guerra mondiale* (Florence: La Giuntina, 1998), pp.31–45; regarding the conflicts within the Roman community, see F. Del Canuto, 'La ripresa delle attività sionistiche', pp.197–9.
46. Regarding the 'Prato case', see F. Del Regno, 'Tendenze politiche, religiose e culturali nella Comunità ebraica di Romaì', pp.91ff.
47. After his conversion, he took the name Eugenio Maria, publishing, among other things, a study on anti-Jewish persecution and prejudice through the centuries (*Antisemitismo*, Rome: A.V.E., 1945), in which he absolved the Church of any blame, as well as an autobiography: *Before the Dawn: Autobiographical Reflections* (New York: Sheed and Ward, 1954). For a first attempt to analyse this peculiar case, see G. Rigano, *Il caso Zolli. L'itinerario di un intellettuale in bilico tra fedi, culture e nazioni* (Milan: Guerrini e Associati, 2006).

48. For example, the Rabbi of the Jewish Brigade wrote an alarmed account, being particularly hard on Zolli and worried about the possible repercussions of his decision on the community as a whole; see J. Hochman, *Memorandum on the Conversion of Rabbi Zolli*, 11 April 1945, in AHJP, f. It. 1925. For a review of the reactions in English and American Jewish circles, see L.I. Newman, *'Chief Rabbi' of Rome Becomes a Catholic: A Study in Fright and Spite* (New York: Renascence Press, 1945), pp.174ff.
49. See D. Carpi, 'Il movimento sionista', pp.1361–2.
50. UCII, b.11f, letter of 1 October 1944 addressed to the Minister of the Interior and CC. to the Prefecture, Office of Religious Affairs.
51. In ACS, PCM, 1944–1947, cat.3.2.2, f.13680. As regards the dating of the document, between July and October 1944, cf. the observations of M. Toscano, *La 'porta di Sion'. L'Italia e l'immigrazione clandestina ebraica in Palestina (1945–1948)* (Bologna: Il Mulino, 1990), pp.23–4.
52. Verb. Giunta, 27 August 1944 (those present included the President Dante Almansi, Engineer Marco Segrè of the Committee, and the members of the Council Lawyer Ugo Foà, Commander Federico Jarach, Col. Alessandro Passigli and Lawyer Ugo Volli; secretary Lawyer Francesco Polgar).
53. Verb. Cons., 6 September 1944.
54. See M. Sarfatti, *Gli ebrei nell'Italia fascista. Vicende, identità, persecuzione* (Turin: Einaudi, 2000), pp.212–14.
55. Verb. Giunta, 6 September 1944.
56. S. Caviglia, 'La speranza tradita: i primi due anni di attività dell'Unione delle Comunità Israelitiche Italiane', in M. Sarfatti (ed.), *Il ritorno alla vita*, pp.184ff. Regarding the figure of Nathan, see also the account of his daughter: V. Nathan, *Roma 1943–45. Una famiglia nella tempesta*, preface by F. Boesch, introduction by M.I. Macisti (Rome: SEAM, 1998).
57. *Israel*, 12, 24 May 1945.
58. S. Caviglia, 'La speranza tradita', pp.181–200.
59. See S. Caviglia, 'La speranza tradita', p.188. On 16 October 1945, the Commissioner of the Union, Nathan, and the President of the Italian Zionist Federation signed a *Message to the United Nations* in which it was stated that 'the Union of Italian Jewish Communities and the Italian Zionist Federation ... make themselves interpreters of the *unanimous feeling of Italian Judaism* maintaining that, in the face of the ruins and the massacres of their brothers in Europe ..., it appears indispensible that Palestine should be opened up to the free immigration of all those who need asylum. They fervently appeal to the United Nations so that they expedite the solution to the problem' (my italics). On the same day, Nathan also signed other letters with the same content, addressed to the embassies of the United States, of the USSR and of Great Britain. Copies of these documents were sent CC. to the Prime Minister. See ACS, PCM 45–53, Segr. Part. De Gasperi, b.3, f.21.
60. The following were elected councilors: Vittorio Fano, Astorre Mayer, Renzo Bonfiglioli, Alessandro Graziani, Giuseppe Ottolenghi, Raffaele Jona, Mario Stok, Raffaele Cantoni, Romeo di Castro, Renzo Levi, Lelio Vittorio Valobra, Anselmo Colombo, Carlo Alberto Viterbo, Gino Vitta, Guido De Angelis. The following were called upon to represent the Italian Rabbinate: David Prato, Alfredo Toaff, Ermanno Friedenthal. The new Council met on 28 March 1946 electing by acclamation Raffaele Cantoni as President and Renzo Levi as Vice-President. The following were elected as members of the Committee: Guido De Angelis, Astorre Mayer, Lelio Vittorio Valobra; David Prato was chosen to represent the Rabbinate within the Committee. See Verbali del III Congresso dell'UCII, in Verb. Cons.
61. See K. Voigt, *Il rifugio precario*, vol. I, pp.375ff. and also vol. II, pp.335–51 and 491–510; see also M. Leone, *Le organizzazioni di soccorso ebraiche in età fascista (1918–1945)* (Rome: Carucci, 1983); S. Sorani, *L'assistenza ai profughi ebrei in Italia (1933–1947). Contributo alla storia della 'Delasem'* (Rome: Carucci, 1983).
62. Raffaele Cantoni, Renzo Levi, Guido De Angelis and Primo Perugia were appointed Associate Commissioners of the UCII by the Commissioner (16 March 1945): cf. Verb. Giunta. Shortly afterwards, the Commissioner of the UCII contacted the Foreign Minister to expedite Cantoni's promptreturn to Italy. See ASMAE, Gab., 1943–1958, P.107, classe II 1944–47, f.102 'Rimpatri dalla Svizzera', letter of 10 April 1945 from Giuseppe Nathan to the Foreign Minister.
63. Regarding Cantoni's life, see S.I. Minerbi, *Un ebreo fra D'Annunzio e il sionismo. Raffaele Cantoni*, preface by R. De Felice (Rome: Bonacci, 1992), pp.143ff.; regarding the history of the Milan Community and in particular its bulletin, see G. Maifreda, 'La riaggregazione della comunità israelitica di Milano (1945–1953)', *Storia in Lombardia*, 2–3 (1998), pp.619–42.
64. This applied, for example, to Federico Jarach, an important Jewish entrepreneur, a fascist, but not *bandierista*, who in the 1930s was President of the Italian Jewish Community of Milan and then

President of the Union. Immediately after the war, Cantoni tried to get him involved in directing the Milanese Community, but he was forced to renounce his plan because of the bitter protests of Reuben B. Reznik – the representative in Italy of the American Joint Distribution Committee – who found it unacceptable that a man, so closely tied to the ancien regime, could be involved in directing the Milan Jewish Community. See Archivio della Comunità Ebraica di Milano, Verb. Cons. della Comunità Israelitica di Milano, type-written sheet dated 28 June 1945. Regarding Jarach, see I. Pavan, *Il Comandante. La vita di Federico Jarach e la memoria di un'epoca 1874–1951* (Milan: Proedi, 2001).

65. Cf. above, note 60.
66. See Verb. Cons. della Comunità Israelitica di Milano, meeting of 4 April 1946.
67. 'The newspaper "Israel" was the flag of Judaism and knew how to maintain its position. The newspaper must be helped', Verb. Giunta, meeting of 24–25 March 1947; see also the meetings of 11 March 1949 and of 4 April 1954.
68. *Israel*, 18, 23 May 1946.
69. See Verb. Giunta, 24–25 March 1947.
70. Regarding the various standpoints, see I. Musselli, *Chiesa e Stato dalla Resistenza alla Costituente* (Turin: Giappichelli, 1990); regarding the debate during the phase of the constituent assembly, see A. Tempestini, *Laici e clericali nel sistema partitico italiano. La constituente e l'articolo 7* (Milan: Angeli, 1987).
71. The text is reproduced in *Il parlamento Italiano. Storia parlamentare e politica dell'Itlaia 1861–1988*, vol. XIV, *Repubblica e Costituzione. Dalla Luogoteneneza di Umberto alla Presidenza De Nicola* (Milan: CEI, 1989), pp.188–92.
72. While for Catholics there was the possibility of turning to the 'Rota' to obtain, in some cases, the dissolution of the bond of marriage, an analogous possibility – of turning to rabbinical tribunals for matters concerning marriages between Jews – was not granted. The Italian regulations on marriage appeared to be prejudicial to the equality of citizens, also because it attributed to marriage a sacramental character – from which the bond of indissolubility derived – alien to the Jewish concept. In relation to this, see E. Capuzzo, 'Matrimonio e divorzio dalla legislazione giuseppina alla legge sui culti ammessi', in E. Capuzzo, *Gli ebrei nella società italiana. Comunità e istituzioni tra Ottocento e Novecento* (Rome: Carocci, 1999), pp.145–64.
73. G. Fubini, *La condizione giuridica*, p.109.
74. The Council of the Union commented on the outcome of the debate on the constituent assembly as follows: '…it was understood that there had been no desire to render justice to the minorities and that the equality of all the Religions, with respect to the Law, remained a formula, not a reality', *IV Congresso delle Comunità: Relazione del Consiglio*, pp.19–20. In effect, in relation to the penal safeguards for religions and the crime of contempt, the behaviour of the judiciary in the course of Republican history highlighted a disparity of treatment, since a distinction between the Catholic religion and the others, which can be traced back to the fascist regulations, was generally applied. See G. Fubini, *La condizione giuridica*, pp.98ff.
75. Ibid., pp.118ff.
76. *Israel*, 32, 15 April 1948.
77. G.E. Rusconi, *Germania Italia Europa. Dallo stato di potenza alla 'potenza civile'* (Turin: Einaudi, 2003), pp.215–65.
78. Regarding the very heavy atmosphere and the violent and repeated clashes in Italy between the end of the 1940s and the early 1950s about the country's entry into NATO and then about West Germany's rearmament, see P. Soddu, *L'Italia del dopoguerra 1947–1953. Una democrazia precaria* (Rome: Editori Riuniti, 1998), pp.212ff., and G. Caredda, *Governo e opposizione nell'Italia del dopoguerra 1947–1960* (Bari: Laterza, 1995), pp.88ff.
79. The memory of Nazi crimes, and more generally of Germany's guilt, became the battlefield of the opposing fronts. While one side preserved the memory as an exploitable element, in order to support the policy of German rearmament, the other side – equally exploitable – pursued a useful and reassuring oblivion. Particularly enlightening, in this regard, is the testimony of Léon Poliakov, who remembered how his study – *Breviaire de la haine: le III Reich et les Juifs* (Paris: Calman-Levy, 1951) – which came out in Italy with the title *Il nazismo e lo sterminio degli ebrei* (Turin: Einaudi, 1955) 'had an exceptional impact, greater than that of the first edition, for this reason: at the end of 1954, the Paris accords envisaged Germany's joining NATO. It is obvious that the Italian Communist Party was opposed to this and so its newspaper, *l'Unità*, dedicated an entire front page to my book. In order to demonstrate that one cannot ally oneself with a "country

of assassins"; there were other articles of this type.' See L. Poliakov, 'Presentazione all'edizione italiana', in L. Poliakov (ed.), *Storia dell'antisemitismo 1945–1993* (Florence: La Nuova Italia, 1996), p.viii.

80. The entire motion is in S.I. Minerbi, *Un ebreo fra D'Annunzio e il sionismo*, pp.224–5.
81. *Verbali del IV Congresso dell'Unione delle Comunità*, 25–26 March 1951, in Verb. Giunta. The motion on German reparations was also associated with a reference to the State of Israel which was declared to be the only one authorized to represent the interests of Judaism. The last three motions dealt, instead, with praise for the activities of the World Jewish Congress, a reflection on the historical significance of the birth of the State of Israel and, finally, a call to the new Council to involve the young much more in community life.
82. See S.I. Minerbi, *Un ebreo tra D'Annunzio e il sionismo*, pp.228–31; see also E. Toaff, *Perfidi giudei*, pp.164ff.
83. After having been re-elected as, respectively, President and Vice-President, Raffaele Cantoni and Renzo Levi submitted their resignations at the Committee meeting of 16 September 1951, in Verb. Giunta. For an analysis of the events which led to the crisis, see the reconstruction, clearly critical of Cantoni's actions, in the Turinese periodical *L'incontro*, 6, June 1951. See also A. Segre, *I Congressi delle Comunità Israelitiche Italiane 1861–1961* (Rome: UCII, 1961), p.39.
84. A Zionist and anti-fascist, he had also been interned by the fascist regime at the camp in Urbisaglia with Viterbo, Cantoni and various other Italian Jews. He became Vice-President of the Italian Zionist Federation in 1948. For further biographical information, see F. Lo Porfido (ed.), *Renzo Bonfiglioli ebreo ferrarese* (Ferrara: Corbo, 1989).
85. See Bonfiglioli's letter of resignation sent to Lattes dated 16 October 1952, in AUCII, b.11C, f. 'Corrispondenza Presidenza'. See also R. Cantoni's letter to Bonfiglioli, sent in October 1952, ibid. Lattes officially communicated to the Committee the choice of Bonfiglioli during the meeting of 18 October 1952, indicating that the outgoing President had stated that he had found insurmountable clashes of opinion during the Committee meeting of 24–25 September, held in Milan (it appears that no minutes of that meeting were taken); see Verb. Giunta.
86. Verb. Cons., meetings of 19 October and of 30 November 1953.
87. Verb. Cons., meeting of 14 February 1954.
88. See the interventions in the newspaper of the Italian Jewish Youth Federation: F. Della Seta, 'Da un Congresso all'altro', *Ha-Tikwà*, 41, in *Israel*, 21, 19 April 1956; 'Appunti sul Congresso delle Comunità' in *Ha-Tikwà*, 44, in *Israel*, 44, 19 July 1956.
89. Verb. Cons., 17 June 1956. Raffaele Cantoni, Lelio Vittorio Valobra and Giuseppe Ottolenghi were called to join the Committee.
90. Verb. Cons., 11 June 1961. As well as the President and Vice-President, Renzo Levi and, once again, Valobra and Ottolenghi were confirmed as Committee members.
91. On the evolution of the Church of Rome's position regarding the 'Jewish question', see G. Miccoli, *Due nodi. La libertà religiosa e le relazioni con gli ebrei*, in G. Alberigo (ed.), *Storia del Concilio Vaticano II*, vol. 4 (Bologna: Peeters/Il Mulino, 1999), pp.199–219.
92. Regarding the position of the Italian Communist Party, see L. Riccardi, *Il problema Israele. Diplomazia italiana e PCI di fronte allo Stato ebraico* (Milan: Guerrini e Associati, 2006); A. Santese, 'Il partito comunista italiano e la questione palestinese 1945–1956', *Mondo Contemporaneo*, 2 (2007), pp.63–104. See also the testimony of a key figure in the Italian Communist Party's middle-eastern affairs: A. Rubbi, *Con Arafat in Palestina* (Rome: Editori Riuniti, 1996).
93. For a preliminary contextualization, see M. Toscano, 'Tra identità culturale e partecipazione politica. Aspetti e moment di vita ebraica in Italia (1956–1976)', in M. Toscano, *Ebraismo e antisemitismo in Italia. Dal 1848 alla guerra dei sei giorni* (Milan: Angeli, 2003), pp.280–305.
94. Among the other organizations which influenced the development of Jewish life mention should be made of the Organizzazione per la Rieducazione Tecnica (ORT) and L'Oeuvre de Secours aux Enfants (OSE). The ORT was established in Russia with the aim of training Jews for agricultural and manual work. In post-war Italy, it played an important role in the refugee camps, as well as setting up some centres for professional training. The OSE, instead, created in 1912 to provide medical assistance for the children of St Petersburg, extended its activities to other areas of Europe. After the war, Cantoni made agreements in order to realize outpatient clinics and summer camps, primarily for refugee children. The activities in Italy of both these bodies were also made possible by funding from the AJDC. For some relevant references, see S.I. Minerbi, *Un ebreo fra D'Annunzio e il sionismo*, pp.200–2.

95. See R.W. Zweig, *German Reparations and the Jewish World: A History of the Claims Conference*, 2nd ed. (London: Frank Cass, 2001), in particular on the role of the Joint see pp.67ff. On the delicate political-diplomatic context of those agreements, see D. Trimbur, *De la Shoah à la réconciliation? La question des relations RFA-Israël (1949–1956)* (Paris: CNRS, 2000).
96. In the West, the Italian-Jewish institutions, apart from the German and Austrian ones, were the most in need of financial and organizational support. See R.W. Zweig, *German Reparations and the Jewish World*, p.97.
97. Between 1954 and 1964, the Union of Italian-Jewish Communities received financial aid equivalent to 7,271,884 dollars, see ibid., p.151.
98. On the activities of the Joint in France, see Y. Bauer, *Out of Ashes*, pp.30–3, 237–45; R.W. Zweig, *German Reparations and the Jewish World*. On the CRIF and its history, see H. Bulawko and R. Berg, *Le CRIF a quarante ans* (Paris: SED, 1983). S. Ghiles-Meilhac, *Le CRIF. De la Résistance juive à la tentation du lobby. De 1943 à nos jours* (Paris: Éditions Robert Laffont, 2011).
99. See M. Brenner, *After the Holocaust*, pp.41–50 and 77.
100. Intervening at a meeting of the UCII Council, the representative of the Joint, H. Trobe, called for the 'simplification of the relations between the various Communities, by concentrating their surveillance and economic control in the Union in order to know their needs'. He also asked that it should be 'the Union which should be solely responsible for the various requests addressed to the Joint'. Suggestions which were promptly accepted by the Council. See Verb. Giunta, meeting of 24 July 1946. An effective centralization remained, for a long time, a difficult goal to attain, as emerges from the discussion of 26 August 1948, in Verb. Cons.
101. See R.W. Zweig, *German Reparations and the Jewish World*, p.98.
102. For the history of this association, see Institute of Jewish Affairs, *Unity in Dispersion: A History of the WJC*, introduction by A.L. Kubowitsky (New York: World Jewish Congress, 1948). See also J. Fraenkel, *The History of the British Section of the World Jewish Congress* (London: World Jewish Congress, 1977).
103. Regarding the UCII's contacts in the early 1930s, see M. Sarfatti, *Gli ebrei nell'Italia fascista*, pp.101 and 115–17. Regarding the relations of Cantoni and in general of the COMASEBIT and of the DELASEM with that body, see S.I. Minerbi, *Un ebreo tra D'Annunzio e il sionismo*, pp.45ff.
104. From spring 1946, the Union sent twice-weekly reports on the Italian situation (process of reintegration, anti-Semitism, reorganization of the communities, etc.) to the British Section of the WJC. Instead, from 1947, in order to publicize the activities of the WJC among Italian Jews a special *Bollettino sull'attività del CME* was published. It appears, according to a 1949 report, that about 3,000 copies of the latter were published, distributed to every community, but also to various Italian ministries and libraries; see CZA, British section WJC, f.C2/476.
105. For example, one can see that the law – approved by Italy in 1947 – which envisaged the inheriting by the Union of the estates of intestate Jews did not originally derive from the Italian-Jewish leadership. It was one of the measures thought up and promoted, in various European States, by the British section of the WJC, with the aim of providing funds to support the rebirth of community bodies. It should however be noted that this measure did not yield substantial funds for the UCII. See S.I. Minerbi, *Un ebreo tra D'Annunzio e il sionismo*, pp.187ff.
106. A. Luzzatto, 'Autocoscienza e identità ebraica', p.1873.
107. See the criticisms and complaints expressed in UCII, *IV Congresso delle Comunità*, and in UCII, *V Congresso delle Comunità*.
108. G. Romano, 'Ebrei d'Italia di ieri e di oggi', in *Israel*, 35–6, 20 May 1956.

3

A Zionist Awakening

The UCII took many measures, in the post-war period, to support the Zionist cause. In a first phase (1945–48), illegal immigration to Palestine was favoured: because of its geographical position Italy represented a natural embarkation point for over 30,000 Jewish refugees who were crossing Europe, fleeing from the death camps and looking for a homeland. Italy was one of the bases of the emissaries of the Jewish Agency run by Ben Gurion, who were responsible for the numerous ships full of refugees leaving the ports of the peninsula, trying repeatedly to overrun the blockade, imposed by the British, against the Jewish immigration to Palestine. In carrying out that operation they could count on the partial and tacit support of the Italian government – which wished to avoid the settlement of those refugees in the peninsula and which, in favouring such population movements, was beginning to undermine British control of the area and delineate its own autonomous Mediterranean policy – as well as the support of the Italian-Jewish leadership, actively involved in assisting the refugees and in mediating with the Italian political authorities.[1]

After the birth of the State of Israel, the Union of the Communities showed in different ways, and explicitly, its full support for the new nation-state: funds were raised, emigration was encouraged and numerous initiatives were undertaken to promote commercial and cultural relations between the Italian Republic and the Jewish State.[2] These activities overlapped, to a certain extent, with those of the FSI (Federazione Sionistica Italiana – Italian Zionist Federation), which constituted the coordinating body for the various local Zionist groups present in almost all the communities and which represented the Italian Zionists at the World Zionist Organization. The main activity of the Federation, as of the single Zionist groups, was propaganda, which found expression through lectures, publications, films and documentaries.[3]

The voice of the representatives of Italian Judaism did not fail to make itself heard on the occasion of the serious crises which punctuated the history of the Middle East. During the Suez Crisis, when the Israeli army invaded the Sinai peninsula, followed by a joint Anglo-French military action aiming at re-establishing control over the Suez Canal, nationalized by President Nasser's Egypt, Raffaele Cantoni – together with Carlo Alberto Viterbo and Gino Luzzatto, a prominent Jewish academic and member of the Academy of the Lincei – launched a campaign, in which numerous political and cultural figures also participated, against the Arab boycott of the State of Israel.[4] Almost ten years later, on 29 May 1967, on the eve of the Six Day War, the President of the UCII called upon all the Jewish communities to mobilize in favour of Israel, a few days later, on 4 June, the Committee of the UCII sent, to the press, an 'Appello agli Italiani' ('Appeal to the Italians') which asked the nation to support the cause of the small State whose existence was under threat.[5] Having said that, it should be remembered that the support for Israel was unwavering and yet discrete, careful not to clash with the needs and the choices of Italian diplomacy, which only recognized the new State in February 1949 and which then maintained limited contacts with it, concerned, as it was, not to upset the sensibilities of the Vatican regarding the fate of Jerusalem and not to jeopardize its good relations with the Arab States.[6]

More than on the strictly political-diplomatic front, the UCII's support for the cause of Israel was perhaps able to influence the cultural climate and – in more general terms – Italian society's perception of Middle Eastern events. The activities of the Jewish leadership and of individuals of Jewish extraction constituted, between the two shores of the Mediterranean, a bridge, slight but long-lasting and resistant, operating as a source of cultural mediation. The role played by the drama of the Middle East in the Italian collective imagination would deserve detailed study.[7] Certainly the Italian perception of that reality would have been different if it had not been for the Jewish community institutions and the numerous figures with Jewish roots strongly interested in Middle Eastern events and exhibiting a very wide range of varying positions regarding the State of Israel, from blind support to harsh condemnation. Apart from well-known political figures such as Emilio Sereni[8] or Umberto Terracini[9] of the Communist Party – whose relationship with the Zionist question and in general with Judaism should receive further study – mention should also be made of a numerous group of journalists and cultural figures from a variety of different backgrounds.[10] Without being able to alter radically the evolution of political and cultural policies, during the post-war period single individuals and Jewish institutions made up for the lack of attention for the history of Zionism and Israel, on the part of a large sector of Italian society and culture: suffice it to mention that one of the rare instances of serious interest from an important cultural periodical was the special issue of the review *Il Ponte*, published on the tenth anniversary of the birth of the State of Israel, which had been promoted by the Union of the Communities.[11]

Israel was a crucial reference point for the concrete actions undertaken by the Jewish institutions in the post-war period, which not only played a very delicate role of mediation with Italian society, but also committed themselves just as much to mobilizing the Jews in favour of that cause. It should, however, be noted that the UCII and FSI's determined propaganda activities, and which had as their main instruments Jewish schools and the Jewish press, could influence the overall climate and above all the youngest, but did not produce massive waves of migration. The most evident results of that action among the Italian Jews were probably the donations: thanks to the initiative undertaken by the leaders of the communities, there was an almost uninterrupted flow of funds, year after year, in Republican Italy, in favour of the fragile overseas democracy. Between January and November 1948, the first fund-raising campaign launched by Cantoni and called 'For life, honour, and the defence of Israel' raised 159 million liras;[12] the commitment continued in the following years and from an internal report of the UCII of 1953 we come to know that such campaigns resulted in the raising of between seventy and a hundred million liras every year: considerable sums when one remembers that the Italian Jews were about 30,000 and that their economic position had been seriously impaired by the persecution.[13] Those donations were, partly, the result of the very strong pressure exercised by the Jewish ruling class,[14] nevertheless, they bear witness to a form of identification with the cause of Israel.

In the majority of cases, that type of identification was not, however, strong enough to break the ties with Italy and convince them to go to the 'Promised Land'. In fact, up to 1955, a total of 1,041 people made *aliyà*, in other words they migrated to Palestine/Israel; shortly afterwards, 161 of those emigrants chose to return to Italy. The migration from Italy to Israel was numerically modest, even if constant, continuing throughout the whole post-war period.[15] The persecution, the difficulties encountered in reintegrating after the Liberation and the UCII and the FSI's propaganda did not succeed in convincing most of the Jewish minority to emigrate: in Italy, as after all in the other Western-Jewish communities, one witnessed the following paradox: 'Zionism has conquered its opponents, and inertia has conquered Zionism'.[16] The decision to go to Israel called for strong motivation and a strong spirit of self-sacrifice; in contrast with their co-religionists in other parts of Europe, Italian Jews had the possibility of taking up again, despite not insuperable difficulties and obstacles, the lives which had been interrupted in 1938: in the absence of imminent danger, it was only with a strong motivational drive that one could think of dedicating oneself to the realization of the Zionist dream, also because the standard of living which awaited the *olim* (those who make *aliyà*) was much lower than that to which they could aspire in their country of origin.[17]

A BREAK WITH THE PAST

The clearly pro-Zionist approach which we have briefly outlined, and which influenced the activities of the UCII leadership, marked a significant turning point with respect to preceding decades. In order to appreciate it, it is necessary to summarize briefly the climate of divisions and internal strife which, particularly starting from the 1930s, but in fact present throughout the 1900s, had characterized the internal dynamics of the Italian-Jewish ruling class. On the one hand, a small group of 'Zionists' had organized themselves, intent on following a path of rediscovery of their religious and cultural tradition and anxious to promote, in the whole Jewish minority, a revitalizing process which would enable them to find their roots and avoid assimilation. On the other hand, there were individual figures or organized groups who did not respond to the Zionist appeal and tended to consider their own Judaism exclusively as a matter of individual conscience, to be fostered within the family: a private question which did not involve any desire for a renewal of community life. The latter was undoubtedly the most widespread feeling throughout the first part of the twentieth century. Starting from the 1930s, the hostility towards Zionism had consistently grown, as many saw it as a threat; while the dictator's attitude towards the Zionist option was slowly evolving,[18] within the ranks of Italian Judaism there had also been those who had thought they could avoid persecution by fervently testifying to their own anti-Zionism and unwavering loyalty to their homeland and Mussolini himself. This applied to the group led by Ettore Ovazza and gathered around the periodical *La Nostra Bandiera* (*Our Flag*) (1934–38), which had entered into a bitter struggle against the Zionists, condemning any extension of the communities' tasks beyond the cultural sphere, resolutely denying the legitimacy of relationships with foreign or international Jewish organizations, namely, trying to remove all those factors which were considered obstacles to a harmonious relationship with fascism. That group had tried to take over the leadership of the UCII and then, not having succeeded, it had tried to delegitimize it, by establishing, between 1936 and 1937 a series of Comitati degli Italiani di Religione Ebraica (Councils of Italians of the Jewish Religion), which aimed at replacing the communities. Such manoeuvres, although winning considerable approval in the Italian-Jewish world, had not evoked particular appreciation on the part of the dictator, who had confined himself to observing without intervening directly. It was only with the approach of the persecution, in March 1938, that the rival groups arrived at a compromise and a relative peace.[19]

Conflicts of this type did not recur in the post-war period and the most important Italian-Jewish institutions were unreservedly and openly pro-Zionist. This reflects a widespread tendency in Western Judaism, among whose ranks Zionism had, for a long time, been viewed with a suspicious detachment, fearing that it could adversely affect the process of integration. It was only after the Second World War, and particularly after the birth of the State of Israel, that one could detect a significant about-turn: while Zionism had remained a dream, an ambitious project, it had been rejected by much of the leadership of the Western-Jewish associations, but after the catastrophe and, above all, after the realization of the project itself, when the State became a concrete reality, it engendered enthusiasm and active support, until then unthinkable. During the post-war period, the leading groups of the Jewish communities in Western Europe and the United States were explicitly more and more in favour of the State of Israel.[20] The influx of the Palestinian soldiers and the rapid turnover in the leadership groups imposed by the fall of the regime and the transition to democracy resulted in the Italian situation following this general trend, although anticipating, by a few years, the change to a pro-Zionist approach in Western-Jewish bodies.

In the post-war period, anti-Zionist feelings were still present within Italian Judaism, but they remained for the most part in the private sphere; even when, in the 1970s, disapproval of Israeli policy began to emerge with increasing insistence, this would not have significantly altered the UCII's pro-Israeli line. It was only in the very first months of the post-war period that there was an, albeit unsuccessful, attempt to recreate the anti-Zionist block which had found so much approval among Italian Jews in the 1930s: in the lively climate which characterized the newly liberated capital, some figures of Roman Judaism tried to set up a movement, the AEI (Azione Ebraica Italiana – Italian Jewish Action), motivated by the same fears and anxieties which had marked anti-Zionist Jews for so long. The promoters of the AEI feared that their rights and their future could be endangered by the emergence of the Zionist current and they did not hesitate to ask for a distinct separation: the AEI suggested to the Allies and the anti-fascist coalition government that the Zionists should be deprived of their Italian citizenship, while it asked for the reorganization of the communities in line with the programmes of the Comitati degli Italiani di Religione Ebraica (Committees of the Italians of Jewish Religion) formed by the movement that developed around the review called *La Nostra Bandiera* in the second half of the 1930s.[21] It was a desperate operation, which testified to a scarce understanding of the changes underway and which did not have significant consequences: the AEI did not find sufficient support and soon disappeared from the scene; for many years there would not have been any organized group capable of challenging the 'new' ruling class for the control of the community institutions.

Thus, Raffaele Cantoni and the small group of his close collaborators, also counting on the support of the Rabbinate, were able to develop a policy of active intervention in Italian-Jewish life, aimed at driving the community towards the development of a different and stronger self-image. At the heart of this new vision was the idea of a Jewish identity not relegated to the realm of individual conscience, but which should go beyond this and move towards a more united and participatory collective life, in accordance with a model which retraced the ideals and the aspirations traditionally nurtured by the Italian Zionists. The support for Israel was intertwined with the rediscovery of Jewish roots and the building of more intense community ties, in an overall cultural plan in which the memory of the extermination played a key role.

CATASTROPHE AND REBIRTH

Immediately after the end of the war, when there was a full realization of the enormous catastrophe which had occurred, its commemoration became an imperative felt not only by single individuals, but taken up by the Italian-Jewish associations and institutions as one of their fundamental duties. As early as a few months after the end of the war, pilgrimages to Auschwitz were organized and commemorative plaques of the deportees were placed in almost all the communities,[22] while, in the Jewish press, there were frequent reminders of the various massacres carried out on Italian soil, in particular the mass slaughters of the Ardeatine Caves in Rome or in Meina by Lake Maggiore, as well as, naturally, the raid of the Roman Ghetto of 16 October 1943.[23]

The representative institutes of Italian Judaism found themselves developing their own commemorations together with a myriad of movements, associations and parties all concerned with working through the bereavement, recovering the scattered bodies of the fallen and keeping their memory alive through public ceremonies, the building of monuments or the erection of memorial tablets. The role played by Jewish institutions and associations in keeping alive their own particular, in many ways separate, memory, corresponds with the overall conduct of commemorations in post-fascist Italy, and more generally with so much of the Western world after the Second World War. In Italy, as elsewhere in Europe, while the State seemed increasingly unable to provide convincing answers for a population devastated by the war, it was parties and movements, the expression of an exceptionally vital civil society, which played an essential role in responding to the citizens' desperate need for meaning and consolation.[24] In that climate, it was natural that the memory of the massacres perpetrated in accordance with Nazi ideology should be conducted primarily by bodies and associations which represented the victims.

The premise and essential key to understanding the commemoration promoted by the Italian-Jewish ruling class was the necessity of fostering the feeling of belonging to the Jewish group. For many, the extermination confirmed the failure of integration as a solution to the Jewish problem; therefore the only possible answer seemed to be the revitalization of community ties and a return to tradition. All this appears to be epitomized in the words of Sally Mayer, the President of the Milan Community, when he invited young Jews to attend Jewish Schools:

> We believe that our countless martyrs only ask one thing of us: avenge us in the only way possible for Jews, namely to be Jews![25]
>
> The prompting to reaffirm their own Jewishness as a moral duty in the light of the genocide also emerges as the dominant idea of the 'Invitation to Zionism' addressed to Italian Jews in the first page of the second issue of the 'Bulletin of the Milan Jewish Community':

> After the storm which has dispersed and swept away everyone and which has left such a void, we survivors can now gather together and resume our work, today more than ever necessary to save what remains and to prepare a calmer and more serene future.
>
> We want to unite here, to mould a serious culture and a Jewish conscience, to prepare for ourselves and the others the way to return to Zion, to become a free people in our own land, as our ancestors in the ghettoes and the martyrs in the death camps, the victims of the pogroms and the heroes of Warsaw wanted and hoped for.
>
> If we want it, it will be granted to us survivors to see what for them was only a dream; but if we do not want it, our dead will have died in vain; and if the next generations suffer what their forebears have already suffered, history will hold us, the inert witnesses of so many horrors, responsible for their blood.
>
> Respond to this appeal![26]

The wish to give a meaning, through leading their lives in a Jewish manner, to the deaths of millions of men is the dominant element of this invitation to Zionism. The Shoah and Zionism did not come to be associated as a result of a precise plan; it was not a question of a contrived formulation or of an opportunistic choice, developed for propaganda purposes, but of a spontaneous reaction which found its origin in the mentality and culture of the supporters of the Zionist cause. 'We will also infuse in our veins the blood of our fallen brothers so that it may help us to continue on our path', wrote significantly the young Zionist Giacomo Viterbo in the pages of the weekly *Israel* in spring 1945;[27] they wanted the horrors of the death camps to be worked through and transformed into a focus of strength, a spur to more energetic and determined action.

The survivors were charged with an enormous responsibility, according to a way of reasoning typical of Jewish thinking. As Stefano Levi della Torre observed:

> the idea of a 'remainder' – is imprinted as much in Judaism, as in the concrete history of the Jews – that remainder of a people, or that remainder of identity or memory which remains after every catastrophe, and which has no particular quality if not that of having once again a possibility. The 'remainder' (according to the prophet Isaiah) are not the good who are saved; the 'remainder' are those who have the privilege of surviving, and therefore of relaunching history.[28]

Failing to support the Zionist cause would have been an affront to the memory of the 'countless martyrs' and an act of irresponsibility towards future generations. It followed that whoever had been lukewarm or even hostile towards the Zionist message was considered a desecrator. In fact, Raffaele

Cantoni replied severely to the protest of a Milanese Jew, who responded with scepticism and unease to the above-mentioned appeal published in the second issue of the bulletin, stating on the one hand that he felt 'the value of the Zionist idea', but on the other hand also expressing his desire to hear other voices and preferably dissonant ones, asking namely that 'in the Community's demonstrations, the Zionist idea should have the function and the role of a tendency, of a movement, and not of a unanimity'. A request made out of love for pluralism? Perhaps. However, one can also detect the fear that too much enthusiasm for the Zionist plan could have put Italian Jews in a bad light; the author asked for greater detachment and due caution to avoid furnishing 'pretexts and arguments for future Rosenbergs and Preziosis', foreseeing that in a not too distant future the position of the nascent State of Israel could have compromised or damaged the image of the Diaspora Jews, fuelling a new anti-Semitism. In concluding his letter, he stated: 'It is all right to be Zionists; but our Community – we believe – gathers together above all Italian citizens of the Jewish religion'.[29] Cantoni took up the challenge and, after having invited all the Jewish forces to a fruitful union, concluded his intervention by peremptorily declaring: 'There aren't two ways of living as a Community: there's only one, as Jews! As Jews who have as their emblem never to renounce anything which represents the spiritual heritage of Israel, never to be afraid of anything and to go forward, guided only by a strong sense of dignity!'[30] The vehement determination which characterizes this reply certainly reflects the impatience of those who, in the 1930s, found themselves at odds with the concerns and uncertainties of those who defined themselves as 'Italians of the Jewish religion', but it can also be understood in relation to the weight of the immense tragedy which the Zionists felt obliged to take upon themselves.

We find a clear parallel in the choice of symbols. It was also through the building of appropriate commemorative monuments that the devastating event could be worked through and in fact, just a few weeks after the Liberation of Rome, the temporary commissioner of the Union of Italian Jewish Communities, Giuseppe Nathan, proposed the building of a monument to commemorate the victims of the extermination. He was not able to finalize the plan, which was however taken up and developed by the group which took his place as the leaders of the UCII. After a few years, in 1947, at Cantoni's behest, a Monument to the Jewish Sacrifice, designed by the architect Manfredo D'Urbino, was erected in the Monumental Cemetery of Milan. That monument was supposed to represent the sufferings and the vicissitudes of Italian Jews, it therefore held the remains of twelve members of the community killed in different places, in Bolzano, Meina, the Ardeatine Caves, the prison of San Vittore in Milan and the hills where the Partisan war had been waged; the monument also contained ashes coming from Dachau camp.[31] Analysing the inaugural ceremony and the symbology of that monument constitutes a good opportunity for examining both the vision of the past and the plan for the future nurtured by the Jewish ruling class in the post-war period.[32]

The Monument to the Jewish Sacrifice was solemnly inaugurated 13 July 1947, with the participation of the Mayor of Milan, the representatives of all the Jewish communities of the country,[33] Umberto Terracini, the President of the Constituent Assembly, the Minister Fanfani representing the government, the Polish Ambassador, the French Ambassador and Gerhardt Riegner representing the World Jewish Congress.[34] The desire to have the participation of illustrious personages is symptomatic of the wish to see the sufferings of the Jewish people acknowledged and respected, of the need for legitimization which characterized the Italian-Jewish ruling class, as well as, obviously, the importance and the solemnity attributed to the event.[35]

The ceremony was followed by the affixing of commemorative plaques in all the communities and the printing, by the Union, of certificates in memory of each of the fallen: a drawing of the monument under which was written the name of the deceased and the cause of death. Each family which had suffered a loss should have received a certificate with the following wording:

> The Italian Jews bring to the attention of the world the memory of their six million innocent brothers brutally suppressed and pass on to future generations, in the victims buried here, an example of the centuries-old martyrdom suffered by the Jewish people for justice, liberty and human brotherhood.[36]

It is important to note that through these words the tragedy came to be placed in an ahistorical context: the sufferings undergone by the Jewish people were placed within an interpretative framework which, leaving aside the consideration of the different situations in which the various persecutions developed, tended to cancel their specificity and presented them as variations on the same theme which recurred through the millennia. That way of reasoning had deep roots in the Jewish cultural tradition with which all Jews had, more or less, come into contact: Primo Levi remembered how the youths who were being prepared for the *Bar Mitzvà* were instructed in accordance with this type of historical vision: 'we were gathered in the gymnasium of the "Talmud Torà" of the School of the Law … and we taught each other to find, in the Bible, justice and injustice and the force which defeats injustice: to recognize in Assuerus and Nebuchadnezar the new oppressors'.[37] Such a stand reflects a specifically Jewish cultural heritage; it was inevitable for those rhetorical frameworks to be re-activated after the war, when the need to work through the catastrophe became intertwined with the need to develop an effective Jewish national mythology, which would have had to support the Zionist State-building project.[38]

The use of the tools provided by the religious tradition could lead to a denial of the historicity of the past and an interpretation of events in the light of a 'paradigmatic memory' which does not seek causes and explanations for historical events, but analyses them in relation to their affinity with paradigms sanctioned by tradition.[39] Thus, it could happen that recent events could be detached from history and interpreted exclusively in relation to the problem of the relationship between God and the Jewish people: a striking example of this attitude is the tendency, typical of some orthodox circles, to see the persecution as a kind of divine punishment for assimilation and the lack of respect for religious norms.[40] Although this particular religious type of interpretation found little support in the Italian-Jewish world, this turning to a 'paradigmatic memory', even though not taken to its extreme consequences and not representing the only interpretative key, carried a certain weight by virtue of its reassuring function: turning to the cultural archetypes sanctioned by the prescribed memory helped to give meaning to the devastating event which had been experienced. In so doing the recent catastrophe lost its singularity, but also became less terrible inasmuch as finally, at least in part, it became intelligible.

However, it was not only by evoking a past transformed by myth that it was possible to deal with this immense massacre. A frequent answer was to associate the genocide with symbols representing a possible rebirth: Resistance and/or Zionism. An act which had a particular symbolic significance was the inclusion of the remains of Israel Epstein in the aforementioned monument. He was a Jew who had arrived in Italy from Palestine a few days before the bombing – organized by the Irgun Zwai Leumi (the nationalist, extremist wing of the Zionist forces, which was waging a very hard struggle against the British occupation of Palestine) – of the British Embassy in Rome (31 October 1946),[41] and was arrested by the Italian police because he was suspected of having participated in that terrorist attack. He was later killed while trying to escape, in December 1946. The body of another Jew – a foreign Jew – was therefore placed next to twelve Italian Jews, who had died during the war: he was not Italian, but a Zionist and active supporter of the Irgun, killed by the Italian police after the Liberation. That decision, strongly desired by Cantoni himself,[42] had a clear significance: it amounted to a claim of a supranational Jewish identity, while the extermination and the struggle for the creation of a Jewish State were placed in the same symbolic context.

The active Irgun supporter embodied, in some way, an ideal of courage and voluntary activism which was in stark contrast with the passiveness with which millions of unknowing innocent victims had been killed. Albeit in a different way, the inclusion of the bodies of some Jewish partisans in the monument recalled the same symbolic goal: also in this case one can see the wish to bear witness to the resistance to the persecution, and to a resolute response capable of opening new horizons. By means of the evocation of such figures involved in an unequal struggle it was possible to try and mitigate the effects of the tragedy, linking the catastrophe with the romantic paradigms of courage and heroism.[43]

The reference to the anti-fascist struggle, evoked by the bodies of the Jewish partisans placed in the monument, had, nevertheless, a wider symbolic significance and also recalled other issues. To think of the Resistance to fascism and Nazism in liberated Italy meant, first of all, evoking the myth of Italian non-involvement in the regime and its evil deeds. This ideological representation would also have won over the Jewish minority which, identifying itself in the *epos* of the Republic born from the Resistance, succeeded naturally in concealing, like many Italians, its own compromise with Mussolini's dictatorship, but also – and above all – to justify its own enduring attachment to Italy.

In the symbology of the Monument to the Jewish Sacrifice the extermination did not constitute an absurd drama, but was imbued with meaning being symbolically associated with the Resistance, represented by the bodies of the Jewish partisans in the monument, and with Zionism, represented by the body of Epstein. Extermination, Resistance and Zionism were thus presented as three aspects of a single issue, the persecution of Judaism and the struggle for freedom and independence. At the root of this symbolic association one can recognize the biblical narrative model of catastrophe and rebirth, which finds its original formulation in the account of the slavery in Egypt, of the Exodus, and of the conquest of the 'Promised Land'.[44] The meaning and import of this symbolic association are conveyed in the words of Stefano Levi della Torre:

> The Exodus [is in Jewish culture] a remote liberation and at the same time a paradigm of every liberation present and future: a precedent which, having once occurred, could once again happen. The memory of what has happened confirms its immanence, the possibility of its recurring today, in any moment of life and history ...
>
> The Jewish sense of history places the new occurrence in a context which has at its heart an event sanctioned by the prescribed memory and by the written word: in the latter the new event finds its paradigm, not its cause. So the paradigm reveals its immanence in the present; and the present event draws its intelligibility from evident or hidden structural similarities with the paradigm.[45]

Placed in this line of reasoning, the extermination did not have a meaning, in itself and of itself, but only as part of a formula which reproduced the biblical paradigm. The extermination represented catastrophe, but it became fully intelligible, and therefore less terrible, in being linked with a second element which symbolized the concept of redemption/rebirth. This second element comes to be identified, in the symbology of the monument of Milan, with both Zionism and the Resistance. In this way, two questions were proposed, the expression of two different versions of the paradigm *catastrophe-rebirth*: Shoah-Zionism and Shoah-Resistance. Symbolically represented in the monument, they can be interpreted as the foundation of the two principal ideal poles which constituted reference points for the Italian-Jewish collective consciousness in the post-war period. Zionism and Resistance offered, in fact, hope for the future, the dream of a new beginning, perhaps in the mythical 'Promised Land' or more prosaically in a new democratic Italy. Next to, and parallel with, the most impassioned revolutionary plans, there was room, nevertheless, for traditional and religious interpretations of the collective drama, which could be linked with the remote past and place the recent tragedy in a cyclical interpretation of history which, as such, would have been extremely reassuring, since the final result could, to a certain extent, appear predetermined. Three narrative formulas, or three paradigms, which can be seen as distinct in an analytical context, but which coexisted, intertwined in different ways, in the commemorations, as in people's hearts.

The variety and multiplicity of the references and the symbolic allusions, identifiable in that commemorative work, should not be regarded as surprising: no mythical representation capable of attributing a new meaning to the life of a community draws its energy from the consistency of the message; the real strength of such symbolic systems lies, rather, in syncretism and polysemy. Monuments and inauguration ceremonies of that type are the expression of a non-verbal communicative strategy which appeals to deep motivations, emotions and feelings, in the first place, rather than to each person's logic: the wealth of references and the structural 'ambiguity' of such constructions enable them to impose themselves on the multifaceted sensibilities of the public, which is asked to share feelings, rather than ideas, identifying with the common drama to gain strength and unity.[46]

THE ZIONIST ETHOS: SCHOOLS AND CULTURAL ACTIVITIES

Radical transformations of a socio-cultural setting produce the need for a ritual sanction. The consequent ceremonies provide the acute observer with an exceptional opportunity to see, in operation, the spiritual forces which are the foundations of social ties, as well as the proposals for the renewal of the social fibre of the community fostered by the leading groups. Not very long after the time of tears and sorrow, there was a clear need for another important ritual, happier and more joyful, also suitable for correlating the community's mythical past with the radical changes and the exceptional novelties which were appearing on the horizon.

To celebrate the approval of the United Nations Partition Plan for Palestine of 29 November 1947, which recognized the right of the Jewish people to have their own State in the region, the UCII invited the leaders of all the communities, through the national press, to explain, at a local level, both to its own members and to the wider public, the importance of the United Nation's decision. Hoping that the new State should incur the favour of the Italian people and authorities, the UCII contacted the President of the Council of Ministers Alcide De Gasperi; it also sent a letter to the Soviet Embassy, to thank the USSR for its vote in favour of the UN partition plan. This activity culminated, on 2 December 1947, in a joyful march under the Arch of Titus.[47] Marching under that arch symbolically marked the end of an era: 'for almost nineteen centuries, generation after generation of Jews had felt inhibited in passing under that monument which celebrated the triumph of the Emperor Titus over the Jews of Palestine ... Now history had come full circle and the infamy could be considered wiped out'.[48]

The Chief Rabbi of Rome, David Prato, solemnly annulled the prohibition according to which no Jew could ever pass under the arch which glorified the destruction of the Jerusalem. Since the United Nations had sanctioned the right of the Jews to reconstruct their State in Palestine, the Rabbi passed under the arch, followed by a vast crowd of people.[49] That symbolic act testified publicly to a sharp break with the past. It was the end of a cycle: the condition of Jews was changing, new challenges faced the communities of the Diaspora.

The realization of the Zionist plan was, of course, greeted with great joy and enthusiasm by the Jewish ruling class: it had struggled for that goal, if nothing else favouring illegal immigration to Palestine in the years immediately after the Liberation; spreading those ideals among the Jews of the peninsula had certainly been among its objectives. In fact, at the same time as the preparation for the imposing ceremony which had taken place under the Arch of Titus, there were also other initiatives aimed at highlighting the importance and solemnity of the moment: in the Jewish school of Milan – as the *Bollettino della Communità* relates – 'in every class the teacher has highlighted, to the small children of the Primary Schools and the older ones from 11 to 14, the significance for Israel of the UN's decisions; later, the Sub-Headmaster Schaumann spoke to the gathered pupils, evoking great enthusiasm'.[50] This episode is not surprising and it enables us to understand the role of the Jewish schools and the opportunities that such a resource made available: the schools were, in effect, the best means of influencing the evolution of Italian Judaism and educational policy constituted a crucial test bench for Cantoni and his collaborators.

Italian Judaism had inherited from the persecutions numerous schools, mainly hurriedly organized in 1938, responding to the urgent need to create, practically from scratch, an educational system for all the students of 'Jewish race' expelled from all the schools of the Kingdom.[51] In the post-war period, the ruling class established at the head of Italian Judaism was in no way inclined to favour a return to the pre-1938 conditions and tried, where possible, to keep those schools in existence. This was, in fact, the post-war problem: was there still a need for those schools and what educational programme should they have?

Discordant opinions were not lacking; they reflected, in large measure, the themes of the debate, within the Jewish world, which had developed in the preceding decades. Following the emancipation, the public school system had, in fact, been for very many Jews, eager for integration, a real 'training ground for Italianization'[52] and, as early as the beginning of the 1900s, Jewish schools or educational structures only survived in a few communities, where they catered for children from the poorest and most deprived families, who were not so much attracted by a thirst for Jewish culture but by a more prosaic need for economic assistance.[53] The need to have their own schools would only have made itself felt when, with the Gentile Reform, the Italian school system lost its secular and liberal character. From the beginning of the 1920s the regime had assigned a pre-eminent role to the Catholic religion in Primary School education and at the same time had ordered that crucifixes should be put back into all the classrooms. That transition, apart from casting a shadow on the dream of integration, seemed to threaten the very possibility of the community's survival. A fear which was not unfounded, since the Minister Gentile had not felt inclined to exclude that, as a consequence of the reform, there could be an attempt, on the part of the Primary School teachers, to convert the Jewish pupils.[54] The first Jewish response to that threat was the establishment of the Jewish Primary School of Rome, and the appeal made to all the communities by the national representative Jewish institution of the time – the Consorzio Israelitico – to set up suitable Primary Schools wherever possible. Then, after 1930, with the birth of the Union, stronger and with more powers on the single communities than the old Consorzio, there were renewed efforts to set up a network of Jewish Primary Schools.[55]

This evolution, wholly in a defensive key, had been accompanied by divisions and clashes between a 'Zionist' militant minority, which focused on Jewish education and the rediscovery of culture and traditions seen as opportunities to revitalize the life of the community, and other groups which acted to avoid standing out and distancing themselves from the rest of the national community and which conceived their Jewishness exclusively as a matter of individual conscience, subordinated, however, to the reaffirmation of their total and sincere commitment to Italian life and culture.[56] Controversies about this subject continued even after the beginning of the racist campaign, when Jewish schools had become a tragic necessity.[57]

Immediately after the Liberation, it became necessary to consider the advisability or otherwise of maintaining the schools created very hurriedly in September 1938. We have seen how, in Rome, an essential impetus had been given to the revitalization of the Jewish School by the soldiers of the Jewish Brigade, and how in Milan, the other major community, Cantoni, in the role of commissioner appointed by the CLNAI, had determinedly imposed the re-opening of the school, refusing to follow the line proposed by those who felt that it was neither necessary nor opportune, once freedom had been regained.

The leadership, which had established itself after the 1946 Congress, energetically committed itself to the education of the youngest pupils and to maintaining in operation, wherever possible, the schools which had arisen in

1938. Starting from the recording of the failings of the Jewish educational system,[58] there was an attempt to intervene by organizing a centralized direction of the schools and the educational programmes. In order to coordinate all this, in 1946 a specific Culture and Education Committee (Comitato Cultura e Educazione) was established.

Dante Lattes was called on by Cantoni to direct that Committee, and thus returned to Italy from Palestine where he had settled in 1939.[59] Lattes had been among the protagonists of the Zionist revival movement which had inspired restricted but lively sectors of the Italian-Jewish world, between the end of the nineteenth and the beginning of the twentieth century.[60] For many years he guided the cultural activities of the UCII. He restarted the publication of the *Rassegna Mensile di Israel* (*Israel Monthly Review*), whose third edition came out in 1948 and which – under the direction of Lattes – dedicated ample space to the history of Zionism, contributions to the history of Judaism, as well as to the publication of short stories. Through translations of articles already published in foreign periodicals, the *RMI* aimed at offering the Italian public a glimpse of the ideas and themes which characterized the debates within the Jewish world. At the same time, Lattes also took on two other editorial tasks. One concerned the publication of weekly instalments, edited by the UCII, in which there were concise commentaries on parts of the Torah, ideally to be complemented by public readings and discussions. On a completely different plane, was the publication of a series of Jewish and Zionist Works, by the *RMI*, as well as the edition, by the publisher, Casa Editrice Israel of Florence, administered directly by the UCII, of varied essays and studies: ranging from textbooks for learning Hebrew, to historical essays and editions of the diaries of Herzl and other contributions dealing with Zionism.[61]

The Comitato Cultura e Educazione also produced specific textbooks for Jewish schools. A report on the condition of Italian-Jewish schools, drawn up by the Union in 1946, provides a useful means for understanding the educational approach supported by the UCII. In analysing what was considered a 'serious crisis', it was seen that, after a first period in which the Jewish spirit of some had enthusiastically emerged, there was a growing tendency to return to the 'hardly brilliant pre-war situation, whose fruits we now see in the ignorance, not to say Jewish illiteracy of today's adults'. This was therefore a confirmation of the need to impede what was considered a dangerous involution and it was proposed to give a new impetus to the schools, also by drawing up suitable programmes, 'the result of a comparison between the programmes currently in use in the main schools, trying to reconcile religious tradition, Italian culture and the educational approaches of Eretz Israel'. Religious education – defined as 'the backbone of Jewish schools' – had to be developed in conjunction with the teaching of the Hebrew language, to be studied as a 'living language', while the history and geography of Israel were to be taught side by side with the relative

Italian subjects. In effect, it was being proposed that *schools for Jews*, generated by the fascist ostracism, should be transformed into authentic *Jewish schools*, or rather into institutes which aimed at transmitting a Jewish education.[62] Plans were put into practice, when in 1950, the Commissione Educazione e Cultura finished preparing the special textbooks in which – as the *Bollettino della Comunità di Milano* stated – 'Jewish history is naturally intertwined with the history of humanity, which is written in accordance with ministerial programmes, based on the criterion of calm impartiality. Geography, as presented by the programmes, is complemented by the geography of the State of Israel'.[63] At the same time, attention was paid to giving a properly Jewish cultural framework to the teachers, for whom training courses were organized in close conjunction with the educational approaches of the World Zionist Organization and the World Jewish Congress.[64]

Following this path, there developed a cultural plan which had had a long period of gestation before the persecutions, when it had been cultivated by very small circles of the Italian-Jewish world. That political-cultural line was reinforced by converging factors, the leading group's commitment, the renewed and unprecedented adherence to that line, stimulated by the persecutions, on the part of much of Italian Judaism, and the strong confirmation, by the government, of the choices made at the beginning of the 1920s regarding the role of Catholicism in the educational system. It should be noted that the gradual disappearance of the last resistance to the Church's influence in society[65] removed, in a Jewish context, the old reluctance to consider the establishment of separate, appropriate Jewish schools. The battle for a fully secular national educational system would have been even more difficult in Christian Democrat Italy and this meant that, in the Jewish world, other hypotheses should find increasing favour, other ways of safeguarding its own identity as a minority. Those who feared the 'Catholicization' of the nation's educational system and who wanted the Union to commit itself totally to fight for a non-confessional education system soon found themselves in a minority, while the supporters of the predominant opposing line saw, in an ever-greater 'Catholicization' of schools, a favourable opportunity, presuming that it would encourage a greater attendance of Jewish schools.[66]

The plans for a renewed system of Jewish schools could begin to take shape in concrete courses of action, directly influencing the activities and character of the Jewish schools in Italy, by means of the marked policy of centralization carried forward by the group which had taken over the leadership of the UCII, which could count on the essential financial support of the American Joint Distribution Committee. It was not sufficient, however, to reorganize the structures, to revise the syllabuses and train the teachers, it was also imperative to attract as many students as possible. Thus, from the very first years of the post-war period, a relentless propaganda campaign was developed, above all through the Jewish press, which was a partial success: in August 1948, out of an estimated population of school-age Jews of between 6,000 and 9,000, 1,339 attended Jewish schools. The main primary schools, which were in Rome, had 545 pupils, Milan had 131, Livorno and Turin each had 90. The secondary schools had 160 pupils in Milan, 50 in Turin and only 25 in Rome.[67] Not very high figures, but noteworthy if compared to those of the pre-1938 decades. That was only the beginning: the attraction of the Jewish schools grew with the passage of time, resulting in a considerable increase in the number of pupils.[68]

In the post-war years, the system of Jewish schools became one of the characteristic features of the life of Italian Judaism. It perceptibly altered the aspect of the whole Jewish community, modifying the course and networks of social life, contributing to the consolidation of many young people's relationship with the religious tradition and the Zionist message,[69] but also increasingly leading to a differentiation in the collective life of the major communities (Rome, Milan and Turin), in which there were greater numerical possibilities for the creation of schools, than in the smaller communities. The fact of belonging to fairly large Jewish communities was the determining factor because of the two-fold character of those educational institutions: both *Jewish schools*, that is schools which gave a 'Jewish education' in the broadest sense – which includes the teaching of the language, the transmission of religious traditions and a deeper knowledge of the history of the Jews – and *schools for Jews*, meaning institutes in which appurtenance to the Jewish community constitutes the necessary premise for admission. The only exception was the case of the schools in Turin which, since 1946, have also admitted, amongst others, the children of the Waldensian Community and of mixed marriages, maintaining an openness in contrast with the generalized call for intra-socialization which instead characterized the other communities. The latter is a delicate issue which has not failed to arouse lively controversies in the last decades: the exclusion of children of mixed marriages from the schools reflects a defensive attitude on the part of the Italian-Jewish world and – taking into account the high percentage of such marriages – poses the risk of leading to the suffocation of Jewish educational institutes.[70]

In any case, it is important to highlight how deeply the presence of Jewish schools affected the communities: those schools constituted 'a privileged channel of socialization to Jewish life', rekindling the sense of belonging to the community and creating a favourable environment for the birth and development of various youth movements and associations.[71] The influence of the schools combined with that of other factors, namely, the echoes of the recent tragedy and the existence of the State of Israel, stimulated the development of a greater sense of internal cohesion, leading to Judaism being subtracted from the individual and family spheres and more and more felt as a collective experience, in which the context of the community became increasingly important. It was no longer simply a matter of personal conscience, to be cultivated within the confines of the home. The form in which belonging to Judaism had manifested itself after the emancipation was undergoing a significant transformation.

Certainly it should be remembered that such changes did not affect all Italian Jews to the same extent. Many of those who could have sent their children to Jewish schools continued to take other courses of action and not simply because of the expenses of private schools set up by the communities. Certainly, many remained at the margins or even completely outside the life of the community, interpreting their own Jewishness in autonomous and particular forms. Nevertheless the changes so far referred to, the plans developed by the leading group and their reception – which we will consider in greater detail – suggest that, generally, there was a clear evolutionary trend in the opposite direction.

NOTES

1. M. Toscano, *La 'porta di Sion'. L'Italia e l'immigrazione clandestina ebraica in Palestina (1945–1948)* (Bologna: Il Mulino, 1990). See also the testimony of a female protagonist of the Zionist campaign for illegal immigration: A. Sereni, *I clandestini del mare. L'emigrazione ebraica in terra d'Israele dal 1945 al 1948* (Milan: Mursia, 1973).
2. See S.I. Minerbi, *Un ebreo tra D'Annunzio e il sionismo: Raffaele Cantoni*, preface by R. De Felice (Roma: Bonacci, 1992), pp.214–18 and 222–3.
3. CZA, Arvhives of the Federazione Sionistica Italiana, files, f.10/2 and f.10/7. It should be noted that between 1945 and 1947 there was, in Italy, a parallel organization of revisionist Zionists led by Leone Carpi. The organization was under the New Zionist Organization created by Zeev Jabotinsky in contrast with the World Zionist Organization (WZO); when in 1947 the New Zionist Organization of Jabotinsky went back to being part of the WZO, the movement led Carpi was also reabsorbed in the FSI, however maintaining a distinct and often strongly critical position. As its worried leader recognized, the revisionists constituted a small section which never enjoyed a great consensus among Italian Jews, while it could find some support among the refugees who between 1945 and 1948 settled in the peninsula. CZA, private archive of Leone Carpi, an internal report of 1947 in f.A 73/47.
4. See S.I. Minerbi, *Un ebreo fra D'Annunzio e il sionismo*, pp.239–41. The signatories of the manifesto included Gaetano Salvemini, Umberto Zanotti Bianco, Tristano Codignola, Delio Cantimori and Nino Valeri.
5. Verb. Giunta, meeting of 4 June 1967. In the meeting of eighteen, formal thanks were expressed to the socialist leader Pietro Nenni for his support for Israel.
6. For the position of Italian diplomacy, see L. Riccardi, *Il problema Israele. Diplomazia italiana e PCI di fronte allo Stato ebraico 1948–1973* (Milan: Guerrini e Associati, 2006); see also I. Tremolada, *All'ombra degli arabi. Le relazioni italo-israeliane 1948–1956. Dalla fondazione dello Stato Ebraico alla crisi di Suez*, preface by S. Romano (Milan: M&B Publishing, 2003). Also useful for a general contextualization: G. Calchi Novati, *Mediterraneo e questione araba nella politica estera italiana*, in F. Barbagallo (ed.), *Storia dell'Italia repubblicana*, vol. 2, pp.197–263, but in particular see pp.206–14 and 229–38. On the attitude of Catholic press towards the situation in the Middle East, see E. Mazzini, '"Terra Santa, Luoghi Santi, tali restano integralmente per il Cristianesimo". Lo Stato di Israele nella stampa cattolica italiana (1948–1967)', in A. Marzano and M. Simoni (eds), *Roma e Gerusalemme. Israele nella vita politica e culturale italiana 1949–2009* (Genova: ECIG, 2010), pp.97–116. On the Vatican's relations with Israel, see M.J. Breger (ed.), *The Vatican-Israel accord: Political, legal and theological contexts* (Notre Dame, IN: Notre Dame University Press, 2004); G.E. Irani, *The Papacy and the Middle East: The Role of the Holy See in the Arab-Israeli Conflict 1962–1984* (Notre Dame, IN: Notre Dame University Press, 1989); P. Pieraccini, *Gerusalemme, luoghi santi e comunità religiose*

nella politica internazionale (Bologna: EDB, 1997). S. Ferrari, *Vaticano e Israele. Dal secondo conflitto mondiale alla guerra del Golfo* (Florence: Sansoni, 1991).

7. A fundamental starting point would have to be the following volume: A. Marzano and M. Simoni (eds), *Roma e Gerusalemme. Israele nella vita politica e culturale italiana 1949–2009* (Genova: ECIG, 2010).
8. See the lucid observations of D. Bidussa, 'La nostalgia del futuro', introduction to Enzo Sereni and Emilio Sereni, *Politica e utopia. Lettere 1926–1943*, edited by D. Bidussa and M.G. Meriggi (Florence: La Nuova Italia, 2000), in particular pp.viiiff.
9. Terracini posed an important parliamentary question on 25 May 1948 asking that Italy should recognize the State of Israel; his policy of supporting Israel continued through the years, going so far as to criticize the stand taken by the press of the PCI (Italian Communist Party): in a letter to *Unità* of 25 July 1969 he complained that the newspaper often denied 'the legitimacy in terms of international law of a Jewish State and, in the historical-political context, its right to exist'. For a preliminary contextualization of the figure of Terracini, see A. Agosti (ed.), *La coerenza della ragione. Per una biografia politica di Umberto Terracini* (Rome: Carocci, 1998); in particular, for a preliminary reconstruction of his minority position in the PCI with regard to events in the Middle East, see the study by M. Galeazzi, 'Terracini e i movimenti di liberazione nazionale', in ibid., pp.175–92.
10. Among the many which could be recalled, we would here like to point out the interesting path followed by Guido Valabrega who, from being a volunteer in Israel's 1948 war of independence and then having experienced life on a *kibbutz*, developed the conviction that Zionism and the egalitarian ideals of communism were irreconcilable. On his return to Italy, he concentrated on historical research, maintaining a particular interest in the contemporary history of Judaism and the events in the Middle East. Thus we see him, on the one hand, as a very active protagonist in the activities of the nascent CDEC (editing, among other things, the three volumes entitled *Gli ebrei in Italia durante il fascismo*, 'Quaderni della Federazione Giovanile Ebraica', vol. I (Milan: Fgei, 1961); vol. II (Milan: CDEC, 1962); vol. III (Milan: CDEC, 1963), while in the pages of the cultural review of the communist party – *Rinascita* – with the pseudonym of Massimo Robersi, he developed from the early 1960s, an increasingly ferocious and intransigent criticism of the realization of Zionism. In the fairly inactive scenario of Italian studies on the Middle East he was among those who, even though from a militant perspective, gave uninterrupted attention to the question.
11. See 'Israele', special issue of *Il Ponte,* 12 (1958). On the role of the Union, see UCII, *VI Congresso, Relazione del Consiglio* (Rome: 1961), p.23.
12. S.I. Minerbi, *Un ebreo fra D'Annunzio e il sionismo*, p.211.
13. AUCII, b.11C, f. 'Corrispondenza Presidenza 1953–1956'.
14. For the campaign of 1948, in Rome, taking into account the fact that many Jews still lived near the old ghetto, 'tax collectors' were sent to knock at every door. See CDEC, private collection Aldo Ascoli, b.13, f. 'Community of Rome'. An analogous operation of persuasion, door to door, was carried out in Venice; the Rabbi Elio Toaff, who himself participated in this operation, remembers 'I went from house to house and collected generous contributions from everyone', see E. Toaff, *Perfidi guide fratelli maggiori* (Milan: Mondadori, 1987), p.153. During a meeting of the Council of the FSI of 12 February 1950, it was stated that the *shekel* (thus was defined the contribution to be given for Israel) should be 'requested' from every member of the community, 'excluding only those who explicitly stated that they did not want to pay it'. See CZA, FSI collection, f. F10/2.
15. A sizeable part of these emigrants was made up of young and very young. See A. Fano, 'L'alyjà dall'Italia dal 1928 al 1955', *RMI*, 7, XXI (1955), pp.263–76, but in particular pp.267–8. But see also the data proposed in S. Della Pergola and A. Tagliacozzo, *Gli italiani in Israele. Risultati di un'indagine socio-demografica* (Milan: La Rassegna Mensile di Israel and Federazione Sionistica Italiana, 1978), pp.19–21.
16. The quotation is taken from A. Finkielkraut, *The Imaginary Jew* (Lincoln, NE: University of Nebraska Press, 1994 [1980]), p.121.
17. An account of the bitterness which characterized the lives of the *olim* can be found in the correspondence of Alfredo Sarano (for many years the secretary of the Jewish Community of Milan and a member of the local Zionist group) with his son who had gone to Palestine. The young man gave vent to his feelings in a letter sent from Jerusalem on 7 October 1945: 'High school diplomas in Palestine almost become waste paper, because there are many high school graduates who work for chicken feed when they aren't washing dishes in a caffé or when they aren't breaking stones to repair the roads', CZA, private archivi of Alfredo Sarano, b.A433/1, f. 'Lettere ricevute'. To put the issue of Italian-Jewish immigration to Israel into context, see A. Marzano, '"Prisoners of Hope" or "Amnesia"? The Italian Holocaust Survivors and their Aliyah to Israel', *Quest. Issues in Contemporary History*, 1 (April 2010), available at http://www.quest-cdecjournal.it/focus.php?issue=1&id=194; M. Simoni, 'Gli ebrei italiani

e lo Stato di Israele. Appunti per un ritratto di due generazioni (1948 e 1967)', in A. Marzano and M. Simoni (eds), *Roma e Gerusalemme. Israele nella vita politica e culturale italiana 1949–2009* (Genova: ECIG, 2010), pp.47–74.

18. Mussolini's attitude was seesawing: at first the dictator tried to play the Zionist card to his advantage, trying to gain credit as a pro-Zionist in his policy of expansion in the Mediterranean, in competition with the British. Then, following the failure of this attempt, after 1934 when Italy was in the vice-like grip of sanctions, the regime's attitude changed. Some facts suggest that it was also an overestimation of Zionist influence on Italian Judaism which made Mussolini think that it was a minority which could not be assimilated and which was not fascistizable, thus favouring the progressive slide towards the racial policy. See M. Sarfatti, *Gli ebrei nell'Italia fascista. Vicende, identità, persecuzione* (Turin: Einaudi, 2000), pp.77ff., 129–30. See also V. Pinto, 'Sionismo e "movimento Ebraico". La percezione del nazionalismo ebraico nelle carte della Direzione Generale Pubblica Sicurezza conservate nell'Archivio Centrale dello Stato (1927–1939)', *RMI*, 3, LXVI (2000), pp.37–62.
19. For a contextualization of the dynamics within the Jewish leadership, see M. Sarfatti, *Gli ebrei nell' Italia fascista*, pp.86ff. On the nature of the movement led by Ovazza, see L. Ventura, *Ebrei con il Duce. La Nostra Bandiera 1934–38* (Turin: Zamorani, 2001).
20. B. Wasserstein, *Vanishing Diaspora: The Jews in Europe since 1945* (Cambridge, MA: Harvard University Press, 1994), pp.85ff.; H.M. Sachar, *A History of the Jews in America* (New York: Knopf, 1992), pp.591ff.
21. In ACDEC, Private Archive of Aldo Ascoli, b.13, f. 'Istituzioni ebraiche dopo la seconda Guerra mondiale', there is a pamphlet of the AEI entitled *Decidersi!* in which it is stated that 'The nation of the Italians of the Jewish faith IS ITALY! Those who do not feel this absolute imperative cannot be considered Italians; they may live in Italy only as belonging to another nationality, resident in Italy, with all the rights and all the dutied of the foreigners in Italy'. References to the AEI are made by D. Carpi, 'Il movimento sionistico', in C. Vivanti (ed.), *Gli ebrei in Italia. Storia d'Italia, Annali*, vol. XI/2 (Turin: Einaudi, 1997), pp.1359–60, and F. Del Canuto, 'La ripresa delle attività sionistiche e delle organizzazioni ebraiche alla Liberazione (1944–1945)', *RMI*, 1–3, XLVII (1981), pp.201–8.
22. AUCII, b.74b, f. 'Lapidi memoria'.
23. A useful review of the main themes in relation to which the Jewish press organized the remembrance of the persecution has been carried out by Elena Mazzini, *Ebrei dopo la Shoah. Politica e cultura nella stampa ebraica italiana 1945–1970*, Degree thesis, supervisor Prof. Marco Palla, University of Florence, Academic Year 2001–2002.
24. I take the liberty of referring the reader to my work 'La morte e la patria. L'Italia e i difficili lutti della seconda guerra mondiale', in *Quaderni Storici*, 113 (2003), pp.551–87.
25. *BCIM*, 2, October–November 1947.
26. *BCIM*, 2, 6 July 1945.
27. *Israel*, 24, 24 May 1945.
28. S. Levi della Torre, *Mosaico. Attualità e inattualità degli ebrei* (Turin: Rosenberg & Sellier, 1994), pp.42–3.
29. *BCIM*, 3, 20 July 1945.
30. R. Cantoni, 'Ebrei', in *BCIM*, 4, 8 August 1945.
31. See Verb. Giunta, Delibere del Commissario, decision of 10 October 1945.
32. The stylistic and symbolic choices made for that work reflect a common tendency of that age. For an overall view of the different monumental styles with which the Shoah was commemorated see the research conducted by James E. Young, *The Texture of Memory: Holocaust Memorials and Meaning* (New Haven, CT and London: Yale University Press, 1993); James E. Young (ed.), *The Art of Memory: Holocaust Memorials in History* (New York: The Jewish Museum, 1994).
33. The President of the Union sent a circular to all the Italian-Jewish Communities asking that each one should send its representatives and 'the greatest possible number of brothers'. AUCII, b.74c, f. 'Il Monumento di Milano'.
34. The Union sought the participation of the Prime Minister De Gasperi, who however could not be present, and of the President of the Constituent Assembly Terracini, finding it strange, however, that 'being a co-religionist he appreciates so little the value of representation'. AUCII, b.74c, f. 'Il Monumento di Milano'.
35. The Italian-Jewish press gave wide coverage of the event; see *Israel*, 40, 17 July 1947; *BCIM*, 10, 20 July 1947.
36. AUCII, b.74c, f. 'Corrispondenza con Milano', document entitled 'Il Monumento di Milano', dated 9 May 1947.
37. P. Levi, *Il sistema periodico* (Turin: Einaudi, 1975), pp.53–4.

38. See Y. Zerubavel, *Recovered Roots: Collective Memory and the Making of Israeli National Tradition* (Chicago, IL and London, University of Chicago Press, 1995).
39. 'The event which has been related to its paradigm, and with which it can identify, is not linked to it like an effect to its cause, but in the timelessness of a structural similarity: the event is "in the image and likeness" of the paradigm. According to the historical criterion, an event is explained by means of causality; according to the paradigmatic criterion, by means of structural consistency'. S. Levi della Torre, *Mosaico. Attualità e inattualità degli ebrei* (Turin: Rosenberg & Sellier, 1994), p.65. See also Y.H. Yerushalmy, *Zakhor: Jewish History and Jewish Memory* (Seattle, WA: University of Washington Press 1996); he observed: 'those Jews who are still within the enchanted circle of tradition, or those who have returned to it, find the work of the historian irrelevant: they seek not the historicity of the past, but its eternal contemporaneity', p.96.
40. For a theoretical and philosophical contextualization of this approach, which can be traced back to the Talmudic interpretation of the destruction of the second Temple by the Romans, see R.L. Rubinstein, 'Alliance et divinité. L'Holocauste et la problematique de la foi', *Pardès*, special issue edited by S. Trigano, *Pensèr Auschwitz*, 9–10 (1989), pp.99ff.
41. The attack was part of a broader strategy in the anti-English struggle conducted at that time by the Irgun also including repeated terrorist attacks. The choice of the Embassy in Rome reflected not only the importance of the Italian theatre in the battle being waged on the theme of Jewish immigration to Palestine, but also a search for attention and international visibility. The terrorist attack was condemned in a joint statement made by the UCII, the FSI and the Organization of Jewish Refugees in Italy through a communiqué of 4 November; Italian Judaism distanced itself from the stand, critical but not an explicit condemnation, taken instead by Umberto Nahon, the representative in Italy of the Jewish Agency for Palestine. Regarding this event, see M. Toscano, *La 'porta di Sion'*, pp.133ff.
42. See AUCII, b.74c, f. 'Epstein'; see also S.I. Minerbi, *Un ebreo fra D'Annunzio e il sionismo*, p.207.
43. It was precisely on these themes – insisting in particular on the epic and glorious representation of the desperate uprising in the Warsaw Ghetto as an anticipation and foreshadowing of the military glories of the 'new Jew', a free author of his emancipation – that the State of Israel insisted on creating its own patriotic mythology. In this regard, see the observations of T. Segev, *The Seventh Million: The Israelis and the Holocaust* (New York: Hill & Wang, 1993), pp.434ff.
44. I refer back to the observations formulated by S. Friedlander, 'La Shoah come mito israeliano', in D. Bidussa (ed.), *Ebrei moderni. Identità e stereotipi culturali* (Turin, Bollati Boringhieri, 1989), pp.63–76. The Israeli scholar observed that in the Israeli mythopoetic processing of the Shoah one can see various narrative *models* which can be traced back to the paradigm of the fall and redemption of biblical origin. He identifies three variations on the above-mentioned paradigm: 'catastrophe-redemption', 'catastrophe-rebirth' and finally 'catastrophe and heroism'. Originally the article was published in German: 'Die Shoah als Element in der Konstruktion israealischer Erinnerung', *Babylon*, 2 (1987), pp.10–22.
45. S. Levi della Torre, *Essere fuori luogo*, p.62.
46. In this regard, see D.I. Kertzer, *Ritual, Politics and Power* (New Haven, CT: Yale University Press, 1989), pp.19–22. The key of such a mechanism is the *performative* and not *discursive* nature of the communication; in this regard, see the solid and cogent reflection proposed by P. Connerton, *How Societies Remember* (Cambridge: Cambridge University Press, 1989), pp.72ff.
47. Verb. Giunta, meeting of 2 December 1947.
48. A. Milano, *Storia degli ebrei in Italia* (Turin: Einaudi, 1992 [1st. ed. 1963]), pp.414–15.
49. This turning point was celebrated with demonstrations in virtually all the communities, for example regarding Venice see the account given by E. Toaff, *Perfidi giudei fratelli maggiori*, pp.152–3.
50. *BCIM*, 4, December 1947–January 1948.
51. A. Minerbi, 'Tra nazionalizzazione e persecuzione. La scuola ebraica in Italia 1930–1943', *Contemporanea*, 4, I (1998), pp.716ff.; D. Fishman, 'Una risposta ebraica alle leggi. L'organizzazione delle scuole', *RMI*, 1–2, LIV (1988), pp.335–64.
52. T. Catalan, *La comunità ebraica di Trieste (1781–1914). Politica, società e cultura* (Trieste: Lint, 2000), pp.147ff.
53. It was noted with regret by E.S. Artom, *La scuola ebraica in Italia*, Tipografia (Florence: La Giuntina, 1913), pp.13ff.
54. This was reported by the President of the Association of the Communities, Angelo Sereni, who had spoken about it directly with Giovanni Gentile. See M. Sarfatti, *Gli ebrei nell'Italia fascista*, p.61, but see, in more general terms, pp.54–63.
55. In 1932, a syllabus was prepared for courses in Jewish culture for those who were attending the State secondary schools, while in 1936 a guide was drawn up for teachers of Jewish primary schools. See A. Minerbi, 'Tra nazionalizzazione e persecuzione. La scuola ebraica in Italia 1930–1943', pp.710–14.

56. An example of such clashes is to be found in the treatment of the Venetian case by S. Levis Sullam, *Una comunità immaginata. Gli ebrei a Venezia (1900–1938)*, postface by A. Cavaglion (Milan: Unicopli, 2001), pp.113ff.
57. See M. Sarfatti, *Gli ebrei nell'Italia fascista*, p.220.
58. Leo Levi made a preliminary analysis of the condition towards which the schools were going in a heartfelt letter sent to Cantoni on 8 November 1946. He underlined the lack of homogeneity which characterized the syllabuses and called for the creation of a central committee to coordinate the cultural activities. Cf. AUCII, b.74c.
59. President Cantoni communicated the appointment of Lattes as head of the Union's Culture and Education Committee during the Council meeting of 13 November 1946, in Verb. Cons.
60. Dante Lattes (Pitigliano 1876–Venezia 1965) studied at the Rabbinical College of Livorno, under the guidance of Elia Benamozegh. In 1898 he moved to Trieste to work at the Italian-Jewish journal *Il Corriere Israelitico*, of which he became Editor in Chief in 1903. He held that position until the beginning of Great War, when he fled from Trieste and took refuge in Florence, in the house of the young Alfonso Pacifici, a Jewish lawyer who had passionately taken up the Jewish and Zionist cause. In that same period began the publications of the Zionist journal *Israel*, directed by the same Pacifici. He then was briefly Rabbi of the tiny Jewish community of Siena in 1916 and in 1917 moved to Rome, continuing his contribution to *Israel*, and two years later he opened there a local office of the World Zionist Organization. In 1925 he founded the *Rassegna Mensile di Israel*, a monthly cultural review loosely connected to the *Israel* journal; this review became a key instrument for the transimission to the Italian public of the major debates that were taking place in the European Jewish circles. He was active in the Italian-Zionist movement and in October 1936, with Angiolo Orvieto, he was sent to London by Mussolini to try move the Zionist circles to put pressure on the British government against the application of sanctions on Italy as a retaliation for its war against Ethiopia. He left Italy for Palestine in 1939, and returned in 1946 when he was called by Raffaele Cantoni to head the cultural offices of the UCII. In 1948 – under the auspices of the UCII – he resumed the pubblication of the *Rassegna Mensile di Israel*, holding the position of Chief Editor until his death. He was Vice-Presidente of the UCII from 1952 to 1956. Regarding Lattes and specifically his cultural formation, see G. Luzzatto Voghera, 'La formazione culturale di Dante Lattes', in D. Bidussa, A. Luzzatto and G. Luzzatto Voghera, *Oltre il ghetto. Momenti e figure dell'emancipazione ebraica* (Brescia: Morcelliana, 1987), pp.17–95.
61. For a preliminary analysis of Lattes' publishing activities, see D. Fubini, *Dante Lattes e la ricostruzione delle comunità ebraiche italiane dopo la Shoah*, Degree thesis, supervisor Prof. Paolo Pezzino, University of Pisa, Academic Year 1999–2000.
62. See AUCII, b.44b, f. 'Rapporto sulla condizione scolastica in Italia'.
63. 'Libri di testo per bambini ebrei', *BCIM*, 1, January 1950, p.6.
64. See S.I. Minerbi, *Un ebreo fra D'Annunzio e il sionismo*, pp.189ff. It should be noted that a total uniformità in the syllabuses would never have been attained. For an overall view of Jewish educational institutions in the post-war period see A.M. Piussi, 'Sguardo sull'educazione ebraica, Ragioni e percorsi di una ricerca', in *E li insegnerai ai tuoi figli. Educazione ebraica dalle leggi razziali ad oggi*, ed. A.M. Piussi (Florence: La Giuntina, 1997), pp.15–145.
65. See the observations made by A.C. Jemolo, *Anni di prova*, preface by F. Margiotta Broglio (Florence: Passigli, 1991), p.246.
66. In this regard, the debate which took place within the Council is significant: see Verb. Cons., 23–24 July 1946.
67. See *Israel*, 51, 26 August 1948. For information regarding all the educational activities carried out in the individual communities see the report dated 26 January 1950 prepared by the UCII at the request of the Israeli Foreign Ministry, in AUCII, b.34.
68. Considering the schools of every type and level, from nursery schools to high schools, in all the communities, we can record, in 1963–64, 2,473 students; in 1973–74, 2,812; in 1982–83, 2,368; in 1992–93, 1,807. The decrease in the 1980s and 1990s can be attributed to many factors, including a generalized demographic decline. In this regard, see the summarized tables in A.M. Piussi, 'Sguardo sull'educazione ebraica', pp.129ff.
69. This is what is suggested by the demographic-statistical research carried out by S. Della Pergola, *Anatomia dell'ebraismo italiano* (Assisi: Carucci, 1976), p.200.
70. Starting from the not dissimilar numerical data, the decision to accept students of other faiths has guaranteed the survival of the Jewish schools in Turin, while the opposite decision has led to the closure, between the 1970s and the 1990s, of the primary and secondary schools of the Community in Florence. See A.M. Piussi, 'Sguardo sull'educazione ebraica', p.53, note 55.
71. Ibid., p.59.

4

Youth Movements

A useful indicator for understanding the nature and extent of the changes produced in the Jewish community by the persecution is the vitality of associations which arose in the post-war period. After 1945, Jewish social life changed deeply; in particular, there was an exceptional youthful vigour, which, because of the number of young people involved and the type of activities undertaken by the associations, appears decidedly different from the experience of the Jewish youth movements which had arisen at the beginning of the twentieth century. Before the persecutions there had been only very small groupings of a few tens of people,[1] while, after the Second World War, a multiplicity of various youth organizations and associations came into being: sporting and cultural, religious and secular, Zionist and non-Zionist (but none anti-Zionist), which involved and mobilized hundreds, perhaps thousands, of young Italian Jews. The proliferation of such groupings can be considered the product of various factors, among which figure prominently the Shoah, the influence of the soldiers of the Jewish Brigade on many young Jewish people which contributed to the rebirth of the communities, the energy reawakened by the creation of the State of Israel, the closer inter-ethnic ties favoured by the continuing existence of the Jewish schools and finally also the UCII's active support for such activities.

Undoubtedly, at the root of that phenomenon was the deep rift in the social fabric and in the Jewish identity caused by the beginning of a persecution. A particular self-awareness developed in many young people, an attempt to respond to the questions posed by fascist racist policy. By denying the rights of equality Mussolini had destroyed the fragile structure of convictions, hopes and aspirations on which barely three or four generations had been able to place their trust and shape their own identity.

Various types of memories and testimonies enable us to enter a young Jewish universe in tumult, in which we can see boys and girls marked by an extraordinary trepidation. After Liberation many seem to be searching for a new beginning rather than closing this parenthetic episode and returning to the way of life of their parents and grandparents. For very many of the young, the persecution represents the beginning of a tortuous path of rediscovering their identity:

> The fascist persecution, the war and all the rest came and we young people all suffered a great shock. When I say we young people I'm talking about

> those who were my age, namely those who, like me, had entered that wretched period between fourteen and sixteen, the formative years, when one begins to think, believe and live. The older people were less affected (I'm naturally referring to the moral context), they had more or less found their way of life and simply hoped that this ugly parenthesis would come to an end as soon as possible, in order to be able to resume their way of life. It was also a different matter for the youngest and this is natural … Then began the reaction; the best of us … began to search for our identity.[2]

These thoughts which, a few months after the liberation of the capital, were addressed by a young Roman Jew Giorgio Piperno, born in 1923, to his friend Joel Barromi, who had emigrated to Palestine quite some time earlier, are an invaluable indicator which helps us to understand what were the enduring consequences of the racial campaign, which cast the condition of the Jews in the West into an unprecedented context, not affecting an abstract Judaism, but the life and the processes of self-representation of single individuals as of entire communities.

Inevitably, dramatic and extreme experiences such as the persecution and the war gave people's lives an unforeseen impetus, causing a separation between generations: the rifts between the young and the world of their parents were too many and too significant, the latter seemed to be merely ruins. This was bitterly noted by Emanuele Arton, slightly older than Piperno, and among the most acute and lucid observers of his age: 'the abyss separating fathers and sons … is unbridgeable. The abyss opened by the biased judgements of the parents and by the reserve which stops sons from revealing the changes they are going through, an abyss which now becomes greater and greater, now that centuries seem to separate one generation from another'.[3]

An emblematic expression of the division which was emerging between generations, although certainly extreme and not paradigmatic, can be found in the autobiography of Vittorio Segre, who between 1944 and 1945 was ascending the Italian peninsula as a liberator – enrolled in the Jewish Brigade, part of the British Army – and who thus recalls the meeting with his father at the end of the war:

> We had both emerged unscathed from the same conflict, in which he had lost his country, Italy, and I had found a new one, Israel. I had returned home a victor in a foreign uniform; he, having survived six years of civilian ignominy and two hiding in the mountains, had witnessed the defeat of his country. Humiliated by the King he had personally served, persecuted by the fascist regime to whose creation he had contributed, he had no other reason for pride if not in my participation in the Zionist cause which he had tenaciously opposed as an Italian nationalist.[4]

Between father and son 'a deeper gulf had opened than that produced by time: between an Israelitic world and an Italian one in ruins and the embryo of a new Jewish world in which I, as Murat put it, was the first of my ancestors'.[5]

The sudden and painful feeling of separation and of alienation from the experiences and sensibility of their parents, the feeling of being uprooted which derived from not being able to follow the path of their forefathers are very frequently recurring themes in the memoirs of those who in 1938, at the beginning of the racist policy, were adolescents or even younger.[6] The choices, replete with often imponderable consequences, which that generation of young people had been forced to make following the persecution, had altered fragile balances, triggering tormented processes of personal reinvention, with the possibility of extremely varied outcomes. If for some, as in the cases referred to of Piperno and Segre, there had been the possibility of adhering to the Zionist cause, for others the reaction could have been different and even contrasting: not a few responded to the beginning of the anti-Semitic campaign by recanting or converting to Christianity.

In this regard, the case of the poet Franco Fortini (born Lattes) seems interesting: in the post-war period, he was involved, for a long time, with coming to terms with his paternal Judaism, trying to rationalize the conversion towards which, in 1939, his parents guided him in an attempt – which was successful – to save him from persecution. In 1967, almost thirty years after the event, after the Six Day War, Franco Fortini significantly reflected publicly on his conversion and his relationship with Judaism (and therefore with his father, the Jewish lawyer and anti-fascist Dino Lattes). In a brilliant and provocative pamphlet against the general trend, *The Dogs of the Sinai*, in which he declared his condemnation of Israel's policies and his dismay at the generalized support of Italian public opinion for the State of Israel, he offered an interesting reflection on his conversion and on the residual traces of an ineffable 'Jewishness' from which he, also through that work, wanted to detach himself definitively.[7]

Not without resonances with what we have already seen in the autobiographical reflections of other young people of the period of the racial laws, we often find in *The Dogs of the Sinai*,[8] but also in so many of Fortini's works,[9] the paternal figure seen as a metaphor and embodiment of a tradition and a past with which it is opportune to come to terms, preferably by severing all ties. This is a crucial question for Fortini, which he had at heart, to such an extent that he raised it to a general theory: 'one has to be able to look one's parents in the eye', he declared gravely and solemnly in the 1970s, since that relationship 'implies, or symbolizes, the relationship with one's class, with one's reality'.[10]

In the following pages, we will consider the search for a new balance on the part of those who tried in various ways to deal with the trauma of State racism, defending and reformulating their own Jewishness. Nevertheless, it seems opportune to recall the 'Fortini case', which not only confirms the importance of the problem of the 'relationship with the father' which was posed by the persecution, but which also clearly highlights how there is something 'Jewish' – concerning a 'Jewish condition' – also in some renunciations of Judaism. This can help us to understand how, in attempting to consider the effects of the persecution and produce a history of the Jewish community, one cannot ignore the presence and influence of those who, either through conviction or for opportunism, chose to 'leave', to abandon the life of the community and who also, in many cases, needed a lot of time to resolve their relationship with Judaism, finding themselves at times intervening in various ways in the life of a community to which they were bound, if for nothing else, by ties with friends and relations. A community which is not and cannot be thought of as a closed entity, separated from the rest of society.[11]

The passages we have cited have introduced us to a theme, that of the generations, which had a considerable impact on the processes of self-representation of so many young Italian Jews, strongly affecting the relationships within the Jewish minority in the post-war period. It should be noted, however, that the theme of the generations was not peculiar to the Jewish world. After 1945, very many observers noticed a widespread sense of disorientation and of being uprooted caused above all in the young by the dictatorship, by the war and then by the difficult political-institutional transition. An excellent exemplification of this is *Il lavoro culturale* by Bianciardi, an autobiographical novel which illustrates the slow, and anything but linear, character-forming path followed by a provincial group of young people, an expression of what the Tuscan writer defines 'the burnt out generation: determined to break with tradition and to make a new start'.[12] A generation which was born and grew up under fascism, and later prepared itself to participate enthusiastically in the formation of the 'new' Italy. Correspondingly, Elio Vittorini defined the new generation of narrators which had emerged in the post-war period as the 'generation without a past',[13] and a similar concept, utilized to explain the different effects, provoked by fascism, on different age groups, was formulated by Ranuccio Bianchi Bandinelli in the first issue of the cultural review *Società*. The latter identified three age groups: first of all, those who had faced the beginning of the war being already mature, between the ages of forty and fifty, and who could easily be deceived by the blandishments of a parenthetic interpretation of the conflict; then there were those who were older, who could have extended the parenthesis to cast a veil over the whole fascist period; finally, the youngest 'who have … the feeling that today has not had a yesterday; that everything has to be started over'.[14]

After the war, the generational issue undoubtedly became one of the main talking points of Italian culture which was struggling to come to terms with the period of the dictatorship.[15] The evolution of the relationship with the regime, on the part of those who were young, adolescents or slightly older, at the end of the 1930s, constituted one of the burning issues of the debate about the problem of consent to fascism, finding a first, essential clear expression in 1947 with the publication of the *Lungo viaggio* (*Long Journey*) by Ruggero Zangrandi[16] who presented a view, mainly self-justifying, of the behaviour of a class of young people disillusioned by the regime, who between 1938 and 1939 began to develop a latent anti-fascism, the so-called *existential anti-fascism*. That historical representation enjoyed a certain favour, finding confirmation in various memoirs, in the studies and testimonies published between the Liberation and the 1960s.[17] Works which faithfully reflected the culture and the mentality of the age, as well as the sensibility and the needs of those who were protagonists of the *lungo viaggio* and crossed the stormy river of ideology until, breathless but enthusiastic, they reached the safety of the anti-fascist river bank: that exceptional adventurous journey had forged strong links and it was also because of this that 'those who became anti-fascists despite being "younger" than fascism … could not help but feel part of a generation'.[18]

The generational issue and the perception of a 'youth problem' were typical of Italian society as it returned to freedom. There were significant analogies with the concepts and discussions which characterized, at that time, Italian Judaism. This is not really surprising: Italian Jews – perceived as being well integrated – were immersed in the national culture; it is natural, therefore, to find shared rhetorical formulae and themes to be pondered. On the other hand, it should be noted that the inter-generational relationships of Italian Judaism had a distinct character, a reflection of their particular experiences from the mid-1930s onwards.

GENERATIONS

The problems experienced by the Italian-Jewish community during the fascist era had been different from those of the rest of the country, and the consequent reactions were also different. For the Jewish community there had not been a moment of choice, as was the case for the rest of the nation when, in September 1943, Italians had to take sides: either standing with the Monarchy which had signed the Armistice with the Allies, or supporting the remains of the fascist regime and the Nazis.[19] Instead Italian Jews had to face a long period of anxiety and uncertainty which had begun in July 1938 and lasted for years, during which many desperately hoped that the racist policies would be soon reconsidered. The turning point, the moment when the inter-generational differences became apparent, had come earlier for the Italian Jews than for the rest of the nation: 'it was as if the Jews were already at war, when, however, for everyone else there was peace: a special war totally against them which from one day to the next had made them foreigners in their own country, digging an unbridgeable gap destined to separate them from the other Italians'.[20]

For the victims of racial persecution there had not only been the problem of their own relationship with fascism and of the, anything but rapid, development of an authentic democratic and anti-fascist awareness, since the turning point of 1938 had also brought sharply into question their way of perceiving themselves and of planning their own lives: that date represented a point of no return, the catastrophe swept away everyone, irrespective of their political ideology, permanently marking not only those who lived through that drama, but also subsequent generations. The sociologist Paola Di Cori has conveyed this with great clarity:

> If for the Italians (fascists and anti-fascists) the introduction of the racial laws can be explained on the basis of essentially political considerations – tied to the historical circumstances of the time, a parenthesis concluded with the end of the war and the disappearance of Nazi-fascism – for the Jews it is instead an event which initiates a process of a radical existential devastation, both individually and collectively, anything but resolved in 1945, through which essential concepts of the Jewish condition in the contemporary democratic societies – such as 'citizenship', 'assimilation', 'tradition', 'memory' – taken on a new and tragically unexpected meaning.[21]

The changes, starting from the terrible year of 1938, separated those who had been able to cultivate peacefully the dream of integration from subsequent generations, which – to some extent – all grew under the shadow of the genocide.[22]

Taking this into account forces us to consider the internal segments of the Jewish community too often seen as a monolithic block, an indistinct whole, whose political-ideological divisions are generally the only ones examined. To operate a generational breakdown of the community in terms of the different reactions to the persecution can enable us, from a particular, but not unfruitful, perspective, to perceive some of the evolutionary processes which began in 1938 and reached their full development in the post-war period.

However, a certain caution is necessary: categories like generations are extremely elusive and inevitably imprecise, it is therefore opportune to specify that historical-sociological distinctions, rather than those based purely on age, will be examined, without imposing rigid evaluations. In the following pages, reference will be made to the concept of generations analysed on two different planes: the first, more imprecise, conveys mainly obvious data which is concerned with the different possibilities, the different means by which, depending upon the age group, one can react to a devastating event; the second, more interesting, plane concerns, instead, *generational self-awareness*. It is a question of building a sense of belonging to a common destiny, a generation, in fact, which forms its character in facing epoch-making transformations and events; generational self-awareness is an *a posteriori* formulation carried out by elitist groups who, in presenting themselves as a generation, try to define and legitimize themselves, also in opposition and in contrast with other generations, above all the preceding one.[23]

In order to try and organize the available information, we can begin by identifying three main age groups: firstly, those who were already old in 1938, then those who were between 30 and 50 years of age at the time of the racial laws, and finally, the young, broadly speaking those born between 1914 and 1924; while, on yet another plane, there were those who were at that time too young to understand that experience, but who would nevertheless have been marked by it. In the following pages, only the behaviour of the first three groups will be considered, and in particular the second and third, in view of the importance of the rift which seemed to have opened between fathers and sons.

The oldest were in many ways the most vulnerable, incapable of sudden transfers or flight, when they became necessary following the German occupation; the most reluctant to contemplate exile, but also those who were less able to rethink and reconsider their own relationship with the national community and the State.[24] Incapable of responding, many had simply decided to wait for the 'storm' to pass, as the persecution was often defined in Jewish memoirs. 'My grandmother', as Silvia Lombroso wrote in her diary, 'wants to stay put … she doesn't read newspapers, she doesn't want any news. There is no future for her; there is only the present and her sons, who are ruined and far away; and death, solitary and imminent, is at hand'.[25]

Evidently, the next generation had more time and resources. This group's life and career expectations were particularly marked by fascist policy: in a period of their lives which should have witnessed its full realization, both personal and professional, these people had been suddenly reduced to inactivity, a painful and frustrating wait:

> my father – as Aldo Zargani remembers – was angry with the whole world, he saw his life disappearing in humiliation, indifference and the moral sloth of the majority, wasting away day by day in the most indecent poverty in the face of the fanatical delirium which everyone seemed to accept. He knew that, when the delirium would have disappeared in the hell of the minds which had engendered it, he would have been old, at least as a musician.[26]

The loss of their work represented a real tragedy, undermining, at their roots, dreams and aspirations. A tangible sign of their own exclusion, it meant serious sacrifices, putting at risk the survival of the family.[27] The primary objective, perhaps the only possible objective, from that moment onwards had been taking care of their children, the desperate defence of what remained of the future for which each of them had struggled so hard. Any measure was acceptable to protect one's family, even suicide, an extreme measure to push away the deadly shadow of one's own 'impure' blood from the family; it was precisely in this way that Emilio Foà displayed his lucid desperation:

> My dear wife I am leaving all of you. I can save my family in this way. It would have been ruin otherwise. With the insurance, and taking out a mortgage, you will have sufficient income … You are all, therefore, safe … Don't condemn me … Love one another and remember me. Giorgio and Franco always love your mother … Today, my family is safe.[28]

The feelings of precariousness, frustration, despair, the loss of any hope induced by the persecution would have led some to a deep state of depression; many contemplated suicide, others actually carried out that extreme act, intended as a sensational protest, as in the case of the publisher Angelo Fortunato Formiggini who, on 28 November 1938, threw himself from the Tower of the Ghirlandina in Modena. Almost all the recorded suicides among Italian Jews in the period of the persecution concerned those belonging to this generational group, middle-aged men whose future had suddenly been taken from them.[29] All of a sudden, their lives were shattered, there only remained the anguish of being, little by little, spiritually driven out of Italy, brutally wrenched from all that they held most dear, their country, their work, their children's future: 'a social death without guilt, felt every day and every hour, difficult to bear, called to mind every day by the insults, in the newspapers, towards the Italian citizens belonging to the Jewish race, whose every attempt to do good was seen in a negative light'.[30]

Despite this, despite the fact that the promulgation of the anti-Semitic laws was also often followed by social isolation, indifference, if not stark rejection, on the part of friends and acquaintances,[31] the majority of the persecuted remained inseparably tied to Italy. A striking attitude, to which we will return. In many cases, the deep attachment to their country, the desire to serve and defend the monarchy and – sometimes – even the dictator, survived despite the betrayal undergone. Suffice it to mention the compendium of declarations of loyalty to fascism and of unquenchable patriotic fervour which accompanied the requests, sent by very many, in the summer of 1940, to be able to take up arms side by side with all the other Italians to defend their country.[32] As if the import, the deep meaning, and the irrevocable nature of the choices made by the regime had not been understood. In effect, since 1938 there had been signs of a deep incapacity to grasp, and to respond to, the situation and to cast off visions of the world and, by now, inappropriate behavioural models, the poor remains of a reality overturned by the racist decrees.[33] An indication of this is the widespread conviction that, despite bombastic proclamations and shrill declarations, the racist plans would come to nothing, as well as the idea that it was a question of a serious misunderstanding, which could be resolved by telling the *duce*, certainly ill-informed or badly advised, of the mistake he had made.[34] This explains why, even after the persecution campaign had been well under way, there persisted the custom of addressing Mussolini directly, in accordance with a widespread practice in force since the establishment of the regime, to ask for favours and set forth one's difficulties.[35]

Well-established social practices and cultural conceptions could not be suddenly eliminated, and they gave rise to feelings and behaviours which we today find difficult to understand. This is the case with the distress displayed by Emilio Artom in the face of the Italian surrender to the Allies: somehow the defeat of that State, which had ostracized and humiliated him, disturbed and hurt him.[36] A feeling which also upset his son Emanuele, who had developed a very different political awareness, and who commented in his diary: 'Father is a little mortified by the defeat, but isn't it nice to see justice re-established? And isn't it an advantage for Italy?'[37] It may help us to understand if we consider the words with which the Florentine poet Angiolo Orvieto explained what made exile unfeasible: 'even if a mother mistreats her children, she is always mother and one cannot help loving her'.[38]

Some of the members of Emilio Artom and Angiolo Orvieto's generation had already chosen, before the promulgation of the racial laws, the path of Zionism or of anti-fascism, but the majority did not reach this point and simply remained bereft of a country, of a regime and, above all, of a monarch in whom it had placed its trust. Those who survived found themselves, after the war, living in a world in which the fundamental reference points – such as the crown, their country, their family and, on a different, but no less important plane, work and professional dignity – on which they had constructed their identity, had been overturned. Following the Liberation, some of them looked back on a lost world with nostalgia, like Edgardo Limentani, the protagonist of a short story by Giorgio Bassani:[39] after 1945 he had ardently desired that the times before fascism had started its persecution policy could return, but it had been impossible for him to reintegrate in the new society. 'It was as if the anti-Semitic laws – Stuart Hughes has acutely observed – were a "time-bomb" whose delayed reaction could destroy even those who had apparently come through unscathed'.[40]

And yet, in the midst of a thousand difficulties and bearing many scars, the majority of those belonging to this generation found a way to reintegrate themselves in society. They managed to close the parenthesis, perhaps finding refuge in daily life and in a reassuring memory of the persecutions. A deep rift had opened between them and the nation, too small to separate them definitively, but large enough to leave a permanent mark.

It was decidedly more difficult for the young to repeat their parents' *heri dicebamus*. The differences in perceiving, and responding to, the State racism could already be seen at the start of the persecution campaign, as Giorgio Bassani indicates in his *Romanzo di Ferrara*, a very rich source of stimuli for the scholar who wants to understand how Italian Judaism perceived and represented the persecution. From *Gli occhiali d'oro* to *Il giardino dei Finzi Contini*, we often find the unease and the impatience of the children towards their fathers' vain hopes, the anger of the young at the attitude of the adults who, between the summer and the autumn of 1938, desperately hung on with all their might to the faint indications which could suggest that fascism would never have actually engaged in persecution. *Gli occhiali d'oro* concludes on this note, with the young protagonist embittered and disillusioned:

> I was desperate, absolutely desperate … because I had seen my father suddenly so happy, or rather so eager to be happy again. Therefore, was it precisely this which I couldn't bear? – I asked myself – Couldn't I bear to see him happy? That the future should smile on him once again, as in the past, as before? … My father's joy – I thought – was that of a pupil unjustly expelled, who, called back, on the teacher's orders, from the deserted corridor where he remained for a while in exile, finds himself, all of a sudden, against all his expectations, readmitted to the classroom among his dear classmates. Not only absolved, but recognized as being innocent and fully rehabilitated. Well wasn't it right, after all, that my father should rejoice like that child? However, I did not. The feeling of loneliness which had always accompanied me in those last two months became if anything, just now, even more terrible: all-embracing and definitive. I myself would never have returned from my exile. *Never again*.[41]

It seems reasonable to consider that 'the most serious traumas caused, above all, by the initial period of the racial laws affected adolescents',[42] since they were going through a very delicate phase without finding adequate answers and support from adults, in their turn terribly disorientated.[43] Having lost any possibility of identifying with the institutions, some only found comfort within the family, 'a precarious sense of belonging in which only blood ties could continue to be a reference point, in a "*pre-polis*" regression which could not but distort the development of the personality in the youngest and in adolescents'.[44] Others, instead, were marked by the formation of unprecedented ties among their peers, new companions known in the Jewish schools created after the expulsion of Jewish children from all the educational institutions of the kingdom.[45] Jewish schools offered some kind of refuge, as one of the children wrote:

> The external world was more and more hostile and threatening, we had to blend in to be able to face it every day, trying not to be identified as Jews, always being careful about what we said, avoiding with the greatest care any situation in which we could become embroiled and risk exposure.
>
> But within our school we could talk, discuss things, exchange news and ideas in complete freedom. And we used to do it, also drawing in the teachers … From the first days until it remained in action (in the autumn of 1943) our school constituted a centre of development, training, social cohesion and of mutual support against the external environment, which was very difficult to face.[46]

The resumption of school life in those peculiar conditions had a two-fold significance: on the one hand, there was the trauma of abandoning one's friends, but at the same time new horizons were opening up. A new feeling of brotherhood was being created with one's new classmates, new stimuli and problems were arising in the schools hurriedly organized by the various communities; many later recalled that experience as the beginning of a new life.[47] It is worth noting that such an experience not only resulted in a separation from 'Aryan' peers, but also, to a certain extent, from one's own parents; while, for the adults, Jewish schools were merely the symbol of an enforced marginalization,[48] for the students they could also represent a positive experience, an important opportunity to rediscover and reinvent themselves. Cesare Cases, remembering his time in the Jewish school of Milan, where, after the war, he would also have taught for a brief period, went so far as to state: '[The racial laws] did not change my life and my expectations very much, in fact they improved, inasmuch as they gave me the feeling of belonging to a threatened community.'[49]

Those young people had grown up experiencing fascism as normality: Vittorio Segre wrote, 'I lived — so to speak, in the belly of the monster but, unlike Jonah, having been born in it I didn't realize it'.[50] For very many, who had never felt that they were different, the anti-Jewish policy had led them to consider an unexpected problem, forcing them to reach a precocious maturity. Primo Levi described that passage in the following way, remembering

> the ironic cheerfulness of an entire generation of Italians, intelligent and honest enough to reject fascism, too sceptical to oppose it actively, too young to accept passively the tragedy which was looming and to feel despair about the future; a generation to which I myself would have belonged if the providential racial laws had not intervened to make me mature precociously and to guide me in my choices.[51]

The transition from free citizens to victims of persecution had imposed an abrupt leap from childhood to maturity. Not a few had discovered that they were Jews only in that moment: 'Jews by law', facing difficult questions posed by the persecution, marking the advent of an age of dilemmas and torments which led to a sudden interruption of the time of games .[52] A turning point which some also wanted to sanction symbolically, as did Vittorio Segre who wrote that, shortly after the start of the persecution, in a night-time ceremony, hidden from the adults, he, then barely an adolescent, had buried 'his avant-gardist polished dagger, … his wooden Red Indian tomahawk and his collection of toy soldiers'.[53] A kind of rite of passage, which sanctioned the renunciation of the world of children and perhaps also the rejection of fascism, of its militaristic culture and its warlike rhetoric. Thus, having definitively repudiated a part of himself, of his own identity, there began a phase of uncertainty and reconstruction which, in his case, led to Zionism.

Rather than the closure of a parenthesis or the end of the 'storm', those young people – or at least a significant number of them – were forced by the persecutions to search for a new beginning: 'we started to want to understand our Jewish condition which suddenly lost any trace of marginality in our lives'.[54] With these words, Giorgio Piperno wanted to describe his state of mind and that of a small group of his classmates of the Jewish School of Rome, with which he shared an impassioned search for ways to deal with a reality which had suddenly become elusive. There were different paths in front of those young men: anti-fascism, Zionism, but also the renunciation of their own identity or the revival of tradition and a return to orthodoxy; more often than not, rather than categorical choices, vague attitudes would have prevailed.

The process activated by the persecution would not have been interrupted on the dawn of 25 April 1945, in fact they could develop fully only after the fall of the regime: then a phase of rethinking and reorganization began, it was a question of planning one's existence, of reconsidering the meaning of the dream of integration and the myth of equality which had marked the previous generations, defining the 'Jewish condition' from the emancipation to the 1930s. The emergence of numerous circles, associations and Jewish youth movements in the immediate post-war period can also be traced back to that spiritual anguish.

HECHALUZ

As we have seen, only a few weeks after the liberation of Rome various cultural activities began, promoted by the Palestinian soldiers and aiming at mobilizing the Jewish youth of Italy towards Zionism.[55] Such activities, in the following months, were also extended to the other communities of the peninsula, and led to the establishment of a youth movement which, from the perspective of the realization of Zionism, could find an answer to the suffering provoked in them by the persecution. The Palestinians, among whom there were also some active Italian Jews who had emigrated some years earlier and had now returned to help the community and spread the Zionist message, also promoted the establishment of some agricultural communities (*hacksharot*) in Northern Italy, as they had already done in Rome. Young people with different ideas and sensibilities went there, united at first by the need to redefine themselves and to investigate their own Jewishness in order to prepare themselves to emigrate to Palestine: they were being trained for working in the fields and they were preparing themselves for a collectivistic life in which any individuality was banned. In time, this type of isolated groupings gave rise to a real Jewish youth movement on a national scale: following a Congress held 29 and 30 April 1946 at Ceriano Laghetto, near Saronno, the groups which had come into being in Rome and in Northern Italy fused[56] and so *Hechaluz* (the pioneer) movement was born, bringing together about a thousand young Italian Jews.[57] The ambitious goal of that movement was clearly stated, in the first issue of the eponymous fortnightly magazine: 'In the renewed contact with nature and with productive work, in linking up once again with the sources of Jewish culture and thought … the revolution will bring a harmonious solution to the problems affecting each person … our publication wants to be the banner of this revolution'.[58]

The heart of the movement was made up of a limited number of young people, committed to emigration and the realization of Zionism, who had chosen to go to *hackshara* to prepare themselves for the 'ascent' to the land of Israel. Around that nucleus there was a much larger number of boys and girls curious about the Zionist message, but who still hesitated to make a definitive choice. The latter joined the most committed activists of the movement in the summer months, experiencing life in the *hackshara* and widening their knowledge of Jewish and Zionist history, of Hebrew, but also of agricultural techniques.[59] Aldo Zargani as a very young boy took part in those summer activities in the largest Italian *hackshara*, in S. Marco di Cevoli near Pisa, where, in the course of seven years, hundreds of young people stayed.[60] He has left us a lively portrait of the life led by the young people who identified with that project, remembering the physical effort they undertook in the belief that work was an instrument of redemption and regeneration. This was 'the new secular prayer of Judaism';[61] it was the Zionist version of the nineteenth-century political myth of the *new man*, but had much older roots: the idea that the solution to the so-called Jewish problem was to be found in transforming unproductive bourgeois into hard-working peasants, is typical of the debate which developed at the end of the eighteenth century. And it was also in the framework of such an idea of collective regeneration that, in the nineteenth and twentieth centuries, the 'Jewish question' was tackled both by socialism and Zionism.

Far from expecting the solution to the Jewish problem to be the result of a revolutionary process destined to liberate the entire social body, the Zionists aimed at regeneration through work as the driving force of a process of self-emancipation fostering national self-determination. The *Hechaluz* movement, too, followed this path. After an apolitical beginning, aiming at bringing together as many young people as possible favourable to the Zionist message without ideological distinctions, it became, especially after 1948, an increasingly left-wing movement, socialist and non-religious.[62] Inevitably, there were clashes with important figures of Italian Zionism and this gave rise to debates and controversial dissention in the Jewish press.[63] It should be noted that – although the line followed was often criticized by the Jewish ruling class – the Union of the Communities nevertheless played an essential role in fostering, through suitable financing, the movement's activities.[64] Within the Italian-Jewish world, two different generations of Zionists then faced each other: on the one hand, those who directed Jewish institutions in the post-war period, those 'old Zionists' who had been moulded between the end of the 1800s and the beginning of the 1900s, who had arrived at Zionism following a slow process of soul searching and a rediscovery of the religious aspect, encouraged and supported in this journey by an important part of the rabbinate; on the other hand, the young, who had arrived at Zionism precipitately, as a reaction to the fascist ostracism and the horror of the extermination, guided by the soldiers of the Jewish Brigade more than by the Italian Zionist tradition. A certain amount of rashness and wishful thinking characterized the actions and the debates of the movement, in any case, the ferment provoked in the Italian-Jewish world by the irruption on the scene of the phenomenon of *Hechaluz* testifies to profound transformations which began in the post-war years: within a few years, the original cultural experience of Italian Zionism (represented in the preceding decades by figures such as Alfonso Pacifici, Dante Lattes and Enzo Sereni) withered and conformed to the ideological strands of the Zionist movement in Israel and in other, larger and more vigorous, communities of the Diaspora.[65]

In the very first years of the post-war period, Italian *halutzism* had a brief and intense flowering, benefiting, among other things, from the new attitude of Italian Jews towards Zionism: 'The storm which has uprooted all European Judaism and also the small Italian community has not significantly altered the latter's physical structure, it has, however, had a strong impact on its spiritual structure', noted an anonymous editor of the Bulletin of the Italian Zionist Federation, who went on to point out that there had been a marked improvement, with the emergence of 'new spiritual attitudes especially among the young ... there are no longer, as frequently as before the war, instances of declared and active anti-Zionism, while now the majority of Jewish organizations are in the hands of Zionists'.[66] Nevertheless, the vital impulse of the *Hechaluz* movement was destined to fade away spontaneously with the progressive emigration of its adherents: the cadres which were formed did not stay in Italy very long to prepare the new recruits, but did *aliyà*. The movement and its periodical stopped their activities in 1956, but already in the early 1950s – the great enthusiasm following the Liberation and the general mobilization for the building and defence of the State of Israel having faded – the crisis became obvious, and the attempt to involve the young from thirteen to fourteen years of age, through the Zionist, socialist boy scout movement of the *Zofim* (explorers),[67] proved to be scarcely effective.

At the same time as the *Hechaluz* movement gradually left the scene, within the body of Italian Judaism new and different Zionist youth movements arose. The place of *Hechaluz* was taken by Zionist groupings whose presence reflected, even more clearly, the influence of Israel on the small Italian-Jewish reality: I am referring to the Zionist religious movement *Bnei Akiva* (the children of Akiva), which reached Italy also thanks to the personal initiative of Rabbi Elio Toaff, and the socialist influence of the *Hashomer Ha-tsair* (young guard) movement. Both began operating in Italy in 1956 and are still present and active, especially in the main communities: they are in fact appendages of larger political-cultural movements which have their bases in the State of Israel; some *shalichim* (envoys) are sent out periodically, from the Israel operational headquarters, to the foreign bases, whose task is to organize activities and pass on to the young people the feeling of a strong tie with the culture and society of *Eretz Israel*.[68]

For a moment, let us return to the youth of *Hechaluz*; it is noteworthy that the progressive and inexorable decline of the movement exacerbated the generational feeling of isolation which had characterized those young people's self-image from the beginning;[69] thus, for example, Marco Maestro – reflecting on the weakening of the movement – remembered:

> If the fascist era struck the adult generation hard, it had a much greater impact on the character of the young, depriving them of education and political awareness. At the same time the persecution awakened in them the feeling of nationality, but only in a few cases could such an awakening realize itself in Zionism and *halutzism*. After an ephemeral flowering, this impetus faded.[70]

The recourse to those formulae deserves attention: it enabled young Italian Jews to find their bearings in relation to the past, emphasizing the impact of the watershed of 1938, which became a distinctive mark, a characteristic feature, the generative matrix of identity and the key to interpret the dynamics in which they were imprisoned. After a few years analogous categories, and a shared pessimism, would characterize the thinking of other young people, who did not share the Zionist fervour of the *halutzim*, but who felt a similar unease.

THE ITALIAN JEWISH YOUTH FEDERATION

In the early 1950s, while the *Hechaluz* movement was in crisis, the FGEI (Federazione Giovanile Ebraica d'Italia – The Italian Jewish Youth Federation) was, instead, establishing itself. It was an organization born in 1948 confederating the CGE (Centri Giovanili Ebraici – Jewish Youth Centres), which arose in the main communities following the Liberation.[71]

The FGEI was not a Zionist organization, even though Zionism was considered interesting and appreciated; the young people who adhered to the FGEI were not in tune with *aliyà*, they were, instead, strongly anchored to Italian reality, and at the same time tied, in varying ways and degrees, to their Jewish identity. Its members were not asked for a total adherence to a precise programme, nor a commitment to study and a return to tradition: their appurtenance to the Jewish group manifested itself more in participating with their co-religionists in recreational or cultural activities than in the definition of a specific ideological line.[72] Perhaps precisely because of this, such an organization rapidly gathered hundreds of members,[73] involving them in a variety of activities which ranged from the publication of an independent organ entitled *Ha-Tikwà*, distributed – until 1956 – within the weekly *Israel*, to the organization of recreational activities such as parties, dances and camping. Many of the cadres who led the Italian Jewish community in the following decades developed within that association.

Together with its character as a 'light' movement, without clear and strong identifying labels, what marked the life of the FGEI, especially in the first post-war decades, was a latent conflict with the Jewish ruling class.[74] Issues of contention concerned views about the Royal Decree of 1930 which had instituted the UCII: the FGEI in fact repeatedly asked for greater internal democracy. Apart from this, there were also other important judgements regarding the Italian political scene – there was criticism of the UCII's rigorous policy of neutrality – finally, there were marked differences in the interpretation of one's own Jewishness and the evolution of Jewish life after the Second World War. Such disputes did not fail to produce repeated controversial clashes which found an echo in the Jewish press of the time, and in which, significantly, the generational theme, from which we had started, re-emerges insistently.

The post-war leadership of the UCII had difficulty in coming to terms with the needs expressed by that youth association, remaining disturbed by the non-acceptance of the messages and lifestyles which it aimed at spreading. Dante Lattes, the director of the Cultural Department of the Union, showed, starting from 1947, that he was very interested in young people and their education and character formation; but his judgement of Jewish youth was anything but positive:

> now we are once again at the point where we were at the beginning of the century, for other and for the same reasons. The war has destroyed men and things and because of a tragic event has produced an immense hiatus, namely an abyss, between the generations, since the older one has either disappeared or has emigrated and the younger one has lived in the desert, in the dark and in fear … today's generation is different, even if its tastes have changed people have gone astray.

Lattes insisted for a long time on the importance of serious and in-depth study, inviting the young to work in order to get closer to tradition,[75] but despite the systematic commitment to education and culture, on the part of the UCII and Lattes himself, the future of the Italian-Jewish world was going in another direction, along a path which the schools and the editorial policy developed by the ruling class of Italian Judaism could perhaps deviate, but not modify radically. Also on account of this, since 1947 and with greater insistence at the beginning of the new decade, there emerges from the pages of the Jewish press the unease of the ruling class, dissatisfied at the dynamics of the young people and anxious about the possible return of the pre-war assimilatory processes.[76]

What Lattes, and much of the Jewish ruling class, had difficulty in accepting was that many of those who were 'reborn' to Judaism with the persecution were objectively assimilated, and at the same time developed something of an ineffable *Jewishness*, which mainly expressed itself in the strengthening of Jewish social ties.

As noted by Amos Luzzatto, nephew of Lattes, in 1948,

> The sad truth – is that for very many young Jews fascism has left a void – in fact, it has often created a void – which has not been filled. The majority of young people, who, immediately after the war, tried to find a new path to follow generally found it either in *Hechaluz* or in Italian political life ... most young people remain detached from any type of renewal, they remain disorientated and uncertain, trying to find, in the most varied diversions, a release of their ill-directed energies ... There are those who believe that cultural activity could improve all the youth, but I don't believe this because there are no masses which have resolved their problems merely through cultural activities.[77]

The persecution and then, later, the change in Italian society in the post-war period with the advent of the mass society introduced new and unexpected variables in the internal dynamics of the Jewish community; so that to be 'active in a Jewish sense' no longer only applied to restricted groups of brilliant, motivated young people, as had happened at the beginning of the twentieth century, but instead to multitudes of disorientated and confused young people. Very few, naturally, had the cultural means to try to work through their unease but, in a way, for all those who have not left a written account of their feelings, the evolution of the life of the Jewish associations provides a testimony. The most obvious break with the past concerned numbers: many hundreds of young people variously involved in the activities of Jewish associations, a fact which we have already mentioned and which reflects the strengthening of that generation's esprit de corps.[78] Only a small minority was careful and committed in considering the different possibilities which were available, a handful of young bourgeois, not highly cultured, who even wrote on the FGEI's organ, the periodical *Ha-Tikwà*. The majority was, instead, completely absorbed in playful, recreational activities, involved in the life of their peers, attracted by parties and camping, but it was not, on account of this, more aware of its heritage or mindful of Jewish history and culture. It is easy to understand the bitterness of a ruling class which had grown up in a completely different atmosphere, far from the attractions of mass culture, and which had totally different expectations for the community which it was committed to directing.

It was impossible to reintroduce, in an Italy which was moving towards modernization and the economic boom, the stylistic features and paradigms of the beginning of the century: this was very evident on the occasion of the thirtieth anniversary of the Jewish Youth Conference held in Livorno in 1924 – in which had emerged the figures, and the very different sensibilities, of Enzo Sereni,

Dante Lattes, Alfonso Pacifici and Nello Rosselli.[79] A new conference was organized to celebrate the anniversary (Milan, 27–28 December 1954) with the aim of reproducing, in some way, past experiences and reviving the community. The outcome of the event bore witness to the fact that Italian Judaism was going through another stage and that it was not possible to recapture the spirit of the 1920s: this time, at the heart of the debate there emerged, in particular, the problem posed by the FGEI, which controversially challenged the community institutions, forcibly raising the issue of what Judaism's attitude towards the values of anti-fascism, and therefore towards Italian politics, should be. It was the overall climate which had changed:

> Italy – as Fabio Della Seta, a companion of Giorgio Piperno in the years of the persecution and among the promoters of the initiative, later observed – was no longer the lively proving ground of the period following the Great War and the very early years of fascism's progressive ascent to power, it was already the sombre marshland of the great compromises, of the conformism typical of the great mass parties.[80]

Too harsh a judgement perhaps, but one which rightly highlights the change which, impacting the evolution of the whole country, inevitably also affected the Jewish minority: the ideological conflict exacerbated by the Cold War and the formidable attraction exercised by the great mass parties captured the attention and the energies of very many Italians and also of some of the most active figures of the Jewish world.

The nucleus of 'old Zionists' who in the post-war period had found itself directing Italian Judaism had to deal with multitudes of disorientated young people, upon whom the persecution had imposed – violently – an identity, which had difficulty in finding content. The call to study and revive tradition could hardly satisfy the peculiar and urgent needs created by State racism. Also those who were attempting some kind of intellectual processing of their difficulties turned to other things: in the first place, there was the fascination exercised by politics. All this emerged clearly in the 1950s, when, mainly in the pages of the weekly *Israel*, debates and heated clashes took place. Some of the most enlightened adherents of the Federazione Giovanile Ebraica (Jewish Youth Federation) tried, with different outcomes, to work through their feelings: the perception of their sadness and loneliness, the idea of being – in the words of Vittorini – 'a generation without a past'.

Some interesting ideas are to be found in the controversy surrounding the publication (*Israel*, 10 March 1955) of an article entitled *Pensiero ebraico e pensiero moderno* (*Jewish Thought and Modern Thought*) by the Genoese Luciano Tas, among the most active members of the FGEI at that time and later destined to have a lively career as a freelance journalist. He called upon the Italian Jews to rethink their identity without limiting themselves to taking into account only tradition and Zionism, encouraging them to consider current themes and problems: 'there are Jews who believe in the advent of a better more just society, and who believe that these ideologies are not outside the compass of the Jewish spirit'.[81] The article, which theorized 'the impossibility of resolving everything by means of the law and tradition', provoked an impassioned debate: the responses which came from the Jewish ruling class basically re-presented the State of Israel, Zionism and the religious tradition as essential reference points for Jews. Lattes, in particular, replied in a polemical tone, stating that it was not possible 'to find the Capital of Karl Marx in the Bible or historical materialism in the Sacred Texts' and, once again, calling for a commitment to study and the rediscovery of Jewish culture.[82] The custodians of tradition saw anti-fascism and the strengthening of community ties as positive factors in themselves, but inadequate for the development of the community. For the 'old Zionists' the meaning and nature of the change which had occurred was difficult to understand; they responded to new problems utilizing the cultural instruments formulated in the preceding decades, in the struggle against the organized anti-Zionist movements and the process of integration. There were particularly harsh comments from two figures of the 'young generations', who had renewed their ties with the historical bases of Italian Zionism: Giorgio Piperno, who, after a stay in Palestine, had returned to Italy with the specific aim of guiding towards Zionism the young Italian Jews, did not hesitate to state that those who identified with the statements of Tas were 'the assimilated who don't want to assimilate', while Augusto Segre, slightly older than Piperno, and a pupil of Lattes, noted that 'those who were assimilated in the past were perhaps simpler, more rough, more informal; having adopted this position they didn't speak anymore about Jewish matters nor did they want to hear about them. Those who are assimilated today, however, are proud of their assimilation and woe to anyone who questions it!'[83] Despite the animosity and the inherently polemical nature of such statements they offer us useful hints to understand the situation, inasmuch as they permit us to see a significant aspect of the dynamics set in motion in 1938: the persecution had not stopped the process of cultural integration which had started forcefully after the emancipation, it had raised the problem of appurtenance, provoking in many a vague feeling of *Jewishness* which had difficulty in fusing with an effective return to authentically Jewish cultural roots. In that context, the development of a strengthened feeling of identification with the community, and the clashes with the ruling class, whose message appeared in many ways inadequate and unacceptable, produced a feeling of alienation in many young people. A sense of unease was worked through and often defined in terms of 'generational isolation'; it was precisely through the development of a kind of generational self-awareness that important figures of young Jewish groups interpreted their own condition. I find the following reflection particularly significant:

> however, I ask myself if only the youngest of us, those born after 1930 who have not had our experiences from 1938 to 1945 and who have grown up in an increasingly sheltered context … have the will to … find in themselves and or the others the clarity of their own ideas … there is a great probability of our remaining, those of us born between 1920 and 1930, isolated amidst the oldest and the youngest.[84]

Rivalry and tension between the Jewish world 'of the adults' and that 'of the young' were often interpreted and contextualized in terms of the idea of the crisis, of the inter-generational conflict, an often recurring theme in the Jewish press throughout the 1950s. On the one hand, the community leaders who stress the value of their experience and message,[85] on the other hand, the younger ones who bear witness to their unease and complain that 'there is a lack of communication between the two generations'.[86]

That tension also reflected the irreconcilability of the political positions taken by the FGEI, or at least by some of its dominant sectors, and those of the Jewish ruling class. At the heart of the debate, of which we have quoted a few excerpts, there was the strong need for political identification expressed by some of the young members of the FGEI. This had had an official sanction at the Congress held in December 1953, when the youth of the FGEI stated that they wanted to establish their identity on what, not without an excess of rhetoric, and unmindful of the deep identification of many Jews with fascism, they celebrated 'the indissoluble bond uniting Judaism and anti-fascism'.[87] It was at one and the same time a provocation and a challenge to the leadership of the UCII, but above all the statement of the need to identify with the patriotic anti-fascist myth.

The particular role which the Federation tried to attribute to anti-fascism and the Resistance emerges clearly from what has been one of the most important initiatives undertaken in those years: the creation of the CDEC, Centro di Documentazione Ebraica Contemporanea (Contemporary Jewish Documentation Centre). As early as the beginning of the 1950s, there was a need, in the movement, to create an archive of the history of the Jewish contribution to the Resistance, with the aim of 'providing young Jews with an anti-fascist, as well as Jewish, education'.[88] A commitment repeated several times and formally taken up at the Congress of 1954, when the FGEI undertook to 'collect and disseminate elements which propose documenting and combating the resurgent anti-Semitism and fascism in the world' and, with this aim in mind, it proposed 'the building, as soon as possible, of a permanent archive about the history of the Jewish contribution to the Resistance, and of the history of anti-Semitic persecutions'.[89] The embryo of the institute, which, even in its name, followed the model of the Parisian *Centre de Documentation Juive Contemporaine*, was born in Venice in 1955, under the direction of Roberto Bassi; it was then transferred to Milan in 1960, and in time it has become a real Jewish historical institute.[90] It was created to deal, at the same time, with the history of the recent persecutions and the history of the Jewish contribution to the Resistance, but it is significant that, at least in its initial phase, attention was primarily focused on the second theme: in fact, one of the earliest initiatives was the preparation of a list of Jewish partisans.[91] Other themes, such as the history of Zionism, remained significantly outside the project.

As we will see in greater detail in the second part of the book, the Union would eventually have given that Centre its approval, transferring to it the documentation collected by its Comitato Ricerche Deportati Ebrei (Committee for the Search of Deported Jews) and appointing the former director of the latter – Colonel Massimo Adolfo Vitale – as its own representative within the CDEC. Nevertheless, it was a project which in many ways distanced itself from the line adopted by the UCII in those years. As we have already seen, the most important institution of Italian Judaism tended to posit memory in a wider framework of persecutions, placing recent events in an ahistorical context, turning to the paradigms provided by tradition to support the need for a recovery of Jewishness, understood as a recovery of the religious element, together with an adherence to the Zionist cause. The youth of the FGEI, active in the 1950s, saw different reference points on the horizon: they mainly aimed at conquering a role and room for manoeuvre within the Italian political-cultural context.

The public clash between some figures of the FGEI and Raffaele Cantoni, which took place in the pages of *Israel* between 1953 and 1954, well illustrates the different sensibilities of those involved; the bone of contention was the attitude to be adopted regarding the possible legal equalization of those who had been persecuted on racial or political grounds. The young advocated this change, and saw it as a legitimization of their own tragedy: it was an opportunity to ennoble the racial persecution, associating it with anti-fascism and the active struggle against the regime. Cantoni, consistently following his own policy of rigorous political neutrality, saw it, instead, as posing a danger, because 'with the change of leadership, the former victim of political persecution was considered dangerous … and the Jews who had to endure persecutions not because of a position they had adopted or any action undertaken, but only because they were what they were, might then find themselves in an unjust position of suspicion'.[92] Excessive fears perhaps, and which nevertheless did not obstruct an admittedly long and complex legislative procedure which led, in 1955, to the approval of the Terracini law, a law that provided measures in favour of the victims of political and racial persecution and their families. One can understand the logic of Cantoni's opposition in view of the fact that such a law, proposed by the parliamentary opposition, was the result of a highly controversial operation against the Christian Democratic Party: it was part of a broader strategy of reviving the anti-fascist memory, in response to the policy undertaken, as early as the beginning of the 1950s, by the Christian Democratic Party which was blandishing the extreme right-wing electorate by putting on the same plane, also in terms of social welfare, the soldiers of Mussolini's Repubblica Sociale Italiana (the Italian Social Republic) and their families and those who had fallen in the war of Liberation.[93]

The political and cultural climate of the time could not but deeply affect an association like the FGEI. In the early 1950s, the attempt by the Christian Democrats to incorporate the neo-fascist MSI (Movimento Sociale Italiano – Italian Social Movement) witnessed one of its most sensational exercises in the albeit disastrous 'operazione Sturzo' (operation Sturzo) which, on the occasion of the 1952 local elections in the capital, foresaw – also following pressure from the Vatican – the establishment of an electoral block which should also have included the right wings of the Monarchist and Fascist parties.[94] This could not fail to upset Italian Judaism, especially those sections which had adhered to the national anti-fascist rhetoric, making it one of the main means for its own reintegration in the Republican political-cultural system. All these actions were linked to the internal politics and the precarious balance with which the Christian Democratic regime propped itself up. In the spring and summer of 1953, it was involved in a very hard clash with the opposition parties regarding a hypothesis about a majority-system electoral reform. On top of all this, passions were inflamed concerning the debate about the rearmament of Western Germany, with the PCI (Partito Comunista Italiano – Italian Communist Party), and the PSI (Partito Socialista Italiano – Italian Socialist Party) and the wider galaxy of Peace Committees working towards the reviving of the memory of the massacres, the violence and the persecutions carried out by Germany during the Second World War, with the aim of mobilizing public opinion against NATO and the European Defence Community.[95] All this, combined with the fact that at the time the Italian Left was not at all hostile to Israel – the change in policy started after the Suez Crisis in 1956 and became increasingly marked and obvious during the 1960s[96] – favoured the *approchement* with the Left on the part of many young Jews, including many activists of the FGEI who could not fail to agree with the battle, for the preservation of the memory of the German crimes, conducted at that time by left-wing parties and movements. This produced a certain unease in the Union's leadership, which at all costs wanted to avoid being involved in the political clash which was dividing the country. The UCII did everything possible to stop what it considered perilious youthful excesses; such an attitude triggered protests[97] and repeated clashes, which became particularly marked between the end of the 1950s and the early 1960s. Suffice it to consider the differences between the positions expressed in 1958 by Guido Neppi Modona in the FGEI's organ: 'Those who do not feel the need to move to Israel have the duty to give an immediate contribution to the country's political life', and the obstinate assertion of the political neutrality expressed two years later – at the height of the intense juvenile revolts which broke out in July 1960 as a reaction to the attempt made by Fernando Tambroni to establish a Christian Democratic Government with the support of the neo-fascist MSI – by Carlo Alberto Viterbo in the weekly *Israel*: 'Generally, as an organ of the Jewish press, we do not consider it our task to concern ourselves with the events of internal Italian politics unless the Jews and Judaism are involved; it is not within the compass of our duties to take part in the polemics which always have a hidden party aim'.[98] To those words, which, however, well reflected the needs and the room for manoeuvre really available to the Jewish ruling class, the organ of the FGEI – which in May 1960 had joined the Consiglio Federativo della Resistenza (the Federative Council of the Resistance) and which during the revolt provoked by the Tambroni plan had come out into the streets to demonstrate presenting itself as an 'autonomous protest group'[99] – replied controversially with the cry 'the Resistance continues'.[100] The recurring friction between the cautious UCII leadership and the impassioned, and sometimes naive, young Jewish activists would, in time, have led several young people, spellbound by political passion, to withdraw from active participation in the life of the community.[101]

After a few years the situation became more complicated; in particular, the fascination with the Left of some sectors of the Jewish world produced disappointments, bitterness, as well as a heightening of the tensions and conflicts within the community. After the Six Day War, the hostility of the PCI towards the State of Israel became markedly obvious, threatening the balance of the identities of a Jewish world tormented by the presence of different loyalties which were increasingly difficult to reconcile. As regards in particular the FGEI, it is worth noting that the change in the overall political-cultural picture was not without consequences: while in the XX Congress, held in October 1967, following Israel's lightning victory in the war, an unconditioned support for Israel could still be expressed;[102] just a few years later, different positions began to take shape, the initial attempts at dissociation were eventually followed by explicit criticisms and denunciations on the occasion of the XXIII Congress (1970), when there was an open condemnation of Israel's repression of the Palestinian national liberation movement.[103] A development which further complicated the already difficult relationship with the UCII, and which did not fail to provoke clashes among young Jews.

The events dealt with so far illustrate the significance and the strength of the new esprit de corps within Italian Judaism, stimulated by the persecution, as well as the effects of this feeling which deeply modified the social interaction within the community. Other things which have emerged include: internal conflicts, the difficulties and diverging views between different sectors of the Jewish world and the formation of a specific generational self-awareness among some sectors of the young people. Finally, it has been seen – also because of the instability of the overall national and international situation – how anguished the search for a balance and for a clear perception of their own Jewish-Italian identity proved to be. It was not always easy to reconcile the renewed feeling of appurtenance to the Jewish group – and the ties with Israel – with enduring and very strong roots in the social, cultural and political Italian reality.

NOTES

1. Regarding Jewish youth activities in fascist and pre-fascist Italy, see M. Toscano, 'Fermenti culturali ed esperienze organizzative della gioventù ebraica italiana (1911–1925)', *Storia Contemporanea*, 6, XII (1982), pp.915–61; see also M. Savaldi, 'I campeggi ebraici (1931–1939)', *Storia Contemporanea*, 6, XVII (1988), pp.1121–52.
2. G.J. Piperno, *Ebraismo, Sionismo, Halutzismo* (Rome: Carucci, 1976), p.69.
3. E. Artom, *Diari di un partigiano ebreo. Gennaio 1940–febbraio 1944*, edited by G. Schwarz (Turin: Bollati Boringhieri, 2008), p.149.
4. V.D. Segre, *Storia di un ebreo fortunato* (Milan: Garzanti, 1985), p.14.
5. Ibid., p.16.
6. See, for example, A. Zargani, *Certe promesse d'amore* (Bologna: Il Mulino, 1997).
7. F. Fortini, *I cani del Sinai* (Turin: Einaudi, 1979 [1967]), p.19. In fact, that would not be a definitive break: Fortini returned to the subject, recalling once again his Jewish roots, with his 'Lettera agli ebrei italiani' significantly signed Franco Fortini Lattes, which appeared on the front page of the newspaper *Il Manifesto* of 24 May 1989. Through that text he asked the Italian Diaspora to distance itself from Israel.
8. F. Fortini, *I cani del Sinai*, p.57, but the following pages, up to p.60, should also be read.
9. See, for example, the poignant verses written in 1944 with the title 'Lettera', reproduced in F. Fortini, *Poesia ed errore 1937–1957* (Milan: Feltrinelli, 1959).
10. F. Fortini, 'Difesa del cretino', in *Verifica dei poteri: Scritti di critica e di istituzioni letterarie* (Turin: Einaudi, 1989 [1969]), p.24.
11. If there is one thing which the fascist persecution highlighted, it was, if anything, the opposite or rather the high level of fusion with the surrounding society, born out by the very high number of mixed marriages which were recorded by the regime itself. Regarding this, see G.M. and Ga. Cardosi, *Sul confine. La questione dei 'matrimoni misti' durante la persecuzione anti-ebraica in Italia e in Europa (1935–1945)*, preface by F. Levi (Turin: Zamorani, 1998).
12. L. Bianciardi, *Il lavoro culturale* (Milan: Feltrinelli, 1997 [1st. ed. 1957]), p.12.
13. E. Vittorini, *Diario in pubblico* (Turin: Einaudi, 1957), p.402.
14. R. Bianchi Bandinelli, *A che serve la storia dell'arte antica?*, *Società*, 1 (1945), p.8.
15. See L. Mangoni, *Civiltà della crisi. Gli intellettuali tra fascismo e antifascismo*, in F. Barbagallo (ed.), *Storia dell'Italia repubblicana*, vol. I, *La costruzione della democrazia. Dalla caduta del fascismo agli anni cinquanta* (Turin: Einaudi, 1994), pp.617–718.
16. R. Zangrandi, *Il lungo viaggio. Contributo alla storia di una generazione* (Turin: Einaudi, 1947). The text, reviewed and with the addition of a documentary appendix, was published by Feltrinelli in 1962 with a new title: *Il lungo viaggio attraverso il fascismo*.
17. See, for example, F. Gambetti, *1919–1945. Inchiesta sul fascismo* (Milan: Mastellone, 1953); E.A. Albertone, E. Antonimi and R. Palmieri (eds), *La generazione degli anni difficili* (Bari: Laterza, 1962). The subject was taken up in the cycles of lessons and accounts which multiplied at the beginning of the 1960s: see F. Antonicelli (ed.), *Dall'antifascismo alla Resistenza. Trent'anni di storia italiana (1919–1945)* (Turin: Einaudi, 1961); *Fascismo e antifascismo. Lezioni e testimonianze*, 2 vols (Milan: Feltrineli, 1962). There are many memoirs regarding, in particular, the transition of many young people from fascism to communism. Apart from the above-mentioned Zangrandi, see L. Lombardo Radice, *Fascismo e anticomunismo. Appunti e ricordi. 1935–1945* (Turin: Einaudi, 1946); D. Lajolo, *Il voltagabbana* (Milan: Mondadori, 1963); U. Alfassio Grimaldi, *Autobiografia dei giovani del tempo fascista* (Brescia: La Scuola, 1947). Mention should also be

made of the intervention by A. La Penna, 'I giovani e la cultura negli anni del fascismo', published in two parts in *Società*, 7–8 (1946), pp.678–90 and 3–4 (1947), pp.380–405.

18. L. Passerini, 'La giovinezza metafora del cambiamento sociale. Due dibattiti sui giovani nell'Italia fascista e negli Stati Uniti degli anni Cinquanta', in G. Levi and G. Schmitt (eds), *Storia dei giovani. 2 L'età contemporanea* (Bari: Laterza, 1994), p.389.
19. Regarding the rupture of 8 September 1943 and the mechanisms which determined the different choices made, see C. Pavone, *Una guerra civile. Saggio storico sulla moralità nella Resistenza* (Turin: Bollati Boringhieri, 1994 [1991]), Chap. 1, and regarding important observations on the problem of generations between fascism and Resistance see pp.551–60.
20. F. Levi, *L'identità imposta. Un padre ebreo di fronte alle leggi razziali di Mussolini* (Turin: Zamorani, 1996), p.185.
21. P. Di Cori, 'Le leggi razziali', in M. Isnenghi (ed.), *I luoghi della memoria. Simboli e miti dell'Italia unita* (Bari: Laterza, 1996), p.467.
22. See the testimony of V. Foa, *Il cavallo e la torre. Riflessioni su una vita* (Turin: Einaudi, 1991), pp.7–8; cf. also V. Foa, *Questo Novecento. Un secolo di passione civile. La politica come responsabilità* (Turin: Einaudi, 1996), p.150. For research on how different generations face the memory issue, see also F. Taglicozzo Di Castro and F. Di Castro, 'La memoria della persecuzione antiebraica. Due generazioni a confronto', *Parolechiave*, 16 (1998), pp.159–72.
23. K. Mannheim, 'The Problem of Generations', in *Essays on the Sociology of Knowledge* (London: Routledge, 1972), pp.302ff.; P. Abrams, *Historical Sociology* (Ithaca, NY: Cornell University Press, 1982), pp.273–314.
24. The decision to emigrate depended upon different factors and had concerned three main categories of people: the young, the intellectuals and the well-to-do: see M. Toscano, 'L'emigrazione ebraica italiana dopo il 1938', *Storia Contemporanea*, 6, XVIII (1988), pp.1287–1314.
25. S. Lombroso, *Diario di una madre (si può stampare). Pagine vissute* (Rome: Dalmatia, 1945), p.62. For other accounts, see A. Stille, *Uno su mille. Cinque famiglie ebraiche durante il fascismo* (Milan: Mondadori, 1991), pp.180–1; S. Segre Amar, *Il mio ghetto* (Milan: Garzanti, 1987), pp.123–4 and 142–7.
26. A. Zargani, *Per violino solo. La mia infanzia nell'aldiquà* (Bologna: Il Mulino, 1997), p.82.
27. See the observations of F. Levi, *L'identità imposta*, pp.16–29.
28. Ibid., letter of 4 May 1939, p.144.
29. It has been ascertained that there were at least twenty suicides; apart from the verified instances there could have been a higher number which Sarfatti has estimated between 0.5 and 1 per 1,000 of the 51,000 persecuted. See M. Sarfatti, *Gli ebrei nell'Italia fascista. Vicende, identità, persecuzione* (Turin: Einaudi, 2000), pp.210–11.
30. See L. Orvieto, *Storia di Angiolo e Laura* (Florence: Olschki, 2001), pp.134–5.
31. See the account of Primo Levi, who records the alienation of students and professors in *Il sistema periodico* (Turin: Einaudi, 1975), p.48.
32. Various requests of this type were forwarded to Mussolini; their nature has been well illustrated by M. Mondini, 'L'identità negata. Materiali di lavoro su ebrei ed esercito dall'età liberale al secondo dopoguerra', in I. Pavan and G. Schwarz (eds), *Gli ebrei in Italia tra persecuzione fascista e reintegrazione postbellica* (Florence: La Giuntina, 2001), pp.161–5.
33. The difficulty in interpreting events correctly and in reacting adequately has characterized very many Western Jews, well integrated and totally unprepared for the racial persecutions. Saul Friedländer has dealt with this subject in a work which postulates the importance of the study of Jewish reactions to the racial oppression for a correct understanding of the persecution and its less obvious effects: *Nazi Germany and the Jews. Volume I. The Years of Persecution 1933–1939* (New York: HarperCollins, 1997).
34. A. Mortara, 'In attesa di miracoli. Gli ebrei in Italia dal 1938 al 1940', in *RMI*, 1–2, LIV (1988), pp.37–47.
35. Between 1938 and 1942 about a thousand Jews wrote directly to Mussolini asking for his interession, see I. Nidam Orvieto, 'Lettere a Mussolini. Gli ebrei italiani e le leggi antiebraiche', in *RMI*, special issue edited by L. Picciotto Fargion, *Saggi sull'ebraismo italiano del Novecento in onore di Luisella Mortasa Ottolenghi*, 1, LXIX (2003), pp.321–46. In more general terms, regarding the habit of having a direct relationship, also through correspondence, with Mussolini developed by the Italians as early as the very first years of the dictatorship see the observations of S. Luzzatto, *Il corpo del duce. Un cadaver tra immaginazione, storia e memoria* (Turin: Einaudi, 1998), pp.20ff.
36. He wrote as follows in his diary for 13 September 1943: 'A terrible day. Italy has asked for an

armistice and has not had peace', in B. Treves (ed.), *Tre vite dall'ultimo '800 alla metà del '900. Studi e memorie di Emilio-Emanuele-Ennio Artom* (Florence: Casa Editrice Israel, 1954), p.122.
37. E. Artom, *Diari di un partigiano ebreo*, p.54.
38. Quoted by Laura Orvieto in *Storia di Angiolo e Laura*, p.137.
39. G. Bassani, *L'airone*, in *Opere*, edited by R. Cotroneo (Milan: Mondadori, 2001). I am quoting from the edition reviewed by the author on the occasion of the publication of the account contained in *Romanzo di Ferrara*, in 1980.
40. H. Stuart Hughes, *Prisoners of Hope: The Silver Age of Italian Jews 1924–1974* (Cambridge, MA: Harvard University Press, 1996), p.147.
41. G. Bassani, *Gli occhiali d'oro* [1st. ed. 1980], in *Opere*, pp.312–13, my italics.
42. A. Pinter, 'L'educazione ebraica nelle famiglie', in A.M. Piussi (ed.), *Presto apprendere, tardi dimenticare. L'educazione ebraica nell'Italia contemporanea* (Milan: Angeli, 1998), p.140.
43. D. Levi, 'La psicoanalisi italiana e il trauma dei sopravvissuti', in B. Maida (ed.), *1938. I bambini e le leggi razziali* (Florence: La Giuntina, 2000), p.94. See, for example, the account of L. Treves Alcalay, *Con occhi di bambina* (Florence: La Giuntina, 1994), pp.33–4.
44. D. Levi, 'La psicoanalisi italiana e il trauma dei sopravvissuti', p.99.
45. See A. Luzzatto, 'Autocoscienza e identità ebraica', in C. Vivanti (ed.), *Gli ebrei in Italia. Storia d'Italia, Annali,* vol. XI/2 (Turin: Einaudi, 1997), pp.1851–2.
46. G. Weillier, *La bufera. Una famiglia di ebrei milanesi con i partigiani dell'Ossola*, (Florence: La Giuntina 2002), p. 32. Regarding the Jewish school of Milan see also pp.44–50, 59–61 and 68–73.
47. See with regard to the Roman environment, G. Piperno, 'Fermenti di vita giovanile ebraica a Roma durante il periodo delle leggi razziali e dopo la liberazione della città', in D. Carpi, A. Milano and U. Nahon (eds), *Scritti in memoria di Enzo Sereni* (Jerusalem: Sally Mayer Foundation, 1970), pp.293–313; see also F. Della Seta, *L'incendio del Tevere* (Udine: Gaspari, 1996).
48. See, for example, E. Levi, *Memorie di una vita* (Modena: STEM Mucchi, 1972), p.87; L. Terracini, 'Cacciati dalla scuola. Carteggio ebraico '38', *Belfagor*, 4 (1990), pp.444–50.
49. See C. Cases, *Confessioni di un ottuagenario* (Rome: Donzelli, 2000), p.56.
50. See V.D. Segre, *Storia di un ebreo fortunato*, p.65.
51. P. Levi, *Il sistema periodico*, p.56.
52. See the reflection of S. Valentina Di Palma, 'Storia e memoria di bambini e adolescent nella Shoà', in *RMI*, 3, LXVII (2001), pp.71ff.
53. V.D. Segre, *Storia di un ebreo fortunato*, p.66.
54. G. Piperno, 'Fermenti di vita giovanile', p.297.
55. For some information, see D. Carpi, 'Il movimento sionistico', in *Gli ebrei in Italia, in Storia d'Italia, Annali*, edited by C. Vivanti, vol. XI/2 (Turin: Einaudi, 1997), pp.1355–6.
56. In the summer of 1944, a first *hackshara* had been established at Ponte Nona, near Rome, while an analogous collective farm had been set up after the complete liberation of the country at Brivio, near Lake Como and then transferred to Ceriano Laghetto.
57. See D. Carpi, 'Il movimento sionistico', pp.1367–8. For a wider overview on the movement's history, see A. Tagliacozzo (ed.), *Sulle orme della rinascita. Cronaca e memorie del Movimento Hechaluz italiano dal '44 al '54* (Rome: Litos, 2004).
58. *Hechaluz*, 1 June 1946.
59. See the account of Corrado Israel Debenedetti, who emigrated to Israel in 1949: *Anni di rabbia e di speranze 1938–1949* (Florence: La Giuntina, 2003), pp.120ff.
60. I have taken the information from *Hechaluz*, 6, 9 May 1952.
61. A. Zargani, *Certe promesse d'amore*, p.85.
62. See G. Piperno, *Fermenti di vita giovanile*, p.307.
63. See, for example, the various articles published in *Israel*, 19, 15 January 1948, and the reply of M. Savaldi, *Lavoro e Spirito*, ibid., 22, 5 February 1948.
64. AUCII, b.44b, f. 'Istituzioni temporanee di soccorso', file 'Contributi Unione ad *hackshara* San Marco (Cevoli)'.
65. It has been rightly pointed out by D. Carpi, 'Il movimento sionistico', p.1368.
66. 'Relazione morale', in *Bollettino d'Informazione e Documentazione*, 9, March 1946, issue entirely concerned with the meeting of Italian Zionist groups.
67. See A. Zargani, *Certe promesse d'amore*.
68. The *Bnei Akivà* movement arose in Jerusalem in 1929, with a markedly religious and Zionist character, the *Hashomer Hatzair* came into being in Galicia in 1916, with strong socialist leanings. For some sociological considerations on the movements and their impact on the Italian situation, see G.B.

Novello Paglianti, 'Aspetti socio-antropologici dei movimenti giovanili Hashomer Ha-tsair e Bnei Akiva', in A.M. Piussi (ed.), *Presto apprendere, tardi dimenticare*, pp.112–36; G.B. Novello Paglianti, 'Profilo dell'associazionismo giovanile ebraico', in A.M. Piussi (ed.), *E li insegnerai ai tuoi figli. Educazione ebraica in Italia dalle leggi razziali a oggi* (Florence: La Giuntina, 1997), pp.201–9.

69. Thus, for example, G. Viterbo, 'Hechaluz: una nuova generazione', in *Israel*, 13, 30 May 1946.
70. M. Maestro, 'E se non ora...?', *Hechaluz*, 7–8, 25 February 1951.
71. For some indications about the activities of the FGEI, see S. Della Pergola, *Anatomia dell'Ebraismo Italiano* (Rome: Carucci, 1976), pp.216–22; E. Sabatello and S. Della Pergola, *Inchiesta su venti anni di FGEI*, *Ha-Tikwà*, 4, May 1968. In this regard, see also the account of F. Piperno, a long-time secretary of the juvenile Jewish movement, in FGEI, *Quarant'anni 1948–1988* (Florence: La Giuntina, 1988).
72. This approach was clearly expressed with the publication of the statute of the FGEI of December 1953 and in an article entitled *La funzione dei CGE* in which Fernando Piperno stated that the aim of the centres had to be 'bringing the Jew closer to the Jew, realizing this almost without the parties concerned being aware of it' and that it was sufficient 'to draw the young together even without specific programmes, but simply with the aim that they should get to know each other better', *Israel*, 15, 17 December 1953.
73. In this regard, F. Piperno ('Fuori dall'equivoco', *Israel*, 33–34, 23 April 1948) stated that young Jewish people between the ages of 16 and 36 were about 10,000, while those who had joined the CGE were 800. Nevertheless a remarkable number when compared to the few tens of people involved in the youth organizations before 1938.
74. As has already been mentioned, the FGEI criticized the lack of electoral scrutiny, after the Bonfiglioli crisis, as well as the scarcely democratic procedures which led to the brief presidency of Giorgio Zevi. Useful information about the debate within the FGEI in the early 1950s, and the terms of the clash with the leadership of the Union, can be found in the *Relazione al Congresso* written by the secretary Elio D'Agnelli on the occasion of the FGEI Conference held in 1955. In AUCII, b.44b, f. 'Campeggi, sport, cge, fgei'. The text is also in ACDEC, FGEI Archives, b.1.
75. D. Lattes, 'Ricominciare da capo', *Israel*, 15, 23 January 1947. See also D. Lattes, *Messaggio alla gioventù*, *Israel*, 14, 16 January 1947. At odds with Lattes, there was an intervention on this point by Leo Levi ('Cultura ebraica e vita ebraica', *Israel*, 15, 21 January 1947) who supported the dignity and importance of recreational activities which aimed at fostering the forging of strong community ties. Leo Levi, a strange figure, an anti-fascist and Zionist intellectual, played an essential part in organizing and promoting Jewish youth associations in the post-war period. On this figure, see Arturo Marzano's introduction to L. Levi, *Contro i dinosauri. Scritti civili 1931–1972*, edited by A. Marzano (Naples: L'Ancora del Mediterraneo, 2011).
76. See, for example, D. Lattes, 'Si fa ancora l'elogio dell'assimilatione', *RMI*, 6, XX (1954), pp.199–203.
77. A. Luzzatto, 'Gioventù in crisi', *Israel*, 3–4, 28 October 1948.
78. This had already been highlighted, in its time, by Leo Levi: 'Riflessioni autunnali', *Israel*, 14, 6 December 1956.
79. See D. Bidussa, 'Tra avanguardia e rivolta. Il sionismo in Italia nel primo quarto del Novecento', in D. Bidussa, A. Luzzatto and G. Luzzatto Voghera, *Oltre il ghetto. Momenti e figure dell'emancipazione ebraica* (Brescia: Morcelliana, 1987), pp.239–79. See also M. Toscano, 'Fermenti di vita giovanile'.
80. For an account of the interventions, see *Israel*, 18, 3 February 1955.
81. F. Della Seta, *L'incendio del Tevere*, p.196.
82. D. Lattes, 'In difesa del pensiero ebraico e di una povera Cenerentola', *Israel*, 25, 24 March 1955.
83. Respectively, G. Piperno, 'Bologna è dopo Firenze: ovvero gli assimilati contro voglia', *Israel*, 39, 30 June 1955, and A. Segre, 'Cultura e assimilazione', ibid.
84. 'Sulla difficile arte di gettar sassi nelle acque stagnanti che ci circondano', *Israel*, 32, 5 May 1955.
85. See, for example, D. Lattes, 'Difesa delle generazioni passate', *Israel*, 8, 25 October 1956. The article is part of a broader controversy which lasted a long time.
86. Thus A. Luzzatto, 'Il dialogo delle due generazioni', *Israel*, 8, 3 December 1959.
87. *Israel*, 17, 31 December 1953. See in particular the article by G. Segre entitled 'Sul binomio ebraismo antifascismo'. What is referred to in this formula is in fact a myth, the expression of the adherence of the minority to the anti-fascist paradigm. Without diminishing the contribution of individual Jews to the anti-fascist cause, the fact that one cannot speak of a 'Jewish anti-fascism' is well demonstrated by P. Treves, *Antifascisti ebrei o antifascism ebraico?*, *RMI*, 6, XLVII (1981), pp.32–58.
88. See S. Liberovici, 'Proposta per un Archivio della Resistenza ebraica', in *Israel*, 4, 17 July 1952; but see also F. Piperno, *Ricordiamo i nostri eroi*.

89. 'Le mozioni approvate al Congresso', *Israel*, 21, 28 January 1954.
90. It was the depository of the documentation accumulated by the Comitato Ricerche Deportati Ebrei (Committee for the Search of Deported Jews), while the man in charge of the Committee itself, Colonel Massimo Adolfo Vitale, would have represented the UCII within the CDEC. Regarding the CDEC, see the observations of L. Picciotto Fargion, 'La ricerca del Centro di documentazione ebraica contemporanea sugli ebrei deportati dall'Italia', in P. Momigliano Levi (ed.), *Storia e memoria della deportazione. Modelli di ricerca e di comunicazione in Italia e in Francia* (Florence: La Giuntina, 1996), pp.60–72. See also L. Picciotto Fargion, 'Eloisa e il CDEC', *RMI*, 1–3, XLVII (1983), pp.9–44; M. Sarfatti, 'La Fondazione Centro di Documentazione Ebraica Contemporanea', in M. Sarfatti (ed.), *Funzioni dei centri di storia e cultura ebraica nella società contemporanea* (Milan: Proedi, 1998), pp.45–50; I. Nidam Orvieto, 'Fighting Oblivion: The CDEC and its Impact on Italian Holocaust Historiography', in D. Bankier and D. Michaman (eds), *Holocaust Historiography in Context: Emrgence, Challenges, Polemics and Achievements* (New York and Jerusalem: Berghahn Books/Yad Vashem, 2008), pp.293–304.
91. See *La Voce della Comunità Israelitica di Roma*, 9 January 1956.
92. *Israel*, 15, 17 December 1953.
93. Between 1950 – when war pensions were granted to the soldiers of the RSI (Repubblica Sociale Italiana) – and 1952, when war pensions were also granted to those who had been in the MVSN (Milizia Volontaria di Sicurezza Nazionale, the National Security Voluntary Militia), a major part of the discrimination against the 'fascists' and their families were removed, so that they could also have access to the various benefits envisaged for the war veterans. See P. Ignazi, *Il polo escluso. Profilo del Movimento Sociale Italiano* (Bologna: Il Mulino, 1989), pp.62–7.
94. There is an immense bibliography on this subject; I will simply mention A. Riccardi, *Roma 'città sacra'? Dalla conciliazione all'operazione Sturzo* (Milan: Vita e Pensiero, 1978), pp.358ff.
95. The crisis of centrism has been well set in its historical context by P. Scoppola, *La repubblica dei partiti. Evoluzione e crisi di un sistema politico 1945–1995* (Bologna: Il Mulino, 1997), pp.263–74; but on the very hard political clash of those years and on the repression put into action by the machinery of State see the documented reconstruction of P. Soddu, *L'Italia del dopoguerra 1947–1953. Una democrazia precaria* (Rome: Editori Riuniti, 1998), Chapter 4.
96. The turning point of 1956 is linked to the changing international balance, from that time Israel appeared increasingly tied to the United States and the Western block. This led to a shift in the attitude of the Italian Communist Party, as emerges clearly from the party newspaper: see L. Tas, *Cartina rossa del Medio Oriente. La storia dello stato di Israele raccontata dall'Unità*, preface by A. Cavallari (Rome: La Voce, 1971). This process would have developed further after the Six Day War, introducing explicit anti-Zionist animosity in left-wing cultural reviews; see A. Becherucci, 'Vincere la guerra e perdere la pace. Isarele e la Guerra dei Sei Giorni in tre riviste della sinistra Italiana: "Il Ponte", "L'Astrolabio" e "Rinascita"', in A. Marzano and M. Simoni (eds), *Roma e Gerusalemme. Israele nella vita politica e culturale Italiana 1949–2009* (Genova: ECIG, 2010), pp.117–38.
97. See, for example, *Fondamenti Programmatici* of the FGEI, in *Israel*, 10, 10 February 1955: 'The call which is constantly made, from outside, to the FGEI to attenuate, minimize or even not start initiatives which, although being clearly linked to problems which deeply concern every Jew (for example, peace in Israel and throughout the world, German rearmament, relations with the Jews of Eastern Europe, the re-emergence of fascism, racism and anti-Semitism throughout the world), is a gesture of mistrust which we have to reject'.
98. C.A. Viterbo, 'Augurio', *Israel*, 37, 14 July 1960.
99. F. Segre, 'FGEI anni '60', in FGEI, *Quarant'anni 1948–1988*, p.69; see also P. Foa, '1953–1964', ibid., p.22.
100. See the article with the same title signed by S. Di Castro, *Ha-Tikwà*, 7–8, July–August 1960.
101. P. Bertilotti, 'Contrasti e trasformazioni della memoria dello sterminio in Italia, in M. Flores, S. Levis Sullam, M-A Matard-Bonucci, E. Traverso (eds.), *Storia della Shoah in Italia. Vicende, memorie, rappresentazioni*, vol. II, (Turin: UTET 2010), pp.74–6. See also the testimony of Fernando Piperno, a long-time secretary of the FGEI, published in FGEI, *Quarant'anni 1948–1988*, p. 13; cf. also A. Luzzatto, 'Autocoscienza e identità', p.1884.
102. *Ha-Tikwà*, 8 October 1967.
103. *Ha-Tikwà*, 7–8 September–October 1970.

5

Italian Citizenship and Jewish Identities

The fascist racist legislation, at first, downgraded the citizens of Jewish extraction and only subsequently, with the Manifesto of Verona of 14 November 1943, the fundamental document of the RSI (Repubblica Sociale Italiana – Italian Social Republic), reached the point of denying them Italian citizenship, defining them 'citizens of a hostile nationality', harshened the racial measures and actively organized roundups, collaborating with the German deportation policies.[1] All this caused deep wounds in the psyche of the persecuted, but could certainly not wipe out the profound feeling of belonging to Italy which, not less – and often more – than a vague Jewishness, characterized the identity of very many Italian citizens of Jewish origin.

So far we have considered the organization of the Jewish community and its associations in post-fascist Italy and the changes within the minority's collective identity. It is essential to note that while the restructuring of Jewish self-awareness and identity was taking place, the majority of Italian Jews was reintegrating itself fully in the fabric of the nation. Despite the persecution, the links capable of binding individuals and families of Jewish extraction to Italian society – customs, culture and politics – were numerous and strong.

> The Italy around us, or rather (in a time when people scarcely travelled) Piedmont and Turin, were not our enemies. Piedmont was our real country, the one with which we could identify; the mountains around Turin, visible on clear days, and which could be reached by bicycle, were ours, they were irreplaceable and had taught us to bear physical effort, endurance, and a certain wisdom. It was in Piedmont, in Turin, that we had, in effect, our roots, not massive but deep, wide-ranging and fantastically intertwined.[2]

These words of Primo Levi help explain why very many Italian Jews could not imagine emigrating to escape from the racist oppression. Strong ties, spontaneous and simple, towards family, loved ones and the places in which they had grown up and to which they had become attached, must be taken into account when considering the relatively small scale of Jewish emigration from Italy, during and after the persecution. Analogous feelings to those so well expressed by Primo Levi are to be found in fact in numerous memoirs.[3] The relationship with the simple things of everyday life, with the land and dear places, is apparent even in the memoirs of those who – like Vittorio Segre – chose to leave for Palestine as a reaction to the turning point of 1938: he wrote that at that time he began to distance himself from fascism and 'distance himself even from Italy', but he significantly sets the loss of roots against the inextinguishable ties of affection for the lands of his childhood, Friuli and the Albese: 'the only clods of earth, in short, which were mine'.[4]

Strong ties of affection and culture bound the Jews to the nation; Silvia Lombroso wrote in her diary,

> the Patria, even when you wrench yourself from her in order to survive, stays with you, strong, subtle, beyond suspicion; because your country is a nostalgia which assails you when you least expect it … your country is you, and your youth, it is the woman you have loved, and the old house and its shadows … the sweet rhythm of everyday life, it is the voice of things.[5]

Professions of patriotic loyalty and declarations of uninterrupted love for Italy recur exceptionally frequently in Jewish memoirs. They are naturally present and accentuated in the authors who, before 1938, had been nationalists and fascists,[6] but we find them, in different, perhaps less rhetorical terms, in almost all the memoirs.

Such feelings should not necessarily be considered incompatible with other drives, which moved some to regain their Jewishness: multiple elements of identity coexisted in the hearts of very many. There was, therefore, an inevitable oscillation between different options. Cesare Segre has left us an interesting description of the feelings and the wide range of choices facing him at the beginning of the post-war period:

> Then there was, for a short time, a completely different life, which certainly constituted a self-contained stratum. It was the recovery of Judaism, which was intense for all those who had survived the Shoah. Many soldiers of the Jewish contingent (of the then British Palestine) after having taken part in the war of liberation had remained in Italy, and tried to re-establish a Jewish solidarity aiming at *aliyà*, the 'ascent' to the Holy Land. With attitudes varying from curiosity to adherence, many young Italian Jews participated in the cultural initiatives of these instructors, soon integrated by others
>
> … I thought … that only there [in Israel] I would have been able to raise a family, something which seemed madness in the Europe of the concentration camps …
>
> If I didn't allow myself to be seduced it is because, despite everything, the ties with Europe and Italy are, for me, unquestionable: I know, by now, from experience that any country can take away your nationality even if

> you live there, like my family, for centuries and centuries, but I want to stay there as long as humanly possible. I then thought of the limited interest which my speciality, Romance Philology, could have for the Israelis. Finally, it was easy for me to resist that Middle Eastern temptation because the feeling of solidarity with the Jews of the Diaspora is stronger than the feeling of territorial-national appurtenance to a land, however fascinating (I have subsequently visited it various times with strong emotion), which was left by my ancestors at least two thousand years ago.
>
> The Italian-Jewish communities also tried their best to consolidate and regroup their members: among other things, organizing, every summer, camping in the mountains for the young. I participated in these activities various times, but by then I was only moved by love of the mountains and by the desire for company. Nevertheless, my habitual sense of detachment did not abate. And I also soon said goodbye to the Jewish circles. Now I only have very sporadic contacts.[7]

It is reasonable to maintain that, as also emerges from this significant testimony, the immediate aftermath of the war was marked by particular anxiety and agitation; it was a question of finding one's way in a world which was still very unstable. Drawing close to the community circles did not always necessarily come to an end so quickly, in any case it is important to note that in the vast majority of cases the reinforcing of one's Jewishness and successful integration in Italy were not considered irreconcilable alternatives. Certainly, there were some who felt that, after the persecution, it would not have been possible to resume their lives amidst those who had been passive onlookers or active accomplices of their own torturers. For example, Fernanda Di Segni Sermoneta wrote, in September 1944, to her son Benedetto, who had already gone to Palestine:

> Even if we now enjoy perfect freedom and have resumed our work, we almost feel strangers here. We feel that this is not our country. We feel that we have to create it down there where you are, where all the world's Jews should go. We feel different, we see among these people, these Italians, so many of the spies who have contributed to the ruin of our people in that fateful period. We don't know how to distinguish the good from the bad any more. And then what will be the future of this poor Italy, and ours![8]

Attitudes of this type can mainly be ascribed to the very first months of the post-war period: once the Italian political situation had stabilized, the anxieties and agitation of many people would have subsided. It is also important to note that, once the period of racial discrimination had come to an end, it was more of an ideological maturation which determined immigration to Israel rather than simply an escape from a reality, that of Italy, seen generally in positive terms.

In fact, it should also be noted that many of the most motivated Zionists, who definitively left Italy, have maintained a positive recollection – almost idyllic – of Italy, convinced that Italy and anti-Semitism were antithetical and irreconcilable terms.[9] What was at stake, for those who took such a radical decision as the *aliyà*, was not the specific judgement about the Italian reality, but rather a more wide-ranging criticism regarding the ideal of integration and the future of the Diaspora. Even the most convinced adhesion to the cause of the 'State of the Jews' could coexist with maintaining an equally strong identification with the Italian reality: quite a few of the Italian volunteers, mainly young and very young, who in 1948 went to fight for the survival of Israel, at the end of the conflict returned to Italy where they achieved perfect integration, participating actively in the life of the nation.[10]

Highlighting the enduring link which united very many Italian Jews to the country should not lead one to forget the wrench produced by the persecution. The Jewish community's relationship with State institutions was damaged and weakened by the turning point of 1938. Certainly the betrayal by the ruling House of Savoy, towards which very many Jews had developed a strong attachment and which did not oppose Mussolini's anti-Semitic change of policy, constituted a very serious wound. Also in that case, however, there was an exceptional variety of individual responses to that event: in the post-war period the majority of Italian Jews probably had an anti-monarchist attitude, but it would be a mistake to think of this change as something to be automatically taken for granted. Especially for the elderly, the monarchy continued to be, in spite of everything, a reference point which would be difficult to forsake.[11] Above and beyond the albeit important symbolic value inherent in the transition from monarchy to republic, the link – particularly evident in the second half of the 1800s – which had found the Jews to be amongst the most faithful servants and defenders of the Italian State, even though not disappearing, would have taken on new and different nuances. This partly reflected wider changes which concerned not only the Jewish minority but rather marked the whole of society: following the Second World War, the link which united the citizens and the institutions was subject to a delicate reformulation, coinciding with the rewriting of the laws of citizenship. The Republican State was born weak, deeply scored by ideological conflicts and divisions.

With the transition from fascism to democracy the regime's rhetorical symbols and formulae were rejected without adequate attention being paid to the constitution of a renewed patriotic 'liturgy'; the State apparatus, exhausted by the war, turned spontaneously towards specifically Catholic symbols and liturgy for the bereaved nation's ceremonies.[12] The increasing influence exercised by the majority religion in the life of the nation[13] certainly did not facilitate the reintegration of the Jewish minority, but this was not an insurmountable obstacle to a full integration. In fact, Italy, in the post-war period, was characterized by a great political and cultural liveliness, a plurality of messages and stimuli overwhelmed all the Italians and thus also the citizens of Jewish extraction.

Different forces were competing for the allegiance of the Italians in the post-war period; undoubtedly, those which stand out include Catholicism, the American myth, spread by the advance of the Allied troops and then above all through the cinema, and finally communism and the myth of the USSR.[14] The Jewish minority, like the whole nation after all, was in a situation of very great ideological mobilization, it was a world in which 'one tended … to see things in terms of white and black, or rather of white and red'.[15] The great force of the so-called myth of the USSR – 'based on a feeling of gratitude, as well as admiration for, and wonder at, the great part – heroic and tenacious – played by the Soviet Union in standing up to and defeating Nazism',[16] – must have exercised a notable fascination, above all on the very young Italian Jews.[17] For many, Zionism and communism were the main centres of attraction and, especially in an initial phase, were anything but irreconcilable: in both of them one could find the same need to overturn everything in order to start from scratch.[18]

The problem of the relationship of Italian Jews with the culture and the parties of the Left is a complex question, which needs to be interpreted in a broad chronological perspective: how, in fact, can one not recall the enthusiasm shown by many Italian Jews since the nineteenth century for the egalitarian socialist utopia?[19] In time, from generation to generation, that passion would have engendered real family traditions;[20] transforming itself, in line with changing circumstances, firstly, into adherence to anti-fascism and, subsequently, in many cases, into communism. The episodes of the anti-Semitic purges in the communist block at the beginning of the 1950s (from the 'Slánsky case' to the 'doctor's plot'[21]) and then the evolution of the international situation, which made Israel an American stronghold, would have altered the picture introducing unprecedented crisis factors; nevertheless, the relationship between Italian Jews and the political Left, despite its becoming more complex, would certainly not have been interrupted.[22]

The attractiveness of the communist message for the Jewish minority was undoubtedly notable, but it would be wrong to regard the whole Jewish community as holding those views or even only the whole of the Jewish Youth Federation (Federazione Giovanile Ebraica): there was the greatest variety of standpoints. It was certainly improbable for the Jews to identify with the Catholic Party, or with the Right (monarchist, *qualunquisti* or neo-fascist). It would be very difficult for the Jews to be attracted by the Right which, in its most extreme fringes, was decidedly far from democratic, developing an ideology in which denial of the Shoah and anti-Semitism have a considerable importance,[23] but which even in its mainstream currents has shown itself, for many decades, incapable of coming to terms with its own responsibilities,[24] finding it difficult until recent times to distance itself from the heritage of the Repubblica Sociale Italiana (Italian Social

Republic). It is also difficult to imagine that the timid, uncertain and contradictory signals of an opening towards Israel, as exhibited by some of the leaders of the MSI (Movimento Sociale Italiano – Italian Social Movement) at the end of the 1960s, could elicit a very positive response from the Italian-Jewish world.[25] Nevertheless, it is important to note that, in the absence of sound information, it is difficult to give a precise evaluation. What can safely be stated is that it was certainly possible for that minority to find solid political-ideological reference points both within the moderate forces (Social-Democrats, Liberals, Republicans and finally Socialists), which during the history of the Republic collaborated with the ruling Christian Democratic Party, as well as within the ranks of the left-wing opposition.[26]

The absence of data should require a cautious silence but, wishing to illustrate what were – on the whole – the different ideal options available to the Jews immediately after the war, we can refer the reader to the notes of Cesare Cases, who has recalled how

> amidst the palingenetic hopes of the post-war period the structures of the bourgeois mentality reconstructed themselves, in an unaltered form, like the economy, and the Jews cooperated to satisfy these needs no less than the others. For those who felt uneasy and did not overcome the trauma so easily, the alternatives were Zionism and the left-wing parties, and both led, after many twists and turns, to an acceptance of the status quo. Or one limited oneself simply to try and realize one's own personal existence which had been miraculously saved.[27]

A complex mixture characterized the Italian-Jewish identity following the Second World War. Israel, memory, some religious feeling and esprit de corps constituted a Jewishness whose contours were partially revised, while the fascination exercised by democratic party politics, combining with factors which were absolutely pre-political – the language, the culture, the land, the people – characterized an Italian identity which fascism had challenged, put under pressure, but had not been able to destroy.

After the Second World War the psyche of many of the persecuted was torn apart by conflicting drives: on the one hand, the instinctive and very deep emotional link with one's country and, on the other hand, a rational reflection, critical and disenchanted which highlighted the injustices borne and the extreme difficulty in recovering the fragile certainties on which the process of integration had been based.[28] A *nostalgic memory*, completely focused on the cult of the past and on a desire of happy integration, prevailed for a long time at the expense of a *critical memory*, that was certainly more painful.[29]

The insistence on one's own roots in Italy and the complementary tendency to minimize, even to excess, the significance of anti-Semitism in Italian society are elements which characterized the public and private rhetoric of Italian

Judaism in the first fifty years of the post-war period. It was also, if not primarily, through the playing down of the events of 1938 that many were able to silence their consciences, stifle their own anxieties and resume their lives, side by side with their fellow citizens, to see to the reconstruction of Italy. Those who were more committed to healing the rift were, mainly, members of a specific generational group: those who were middle-aged at the time of the racial turning point preserved in the depths of their soul a clear image of their country and of their own relationship with it; after the Liberation they would have desperately tried to recapture that image, struggling to take up once again a lifestyle and a value system which – as did, after all, very many of their compatriots of another faith – they still considered valid, not adulterated or seriously compromised by the dictatorship or by the war.

NOTES

1. On the persecution of Jews by Mussolini's Social Republic, see M. Sarfatti, *Gli ebrei nell'Italia fascista. Vicende, identità, persecuzioni* (Turin: Einaudi, 2000), pp.245–71; L. Picciotto, 'La macchina antiebraica della RSI e l'Ispettore generale per la razza Giovanni Preziosi', in M. Sarfatti (ed.), *La Repubblica sociale italiana a Desenzano. Giovanni Preziosi e l'Ispettorato generale per la razza* (Florence: La Giuntina, 2008), pp.17–44; M. Raspanti, 'L'ispetorato generale per la razza', in ibid., pp.109–40; L. Ganapini, 'I persecutori italiani', in M. Flores, S. Levis Sullam, M.-A. Matard-Bonucci and E. Traverso (eds), *Storia della Shoah in Italia. Vicende, memorie, rappresentazioni*, vol. I (Turin: UTET, 2010), pp.454–76. For an overall history of the Italian Social Republic, see L. Ganapini, *La Repubblica delle Camicie nere. I combattenti, i politici, gli amministratori, i socialiszzatori* (Milan: Garzanti, 1999). As far as the Nazi initiatives for the murder and deportations of Jews from Italy are concerned, see L. Klinkhammer, *L'occupazione tedesca in Italia 1943–1945* (Turin: Bollati Boringhieri, 1993), pp.399–411. L. Klinkhammer, 'L'occupazione tedesca in Italia e lo sterminio degli ebrei', in M. Flores, S. Levis Sullam, M.-A. Matard-Bonucci and E. Traverso (eds), *Storia della Shoah in Italia*, pp.433–53.
2. P. Levi, *Il sistema periodico* (Turin: Einaudi, 1975), p.53.
3. See, for example, L. Morpurgo, *Caccia all'uomo. Vita sofferenze e beffe* (Rome: Dalmatia, 1945), p.41; E. Levi, *Memorie di una vita* (Modena: STEM Mucchi, 1972), p.102; M. Bemporad, *La Macine. Storia di una famiglia israelita negli ultimi 60 anni di vita italiana* (Rome: Carucci, 1984), p.5.
4. V.D Segre, *Storia di un ebreo fortunato* (Milan: Garzanti, 1985), p.85.
5. S. Lombroso, *Diario di una madre (si può stampare). Pagine vissute* (Rome: Dalmatia, 1945), pp.36–7.
6. See, for example, what the Bolognese Jew Giorgio Sacerdoti wrote: 'Generally, Italian Jews, despite the persecution, remained tied to Italian culture with which they were imbued … Detaching oneself or only trying to detach oneself from the culture of one's own native country is like a suicide', *Ricordi di un ebreo Bolognese. Illusioni e delusioni 1929–1945*, preface by R. De Felice (Rome: Bonacci, 1983), p.65. For another example, always from the cultural area of fascist Jewry, see G. Del Vecchio, *Una nuova persecuzione contro un perseguitato. Documenti* (Rome: Tipografia artigiana, 1945), p.6.
7. C. Segre, *Per curiosità. Una specie di autobiografia* (Turin: Einaudi, 1999). See, for example, the account on pp.112–13.
8. Quoted in F. Barozzi, 'L'uscita degli ebrei di Roma dalla clandestinità', in M. Sarfatti (ed.), *Il ritorno alla vita. Vicende e diritti degli ebrei in Italia dopo la seconda guerra mondiale* (Florence: La Giuntina, 1998), p.41.
9. See, for example, the accounts collected by A. Pezzana, *Quest'anno a Gerusalemme. Gli ebrei italiani in Israele*, with an essay by V.D. Segre (Milan: Il Corbaccio, 1997); see in particular pp.15,

17, 34–5, 37. There is much less information about those who left Italy for other destinations other than Palestine. As far as Argentina is concerned, see E.M. Smolensky and V. Vigevani Jarach (eds), *Tante voci, una storia. Italiani ebrei in Argentina 1938–1948* (Bolgna: Il Mulino, 1998).

10. See M. Simoni, 'Gli ebrei italiani e lo Stato di Israele. Appunti per un ritratto di due generazioni (1948 e 1967)', in A. Marzano and M. Simoni (eds), *Roma e Gerusalemme. Israele nella vita politica e culturale italiana 1949–2009* (Genova: ECIG, 2010), pp.47–73. Regarding the Italian Jews who fell in that war, see also G. Romano, 'Via eroica. Gli olé d'Italia caduti per Erez Israel', *RMI*, 7–8, XVI (1950), pp.106–15.
11. See, for example, L. Levi, *Se va via il re* (Rome: e/o, 1996), pp.108–9.
12. On this point see my book: *Tu mi devi sepplir. Riti funebri e culto nazionale alle origini della Repubblica* (Turin: UTET, 2010).
13. Regarding the problem of the Italian secular religion, see G.E. Rusconi, *Possiamo fare a meno di una religion civile?* (Bari: Laterza, 1999); G.E. Rusconi, 'Religione civile e identità italiana', *Il Mulino*, 4 (2003), pp.832–8.
14. Regarding the influence of the American model on Italy, see V. De Grazia, 'La sfida dello "star system". L'americanismo nella formazione della cultura di massa in Europa, 1920–1965', in D. Elwood and A. Lyttelton (eds), *L'America arriva in Italia*, monographic issue of the review *Quaderni Storici*, 58 (1985), pp.95–133; S. Gundle, 'L'americanizzazione del quotidiano. Televisione e consumismo nell'Italia degli anni cinquanta', *Quaderni Storici*, 62 (1986), pp.561–92; P.P. D'Attorre (ed.), *Nemici per la pelle. Sogno americano e mito sovietico nell'Italia* contemporanea (Milan: Angeli, 1991).
15. P. Ginsborg, *Storia d'Italia dal dopoguerra a oggi. Società e politica 1943–1988* (Turin: Einaudi, 1989), p.245.
16. See P. Spriano, *Le passioni di un decennio 1946–1956* (Milan: Garzanti, 1986), p.149.
17. See, for example, the observations made by G.J. Piperno, *Ebraismo, Sionismo, Halutzismo* (Rome: Carucci, 1976), pp.49–56 and 156. Regarding young Italian Jews and the fascination with communism see the observations of A. Luzzatto, 'Autocoscienza e identità ebraica', in C. Vivanti (ed.), *Gli ebrei in Italia*, in *Storia d'Italia, Annali,* vol. XI/2 (Torino: Einaudi, 1997), pp.1860ff.
18. Regarding the adherence to Zionism and communism as expressions of an identical need to fight for a new beginning, see the autobiographical observations of Saul Friedländer, who was an adolescent in the immediate post-war period: *When Memory Comes* (Madison, WI: University of Wisconsin Press, 1979), p.164 in particular.
19. See A. Cavaglion, 'Gli ebrei e il socialismo', in M. Toscano and F. Sofia (eds), *Stato nazionale ed emancipazione ebraica* (Rome: Bonacci, 1992).
20. See G. Arian Levi and M. Montagnana, *I Montagnana. Una famiglia ebraica piemontese e il movimento operaio (1914–1948)*, preface by A. Luzzatto (Florence: La Giuntina, 2000).
21. In 1952, Rudolf Slánský, a leader of the Czechoslovak Communist Party, was, together with other thirteen Jewish officials, the victim, in Prague, of trial-farce in which he was accused of having supported a kind of 'Zionist plot' against the Revolution. In the same year, there was, in Moscow, a campaign of hostility towards the presence of Jews in the party, which culminated in the trial of the members of the Jewish Anti-Fascist Committee. Analogous trials led to the elimination of the Jewish leaders of the Communist parties of Rumania (Ana Pauker) and of Hungary (Péter Gábor). This wave of anti-Semitism culminated at the beginning of 1953 with the unveiling of a presumed plot by Jewish doctors to assassinate Stalin. There followed intense anti-Jewish campaigns throughout the communist block. Such events fit, albeit in an anything but linear way, into the culture of suspicion and the system of purges which characterized the Soviet system in those years and, regarding which, see M. Flores, *L'età del sospetto* (Bologna: Il Mulino, 1995).
22. In this regard, there is a deplorable lack of studies: the book by Maurizio Molinari, *La sinistra e gli ebrei in Italia 1967–1993*, preface by V.D. Segre (Milan: Il Corbaccio, 1995), turns out to be unsatisfactory.
23. F. Germinario, *Estranei alla democrazia. Negazionismo e antisemitismo nella destra radicale italiana* (Pisa: Biblioteca Franco Serantini, 2001).
24. Significant, in this regard, is the reflection, tending to claim their innocence, sometimes even turning to anti-Semitic arguments, conducted in extreme right-wing (neo-fascist) circles on the issue of Italian responsibilities in the Shoah. See F. Germinario, *L'altra memoria. L'Estrema destra, Salò e la Resistenza* (Turin: Bollati Boringhieri, 1999), pp.58–72.
25. The historical path followed by the Italian right-wing parties, with respect to the Jewish question, should be examined with greater attention and in a more balanced way than has been done in the

book – inspired by immediate political aims and useful, if anything, for understanding the cultural climate of our times – written by the journalist G.S. Rossi, *La destra e gli ebrei. Una storia italiana* (Catanzaro: Rubettino, 2003).

26. In a police report of 1946, it was stated that the Jews of Rome mainly favoured the left-wing parties and in particular the Republican and Action Parties, quoted in M. Toscano, *La 'porta di Sion'. L'Italia e l'immigrazione clandestina ebraica in Palestina (1945–1948)* (Bologna: Il Mulino, 1990), p.146 in a note. It is naturally difficult to evaluate the credibility of these statements. For some observations on the political behaviour of Italian Jews, but dealing with the 1960s, see S. Della Pergola, *Anatomia dell'ebraismo italiano*, pp.282–90.
27. C. Cases, 'Cosa fai in giro?', *Il Ponte*, 11–12 (1978), p.1336.
28. For a comparative perspective, see the thought-provoking book dealing with the Austrian situation by J. Vansant, *Reclaiming Heimat: Trauma and Mourning in Memoirs by Jewish Austrian Remigrés* (Detroit, MI: Wayne State University Press, 2001).
29. I am here turning to the analytical categories proposed by L. Spitzer, *Hotel Bolivia: The Culture of Memory in a Refuge From Nazism* (New York: Hill & Wang, 1999), pp.141–60.

Part 2

PATHS OF MEMORY

6

Memory Lapses

Once the regime had been defeated the reflection on the recent past, analysing the persecutions undergone and the specific Italian responsibilities – the guilts of the State, the world of culture, the economic system and the population as a whole – constituted an obligatory course to be followed for the Jewish community. The judgements developed concerning the tragedy which had occurred were destined to influence the minority's mechanisms of self-representation, delineating the contours of a renewed pact of integration and citizenship. It is necessary to analyse the structure and organization of the Jewish memory in order to understand that minority's identity, but it also offers a useful opportunity to investigate the genesis of cultural stereotypes and historiographic paradigms which have, for a long time, influenced the perception of fascist racism and the self-representation of the Italian nation as a whole.

The victims were the natural custodians of the memory of the racial persecution and for a long time were, in effect, left to deal with it alone. Inevitably, the judgements and the considerations formulated by the persecuted and by their official representatives played an essential role in conferring legitimacy and vigour to cultural representations which were vital and delicate for the Republic born from the Resistance.

Immediately after the fall of the fascist dictatorship we witness the consolidation of an interpretation of the anti-Jewish policy which erased even the slightest reference to a specific Italian responsibility. Italy, it was loudly proclaimed from every rostrum, had never offered fertile ground for the evil seed of anti-Semitism; the persecution must have been the result of foreign constraint, or perhaps the consequence of the delirium of a dictator foolishly pleased to imitate Germanic fashions. In any case, that policy could not fail to have evoked the unanimous hostility of the Italian people, whose moral conscience certainly had stopped it from collaborating with those criminal aims.

It is worth remembering, with Marc Bloch, that there are 'mythomaniac epochs',[1] and the post-war period in Italy was certainly one of these: interpretations of the fascist period in which reality and imagination, historical truth and an ideological reading of the past were inextricably intertwined flourished for a long time. 'The Resistance was – as the historian Claudio Pavone has written – essentially an attempt to come to terms with the past',[2] but a critical and sincere confrontation with reality was, in those conditions, perhaps impossible. The political and cultural climate which characterized the immediate post-war period led to denying that the fascists and fascism were part of Italian history: the fascists were the *Hyksos* – a foreign horde which had occupied the country for a time – the regime a mere parenthesis in national history, the Repubblica Sociale (Italian Social Republic) a puppet of the Germans who had exploited the collaboration of a few renegades: 'in this way, Italy came to terms with the fascist past very quickly with the general casting into oblivion of all the responsibilities and guilt, soon and universally considered venial'.[3]

By celebrating the presumed rejection of the racial campaign by a population which so much historiography thought it right to present as being outraged and offended by that turning point, there was the desire to indicate the gulf separating the Italians from the war, from the horrors of the Shoah and, not less importantly, from the fascist dictatorship. The Italian-Jewish representation of the persecutions fitted perfectly into this context, influencing it and being, in its turn, influenced by it. As this is a study dealing with the Italian Jews and the dynamics – political, cultural and also psychological – which marked their reintegration after 1945, a great deal of attention has, naturally, been paid to the recollection of the persecution which the minority worked through. This does not mean, however, that there is any intention of considering the victims of persecution as the prime movers of the repression of the Italian responsibilities regarding racism and anti-Semitism: the paths followed by the Jewish recollection were – mainly – those already taken by the dominant political and cultural forces of the country. Jewish memory – it should be remembered – is only one of the pieces of a much wider and more detailed mosaic which depicts a Republic founded, to a great extent, on a distorted perception of the dictatorship; reference will sometimes be made to the wider and more complex cultural horizons in which, of necessity, the memories of the Jewish minority fitted, without claiming, however, to write the history – already analysed by scholars, but partly still to be written – of the Republic's relationship with the fascist past.[4]

GEO JOSZ

It is useful to start with a literary text, the work of a writer capable of illuminating small, obscure events, telling us, with a light touch, a story which at times seems surreal. In the short story entitled *Una lapide in via Mazzini* (*A Plaque in Via Mazzini*), Giorgio Bassani has delicately reconstructed the environment of a recently-liberated Ferrara, in which, all of a sudden, a disquieting figure materialized:

> When, in August 1945, Geo Josz reappeared in Ferrara, the only survivor

> of the hundred and eighty-three members of the Jewish Community ... and whom most people thought had, some time ago, ended up in the gas chambers, nobody in the city recognized him at first.
>
> ... after such a long time, after so much suffering which had, to a certain extent, touched everyone and without distinction of political allegiance, wealth, religion, race, this fellow, just now, what did he want? What was he expecting?[5]

On returning to the city he read his name among those on the memorial plaque which listed the deported Jews. Given up for dead, to the eyes of many he was like a ghost: 'as if, pale and swollen, he had emerged from the depths of the sea ... Geo Josz reappeared in Ferrara'.[6] He was a big dark question which seemed to threaten the serenity of a small city determined to square accounts quickly with its own conscience. At first, his fellow citizens had difficulty in recognizing him, and even regaining possession of his family's home was not easy for him as it had become the headquarters of the CLN (Comitato di Liberazione Nazionale – National Liberation Committee). Nevertheless, after the first moment of uncertainty, in its own way the city closed ranks around this new attraction:

> He had been in Buchenwald and, the only one!, he was returning from it ... Well they were there, at his disposal, all ears to listen. Let him tell his story; and they – also to be forgiven for having so tardily recognized him, trying in fact to reject him, to exclude him once again – they would never have tired of listening to him.[7]

Instead they soon got tired. With lightning speed a sentiment arose: 'the conviction ... that for good or ill a new era was just then due to start, incomparably better than the other which, like a long sleep full of atrocious nightmares, was ending in blood'.[8] So it happened that very quickly curiosity gave way to fear, suspicion, intolerance. No one wanted to pay close attention to his accounts, not even his uncle, a lawyer and former fascist, who like all the others wanted to make a new start and go forward. The need for the *future* left no room for someone who wanted to rake up the past: 'Disrupted by the war, and anxious to start with every means the so highly desired and desirable reconstruction, society tried to get back on its feet. Life was starting again, thank God. And when it resumes, it is well known, it goes ahead regardless of everyone.'[9]

As suddenly as he had appeared, Geo Josz disappeared, leaving his Ferrara forever the day after the general elections of 18 April 1948, which lead to the triumph of the Christian Democratic Party. His partially fictitious story, narrated by Bassani with melancholic pessimism, does not – obviously – represent the lives of all Italian Jews in the post-war period, and yet it helps us get a grasp of the spirit of the times.[10]

A FLOOD OF MEMORIES

In the first two or three years after Liberation there was a real flood of memories: a great many diaries and eyewitness accounts – of soldiers, partisans, fascists and anti-fascists, political deportees, and also Jews, the survivors of the death camps and others – were published. They were not all masterpieces and quite soon the publishers stemmed the tide of that production, invoking the need to go beyond the mere preservation of memory. A letter of Cesare Pavese – a key figure at Einaudi publishing house – to Costanzo Aurelio of 19 July 1947 can help to shed light on the unease which developed in many people towards that flood tide:

> For two years we publishers have seen innumerable manuscripts dealing with various aspects of life: partisan, clandestine, prison, mixed – and the author always thinks that the enormity of the events he has experienced, or thinks he has experienced, is enough to constitute literature. No, these books oscillate, instead, between news and emotional outlets, they are essentially 'sentimental' and, aside from any political judgement, they have the same value.[11]

Casting a glance at the memoirs of the post-war period one will notice how from 1947–1948 that production diminished: numerous intellectuals – like Pavese – wanted to set in motion a new and different cultural season, the publishing market had rapidly become saturated and furthermore many of those who had the desire and the ability to tell a story, and to tell their own story, had already done so. All this makes the very first years of the post-war period exceptionally important as in that phase stereotypes were taking shape which had a long life, marking the culture and mentality of the nascent republic. As was inevitable, only a fragment of the heritage of experiences and emotions accumulated by the Italian people under the fascist regime, during the war and then in the course of the civil war, was able to be integrated, and not always successfully, in a nascent national memory, based on the anti-fascist myth and the experience of the Resistance. Thus, many aspects of the fascist past ended up seeming marginal.[12]

In order to imagine the atmosphere of those crucial years we can look at the conflicting, and yet in a way complementary, considerations, of Italo Calvino and Primo Levi. The former masterfully evoked the spirit of an age in which everyone seemed eager to tell his own story:

> With our renewed freedom of speech, all at first felt a rage to narrate: in the trains that were begining to run again, crammed with people and sacks of flour and drums of olive oil, every passenger told his vicissitudes to strangers, and so did every customer at the tables of the cheap restaurants, every woman waiting in line outside a shop. The grayness of

> daily life seemed to belong to other periods: we moved in a varicolored universe of stories.[13]

Nevertheless, it was difficult to expect that that 'rage to narrate' would be matched by an equally intense propensity to listen and understand. The burning need to unburden oneself was accompanied by other, no less urgent and intense, needs, and it was very unlikely that individuals and groups could succeed in setting aside such urgent needs in order to try and really understand others' dramas. Primo Levi, trying to explain the difficulties encountered in publishing the first version of *Se questo è un uomo*, wrote,

> At that time people had other things to do. They had to build homes, find work. There was still rationing; the cities were full of ruins; the Allies were still occupying Italy. People were not interested in this, they wanted something different, dancing for example, to have parties, to have children. A book like mine, and like many others which came later, was almost an incivility, a spoilt party.[14]

As everyone was totally absorbed by his own particular tragedy, the terrible and exceptional stories he had lived through, it was perhaps only that type of story – familiar inasmuch as it also reflected one's own anxiety – that people were prepared to listen to. Very soon different groups formed, custodians of specific and relatively homogeneous memories and experiences. It was primarily within the framework of those groups that those who were suffering would find a friendly ear, fellow feeling, brotherhood and consolation. Such groupings found themselves in competition with each other; at stake were the recognition of merits and sufferings, as well as the reclaiming of rights which had been infringed: naturally, the behaviour of Italian Jews also fitted into this context. They were, for rather a long time, the only custodians of their specific drama, and also the only ones – or almost – interested in putting it in writing.[15]

EARLY TESTIMONIES AND INTERPRETATIONS

Among the very first books dealing with the fascist anti-Jewish persecution, Eucardio Momigliano's *Storia tragica e grottesca del razzismo fascista* stands out.[16] Published in 1946, it was the very first attempt to analyse, in depth, the fascist racial policy and it was an important reference point for subsequent research. One finds, in this book, a thorough reworking of all the characteristic elements of the interpretative path followed, in the immediate post-war period, by dominant sectors of Italian culture, in tune with the majority of the victims of the persecution.

A lawyer and prolific freelance journalist, Eucardio Momigliano – a cousin of the more famous historian Arnaldo – had adhered to fascism in its early days, but had soon distanced himself from it – clashing sharply with Mussolini – after the murder of the socialist leader Giacomo Matteotti in 1924, when he began to participate actively in the Unione Democratica (Democratic Union). Well established in the circles of the anti-fascist intellectual bourgeoisie, he was subsequently a member of the Roman National Liberation Committee and close to the circles of the Democrazia del Lavoro (Labour Democratic Party).

Although he was certainly not a professional historian, he could present an *ex tempore* detailed and, for the times, well-informed reconstruction which met with a certain success also because it reflected very well feelings and opinions – in large measure unproven commonplaces – widespread at the time.

Like many of his co-religionists and like very many Italian intellectuals, Eucardio Momigliano seemed sincerely convinced that anti-Semitism had absolutely no roots in Italian society or its cultural tradition:

> Italy has always ignored anti-Semitism. A tradition of a 1,000 year-old civilization has always inspired, in governments and the people, a broad and benevolent tolerance towards the Jews; and even when the laws, inspired by the religious intolerance of a particular sovereign or pope, limited the freedom of the Jews and even disciplined their lives harshly, the application of these laws was, in fact, always lenient.[17]

The persecution was considered an absolute perversion of Italy's historical-cultural experience imposed, by the Nazis, on Mussolini who in accepting it was not only betraying the country's history and the trust of the Jewish minority, but fascist ideology itself; the author in fact talks at length in his attempt to demonstrate how the well-known 'Manifesto degli scienziati razzisti' ('Manifesto of Racist Scientists') was at variance with the principles enunciated by Mussolini and the fascist doctrine of the preceding years.[18] The anti-Semitic turning point is seen exclusively in connection with the evolution of Italo–German relations in the 1930s, ascribing a crucial importance to Ciano's visit to Berlin in October 1936: 'Germany exerted pressure and Mussolini had to obey'.[19]

This interpretation of events was very widespread in the reflections and testimonies of many Italian Jews,[20] and it was commonly linked to the idea that the anti-Semitic policy had been rejected and resisted by the Italian population. Until the second half of the 1980s – when the general climate changed and a different reading of events gained ground which was finally based on numerous in-depth studies of documents – this concept had been insistently reconfirmed by the vast majority of writers of memoirs and studies of this subject. Let us consider, once again, the words of Eucardio Momigliano, who, for example, does not hesitate to maintain that there was a 'tenacious opposition … of the Italian people towards the application of the racial laws … everything was done without the Italian people believing a single word of what the fascist government tried to make it believe'.[21] Furthermore, he particularly praises and thanks the Church and Catholics; he highlights the help received from many members of the ecclesiastical hierarchy while he does not refer at all to the 'silence' of Pius XII.[22]

There was enormous faith in the goodness of the Italian people and a broad consensus regarding the fact that fascist propaganda could not have significantly influenced the population. Emblematic, in this regard, are the statements of Guido Bedarida – Jewish intellectual from Livorno – in introducing a book which, in supporting the right of the persecuted to a prompt re-integration, put forward a list of Jewish notables – scientists, politicians, jurists, entrepreneurs, etc. – whose contributions to the glory of the country he extolled; in evaluating the outcome of the anti-Jewish campaign Bedarida noted that 'racism had little following', or that 'the masses were indifferent; the Italian people did not understand or did not want to understand the reason for this sudden anti-Judaism'.[23]

The evidence was denied because it was terrible and distressing to think that one's own neighbours, friends, colleagues could have been ready to persecute others. This attitude stands out clearly in the pages of the diary of the Jewish publisher Luciano Morpurgo. The author describes various meetings and conversations with various people, some sincerely anti-Semitic, others indifferent, yet others pro-Semitic or to a certain extent sympathetic towards the sufferings of the Italian Jews: but it is only the latter who, even if representing a minority of the author's interlocutors, is considered truly representative of the feelings of the Italians. Thus, after having reconstructed the discussion he had had with a stranger who had shown his disapproval of the anti-Jewish campaign, Morpurgo writes:

> He did not know how much good he had done me, he did not know that he had given me a great satisfaction, a great joy, and all the more appreciated as it was unexpected. He did not need to convince me, certainly not; because I was certain, very certain, that the bad seed of anti-Semitism, only the result of propaganda and of the friendly Germanic arrogance, is not to be found in Italy.[24]

In Jewish memoirs, understandably, more pages dealt with the help received, the meetings with people prepared to collaborate and offer their understanding, than the pages concerned with those who, instead, displayed a certain anti-Jewish feeling. Almost always, as did Morpurgo, it was those who had shown friendship and had helped that the persecuted saw as truly representing the Italian national character.[25] And one should not forget that those who survived the long months of the German occupation were able to save their lives thanks to the help and support offered by so many Italians, and inevitably in the post-war period that assistance was remembered with gratitude. On the other hand, those who were less fortunate, who did not encounter friendship or charity, or who were even denounced by rapacious acquaintances, found it difficult to survive and make their voices heard.

It is also in relation to this overall picture that it is possible to begin to understand why, in Jewish memoirs, the memory of the help received after 8 September 1943 – when German occupation of Italy began and with it a new bloody phase in anti-Semitic persecution involving massacres, roundups and deportations – tended to prevail over the recollection of the injustices suffered earlier, from 1938 to 1943, amidst the silence and indifference of the majority: the perception of the dictatorship, filtered through the memory of the most recent experiences of civil war and Liberation, thus underwent serious distortions. Obviously, this did not only concern the Jewish minority. The events of 1943–45, and their subsequent commemorations, clouded the perception of the preceding twenty years, leading to the denial of citizenship to fascism and to exalting the Resistance as the authentic embodiment of the collective Italian consciousness. Jewish memory certainly could not be immune to the influences which affected so much of the country's society and culture: the victims of political persecution also found reassurance in the myth of the Resistance which obscured a more inconvenient and disquieting past. The virtuous behaviour of many Italians after 8 September could therefore be taken as incontrovertible evidence of the rejection encountered by racism and anti-Semitism in Italy, 'the most beautiful anti-fascist and anti-racist plebiscite ever seen', in the words of Guido Bedarida.[26] A certainly too emphatic evaluation; the rescues undertaken when Germans where occupying the country perhaps expressed the increasing disaffection of the Italians towards fascism, perhaps the resentment felt towards the foreign oppressors, and certainly also some form of solidarity towards the innocent victims. All this has, however, been seen and interpreted in a distorted manner: both the grateful victims and the self-satisfied anti-fascist circles wanted to interpret it as bearing witness to Italian virtues.[27]

The attitude of those Jews who, in the immediate post-war period, published studies or eye-witness accounts dealing with the period of the persecution was certainly not the most suitable for reconstructing the context in its complexity. There was the tendency to highlight the absurd, senseless and grotesque nature of the persecution rather than reflecting calmly on the origins and consequences of that policy, presented as a parenthesis, tragic as it was unexpected. An appropriate expression of this perception of events is the recurring image of the persecution as a 'storm': a storm is a traumatic and unforeseeable, but transitory, event; it can momentarily disrupt the landscape, but it cannot transform it radically.

What has been described so far was the prevailing attitude. However, dissonant voices, doubts and fears were not lacking. Reintegration in society was often slow and difficult and those who were ready to come to terms with the recent past and gauge the consequences of the persecution were forced to recognize that it was virtually impossible to return to their lives as they had been before 1938. The unease felt by some in the post-war period emerges, for example, in *Otto ebrei* (Eight Jews) by Giacomo Debenedetti, published in Rome a few weeks after the liberation of the city. Taking his cue from a declaration made in the course of the trial of the former Chief of Police of Rome, Pietro Caruso,[28] the author dwells on the difficulties encountered in attempting a complete reintegration in society. He does not confine himself to questioning the value of a mere abrogation of the anti-Jewish law, not supported by a sincere collective reconsideration or by a complete 're-education' of a population which had lived through seven years in a racist State, but also points out that the prejudice had not been overcome or erased, but only transformed, easily adapted to the new situation. The Jew had been an ideological reference point during the fascist era and continued to be so also after the Liberation:

> What were the finger prints of fascism? For heaven's sake, the persecution of the Jews. What, consequently, was the most incontrovertible feature of anti-fascism? The protection of the Jews … What was black yesterday has become white today, and vice versa … Let's show ourselves as having been pietists, of having had this courage and we will undoubtedly be enrolled, officially enrolled, indisputably, in the ranks of anti-fascism.[29]

This situation leads him to state that 'the racial campaign is not over. The persecution goes on';[30] he claims the right to equality and a prompt readmission to the heart of society. He therefore asks that once again people should be judged in accordance with their individual merits or demerits and that the sufferings of the Jews should be contextualized in the more general tragedy provoked by the war:

> And what the Jews, who are already free, have suffered, and what the persecuted are still suffering, is what they wish should be poured, put in common, mixed with the long, collective, unanimous tribute of tears and sufferings, which men worthy of this name have offered, and continue to offer, to ensure the longest series of civilized centuries for the world. If the Jews have a demand to make, it is only this: that their dead, from violence and hunger … should be lined up with all the other dead with all the other victims of this war.[31]

A similar attitude also emerges from the diary of Silvia Lombroso. The author, who had been active in Jewish self-help organizations such as DELASEM,[32] asks herself how to give meaning to her own personal sufferings, and even more so to the murder of millions: 'will it do any good, will it serve a common cause?' She also expresses a yearning for a renewed patriotic communion: 'may our suffering be united with that of everyone, disappear and be assumed in that of the country';[33] on the other hand, she realizes that in order to achieve a real return to the conditions at the outset it would be necessary to re-educate the Italian people: 'In Italy, where there has been a persecution, people would like to see the abolition – not only on paper, but in people's brains – of the premises which permitted the persecution itself, I would not say to be approved, but tolerated, without there having been, on the part of many, a real, deep, moral revolt.'[34]

From these words, one can see both the mistrust caused by years of ostracism, and the inability to accept that part of the population had in effect approved of the racial policy. The author's feelings appear torn between her faith in Italy and the anguish which had developed during seven years of persecution.

Some wrote, like Debenedetti and Lombroso, to give vent to their own anxieties, others, like Eucardio Momigliano – to a certain extent, also Bedarida and Morpurgo – in order to stifle them in the most rigorous and cogent analysis possible. But it was not easy to translate one's own disorientation and anguish into a coherent vision, which would also be, at the same time, fully reassuring in relation to the persecution. In the case of both categories of writers, one can find contradictions and inconsistencies which reveal the difficulties encountered in coming to terms with the recent past. For example, Luciano Morpurgo first emphatically states that the Italians could never have approved of anti-Semitism, then he is forced to recognize the contrary: 'the Italians with whom, a long time ago, I had shared joy and suffering shunned me: the word which had come from Rome had had its effect!'[35] He does not seem, however, to able to bear the weight of this statement and its implications, his rationality is overcome by deep drives and so he nonchalantly returns to praising the virtuous character of the Italians.

More often than not the contradictions could not be resolved: at the heart of the memories, both individual and collective, of the Italian-Jewish world there were disquieting antinomies. In the post-war period, the Jews who, in the various countries of the West, faced the challenge of reintegration, were torn between 'memory and hope',[36] between the opposing forces of the recollection of the injustices borne and of the desire to resume the path of reintegration which had been brusquely interrupted by the racist oppression. For the majority of those who struggled to reintegrate themselves in Western societies hope prevailed; perhaps this explains why many writers of memoirs ended up extolling the virtues of the Italians even if, on a daily basis, they were forced to come to terms with the consequences of the persecution, with the burden of hatred and indifference. The post-war situation was certainly not favourable for the emergence of a richer and more detailed vision of the shared past because of the inconsistencies between reality as it had been experienced and as it had been narrated. Until thirty years ago, the need for tranquillity and peace had prevailed: the most reassuring narrations have prevailed over the more critical ones. After all, the absolving and minimizing interpretations met with the approval and consent of so many politicians and intellectuals of the 'new' Italy who looked with hope at the prospect of freedom.

NOTES

1. M. Bloch, *The Historian's Craft* (Manchester: Manchester University Press, 1992), p.78.
2. C. Pavone, *Una guerra civile. Saggio storico sulla moralità nella Resistenza* (Turin: Bollati Boringhieri, 1994 [1991]), p.560.
3. R. Romeo, 'Nazione', in *Enciclopedia del Novecento*, vol. IV (Rome: Istituto dell'Enciclopedia Italiana, 1979), p.632.
4. In this regard, see E. Gentile, *La Grande Italia: The Myth of the Nation in the 20th Century* (Madison, WI: University of Wisconsin Press, 2009) in particular Parts 4 and 5.
5. G. Bassani, *Una lapide in via Mazzini*, in *Opere*, edited by R. Cotroneo (Milan: Mondadori, 2001), pp.84–5. I am quoting from the revised 1980 edition of *Romanzo di Ferrara.*
6. Ibid., p.89.
7. Ibid., pp.99–100.
8. Ibid., p.100.
9. Ibid., pp.117–18.
10. Giorgio Bassani declared explicitly that the novel dedicated to Geo Josz was based on the life story of his cousin Eugenio Ravenna (see G. Bassani, *Di là dal cuore* [1984], now in *Opere*, p.1323). He was arrested on 8 October 1943 and then led to the Fossoli internment camp. From there, on 22 February, he was deported to Auschwitz with his family. He was the only one to survive and returned to Ferrara on 15 September 1945. Unlike the protagonist of Bassani's novel he remained in his home town, married in 1950 and had three children. He died on 18 February 1977. I wish to thank his daughter, Marcella Ravenna, for this information.
11. Regarding Einaudi's publishing policy and the contrasting inclinations of Cesare Pavese and Elio Vittorini, see L. Mangoni, *Pensare i libri. La casa editrice Einaudi dagli anni Trenta agli anni Sessanta* (Turin: Bollati Boringhieri, 1999), pp.413ff; see p.414 in particular for the quotation.
12. See A. Rossi-Doria, *Memoria e storia. Il caso della deportazione*, preface by P. Jedlowski (Catanzaro: Rubettino, 1998), see pp.41–4 in particular regarding the recollection of the racial deportations. For a stimulating reflection on the conflicting memories of war and deportation, see P. Bertilotti, 'La notion de déporté en Italie, de 1945 à nos jours. Droit, politiques de la mémoire et mémoires concurrentes', in T. Bruttmann, L. Joly and A. Wieviorka (eds), *Qu'est-ce qu'un déporté ? Histoire et mémoires des déportations de la Seconde Guerre mondiale* (Paris: CNRS, 2009), pp.377–402.
13. I. Calvino, 'Preface', *The Paths to the Nest of Spiders* (New York: Ecco Press, 1976), p.vi.
14. C. Paladini, 'A colloquio con Primo Levi', in P. Sorcinelli (ed.), *Lavoro, criminalità e alienazione mentale* (Ancona: Il Lavoro Editoriale, 1987), pp.148–9. On the editorial history of Primo Levi's masterpiece – *Se questo è un uomo* (Turin: Einaudi, 1958) – see: C. Angier, *The Double Bond. Primo Levi: A Biography* (New York: Farrar, Straus and Giroux, 2002), pp.441–53, 503–13.
15. The invaluable contribution of various types of associations in helping the population, upset by the war, to find reassurance and comfort is a theme dealt with by Pieter Lagrou in a brilliant comparative study which investigates the French, Dutch and Belgian situations and the difficult integration of the experiences of the Second World War in the system of symbols and rhetoric of traditional patriotism. See P. Lagrou, *The Legacy of Nazi Occupation: Patriotic Memory and National Recovery in Western Europe 1945–1965* (Cambridge: Cambridge University Press, 2000).
16. E. Momigliano, *Storia tragica e grottesca del razzismo fascista* (Milan: Mondadori, 1946). A virtually identical version of this study had already been published in 1945, *40.000 fuori legge* (Rome: Carboni, 1945).
17. E. Momigliano, *Storia tragica e grottesca del razzismo fascista*, p.29.
18. Ibid., pp.56–7. In effect, as recent studies have suggested, the 'Manifesto degli scienziati razzisti' was at variance with the dominant theses on eugenics and 'racial cleansing' of the preceding decades. There is nothing, however, to suggest that this change was, as Momigliano instead leads one

to understand, due to – direct or indirect – German influences. For a reflection on fascist anti-Semitism in connection to the evolution of Italian–German relations, see A. D'Onofrio, 'I rapporti tra Italia e Germania e il razzismo fascista', in M. Flores, S. Levis Sullam, M.-A. Matard-Bonucci and E. Traverso (eds), *Storia della Shoah in Italia. Vicende, memorie, rappresentazioni*, vol. I (Turin: UTET, 2010), pp.221–55. On the genesis of the 'Manifesto', see M. Sarfatti, 'La preparazione delle leggi antiebraiche del 1938. Aggiornamento critico e documentario', in I. Pavan and G. Schwarz (eds), *Gli ebrei in Italia tra persecuzione fascista e reintegrazione postbellica* (Florence: La Giuntina, 2001), pp.25–54. Many important studies have been dedicated to the reconstruction of the cultural background in which Italian racism could develop: see R. Maiocchi, *Scienza italiana e razzismo fascista* (Florence: La Nuova Italia, 1999). R. Maiocchi, *Scienza e fascismo* (Rome: Carocci, 2004); A. Gillette, *Racial Theories in Fascist Italy* (London and New York: Routledge, 2002); Giorgio Israel and Pietro Nastasi, *Scienza e razza nell'Italia fascista* (Bologna: Il Mulino, 1998); Anna Treves, *Le nascite e la politica nell'Italia del Novecento* (Milan: LED, 2001); F. Cassata, *Molti sani e forti. L'eugentica in Italia* (Turin: Bollati Boringhieri, 2006); C. Mantovani, *Rigenerare la società. L'eugenetica in Italia dalle origini ottocentesche agli anni Trenta* (Catanzaro: Rubettino, 2004); G. Israel, *Il fascismo e la razza. La scienza italiana e le politiche razziali del regime* (Bologna: Il Mulino, 2010).

19. E. Momigliano, *Storia tragica e grottesca del razzismo fascista*, p.49, more generally see pp.45–59.
20. See, for example, L. Morpurgo, *Caccia all'uomo! Vita sofferenze e beffe. Pagine di diario 1938–1944* (Rome: Dalmatia, 1946), pp.33, 61; G. Bedarida, *Ebrei d'Italia* (Livorno: Tirrenia, 1950), pp.12ff.; G. Debenedetti, *Otto ebrei*, preface by C. Sforza (Rome: Atlantica, 1944), p.20; R. Debenedetti, 'La tragedia degli ebrei d'Europa', in the appendix of A. Errera, *Vita del popolo ebraico* (Milan: Garzanti, 1947), pp.316ff. See also the accounts in the book edited by G. Ottani, *Un popolo piange. La tragedia degli ebrei italiani* (Milan: Spartaco Giovene Editore, 1945), p.12.
21. E. Momigliano, *Storia tragica e grottesca del razzismo fascista*, pp.129 and 130.
22. Ibid., p.132. As regards the delicate, but very important, link between traditional Catholic anti-Judaism and anti-Semitism, see G. Miccoli, *Santa Sede, questione ebraica e antisemitismo fra Otto e Novecento*, in C. Vivanti (ed.), *Gli ebrei in Italia. Storia d'Italia. Annali*, vol. XI/2 (Turin: Einaudi, 1997), pp.1380–574.
23. G. Bedarida, *Ebrei d'Italia*, pp.33 and 18. Also on the same wavelength R. Debenedetti, *La tragedia*, pp.316–17, and G. Ottani, *Un popolo piange*, pp.104–5.
24. L. Morpurgo, *Caccia all'uomo*, p.45.
25. In this regard, see the observations of R. Finzi, *L'università italiana e le leggi antiebraiche* (Rome: Editori Riuniti, 2003), pp.49ff.
26. G. Bedarida, *Ebrei d'Italia*, p.35. Regarding the anti-Jewish policy of the RSI and the Italians' responsibility in the deportations, see M. Sarfatti, *Gli ebrei nell'Italia fascista. Vicende, Identità, Persecuzione* (Turin: Einaudi, 2000), pp.271ff. See also G. Mayda, *Ebrei sotto Salò. La persecuzione antisemita 1943–1945* (Milan: Feltrinelli, 1978).
27. See E. Collotti, 'Il razzismo negato', in E. Collotti (ed.), *Fascismo e antifascismo. Rimozioni, revisioni, negazioni* (Bari: Laterza, 2000), pp.359–60, for a justified insistence on this point.
28. Regarding the Caruso trial and the very tense climate in which it developed, see G. Ranzato, *Il linciaggio di Carretta. Violenza politica e ordinaria violenza* (Milan: Il Saggiatore, 1997).
29. G. Debenedetti, *Otto ebrei*, p.8, but see also pp.18–19 and 29–33. Mention should also be made of the classic work by the same author, *16 ottobre 1943*, first published in *Mercurio*, 1 (December 1944), pp.75–97, then in a book by OET (Rome, 1945). In this study, Debenedetti recalled the deportation of the Roman Jews, he did not make particular observations about the events prior to the Armistice and he did not fail to pronounce the usual words of gratitude towards the Italians. Nevertheless the author raised the problem of the collaboration, with the Germans, on the part of the Italian police in collecting and promptly passing on lists of names useful in identifying the Roman Jews.
30. G. Debenedetti, *Otto ebrei*, p.12.
31. Ibid., pp.33–4.
32. See S. Lombroso, *Diario di una madre (si può stampare). Pagine vissute* (Rome: Dalmatia 1945), Part 1, Chapter 1, note 59.
33. Ibid., pp.192 and 198.
34. Ibid., p.199.
35. L. Morpurgo, *Caccia all'uomo*, p.40.
36. I take up the formula from Z.W. Mankowitz, *Life between Memory and Hope: The Survivors of the Holocaust in Occupied Germany* (Cambridge: Cambridge University Press, 2003).

7

Public Uses of the Recent Past

BETWEEN CONDEMNATION AND ABSOLUTION

In the first decade of the post-war period, Italian culture paid very little attention to analysing the fascist anti-Jewish campaign. This was considered the result of the evolution of the regime's foreign policy, or even a product of arrogant German pressure. In the most detailed studies, it was seen in relation to the evolution of fascist ideology in the 1930s (the demographic campaign, the anti-bourgeois drive, the creation of the fascist 'new man') and the efforts to build a totalitarian State; in any case, anti-Semitism was always presented as a phenomenon which was absolutely foreign to the culture, history and character of the Italians.[1]

Carlo Sforza's reflections in 1944 – an important political figure in anti-fascist Italy – are emblematic of the attitude of Italian culture and politics towards the anti-Jewish campaign. In the preface to *Otto ebrei* by Giacomo Debenedetti, he not only did not consider the criticisms raised by the author, but even went so far as to define anti-Semitism 'anti-Italian', noting that

> in every period of national depression – and fascism was one of them – we suffered from pompous fevers based on papier-mâché Roman Emperors; but, at least, our universalism had always made us reject an anti-Semitism which we had even refused to understand…
>
> Were the Germans able to believe seriously in anti-Semitism only because they were converted ten centuries after us?[2]

According to him and many others, the Italians were culturally, and sometimes anthropologically, incapable of feeling hatred towards, or harbouring prejudices against, the Jews. The question, posed in this way, became a problem of civilization and the Catholicism of the Italian people could be seen, paradoxically, as an immunizing agent against the germs of anti-Semitism. The recourse to these arguments is rather interesting as it reveals aspects of national self-representation in the post-war period. We will return to this later, it is sufficient for now to note how in this way every responsibility was attributed to the Nazis, or, in more general terms, to the Germans and Mussolini's regime, their accomplice.[3] The clear and firm denial of any Italian responsibility as regards anti-Semitism is consecrated, in the immediate post-war period, also in the pages of the main encyclopaedias: *L'Enciclopedia Cattolica* (*The Catholic Encyclopaedia*), published in 1948, goes so far as to state that 'anti-Semitism has never existed in modern Italy'. Consequently, it defines the racist Italian law of 1938 as an 'imitation' of National Socialist ideology and, finally, maintains that the regime's propaganda had not been able to change the people's feelings: 'The periodicals *La Difesa della razza* and *La Vita italiana*, the dailies *Regime fascista* and *Tevere*, repeated *ad infinitum* anti-Jewish commonplaces, but they did not influence the Italian mentality, generally well balanced.'[4]

The position adopted, in its tone and content, by the *Enciclopedia Italiana* (*The Italian Encyclopaedia*) was similar. In its updating of 1949, it gives, on the whole, little space to the fascist racial policy, concentrating mainly, instead, on German events. The entries 'Razzismo' (Racism) and 'Ebrei' (The Jews) stress the imitative nature, therefore not autochthonous, of the anti-Jewish policy and concentrate on the help and protection offered 'by the people and the Church'. Any specific Italian responsibility was thus adroitly repressed.[5]

Such stereotypes were fully accepted by all the political and cultural strands of anti-fascism, which, despite being reluctant to intervene in this awkward subject, formulated an unequivocal interpretation of the anti-Jewish policy of Mussolini's regime. Examples of this approach include, with few fine distinctions, politicians and intellectuals like Francesco Saverio Nitti, Carlo Sforza, Benedetto Croce, Luigi Sturzo, Stefano Jacini, Piero Malvestiti, but also very serious scholars like Corrado Barbagallo and Giacomo Perticone, as well as various organs of the press, including those of the Vatican.[6]

In order to understand the dynamics which led to the establishment of such an interpretation, simplistic and broadly self-absolving, and above all its crucial political function, it is worth remembering that the need to reinvent myths and national traditions was particularly strong after 1945, when the need to pay particular attention to the image of the national community became more marked and pressing because of the nature of the last world war. The tragedies which took place during that war raised disquieting ghosts and terrible anguish: what was at issue was not only the guilt of restricted groups of leaders, but also judgement on entire peoples and cultural systems.[7] Every state of continental Europe was therefore forced to define its own position with regard to the actions of the national fascist movements, not only in strictly juridical or diplomatic terms, but also in moral and cultural ones. The strategies adopted then by the ruling anti-fascist groups in each country to tackle the problem and safeguard legitimate national interests had serious and important repercussions, delineating the identity of the respective communities and consequently influencing culture and mentality, as well as contributing to leaving a deep and lasting mark on the set-up of each political system.[8]

At the foundations of the Italian Republic lay, therefore, no less than the constitutional pact, the representations of the past, the idea of Italy and of the Italians, forged – more or less knowingly – by the anti-fascist ruling class in the delicate period going from the fall of the dictator to the signing of the peace treaty (1943–47). At issue was not only an unsteady national tradition offended by the regime. At stake was also the country's place in the scenario the Allies were getting ready to design: were the responsibilities and guilt of fascism – and of Italy – equal to those of Germany? Would defeated Italy be punished and humiliated, or would it succeed in saving face, transforming a military defeat into an at least partial political victory? These were the problems already on the agenda for the government, the parties and more generally the world of information and culture following the Armistice signed with the Allies on 8 September 1943. The fundamental question was whether Italy's fate would be the same as Germany's or better; inevitably, considerations as to the affinity of fascism and Nazism, and the complicity of Mussolini's Italy with the National Socialist crimes carried a lot of weight. While the international community slowly came to know about the terrible horror of the death camps, the role played in that tragedy by the Italian institutions and people acquired a crucial importance, both for the moulding of the nation's collective conscience and for the country's image abroad.

The memory and the interpretation of fascist anti-Semitism were inevitably influenced by the rapid organization of the political-cultural order decided by the Allies with the Nuremberg trials. Those trials constituted a symbolic and political act rather than simply a juridical one, through which there was the representation of 'a purified, but fictitious, image of every European country's conscience and of Europe itself: rather than an act of justice, it turned out to be at the end an integral part of a culture of oblivion instrumental in the construction of a new European identity'.[9] Although Nuremberg condemned the policy of racial extermination adopted by National Socialism, nevertheless – because of a series of juridical and political problems – it could not grasp its historically specific character: the trials emphasized 'the crimes against peace', the responsibility of a restricted group of men in having dragged the world into a terrible war, and so the anti-Semitic policy was interpreted as a secondary variable of the military strategy of aggression of the Hitlerian regime. In those trials, not only was all the emphasis placed on Germany's sole guilt – in fact, on the guilt of a handful of Nazi leaders – obscuring the responsibilities of other regimes and peoples, but there was a distorted perception of the peculiar historical nature of the anti-Semitic policies which developed in Europe well before the beginning of the war.[10] All this, naturally, was to Italy's advantage and felicitously met the psychological needs and the mechanisms of self-representation of a defeated nation, which, nevertheless, vigorously asserted its purity, innocence, and innate anti-fascist vocation.

Also Italy has won the war, loudly proclaimed a famous issue of the magazine *Mercurio*, dedicated to illustrating the activity of the Italian Resistance movement.[11] That issue, together with another number of the magazine, published earlier and dealing with the history of the Resistance in Rome and the South,[12] have been found among the papers of the Secretariat of the Foreign Ministry.[13] This is not surprising, as the officials of the Ministry were actively committed to safeguarding the country's image vis-à-vis the governments and public opinion of the Allies; what stood out among the other activities was the presentation – repeated and documented – of the Italian contribution to the struggle against Germany and therefore the glorification of the Resistance, represented as the embodiment and testimony of the true character of the people, who, it was hoped, would not be punished for the crimes attributed to Mussolini and a restricted circle of his accomplices.[14] In composing their own celebration of anti-fascist and blameless Italy, political leaders and ministry officials did not fail to insist on the presumed Italian non-involvement in racism and the extermination policy, emphasizing the distance and diversity which separated Italy's sins considered venial and the terrible crimes committed, instead, by Germany.

The diplomatic effort and the propaganda campaign, thus orchestrated, did not yield a complete success – by signing the peace treaty, Italy lost all its colonial possessions and suffered considerable territorial amputations (the loss of Istria and the internationalization of Trieste) – but enabled the country to save face and present itself on the post-war scene in conditions which were certainly better than those reserved to its former German ally.[15] The political use of the recent past contributed to legitimizing some interpretations of the fascist experience, constructing a narrative canon and a rhetorical code which, for a long time, marked not only State institutions but, more generally, the nation's collective identity. By avoiding the trials of Italian war criminals,[16] suppressing the horrors of the colonial domination in Africa,[17] and, more generally, cancelling so many of the responsibilities of a nation which had, for a long time, supported the regime's plans, the government and the State apparatus contributed, in the first crucial years of the post-war period, to erecting the pillars upon which rested, for a long time, the conscience of a community which obstinately pursued a convenient oblivion, being happy to look at itself in the distorting mirror of the *myth of the good Italian*.[18]

A 'JEWISH TRUMP CARD' FOR ITALIAN DIPLOMACY

Italian diplomacy made a significant contribution to the creation of that myth; in the following pages, we will illustrate the active role played by the Italian Foreign Ministry and other organs of the State in spreading the image of a country not involved in, and hostile towards, anti-Semitic racism. The attitudes we have seen in Jewish memoirs and the theses which dominated the first historical reconstructions offered useful arguments for Italian diplomacy. While a complicated process of abrogation of the persecutory regulations and the drawing up of appropriate laws for reintegration were starting,[19] the attention of some diligent officials of the Foreign Ministry was captured by the shrill declarations of eternal gratitude to the Italian people, for its support and compassion, which individual Jews and, above all, some Jewish bodies and institutions repeated insistently and with conviction.

From 12–15 January 1945, in the capital, there was the first meeting of the Italian Zionist Groups, which reunited the Italian Zionists present in Rome, as well as the representatives of the Palestinian military units and of the American Joint Distribution Committee and numerous delegates representing foreign Jewish refugees scattered in the South. The first of the unanimously approved motions did not fail to surprise and interest the alert Italian diplomats:

> The Meeting of the Italian Zionists – states the text of the motion – reunited in Rome for the first time since the Liberation: remembers with great gratitude the silent, often heroic, solidarity which so much of the oppressed Italian people – following the lofty humanitarian example of the Catholic Church – offered to the persecuted victims of Italy and to the refugees from other parts of Europe, who, in this way, were able to find refuge here despite the barbaric Nazi laws.[20]

Those words circulated both in the country[21] and abroad: the Secretariat of the Foreign Ministry forwarded copies of the order of the day voted by the Italian Zionists to various embassies and legations abroad, inviting diplomatic representatives to spread the above-quoted declaration in the relevant countries, giving it prominence in the press, as well as among Jewish and Zionist circles.[22] That was only one of the analogous initiatives in which Italian government offices were involved in during the first years of the post-war period.

Every resource which could be useful to safeguard the nation's image was to be exploited fully, furthermore, in the Foreign Ministry, there had developed, over a long time, an awareness that there was a 'Jewish card' to be played on the international scene. In a note dated 24 October 1944 and entitled 'Taluni aspetti internazionali della questione ebraica' ('Some international aspects of the Jewish question'), there was particular emphasis on the Zionist question, which it was thought, rightly, had a certain weight in modifying the balance of the international situation in the following years. In that document it was noted that the issue did not only affect the evolution of the balance in the Middle East and the Mediterranean; there were other aspects considered important and in particular the weight of the Jewish groups of the Diaspora and their (presumed) influence on governments and public opinion:

> This second aspect of the question perhaps has, in certain moments, an international importance even greater than the first even if less obvious; not only because such a question presents itself in varying degrees in almost

> every country, therefore inevitably influencing its foreign policy, but also because it is easy for solid ties of interest and friendship between various Jewish groups to develop both because of the pre-eminence sometimes acquired by individuals of Israeli extraction in the realms of culture, finance and industry in the respective Nations, and because of the persecutions themselves.
>
> This second aspect of the question has acquired a particular importance in recent times precisely in relation to the different and marked attitudes of the internal politics of the most important countries of the world with respect to the Jewish community. To explain the apparently contradictory attitude of such communities with regard to the official politics of their governments, on account of which in some countries the Jews support the established order and in others, instead, they act as revolutionary elements, it is necessary to note that the Jews constitute a factor of political stability only in those countries whose regime is based on broad concepts of freedom and gives guarantees safeguarding the rights and interests of every type of minority.[23]

The memo quoted above appears confused and the analytical categories utilized are rather imprecise. The tendency to consider the very different Jewish groups living in distant countries as a single community which acts consistently pursuing its own objectives, presents traces of a distorted and aberrant perception of Judaism, the result of ancient prejudices and more recent ravings fuelled by fascist propaganda. In any case, what should be stressed here is that the myth of the 'Jewish conspiracy' or, in simpler terms, the overestimation of the political influence exercised by associations representing limited sectors of the Jewish world would, in effect, have conditioned, to a certain extent, the actions of Italian diplomacy. Especially in the very first years of the post-war period, the Foreign Ministry did not fail to try and ingratiate itself with American and British-Jewish circles.

But let us return to the note: the author went on, at length, about the history of Zionism and its many repercussions. Regarding Italy's specific interests, he proposed some considerations which are of a certain interest. Firstly, he noted that the anti-Jewish policy had damaged Italy, compromising the country's image and, in particular, its influence in the Mediterranean area, as the profitable links, established in time, with Jewish groups – in Salonika, Cairo, Alexandria and the Greek islands, communities which had ancient ties of kinship with elements of Italian Judaism and had shown, on several occasions, a pro-Italian attitude – had been severed. Until the start of the anti-Jewish campaign, Italy had been able to profit from the excellent integration of the Jews in the social fabric of the country, thus obtaining some 'not merely moral' advantages in the Mediterranean area.[24]

Among the officials of the Foreign Ministry, the problem of the negative impact of the anti-Semitic turning point had already been considered as early as August 1940 – with the racial campaign in full swing – when, in drawing up an important policy document, some Italian diplomats had tried to hypothesize measures to mitigate the racist policy, with the aim of safeguarding the profitable relations, which had been cultivated for a long time, with the Jewish communities scattered throughout the Mediterranean.[25] The attempts made, in 1940, by the Italian diplomats to find a balance between the racial doctrine and the need to preserve useful relations with the Jewish groups of the region had not produced significant results, nevertheless it is interesting to note that the gist of that reflection was taken up again by the above-mentioned note of October 1944. In fact, in the latter, it was stressed that regaining the lost friendships and restoring the nation's public image was difficult, but necessary: 'Although in Italy the anti-Semitic regulations were generally mild and not openly shared by the majority of the people, it is not an easy enterprise to reconquer completely this trust [of the Jews]; nevertheless, it is undoubtedly convenient to aim in this direction.'[26]

And pursued it was. Hence it comes as no surprise to find that the aforementioned solemn declaration made by the Italian Zionists gathered in Rome was received with great interest. Being able to draw a sharp distinction between Italy and the crimes of Nazism and Germany, being able to claim to be 'saviours of the Jews', would certainly have put Italy in a positive light, favouring the restoration of the friendships lost in the Mediterranean area, but also improving relations with Jewish circles which, it was thought, could influence the decisions of the Allies. Having taken note of the fact that they could have counted on the support of the persecuted themselves, various Italian government offices were very active in fuelling a propaganda campaign to safeguard the country's international image. Thus, for example, in September 1945, the Ministry of the Interior asked all the prefects to send reports on the application of the racial laws in their provinces. The initiative had started from the request of a Belgian journalist, who had asked the Italian Embassy in Bruxelles for information about the fate of the Jewish groups in the peninsula; the ambassador forwarded, to the government, the questionnaire presented to him and – confident, perhaps, because of the declarations of the Italian Zionists in May – he emphasized that it had been his concern to 'highlight the fact that our law on race had not only found a scarce application in single concrete cases, but the whole population and almost all the administrative organs which should have applied it, had instead competed in order to sabotage it completely or, at least, to mitigate its effects as much as possible'. In short, far from being a totalitarian State, the regime was marked – according to this interpretation – by a creeping rebellion, its orders were not followed, its laws remained a dead letter, because the Italian people could never have betrayed their own consciences. These farcical representations were deliberately put together by the State apparatuses. In fact, in asking for more details from the government, the Italian diplomatic representative bore witness to the fact that he did not want a real fact-finding investigation, but rather he wanted to receive reports to support his narration; his letter concludes as follows: 'In providing me with the necessary documentation I would be grateful to this Ministry to stress clearly that the Italian initiatives, as regards race, not only were not spontaneous, but that their formal nature only ceased when the German invaders directly extended their control over the application of the anti-Semitic measures'. The Ministry of the Interior arranged for the forwarding of the request to the prefectures, which, in turn, provided 'adequate' accounts.[27]

That was not the first idea of its kind: other analogous initiatives had already been put into effect by the Roman offices of the Foreign Ministry. Among the protagonists of those activities there stands out the official Roberto Ducci: in the early 1940s he had closely monitored the problem of the Jews in the Italian-occupied zones of Yugoslavia – including the discussion concerning the possibility of handing them over to the German authorities who would certainly have killed them – and had subsequently removed and concealed the relevant dossiers once the German occupation began.[28] After the liberation of the capital, such documents could, however, have been useful to Italian diplomacy, and on 1 September 1944 it was Ducci himself who suggested that they should receive the due publicity. He wrote to Luigi Vidau, the former director of the Confidential Matters section during the regime and destined to continue his career brilliantly in the post-war period:

> I have the honour of returning herewith the paperwork 'The Jews in Croatia 1942–43', put in safekeeping by me on 10 September 1943 and since then kept in my Family's flat.
>
> The paperwork is known to Your Lordship in general terms, since You knew of it when You were Director General of Political Affairs. I do not, therefore, need to point out the interest which the documents contained in it present, with the aim of bearing witness to the attitude of humanity always maintained by the Foreign Ministry, even during the fascist regime and the alliance with Germany, and to its successful efforts to save from certain destruction 3,000 individuals who had placed their trust in Italy's protection.
>
> I permit myself, secondarily, to pray Your Lordship to consider, in agreement with the other higher Authorities of the Royal Ministry, the appropriateness of making known the action undertaken in that period to the Italian (and consequently international) public, through the publication of an article in the periodical 'Politica Estera'.
>
> If the Ministry were to agree, I could begin drawing up the said article, to be submitted, prior to publication, to superior approval.[29]

It was not long before an article did appear in the periodical *Politica Estera*, signed *Verax* but actually written by Ducci himself, entitled 'Italiani ed ebrei in Jugoslavia' ('Italians and Jews in Yugoslavia'), which proposed an account of the policy towards the Jews in the Yougoslav territories occupied by the Italians.[30] It is clear that such a publication was produced to safeguard legitimate national interests in view of the forthcoming peace treaty. The final aim is clear, nevertheless it is worth noting the cultural norms used by the author to absolve Italy of blame: Ducci-*Verax* referred to specific facts in order to reveal 'the irreconcilable difference between the Italian way of life and that imposed on the Germans by the Nazi system', constrasting 'a people who had remained, despite everything, civilized with another people rendered barbarous by a political philosophy which threw it back towards the forests from which it had emerged in the Christian era'.[31] The interpretative key is, therefore, that of the contrast between the barbarity of the Nazis and the superior civilization of Catholic Italy; a theme characteristic of the nation's self-representation already in use during the war, when Italian diplomats and soldiers proudly claimed their moral superiority over the Germans. A superiority which, it was maintained, prevented the Italians from being accomplices of the unspeakable German atrocities: 'the instinct, on account of which our soldiers are revolted by atrocities, comes from Christianity', Luca Pietromarchi – one of the coordinators of Italian diplomacy between the war and the post-war period – stated decisively during a meeting with the Pope on 1 January 1943. Pietromarchi maintained that 'the humanitarian spirit of our people must one day perforce be taken into account';[32] in fact, with a watchful eye on the immediate future, as early as 1 March 1943, he did not fail to take measures so that the documents testifying to the different choices made by the Nazis and the fascists regarding the 'Jewish question' should be 'jealously' preserved.[33]

We can notice here a very intricate web of truth and lies, in which instinctive mechanisms of collective self-representation link up with well thought-out political choices. The country had to use every available resource to avoid a punitive peace, on the other hand, very many people genuinely maintained that the Allies should take into account, among other things, the notable differences between the German anti-Jewish policy and the Italian one. In March 1945, this would be explicitly claimed by a very prominent person such as Benedetto Croce, remembering that aspect together with others in claiming Italy's right to participate in the San Francisco Conference, where on 26 June 1945 the fifty nations who had won the war gathered to approve the UN charter. While the Germans had submitted to the inhuman decisions of their government – argued Croce – 'the Italians, even under fascism, did not become machines, and showed their humanity, among other things, in their tacit and non-tacit opposition and disobedience, and in protecting the Jews who had been wickedly slandered, reviled and persecuted'.[34] Italian politicians, men of culture and diplomats insisted on this argument for a long time, even after the peace treaty had been signed; the idea of Christian Italy's civilizing mission, which is contrasted with the image of a primitive and ferocious Germany, had a long life, marking the language and the self-representation of the anti-fascist Republic. Even after the signing of the peace treaty, in 1948, in a book published for an important series dealing with anti-fascist martyrs, Roberto Ducci again took up and developed the reflection on the massacres and the terrible violence which had happened during the war, re-proposing what he considered 'the enormous difference, on this point, between the followers of Hitler and those of Mussolini: very few Italians – and it was always a question of sporadic and individual cases, without the State ever thinking of organizing the 'atrocities' – have committed crimes which showed that they had destroyed their souls'.[35]

This contention is simply false. Undoubtedly, the cultural and ideological drives which oriented the actions of the German and Italian authorities were different and – sometimes – divergent, but this does not mean that the Italians were intrinsically 'better'. It is of greater importance for the present discussion to understand how these arguments corresponded *inter alia* to a need as latent as it was strong, cherished by ample sections of the European cultural and political world. These elements, after a terrible and devastating war, were more than ever bent on justifying their belief that the civilization of honour, an ideal that had stood at the basis of the traditional conception of war, had not been irrecoverably swept away between 1939 and 1945.

In effect, Europe had witnessed the intimate coexistence of two opposite concepts of war. One continued to be informed by traditional rhetoric and ideals of Romantic origin, founded on the ideal of a fair and honourable conflict; the other was more cynical and brutal, definitely amoral, and became incarnated in a total war that included war against civilians.[36] In the post-war period, the forms of historical self-representation of the Italians could be felicitously reconciled with the deep desire, cultivated by a large part of the ruling classes of the West, to blame only Germany, or rather only Nazism – pointing an accusing finger at the SS and saving, instead, the Wehrmacht – for the perversion of traditional culture and the betrayal of the civilization of honour.[37]

In this cultural and psychological climate, it is possible to locate and to appreciate the success, both in Italy and elsewhere, of the myth of the 'good Italians'. A myth which was deliberately exploited by the Italian political leadership in the post-war period. With the aim of upholding Italy's public image, Italian officials fed the international press information about the protection offered until the summer of 1943, for a variety of motives, to some thousands of Jews in southern of France, saving them from deportation. At the same time we must remember that they consciously abandoned others to their fate.

In the summer of 1946, the Foreign Ministry informed the Prime Minister's Office about the publication of an important and lengthy article in the *New York*

Times on May 22 with a sensational title: 'Fascist Rescues of Jews Revealed'.[38] With considerable emphasis, the article reported, what emerged from Italian and German documents which Angelo Donati, the organizer in the 1940s of detailed, but unsuccessful, plans to save the Jews in the South of France and who became, after the war, Vice-President of the Italian Red Cross, made available, confidentially, to the Editor of the important daily. From those documents it could be deduced, according to the analysis of the New York newspaper, that 'Mussolini was continually deceived by his subordinates', diplomats and officials were motivated by the insuppressible desire to save as many Jews as possible. Such feelings reflected the character, the nature, typical of the Italian people whom the dictator had tried, unsuccessfully, to pervert: 'There is no doubt that these dossiers reflect the instinctive spirit of tolerance and the kind heartedness of the Italian people, a quality which made them despise the Germans and rebel against the promulgation of laws so contrary to its values'.[39] Such ravings, presented as indisputable truths, leave one speechless; the influence exerted by Italian diplomacy is evident. It wanted to convince the world of Italy's innocence, but also to safeguard itself, making every effort to highlight falsehoods, namely, trying tenaciously to convince public opinion that it had never been totally compromised with the regime.[40] No one wants to deny – in any way – the gratitude which is owed to individuals or institutions for having obstructed the policy of extermination. But what makes the quoted assertions unacceptable are the tone and accents, the superficiality of considerations that overflow with rhetoric in their inability to comprehend the intimate complexity of fascist policies.

An article of such workmanship, which appeared in a very prestigious organ of the American press, was undoubtedly a success for Italy; but a result like that cannot only be explained in terms of the abilities, authoritativeness and contacts available to those who – inside and outside the Foreign Ministry – promoted that type of historical representation. It has to be acknowledged that there had really been cases, even sensational and very remarkable, of help and support for the persecuted, especially in the face of the strength of the Nazi commitment to the total extermination of the Jewish people. The cases in which assistance had been offered could easily be read outside their context, so as to engender a mythological and essentially unreliable representation. There was, it is obvious, a background which was very favourably inclined to accept that message; it was possible to reach positions which were so clearly absolutory, rhetorically bombastic, so firmly held, also because of the essential lack of understanding of the fascist phenomenon as a whole, from which derived, in specific terms, the misunderstanding of the Italian anti-Jewish policy. The lack of the suitable political and cultural conditions meant that there was neither the appropriate contextualization, nor a proper understanding, of the particular choices made by fascist Italy, which, on the one hand, had rejected the Jewish refugees fleeing from the territories controlled by the Germans or the Croats, but, on the other hand, had protected – at least in some cases – the Jewish groups resident in the territories under its own control. These different behaviours aimed at safeguarding concrete and well-defined economic and political interests. They reflected an autonomous and particular anti-Jewish strategy: in recent years all this has been excellently documented and acutely analysed,[41] nevertheless that thorny ensemble of problems and questions has long escaped the understanding of most people and even that of the many serious scholars.

This also holds true for Léon Poliakov who, in October 1946, wrote an important book, published by the Centre de Documentation Juive Contemporaine of Paris, concerned with analysing the attitude of the Italian occupying forces towards the Jews in the South of France. The text is based on the examination of the papers found in the Paris offices of the Gestapo, abandoned by the fleeing Germans. The same documents which, with a great fanfare, had been presented barely five months earlier by the *New York Times*, were, with Poliakov's work, reproduced in their entirety and placed in a much more detailed analytical framework than that of the article in English, but followed a similar interpretative line as regards the overall judgement on fascism and the Italians.[42] In fact, the French scholar referred to the good heartedness of the Italians in order to explain

> the attitude in fact adopted by the Italian authorities. It appears obvious that the poison of racial propaganda has only totally infected the most barbaric populations, and that it spreads easily only in the midst of the Northern fog. With their Mediterranean lucidity, the Italian people have been, in the vast majority of cases, totally refractory to these influences. They have reacted with irony or indignation to the propaganda of *Tevere* and *Difesa della Razza*. And it was this spirit which influenced the attitude of the military and civilian authorities and the behaviour of the officials at all levels of the bureaucratic hierarchy.[43]

That first work by the young Poliakov fitted into the context of the research and study plan of the Centre de Documentation Juive Contemporaine,[44] but it also had an internal political significance: by emphasizing the merits and virtues of the Italians it was possible to point an accusing finger at French collaborationism.[45] The publication of the article in the *New York Times* can, instead, be more easily traced back to the Italian political strategy of spreading, in Allied public opinion, the image of an upright and honest Italy, subjected against its will to a policy which was alien to its nature. In any case, both the texts well reflect the climate of the age and the easy and rapid spread of cultural stereotypes which, by extolling Italian non-collaboration in the deportation of foreign Jews until September 1943, ended up by casting a falsifying veil over the reactions of the Italians to the fascist regime's anti-Semitic policy: the protection offered from 1941 to 1943 by the Italian administration to the Jews in the Balkans, France and

Greece has greatly complicated an understanding of the anti-Semitic campaign which began in Italy towards the end of the 1930s.

The active practice of historical disinformation to which the Italian Foreign Ministry dedicated itself, between 1945 and 1946, certainly did not favour a correct interpretation of events. The campaign carried forward, on these themes, by Italian diplomacy culminated in the publication of a book entitled: *Relazione sull'opera svolta dal Ministero degli Affari Esteri per la tutela delle comunità ebraiche (1938–1943)* (*Report on the Work Carried Out by the Foreign Ministry to Safeguard Jewish Communities, 1938–1943*). It was published by the Ministry itself between the spring and autumn of 1946, and was part of the documentation presented by the Italian government to the Allies in view of the drawing up of the peace treaty.[46] The cited documents of the Paris Gestapo, mentioned by the American article and reproduced in the French book, were re-published – with slight differences in relation to Poliakov's book – as an appendix to the book published by the Foreign Ministry, but it also contains a more voluminous and original documentation, preserved by the records office of the Foreign Ministry and suitable for demonstrating, with a wealth of details, the real contribution made by the Italian authorities to save the Jews of the Balkans and the South of France from their fate of deportation and death. The text presents an abundant collection of documents, which nevertheless sometimes appears defective or imprecise, and which in any case is presented in a factious and unreliable way, so far as to theorize explicitly a deliberate boycotting of Mussolini's persecutory choices by those responsible for Italy's foreign policy.[47]

It is beyond the scope of this book to discuss in detail the limitations and the imperfections of that work. It is, however, worth stressing that fascism's racial policy is presented in static terms, theorizing a persistent opposition to National Socialism's extermination policy which does not correspond with the truth. We should, in fact, remember that, from its inception in 1938, the anti-Jewish policy had been subject to various adjustments. In particular, between the spring and summer of 1943, Mussolini's anti-Jewish policy had become more radical: the internment of all the Italian Jews had been organized – then, in fact, realized by the Repubblica Sociale (Social Republic) – the transfer of foreign Jews had been planned from Ferramonti (Calabria) to Bolzano, perhaps in view of their being handed over to the Germans; the internment of the Jews in Yugoslavia had been prepared, a measure which could be seen as the logical premise for their deportation. Finally, on 15 July an explicit order had been issued for the handing over to the German authorities of the Jews resident in the zones occupied by the Italians in the South of France; an event avoided, even if only temporarily, by the conspiracy of 25 July which brought about the fall of Mussolini.[48]

There is no trace of these developments in the documentation drawn up and distributed by the Italian government, while emphasis is repeatedly placed on the Italians' superior conscience, which made it impossible for them to collaborate in the Nazi regime's plan of a 'final solution of the Jewish Question'. Certainly, it cannot be denied that some Italians, and sometimes apparatuses and institutions such as the diplomatic service and the Armed Forces, saved many lives; but the motives of such acts should be very carefully evaluated, while it should not be forgotten that the non-adherence to Nazism's policy of extermination did not imply *ipso facto* the absence of anti-Semitism, nor even less did it reflect an innate good heartedness,[49] as some commentators have suggested in the immediate post-war period and also in more recent times.[50] The choice of obstructing or not actively collaborating with the Nazi policy of extermination – which can be recognized in some cases – rather suggests how Italy had cultivated its own different, autonomous, persecutory plan, which had been harmonized with the need to safeguard precise national interests also in the management of the territories occupied by its own army.[51]

The propaganda campaign put into effect by the government apparatuses contributed to the consolidation of a distorted and ambiguous interpretation of the Italian occupation policy, which only in very recent times has received an opportune critical revision also following important in-depth studies. Thanks to the general consensus, the virtual absence of criticism or of challenging replies to such attitudes, the myth of the good Italian was widely accepted. The official representatives of Italian Judaism played an important part in corroborating and confirming the totally absolutory reconstructions which were emerging insistently in government pronouncements, journalists' comments, the writings of survivors and scholars.

THE MEMORY POLITICS OF THE JEWISH LEADERSHIP

The interpretative canon which has been outlined is also to be found in the statements of the official representatives of the Jewish community. The Italian-Jewish ruling class did not make a thorough, in-depth investigation of fascist anti-Judaism and the Nazi extermination policies, nevertheless the representatives of Italian Judaism produced a long series of statements which tended to extol a civilized and honest Italy, immune to Mussolini's racist policy. In the immediate post-war period, those who took up the role of guiding the Italian-Jewish community did not hesitate, on several occasions, to express their faith not only in the new ruling class, but also in all Italians.[52] The deep roots in the country's social and cultural fabric as well as the ties, also personal, with the new anti-fascist political class could easily lead to denying that Italy, the 'real' Italy, would bear any guilt. Speaking on the radio on 30 April 1945, Raffaele Cantoni remembered, in fact, the contribution made by many Italian Jews to the Resistance movement, seen as a moment of renewed brotherhood: 'the blood shed together had the value of a symbolic sacrifice which could cancel forever the disgrace which fascism ... heaped upon Italy with the adoption of measures unworthy of its millenary civilization'. Then, after having referred to the many Jews who were still languishing in pitiful conditions in other parts of Europe, he expressed his gratitude towards the Italians: 'the human solidarity manifested by the good part of the Italian people, many times putting their lives in peril, gives a solid certainty that in Italy the evil of the theories imposed upon us by the Nazis will be eradicated. With such hopes, we take up our lives again, certain of finding the traditional affectionate warm-heartedness'. There was also heartfelt gratitude towards the Church which 'in the name of the most sincere brotherhood' helped the persecuted.[53] Almost a year later, Carlo Alberto Viterbo greeted the Republican victory in the referendum of 2 June 1946 noting that in this way 'all the power would have gone to the Italian people whose innate kindness and sense of justice we Jews, in the sad times, have been able to gauge'.[54] These and many other statements, similar in tone, undoubtedly contributed to creating a climate favourable to the rapid suppression of the Italian roots of the racial persecution.

Carlo Alberto Viterbo, like other community leaders, did not fail to join battle so that Mussolini's responsibilities[55] – or those of other prominent figures of Italian racism, such as the scientist Nicola Pende[56] – would not be denied; this however did not make people reflect more critically on the recent past and to question the tendential denial of the culpability of Italian society and culture. The persecutions were rapidly pushed aside as something only linked to Teutonic barbarity, imposed in Italy by a minority of individuals who had betrayed the true spirit of the nation; thus the Jewish statements about the racial laws became part of the chorus of those who, from different sectors of society, denied that fascism could really have represented the Italians. 'Everyone knew that the real Italy was represented by other circles, other ideas, other people', wrote Giacomo Viterbo, a leader of the Zionist youth movement *Hechaluz*, referring to the intensification of the anti-Jewish campaign under Mussolini's Social Republic.[57] Words which well reflect a widespread cultural climate – and, I would say, characteristic of the Italy of those years – in which the Jewish citizens, like everyone else, were immersed.

Another example, which helps us to understand the attitude of prominent figures of the Jewish ruling class, is the speech given on 19 December 1945, the first after his return to Italy from Palestine, by the Chief Rabbi of Rome David Prato. On that solemn occasion, he could not help casting a glance at the very recent past: he referred with contempt to Nazi Germany – 'fanatical hordes led by a man who embodied all that the human mind can imagine as satanic and bestial' – while obviously his judgement was very different concerning 'that good and generous Italian population which astutely and in a contrived manner wanted to seem bad, incapable of conceiving racial hatred, and which at the right moment, following the bright example was set by the highest dignitaries of the Church, knew how to express generosity in saving the persecuted'.[58] The absolution of the Italian people acquires a particularly sensational significance if it is compared to the statements about the responsibilities of the German people. This was written, for example, in the *Bollettino della Comunità Israelitica di Milano* in July 1947: 'now one thing is certain and at this point indisputable: all the German people participated, approved, supported the atrocious extermination; all the German people must, therefore, expiate this guilt'.[59] There is a notable contrast between the collective guilt with which the Germans were marked and the great readiness to absolve the Italians: almost all innocent, except for a few irresponsible fanatics.

Care must be taken when reflecting on the factors which determined such an attitude among Jewish leaders, weighing up carefully a plurality of causes which interacted and influenced consciences. It is probable that the statements made by prominent figures of the Jewish world also reflected diplomatic needs; on the other hand, there is no doubt that the leaders of Italian Judaism shared the ideas and feelings typical of their age.

In the crucial years of the post-war period, in the very first years of the governments of anti-fascist coalitions when the country's future was still in doubt, the Union of Italian Jewish Communities played an important role in acquitting the Italians of the charge of anti-Semitism. In that period, the UCII found itself in an extremely delicate position: it had to struggle to achieve the reintegration of the Italian-Jewish minority. Furthermore – from the Liberation until 1948 – it was committed to encouraging a constant flow of refugees who were crossing Italy, fleeing from death camps and heading for Palestine, playing a crucial role of mediation between various Jewish and Zionist institutions (particularly concerned with the problem of the refugees) and the Italian government, which, as we have seen, was trying to play every card at its disposal, including the one which it considered the 'Jewish card'.

The Italian government found it easy to encourage *aliyà beit* (as the plan of clandestine Jewish immigration to Palestine is defined), which contributed to creating difficulties for the British control of the Mediterranean, thus laying the foundations for the reconstitution of its own political influence in the area.[60] And that policy favourably impressed both the representatives of Italian Judaism and members of foreign Jewish bodies, among which stands out the World Jewish Congress, which tended to develop an interpretation of the recent past which provided Italian diplomacy with the support necessary for the construction and propagation of the so-called myth of the good Italian. It is an event which is sometimes obscure, and it would be foolish to explain it, in trivial terms, as being the result of cold and deliberate calculations. This is a complex issue to unravel: it is difficult to deny absolutely that there could be, on both sides, hidden agendas which contributed to determining certain choices. What can unequivocally be stated, at the present state of research, is that there was a convergence of interests regarding the question of *aliyà beit*, and a shared sensibility in perceiving and representing the anti-Jewish fascist policy.

As regards the particular role of the UCII, it should be remembered that in the post-war period it found itself having to manage a situation which was in many ways tragic and desperate: the desire to safeguard the Jewish community and to free it from its condition of utter prostration could have led some leaders to take into consideration the potential political-diplomatic implications of the Jewish question in order to bring to the attention of governments and authorities – often distant and uninvolved – the problems which were afflicting the former victims of persecution. From the end of 1944 and at least until 1947, in a phase when the country's future was uncertain and the regaining of rights was still in progress, good relations with foreign Jewish bodies – especially American – were, for the Italian-Jewish leadership, among the most important resources they could utilize in their dealings with the Italian political authorities. This emerged as early as the first months of Giuseppe Nathan's activity as the Union's temporary commissioner: on 19 January 1945, in a long letter sent to Prime Minister Ivanoe Bonomi, he began by referring to the condition of 'economic ruin' caused by the persecution of individual Jews and the impossibility, for the UCII, of dealing effectively with the needs of the former victims of persecution, and he therefore asked the government to engage in 'an act of just reparation' allocating funds so that the Union and the individual communities could resume their activities and commit themselves productively to helping the many who were in need. At the same time he also asked for a solemn reconfirmation of the commitment to restore the rights of the persecuted and also called upon the government to give asylum to all the foreign Jews resident in Italy, making it easier, for those who wanted it, to be granted Italian citizenship. Significantly, in urging such an intervention, he was not only recalling national traditions, that is the season of happy integration before the persecution, providing an idyllic picture of an Italy in which there had never been 'any trace of anti-Semitism', but he also raised a different argument: in the last paragraph of the letter he noted that 'such an understanding policy would certainly be warmly welcomed in the Jewish communities of the United States and the British Empire, which are very powerful and could exercise benevolent pressure, towards us, on the respective governments'.[61]

There is undoubtedly an exploitative aspect in such statements, which try to make use of the stereotype of Jewish solidarity. It is worth noting that such an attitude was the result of a real desperation on the part of the Italian-Jewish leadership which, in the aftermath of the war, had to come to terms with its own impotence: its inability to adequately help Italian Jews. The UCII did not have many means at its disposal with which to gain favour with the Italian government, so that particular argument was insistently repeated in the following years: the representatives of Italian Judaism were able to play the role of political and cultural mediators between the Italian government and various foreign Jewish and Zionist organizations.

In its contacts with foreign Jewish bodies and representatives, the UCII leadership promoted the propagation of a very positive image of the Italian people and the new anti-fascist ruling class. The voice of Italian Jews made itself heard abroad at the conferences and meetings of the World Zionist Organization: at the Conference of 6 August 1945, the Italian delegate, Carlo Alberto Viterbo, pointed out that the Parri government had paid attention to, and shown understanding towards, the Zionist plan,[62] while, about a year later, during the XXIII Conference of the WZO (Basel, 22 December 1946), a motion was passed which thanked the Italian people for their opposition to the persecution, their understanding of Jewish problems and their support for the Zionist cause, demonstrated after the Liberation. Cantoni, representing Italian Jews and the WZO, personally handed De Gasperi the text of the motion, which the latter did not fail to cite in a speech, given at the Angelicum Pontifical Institute on 3 January 1947, in which he listed the many virtues of an Italy which certainly did not deserve to be punished by the Allies.[63]

On another, perhaps more important, front, mention should be made of the relations between the UCII and the WJC. A note dated 27 August 1945 of the General Administrative Department of Political Affairs of the Foreign Ministry reports that Raffaele Cantoni, at the time deputy commissioner of the UCII, made known 'the atmosphere … very favourably disposed towards Italy' in the circles of the WJC. Returning from a meeting with the London Executive Committee of that body, he stated that 'the Head of the Political Office of the World Jewish Congress, Kubovinsky [*sic*] very influential in America' would be going to Rome on 4 September. Cantoni therefore suggested that a meeting with the Foreign Minister should be organized and, on that occasion, the important foreign guest should be given the documentation regarding 'the main Italian problems [he suggested in particular Trieste] which could serve as guidelines for Kubovinsky [*sic*] and the other influential Jews of the WJC so that they could undertake appropriate action in American and English circles'.[64]

It has not been possible to ascertain whether the meeting proposed by Cantoni took place, but from the documents of the London Section of the WJC it transpires that Leon A. Kubowitzky (this is the correct name) had actually gone to Italy where he had met the representatives of Italian Judaism. He referred to it in an 'Interim Report in Preparation for Peace Treaties with Satellite Countries', which tackled the problems of Jewish communities throughout the European Continent (apart from Germany). Kubowitzky also referred to the Italian situation, noting, first of all, that Italian Jews were not putting forward any request for international protection, as they had full trust in the new anti-fascist government;

moreover he pointed out, not without surprise, that 'the only two issues Italian Jews seem worried about are the future of Trieste and the future of Libya, with its ancient Jewish community'. An attitude which had surprised the Executive Committee of the WJC, whose members declared that they were not 'satisfied that this was really the last word on Italian Judaism'. Finally, in concluding the paragraph dealing with Italy, he wrote: 'Furthermore, we have taken into consideration the just and thorough legislation dealing with reinstatement in Italy, as also the admirable attitude of the Italian people during the anti-Semitic persecutions of the fascist era and the excellent history of Jewish-Italian relations over the last thousand years'.[65]

Bearing in mind Cantoni's formative years – he had been deeply affected, in his youth, by the irredentist ferment which had led him to volunteer for military service in the Great War and then to participate with D'Annunzio in the Fiume expedition – it is not surprising that Trieste should be close to his heart, just as one is not surprised by his concern for Libyan Jews, with whom Italian Judaism had solid ties and who were officially represented by the UCII. Nevertheless, the loyalty towards national interests displayed on that occasion is notable.

Despite being perplexed by such an attitude, the WJC leadership was not particularly interested in the situation of the very small Italian-Jewish minority, a distinctive community, different from many others, and whose history appeared difficult to interpret;[66] other much more dramatic situations, in various areas of Europe, required their attention. Italy had, if anything, a certain importance because of its geographic position: for those who were nurturing the plan of Jewish settlement in Palestine the collaboration of a defeated power, but which was destined to exercise a significant influence in the Mediterranean, was precious, also in view of British hostility and the ambiguous and uncertain line followed for many years by the USA and the USSR towards the Zionist plan.[67] This interest, it seems to me, emerges from an important letter, dated 13 February 1946, which the Swiss Jew Gerhard Riegner, the Secretary General of the WJC, wrote to Raffaele Cantoni, asking him to forward the gist of his letter to the Italian government. A copy of the letter, translated into Italian, can in fact be found among the documents of the Foreign Ministry. In a crucial and delicate passage of that letter, after having paid the ritual homage to Italy always immune to the germ of anti-Semitism, Riegner stated:

> We well know the precarious situation in which Italy finds itself today, after the tragic years it has been through. We therefore appreciate all the more the generous attitude of its government, which despite all these difficulties has opened, after the Liberation, its frontiers to thousands of our brothers from Central and Eastern Europe and has allowed them to find a fraternal hospitality in Your Country, and at a time when, unfortunately, in many nations the persecutions have not stopped. I pray you to

> convey to the Italian government the gratitude and sincere appreciation of the World Jewish Congress for the attitude it has adopted so far with regard to this sad problem.
>
> You can be sure that the leaders of the World Jewish Congress will not forget, in the years to come, either the attitude of the Italian people during the tragic years of the persecution or the warm welcome which the Italian government reserves, at this time, for the Jews of Central and Eastern Europe, and that they will continue, as far as they can, to give their support to the work of reconstruction of a free and democratic Italy.[68]

Not very long afterwards, the assurance given by Riegner was embodied in a concrete political act when, on 20 August 1946, the WJC submitted a Memorandum on the problems of European Jews to the Peace Conference; the report also touched on the Italian situation, the object of a particularly benevolent glance which pointed out the many merits of the people and the government.[69] Even if this could not significantly affect the political-diplomatic balances which made Italy's position, at the Paris Conference,[70] particularly weak, it should in any case be noted that such standpoints, on the part of Jewish bodies, in an official setting, represented the crowning achievement of the campaign pursued by Italian diplomacy. And, in large measure, it was the result of the good auspices of Cantoni and the Italian-Jewish ruling class, which had felicitously mediated – favouring a convergence of interests, even if partial and momentary – between the WJC and the Italian government.[71]

As regards the specific role played by the UCII in favouring the efforts made by Italian diplomacy, it should be remembered that on 6 July, a month before the submission of the cited Memorandum of the WJC, the UCII and the Organization of Jewish Refugees in Italy had sent to the UN a letter in which they expressed their gratitude for the protection offered by the Italians during the dark years of the persecution. 'In the letter which accompanied the proposals to be kept in mind in compiling the treaties – Cantoni told the Council of the UCII *– there has been an official recognition of the benevolent attitude adopted by the Italian people towards the Jews*'. During the same session of the Council of the UCII, Cantoni informed of the 'intervention of the WJC in supporting Italy's request to become a member of the United Nations Organization and the satisfaction of the Italian government for such an initiative'.[72] He also stated that the UCII had not only expressed a favourable judgement about Italy in its relations with foreign Jewish bodies, but had also approved the operation which led to the publication of the above-mentioned *Relazione sull'opera svolta dal Ministero per gli Affari Esteri per la tutela delle comunità ebraiche (1938–1943)*. In this regard, he spoke of contacts with officials of the Foreign Ministry, stating that 'he had received some copies of a secret report, published by the Foreign Ministry, about the activities undertaken by the Italian government to help the Jews from 1939 to 1943'. He did not fail to underline the spirit and importance of that initiative: 'the Italian government wants to put Italy in a good light and, with this aim in mind, considers of the utmost importance the help given to the Jews during the persecutions'. From the minutes it appears that no one in the Council opposed the legitimacy of those claims or raised any doubts as to the advisability of the UCII corroborating such a standpoint.

How can one explain such behaviour on the part of the official representatives of the Italian-Jewish community? We could say that these were the terms to be accepted in order to achieve peaceful integration in the society born following the Liberation: it was necessary to identify Italy with anti-fascism, to interpret fascism, and with it also the anti-Jewish policy, as a parenthesis or a tragic accident, easily overcome. An interpretation of that kind well reflected the needs of the Jewish minority and of all the national community; the concealment of the racial persecution was only one aspect of a wider attempt to push away the past seen as a useless burden, or even as a disquieting threat. If it could be stated that the whole of fascism had been a betrayal of national history, if it could be stated that the 'real Italy' was the daughter of the values of the French Revolution and of the Risorgimento, then it would certainly be possible to convince oneself that anti-Semitism had been one of the most sensational distortions of the national tradition carried out by Mussolini.[73]

Perhaps, this is part of the explanation. The above-mentioned statements expressed a clear desire for reconciliation with the national community: it is obvious that the Jewish leadership which had established itself in the post-war period thought it could safeguard the community's interests better by avoiding reproaching Italy with its own crimes. In any case, it is important to remove the idea that the leaders of the Union could have carried out a kind of *appeasement of memory* just to avoid damaging relations with the government. There was a deep conviction, shared at the time by all the political and cultural circles, as well as by very many Italian Jews, that fascist anti-Semitism had really been an imported phenomenon. Several leaders of the Jewish communities also sincerely believed this; the UCII subscribed to this idea and its consequent policy for very many years.

NOTES

1. Among the main studies published in the first post-war decade mention should be made of: A. Spinosa, 'Le persecuzioni razziali in Italia', *Il Ponte*, 7 (1952), pp.964–78; 8 (1952), pp.1078–96; 11 (1952), pp.1604–22; 9 (1953), 7 (1953), pp.950–68; L. Salvatorelli and G. Mira, *Storia d'Italia nel periodo fascista* (Rome: Novissima, 1952), then later (Turin: Einaudi, 1956.) See also C. Roth, *History of the Jews in Italy* (Philadelphia, PA: Jewish Publication Society of America, 1946), in particular the last chapter, drawn up with the guidance of Gino Luzzatto (see C. Roth, 'Gino Luzzatto and Jewish

History', *Nuova Rivista Storica*, 49 (1965), pp.166–9); L. Poliakov and J. Sabille, *Gli ebrei sotto l'occupazione italiana* (Milan: Comunità, 1956). Some information about the fascist racial policy is also present in the classic work L. Poliakov, *Breviaire de la haine: le III Reich et les Juifs* (Paris: Calman-Levy, 1951).

2. C. Sforza, preface to G. Debenedetti, *Otto ebrei* (Rome: Atlantica, 1944), pp.ii–iii.
3. With regard to the Germans as an ideological and cultural reference point for the Italian national self-representation, see E. Collotti, 'I tedeschi', in M. Isnenghi (ed.), *I luoghi della memoria. Personaggi e date dell'Italia unita* (Bari: Laterza, 1997), pp.65–86.
4. A. Romeo, 'Antisemitismo', in *Enciclopedia Cattolica*, vol. I (Vatican City: Ente per l'Enciclopedia Cattolica e il libro cattolico, 1948). On this, see E. Mazzini, 'The Presences of Anti-Semitism in the Catholic World. The Case of the "Enciclopedia Cattolica" (1948–1954)', *Quest. Issues in Contemporary History*, 1 (April 2010), available at http://www.quest-cdecjournal.it/focus.php?issue =1&id=196.
5. Entry 'Ebrei' and 'Razzismo', in *Enciclopedia Italiana, Appendice 1938–1948* (Rome: Treccani, 1949. On this same entry, see G. Turi, *Il mecenate, il filosofo, il gesuita. L' 'Enciclopedia Italiana' specchio della nazione* (Bologna: Il Mulino, 2002), p.245.
6. For the various references, see the documented work by F. Focardi, 'Alle origini di una grande rimozione. La questione dell'antisemitismo fascista nell'Italia dell'immediato dopoguerra', *Horizonte*, 4 (1999), pp.135–69; the quotation is taken from p.141; see also F. Focardi, 'La percezione della Shoah, in Italia nell'immediato dopoguerra: 1945–47', in M. Flores, S. Levis Sullam, M.-A. Matard-Bonucci and E. Traverso (eds), *Storia della Shoah in Italia. Vicende, memorie, rappresentazioni*, vol. II (Turin: UTET, 2010), pp.10–35. As regards the attitudes of the Catholic hierarchy, see G. Miccoli, 'Tra memoria, rimozioni e manipolazioni. Aspetti dell'atteggiamento cattolico verso la "Shoah"', *Qualestoria*, 3 (1991), pp.161–88.
7. The themes of responsibility and guilt were soon at the centre of the cultural and political debate in the post-war period and, to a greater or lesser extent, remained there for a long time. In this regard mention should be made, first of all, of the detailed and stimulating reflection by K. Jaspers, *The Question of German Guilt* (New York: Capricorn Books, 1961 [1947]). This text presents the revised version of the lectures given at the University of Heidelberg in 1946. No less important and significant is the slightly earlier intervention of Hannah Arendt: 'Organized Guilt and Collective Responsibility' [1945], now in R.H. Feldman (ed.), *The Jew as Pariah: Jewish Identity and Politics in the Modern Age* (New York: Grove Press, 1978), pp.225–36.
8. In this regard, Tony Judt has proposed some stimulating observations of a comparative nature: 'The Past is Another Country: Myth and Memory in Post-War Europe', in I. Deak, J. T. Gross and T. Judt (eds), *The Politics of Retribution in Europe: World War II and its Aftermath* (Princeton, NJ: Princeton University Press, 2000), pp.293–324.
9. M. Battini, *The Missing Italian Nuremberg: Cultural Amnesia and Post-War Politics* (New York and Basingstoke: Palgrave Macmillan, 2007), pp.97–8.
10. See ibid., p.109. But see also D. Bloxam, *The Holocaust on Trial: The War Crimes Trials and the Formation of History and Memory* (Oxford: Oxford University Press, 2001).
11. *Mercurio*, 16 (1945).
12. *Mercurio*, 4 (1944).
13. ASMAE, General Secretariat, 1945, cat.11/12, pacco 28/2, f.34 'Contributo italiano alla guerra'.
14. To summarize, it could be said that various bodies were charged with gathering information about the partisan struggle and the relationship between the Italians and the regime, and that, subsequently, it was the Foreign Ministry which reviewed everything and decided how to utilize that information. The two main texts produced by that ministry for propaganda purposes were *Relazione sull'opera svolta dal Ministero degli Affari Esteri per la tutela delle comunità ebraiche (1938–1943)* (Rome, 1946); *Il contributo italiano nella guerra contro la Germania* (Rome, 1946). Mention should also be made of the intense activity in political journalism conducted by the ministry of Occupied Italy in its brief period of existence (from February to July 1945) and continued later by the Historical Office of the War of Liberation, set up by the Parri government at the Prime Minister's Office. That office was definitively closed on 31 January 1946, only ten days before the signing of the peace treaty.
15. Regarding the international scene and the path which led to the drawing up of the peace treaty, see I. Poggiolini, *Diplomazia della transizione. Gli Alleati e il problema del trattato di pace italiano (1945–1947)*, preface by E. di Nolfo (Florence: Ponte alle Grazie, 1990; S. Lorenzini, *L'Italia e il trattato di pace del 1947* (Bologna: Il Mulino, 2007).
16. F. Focardi and L. Klinkhammer, 'La questione dei "criminali di guerra" italiani e una commissione di

inchiesta dimenticata', *Contemporanea*, 3 (2001), pp.497–528; F. Focardi, 'La questione della punizione dei criminali di guerra in Italia dopo la fine del secondo conflitto mondiale', *Quellen und Forschungen* (2000), pp.543–624; F. Focardi, *Criminali di guerra in libertà. Un accordo segreto tra Italia e Germania Federale 1949–1954*, preface by L. Klinkhammer (Rome: Carocci, 2008). Linked with this issue is the question of the trials of the Germans responsible for massacres in Italy; regarding the complex cultural, political and judicial scenario, see M. Battini, *The Missing Italian Nuremberg*.

17. The best-known and most sensational example concerns the deliberate cover-up of the use of gas in the Ethiopian War. See in this regard A. Del Boca, *I gas di Mussolini. Il fascismo e la guerra d'Etiopia* (Rome: Editori Riuniti, 1996). In more general terms, see A. Del Boca, 'Il mancato dibattito sul colonialismo', in *L'Africa nella coscienza degli italiani* (Bari: Laterza, 1992), pp.111–27.
18. D. Bidussa, *Il mito del bravo italiano* (Milan: Il Saggiatore, 1994).
19. See M. Toscano, 'L'abrogazione delle leggi razziali', in M. Sarfatti (ed.), *Il ritorno alla vita. Vicende e diritti degli ebrei in Italia dopo la seconda guerra mondiale* (Florence: La Giuntina, 1998), pp.59–76.
20. The text is reproduced in ASMAE, General Secretariat, folder 42, cat.11/17, 1946 'Questioni israelitiche'.
21. Particular importance was given to that statement by G. Dalma, *La verità sugli ebrei* (Rome: OET, 1945), pp.149ff.
22. The text was forwarded to the embassies and legations of London, Moscow, Madrid, Ankara, Buenos Aires, Washington, Berne, Sofia, Dublin, Lisbon, Bucharest and Stockholm, as well as the Consulate of Tangiers. The instructions received were promptly executed and the text circulated in different countries in the spring of 1945. In particular, in Bucharest in June the document was published by the main newspapers and handed personally to the Great Rabbi of Rumania Alexander Safran. See ASMAE, General Secretariat, folder 42, cat.11/17, 1946 'Questioni israelitiche'.
23. C. Calenda, 'Appunto. Taluni aspetti internazionali della questione ebraica', pp.1–2, in ASMAE, Gabinetto 1943–1948, folder 107, cat. II, 1944–1947, f.84 'Comunità Israelitica Italiana'. Mario Toscano has referred to the document, which he has opportunely linked to the development of an Italian policy towards the Zionist question. See M. Toscano, *La 'porta di Sion'. L'Italia e l'immigrazione clandestina ebraica in Palestina (1945–1948)* (Bologna: Il Mulino, 1990), pp.17–21.
24. C. Calenda, 'Appunto', p.12.
25. In an interesting memoir dated August 1940 it was theorized: 'in the Mediterranean Basin the Jewish population must become our ally: therefore nothing should be done which can offend its sensitivity and self-respect. What has been done in Italy, and has to remain in place, is something by now outdated which few people still think about, but it is necessary that the memory is not revived and that new measures do not alienate the sympathies of this people who, as long as it exists, should be taken into account'. The reflection concluded with a final attempt to find a way to work out a flexible strategy within the context of the racist policy: 'Finally, it should not be forgotten that the Mediterranean Jews are Sephardi who are very different from the Ashkenazi of Central Europe against whom measures have been taken by the German Government. The former are closer to the Latin culture and the Western mentality'. See 'Palestina e Transgiordania. Cenni Storici. Periodo mandatario, possibile assetto futuro', in 'L'Italia fascista e la "questione palestinese"', edited by V. Pinto, in *Contemporanea*, 1 (2003), pp.102–25. Pinto attributes the text to Count Quinto Mazzolini, Italian Consul General in Jerusalem from 1936 to 1940 and then head of the Historical Diplomatic Service; as regards the importance of the document, see the observations of Pinto in pp.101–2.
26. C. Calenda, 'Appunto', p.12.
27. The passages quoted are taken from the text of the letter of the Italian Ambassador in Brussels, reproduced in the circular forwarded by the Ministry of the Interior to all the prefectures on 21 September 1945. The text and the replies from the prefectures are in ACS, Min. Int., DGPS, A.G.R., cat. A5G-IIG. M.1944–1948, v.3, f. 'Rimpatrio degli ebrei italiani deportati in Germania'. Information about this issue was given by M. Sarfatti, 'Razzisti per ordine superiore', *Diario*, special issue of 27 January 2001, pp.78–82.
28. See the account of Ducci himself in N. Caracciolo, *Gli ebrei e l'Italia durante la guerra, 1940–45*, preface by R. De Felice (Rome: Bonacci, 1985). Regarding Ducci's role in helping the Jews in the territories occupied by the Italians, see A.J. Steinberg, *All or Nothing: The Axis and the Holocaust 1941–1943* (London and New York: Routledge, 1990).
29. Letter of 1 September 1944, in ASMAE, General Secretariat, folder 42, cat.11/17, 1944 'Ebrei'.
30. *Politica Estera*, 1 (1944), pp.21–9.
31. Ibid., p.21.

32. Quoted in D. Rodogno, *Il nuovo ordine mediterraneo. Le politiche di occupazione dell'Italia fascista in Europa (1940–1943)* (Turin: Bollati Boringhieri, 2003), p.481; see also the similar statements by General Pièche in pp.479-481.
33. Quoted in ibid., p.482.
34. The statement was made by Croce to Cecil Sprigge, a Reuters correspondent, and appeared in various Italian, English and American dailies between 30 and 31 March 1945, and later reproduced in B. Croce, *Scritti e discorsi politici 1943–1947*, vol. II, edited by A. Carrella (Naples: Biliopolis, 1993), pp.248–9, in a note. That intervention is part of a broader initiative by Croce aiming at putting forward Italy's merits and avoiding a punitive peace treaty for Italy; see the letter to the Editor of *The Times*, 'L'Italia e la conferenza di San Francisco', published on 7 April 1945 on the same daily and also in Italian newspapers, and the letter to the Editor of the *Manchester Guardian*, 'Pace punitiva o pace costruttiva?', published by the same daily as also by Italian dailies 11 September; later reproduced in B. Croce, *Scritti e discorsi politici*, pp.244–8 and 249–51, respectively. These writings have been referred to by F. Focardi, *Una grande rimozione*, pp.149ff.
35. R. Ducci, *Questa Italia* (Milan: Mondadori, 1948), p.191.
36. Some useful thought-provoking ideas are offered by L. Klinkhammer, *Stragi naziste in Italia. La Guerra contro i civili (1943–1944)* (Rome: Donzelli, 1997), pp.98–103.
37. I here refer back to the reflection of Michele Battini, to explain the mobilization of so many prestigious figures of the British establishment to save General Kesselring from the death sentence: cf. *The Missing Italian Nuremberg*, pp. 41 and 117-119.
38. The article, signed by Delbert Clark, has in its title a reference to 'Rome, 11 May'. The text of the article and an Italian translation were sent by the Foreign Ministry to the PCM with a brief covering note – dated 1 July 1946 – in which it was stated that the article was the result of the initiative of the lawyer Angelo Donati, who lived in Paris. See ACS, PCM, 1944–1947, cat.3.2.2, f.15539. Regarding Donati and his commitment in helping the Jews present in the territory controlled by the Italians in the South of France, see K. Voigt, *Il rifugio precario. Gli esuli in Italia dal 1933 al 1945*, vol. II (Florence: La Nuova Italia, 1996), pp.293–334.
39. ACS, PCM, 1944–1947, cat.3.2.2, f.15539.
40. As Rodogno has shown, the Foreign Minister worked 'towards the Duce' and certainly not to oppose Mussolini's orders: D. Rodogno, *Il nuovo ordine mediterraneo*, pp.149–51 and 433ff.
41. Ibid., in particular, pp.432–84. On the logics that inspired the differentiation between Germany's and Italy's anti-Semitic actions, see C. Moos, *Ausgrenzung, Internierung, Deportation. Antisemitismus und Gewalt im spaten italienischen Faschismus, 1938–1945* (Zurich: Chronos, 2004); M. Knox, 'Das faschistische Italien und die "Endlösung", 1942/43', *Vierteljahrshefte für Zeitgeschichte*, 1 (2007), pp.53–92.
42. The author of the article published in the *New York Times* (see note 38) pointed out, among other things, the imminent integral publication of the documents in English, in a book edited by Angelo Donati and Chaim Weizmann, a very prominent leader of political Zionism since the time of the Great War anddestined to become the first president of the State of Israel. No confirmation of such a plan has been found, nor has the publication announced as imminent been found. It seems reasonable, however, to recognize the accomplishment of that plan in the book by Léon Poliakov, *La condition des Juifs en France*, foreword by L. Schneersohn, preface by J. Godard (Paris: Édition du Centre, 1946). A revised version of the work would have been published a few years later, combined, in a single book, with the observations (in an amplified version) which Jacques Sabille had made about the fate of the Jews in Croatia and Greece occupied by the Italians (see J. Sabille, 'L'attitude des Italiens envers les Juifs persecuté en Croatie', *Le Monde Juif*, 46–7 (1951), pp.5–8; J. Sabille, 'L'attitude des Italiens à l'égard des Juifs en Grèce occupée', *Le Monde Juif*, 49 (1951), pp.7–10). This last-named work by two authors appeared in Yiddish in 1952 and in English in 1956, in both instances being published by the Centre de Documentation Juive Contemporaine, and finally in Italian: *Gli ebrei sotto l'occupazione italiana* (Milan: Edizioni di Comunità, 1956).
43. L. Poliakov, *La condition des Juifs en France*, p.18. The translation from the French is mine.
44. Utilizing the German documentation recovered following the liberation of Paris, the Centre produced different works dealing with the history of the persecution; see *Catalogue des ouvrages publiés par le Centre de documentation juive contemporaine, 1945–1958* (Paris: CDJC).
45. This point is touched on in the J. Godard's preface to L. Poliakov, *La condition des Juifs en France*, p.14.
46. From a note by Luigi Vidau we learn that a favourable view of the publication of the report, whose data must have been collected and organized in the preceding months, had been given on 4 April

1946 by the Undersecretary of State at the Foreign Ministry, Negarville. In ASMAE, General Secretariat, folder 42, cat.11/17, 1945, f. 'Questioni Israelitiche varie'.

47. In fact, the introduction stated: 'When the Fascist government, failing also in this to keep faith with the Italian tradition of freedom, equality and tolerance, began the evil racial policy, the Foreign Ministry immediately realized the dangers which have ensued from such a policy for our material, moral and political interests in the world. The Foreign Ministry obviously not being able to ignore the laws issued as a consequence of the racial policy, nor to adopt an attitude of open opposition with the regime's directives, nevertheless maintained that it was its duty to impede as far as possible, within the context of its remit, the application of such laws and directives'. See Ministry of Foreign Affairs, *Relazione sull'opera svolta dal Ministero degli Affari Esteri per la tutela delle comunità ebraiche (1938–1941)* (Rome, no date [1946]), p.1.
48. See K. Voigt, *Il rifugio precario*, vol. 2, Chapter 3 about Yugoslavia and Chapter 4 about the Jews in the South of France; M. Sarfatti, *Gli ebrei nell'Italia fascista*, pp.174–5, regarding the planned transfer of the internees of Ferramonti, and pp.245ff., as regards the policy of the RSI. See also the documents reproduced and commented on in M. Sarfatti, 'Fascist Italy and German Jews in South-Eastern France in July 1943', *Journal of Modern Italian Studies*, 3 (1998), pp.318–27.
49. Among those who claimed the title of 'saviours of Jews' there was also a character who was anything but noble and in fact dramatically compromised with the policy of violent repression against the local populations carried out by the Italian Army in Yugoslavia. The reference is to M. Roatta, *Otto milioni di baionette. L'esercito italiano in Guerra dal 1940 al 1944* (Milan: Mondadori, 1946), pp.170ff.
50. Even in recent years works have been published, dealing with the treatment of the Jews in the territories occupied by the Italians, strongly imbued with the persistent 'myth of the good Italian'. I am referring in the first place to the above-mentioned study by Jonathan Steinberg, *All or Nothing*, which presents detailed documentation, but which appears totally unsatisfactory as regards analysis, utilizing vague references to national characters to explain the different behaviour of the Italians and Germans towards the Jews. Mention should also be made of the text of a Yugoslav Jew who was arrested by the Italians and deported to Ferramonti and thus survived being soon freed by the Allies. This last-mentioned work provides an important legitimization of some of the rhetorical topos upon which the mechanisms of self-representation of the State institutions had been based and it is not surprising that it was translated and published by the Historical Office of the Army General Staff; the reference is to M. Shelah, *Un debito di gratitudine. Storia dei rapport tra l'Esercito Italiano e gli ebrei in Dalmazia (1941–1943)* (Rome: USSME, 1991 [1986]).
51. D. Rodogno, *Il nuovo ordine mediterraneo*.
52. See, for example, *Israel*, 31–32, 12 July 1945.
53. See R. Cantoni, 'Il saluto dell'Unione delle Comunità Israelitiche Italiane', *RMI*, 2–3, XVI (1950), *Scritti in Onore di Riccardo Bachi*; the entire text is also reproduced in S.I. Minerbi, *Un ebreo fra D'Annunzio e il sionismo. Raffaele Cantoni*, preface by R. De Felice (Rome: Bonacci, 1992), pp.148–50, in a note.
54. *Israel*, 39, 13 June 1946.
55. C.A. Viterbo wrote as follows in *Israel*, 7, 11 October 1945: 'the legend of a Mussolini dragged unwillingly in tow by the German anti-Semitic policy has fallen and is falling to pieces even more. He made that policy his own out of political expediency. Therefore he also carries the ignominious responsibility before men and God'.
56. See *Israel*, 14–15, 13 January 1949. Viterbo and the UCII did not fail to intervene to block the hypothesis of the conferring of the Nobel Prize for medicine on Nicola Pende, a prominent figure of Italian racism.See Viterbo's letter in the appendix to A. Spinosa, 'Le persecuzioni razziali in Italia. L'azione della stampa', *Il Ponte*, 8, 11 (1952), pp.1621–2; see also the letter of 9 October 1950 sent by Cantoni to the board of the WJC of London, in which he communicated his decision to oppose the possible awarding of the Nobel Prize to Pende, in CZA, Archives of the British Section of the WJC, C2, f.466. Regarding Pende see R. Maiocchi, *Scienza italiana e razzismo fascista*, pp.145ff. On the post-war stories of Italian racial scientists, see T. Dell'Era, 'Destino degli scienziati razzisti nel dopoguerra', in M. Flores, S. Levis Sullam, M.-A. Matard-Bonucci and E. Traverso (eds), *Storia della Shoah in Italia. Vicende, memorie, rappresentazioni*, vol. II (Turin: UTET, 2010), pp.234–47.
57. *Israel*, 24, 24 May 1945.
58. D. Prato, *Dal Pergamo della Comunità di Roma* (Rome, 1950), respectively pp.2 and 3.
59. *Bollettino della Comunità Israelitica di Milano*, 10 July 1947.

60. The many and complex implications of such a policy undertaken by the Italian government, and the evolution of its positions on this issue from 1944 to 1948 have been well outlined by M. Toscano, *La 'porta di Sion'*.
61. On 3 May 1945, Nathan forwarded a copy of the letter to Alcide De Gasperi, the Foreign Minister. See ASMAE, General Secretariat, folder 107, c.II, 1944–1947, f.84 'Ebrei'.
62. *Israel*, 6, 13 September 1945. See also M. Toscano, *La 'porta di Sion'*, pp.48–9.
63. De Gasperi's speech is reported in the *BCIM*, 11, 24 January 1946. The text of the motion, a synthesis of the meeting between De Gasperi and Cantoni and a letter of De Gasperi to the Union are reported, in an English translation, in the memorandum sent by the Union to the London office of the World Jewish Congress. See 'Jewish life and activities in Italy in the period 16–31 December 1946', CZA, archives of the British section of the WJC, C2, f.464.
64. See ASMAE, General Secretariat, 1945–1949, folder 42, cat.11/17, f.1946 'Questioni israelitiche'. The reference is to Leon Kubowitsky, a prominent figure in the WJC.
65. See 'Interim Report on Preparations for Peace Treaties with Satellite Countries', p.8, in CZA, Archive of the British Section of the WJC, C2, f.183, my translation. It should be noted that, also because of reasons tied to its early liberation by the Allies, Italy had been one of the very first countries to start the process of abrogating the persecutory legislation, however the Italian legislation would not – comparatively speaking – have appeared to be among the best. On the contrary, it was one of the most restrictive as regards the problem of the restitution of goods stolen or sold, under blackmail conditions, following 1938. A comparison between the relevant Italian laws and those of other European countries has been carried out by Ilaria Pavan, *Tra indifferenza e oblio. Le conseguenze economiche delle leggi razziali in Italia (1938–1970)* (Florence: Le Monnier, 2004).
66. The action of the representatives of Italian Judaism, combined with the independent action of Italian diplomacy, was in felicitous accord with the prejudices towards, and the lack of understanding of, the Italian situation, particularly the Jewish one, which characterized the views of many foreign observers. If one reads, for example, the accounts of the period 1938–1940 in an important masthead of the Jewish British press such as the *Jewish Chronicle*, one will notice how the start of the racist policy was presented as simply a political-diplomatic concession, while it was maintained that anti-Semitism could not find any consensus and even less be seriously applied. See for example 'Italy's Drift to Anti-Semitism', *Jewish Chronicle*, 29 July 1938, p.13 (for an overall view of the periodical's attitude to the tragedy of the Continental Jews, see D. Cesarani, 'Le Jewish Chronicle et la Shoah', *Revue d'Histoire de la Shoah*, 163 [1998], pp.183–202). Such interpretative distortions later found confirmation and legitimization in the post-war period and so there was – especially in the Jewish Anglo-Saxon world – the propagation of a misrepresented and misleading vision of the fascist racial persecution, which tended essentially to confirm the idea that it had only been a sort of tragic farce. See, for example, A. Boyars, 'No Jewish Problem – and Little Judaism', *Zionist Review*, 1, 23 September 1949, p.11: 'Under fascism these [Italian Jews] suffered virtually no racial persecution and it was only later, when Hitler started exerting pressure … that 3,000 Jews were handed to the Nazis – or rather the Nazis were asked to take them – as the fascists themselves had very little idea who should be arrested!' And, as if this were not enough, it carries on noting the irremediable assimilation of the Italian Jews as well as their prompt reintegration after the war: 'All of the Jews I have met here are of the opinion that the laws recently passed by the Italian government have made up for all the losses (that of life, naturally excluded) sustained by Italian Jewry during the war years'. See also 'Report from overseas: Italy', *Congress Weekly*, 6 (February 1947) (the publication is the organ of the British section of the WJC).
67. On the policies of the British and Americans, see A.J. Kochavi, *Post-Holocaust Politics: Britain, the United States & Jewish Refugees, 1945–1948* (Chapel Hill, NC and London: University of North Carolina Press, 2001), regarding in particular the Italian context, see pp.235–56.
68. A copy of the letter is in ASMAE, General Secretariat, 1945–1949, p.42, cat.11/17, 1946 'Questioni israelitiche'. On 7 March the letter was also sent to the Italian diplomatic bodies in Washington, London and Berne.
69. All Germany's allies were forced to include in their new constitutions four principles inherent in the safeguarding of human rights and in particular of the minorities: 1. Respecting individual rights without distinction of race or religion; 2. Freeing prisoners incarcerated on racial grounds; 3. Repudiating discriminatory laws; 4. Declaring illegal the reconstitution of fascist movements. Also because of the intervention of the WJC and Cantoni, present in Paris, in the case of Italy the second and third points were omitted. See Institute of Jewish Affairs, *Unity in Dispersion: A History of the WJC*, introduction by A.L. Kubowitsky (New York: World Jewish Congress, 1948), pp.253ff. See

also S.I. Minerbi, *Un ebreo fra D'Annunzio e il sionismo*, pp.184–5.

70. Among the factors which made Italy's position difficult and precarious were the looming Cold War, which influenced the strategies of the USA and the USSR, and the friction between the conciliatory American approach and the hostile British policy. The combination of these factors led to a peace treaty seen by the politicians and public opinion as a humiliation and a defeat. See R. Quartararo, *Italia e Stati Uniti, gli anni difficili (1945–1952)* (Naples: Edizioni Scientifiche Italiane, 1986), pp.70ff.
71. See M. Toscano, *La 'porta di Sion'*, pp.91–101; A. Sereni, *I clandestini del mare. L'emigrazione ebraica in terra d'Israele dal 1945 al 1948* (Milan: Mursia, 1973), pp.93ff.
72. Verb. Cons., meeting of 24 July 1946, my italics. See also CZA, collection of British section WJC, C2, f.464.
73. We well know how interpretations of this type prospered after the war. Consider, for example, Salvatorelli's definition of fascism as 'anti-Risorgimento', see L. Salvatorelli, *Pensiero e azione del Risorgimento* (Turin: Einaudi, 1963), in particular pp.180–92. That book has been both an interesting study and an anti-fascist political manifesto; written straight off and published in 1943, it also had an important impact in anti-fascist culture after the war; see the account by G. Spadolini, 'Introduzione a Salvatorelli', in F. Tessitore (ed.), *Salvatorelli Storico* (Naples: Edizioni Scientifiche Italiane, 1981), in particular pp.27 and 19.

8

Memory Politics during the Cold War

OFFICIAL RHETORIC AND PUBLIC CELEBRATIONS

Once the peace treaty had been signed, the Italian government's interest in the political use of the memory of the anti-Jewish persecution lessened; nevertheless, fascism, Nazism and the Second World War continued to be very critical and exceptionally delicate themes, subject to repeated political exploitation. In the situation which had been developing since the end of the 1940s, when German rearmament and the building of the Atlantic Alliance were under discussion, evoking the guilt and the crimes of Germany could not be a politically neutral act.

In the first half of the 1950s, the issues of German rearmament and of the treatment of the Nazi war criminals were themes often dealt with by the Jewish press and re-emerged insistently in the ceremonies promoted to commemorate the victims of the Shoah. There were very many such commemorations; they were generally promoted by individual Jewish communities, looking for means to carry out the slow and difficult processes of mourning. These ceremonies were regularly repeated on the anniversaries of the massacres and violence undergone; the ceremonies for 16 October, commemorating the round up of the Roman Ghetto by the Germans in 1943, were particularly important. Inevitably, such anniversaries provided the opportunity for the expression of a desire for justice which was reflected in the collective anguish for the evolution of the international political situation.[1] Considerable anxiety caused a split within the leadership of the Union throughout the 1950s; we have already seen how the UCII, which avoided any direct political involvement, was in crisis in 1952 – with the resignation of the President Renzo Bonfiglioli – precisely in relation to the battle which the Peace Committees and the whole of the Left were orchestrating to impede the Atlantic choice by the Christian Democratic Party. And also in the following years there was deep unease and repeated divisions on how to behave – on how to reconcile the instinctive repugnance for the idea of German rearmament with its apolitical attitude, on how to formulate its own opposition to the project of the European Defence Community while avoiding clashing with the Christian Democratic political majority – which had a painful impact on the Council of the UCII.[2]

In that very delicate situation, there was an explosion of intemperance on the part of some youth groups who openly challenged the choices of the Jewish leadership, displaying a spontaneous and deep identification with the anti-fascist rhetoric of the left-wing parties.[3] As we have already shown in the first part of this book, during the 1950s the UCII's attitude of waiting was challenged by progressive youth groups, who were calling for a greater commitment in seeing memory as an instrument not only for conserving the recollection of the past, but also useful in the present struggles. A militant memory, which wanted to recall the crimes of Nazism to prevent what was seen as the dangerous return on the scene of a German military power in the heart of Europe. In 1952, for the anniversary of 16 October, Jewish youth went so far as to organize its own autonomous commemorations, with the participation of the communist leader Umberto Terracini, in contrast with the official and more moderate ones proposed by the community leadership.[4]

Pressed by the youth groups, the UCII was therefore driven to a greater commitment regarding the policy on commemorations, striving to prevent the memory of the horrors of the Second World War from dragging the community into the political arena, trying instead to ensure that the ceremonies and commemorations would permit the strengthening of the relationship with the governing body. In this respect, it is interesting to analyse the forms and aims of the strong commitment shown by the UCII leadership on the occasion of the anniversary of 25 April 1955.

Since the crisis of the anti-fascist coalition governments, that date had been one of the moments when the ideological fissures which divided the national community were on display: on one side, the official ceremonies with the government orators, on the other, the mass rituals promoted by the opposition parties.[5] The moments of harmony evoked by the ritual of 25 April were few and far between;[6] the memory of the patriotic and anti-fascist consensus could not cancel the conflicts and rivalries accentuated by the Cold War and in fact the commemorations organized by the government for the tenth anniversary were marked by fervent anti-communism.

At the time of that anniversary, the political situation was characterized by the crisis of centrism and mounting American pressure for harsher anti-communist measures. Thus, the Scelba-Saragat government,[7] in response to both international political needs and the requests coming from different sectors of society, was induced to develop a detailed campaign of intervention in the policy of commemoration which, in the first place, concerned the Liberation Day of 1955. In view of the important anniversary, the Council of Ministers considered the issue on various occasions and asked the Vice-Prime Minister Giuseppe Saragat to coordinate the necessary initiatives.[8]

For the first time in Republican history, the government was intervening directly, with energy and determination, in organizing the anti-fascist ritual: by promoting the publication of important books,[9] producing a documentary film,[10] financing scholarships for the orphans of Partisans and soldiers,[11] as well as issuing some commemorative stamps.[12] Above all, the role of the State institutions became a concrete reality in claiming the *monopoly of the commemorative ceremony*: ceremonies organized by parties or associations were banned and the organization of commemorations in the various provinces was entrusted to the prefects.[13] The only authorized commemorative ceremony not directly promoted or managed by the central government was the one organized by the Union of Italian Jewish Communities in Milan on 17 April with the aim of 'remembering the sacrifice of the Jews in the resistance struggle in Italy and the help given to the Jews by the Italians in that distressing period'.[14]

The significance of such an exceptional concession is to be found in the government's overall view of that tenth anniversary. The commemoration of 25 April 1955, so different from those of previous years, was characterized by a sudden reawakening of State authority which, after a long period of quiescence seemed to recognize the importance of such events. The intervention, from above, did not aim at the organization of a shared memory, *super partes*, but rather at stifling the establishment of those commemorative initiatives considered hostile to the government and instead supporting others, useful to it.[15] It was a question of defining hierarchies of memory, selecting some events at the expense of others in the attempt to promote a pacified national memory.[16]

The participation in such important ceremonies was, for Italian Jews, a precious opportunity to re-confirm their own ties with their nation and the State, which, in the view of the UCII, cautious and substantially pro-government, meant underlining the patriotic dimension – not political nor much less revolutionary – of the Resistance, and confirming the myth of the good Italian, which had been tenaciously reinforced since the beginning of the Republic. The ceremony proposed by the Union was in line with government's interests since singing the praises of the virtuous Italians, rehabilitated a potentially negative memory, promoting exactly the model of pacified memory free from controversial traces favoured by the parliamentary majority.

But let us take a closer look at the UCII's initiatives for that anniversary. At the same time as the organization of the Milanese ceremony planned for 17 April, a 'Manifesto agli italiani' ('Manifesto to the Italians') was prepared by the UCII, which arranged for it to be posted on the walls of the provincial capitals of Italy for 25 April 1955:

> On the tenth anniversary of the Liberation the Italian Jews, who, as Italians and as Jews suffered a two-fold oppression by the Nazi-fascist tyranny,
>
> kneel reverently before the memory of the martyrs of every faith who fell for Freedom,
>
> they are moved as they remember the innocent victims deported and

> slaughtered in the name of barbaric laws and inhuman ferocity in the Italian cities and countryside or in the crematoriums beyond the Alps,
>
> they gratefully extol the courageous acts, sometimes as far the sacrifice, of all those Italians – Partisans, soldiers, religious and laymen, modest people of every class and creed – who, redeeming the crimes of a minority – as true Italians they did their utmost to save the defenceless victims of persecution within the borders of Italy and beyond them,
>
> they gratefully remember the support given by the revived democracy in the immediate post-war period to the Jewish refugees who had survived the concentration camps…[17]

This manifesto clearly expresses the idea that the help given by a part of the Italian population had redeemed the crimes of which a minority was guilty, while the reception given after the war to the refugees from the concentration camps and the government's collaboration in the clandestine immigration to Palestine were presented as a confirmation of the virtuous character of the Italians. Moreover, it should be noted how, in remembering the persecutions, reference was only made to the tragic period following the Armistice; in the text, there is no mention of the less sensational, but no less unjust, persecutions imposed with full autonomy by the fascist regime between 1938 and 1943. In this way, the sufferings of the Jews could be correlated with the horrors of the German occupation and associated with the suffering of all the Italian people: thus, the Jewish tragedy could be integrated in the national tragedy; which would have been much more difficult if attention had been focused on the persecutions undergone from July 1938 to September 1943.[18]

The commemorative ceremony promoted by the UCII was an expression of solemn gratitude to the Italian people. At the Alcione Theatre of Milan, the President of the UCII, Giorgio Zevi, the Chief Rabbi Elio Toaff and the President of the Community of Milan Ottolenghi highlighted 'particularly how great was the gratitude of the Jews towards all those Italians who during the terrible period had done their utmost to save the persecuted minority from certain death'. Thus, in order to give a tribute and testimony of their gratitude, twenty-three Italians (including many religious figures) were commended for having protected and saved the persecuted between 1943 and 1945. The Minister Umberto Tupini, present at the ceremony in representation of the government, significantly expressed the hope that that ceremony could represent 'for Italy the end of the post-war period': from then on, it was necessary to proceed 'in harmony, working together for freedom, democracy and peace'.[19] Therefore, it was a question of settling an account, starting a new chapter; it was time to bury anti-fascism, an inconvenient burden for the government, and for everyone to be united, embracing a conciliatory memory which contributed to creating a serene atmosphere.[20]

The statements of the leading figures of the Jewish community fitted in well with that approach. Less than a year later, during a solemn ceremony held on 14 December 1956 in the Capitol in Rome, they repeated their gratitude towards the Italian people.[21] The President of the Union, Sergio Piperno Beer, stated that:

> Everyone had done their utmost; all those who, in some way, were able to follow the moves of the occupier and of his thugs, were careful to warn the predestined innocent victims; all the friends, the acquaintances, the neighbours were ready to take them in, to hide them, to help them; they all did their best to provide the Jews with false documents and to divert the search.

To state that 'everyone did his utmost' is decidedly exaggerated. But what perhaps is more disquieting is that such words were quoted by Renzo De Felice, from the first to the last edition of his book on the Jews in Italy under fascism, in order to maintain the thesis of a collective Italian opposition to German extermination policy.[22] Obviously the statements made by representatives of Italian Judaism eleven years after the Liberation, and eighteen years after the beginning of the persecution, are more useful sources to understand the mentality of the latter than the actual history of the persecution, yet it should be noted that such standpoints characterized the post-war cultural climate, thus also influencing historiographic judgements.

That the reports given by witnesses and protagonists of such a complex situation are inevitably partial, incomplete, unreliable – especially when they do not confine themselves to describing a precise event, but indulge in overall judgements on an age and on the behaviour of a people – is an obvious and foregone conclusion. Nevertheless, it is not surprising that Italian historiography dealing with the theme of the persecution should have been influenced by the weight of Jewish memories. The problem of the utilization of the memories of the victims is not new to those who have followed the international debate which since the 1960s has characterized the historiography of the Shoah: the warning about the mythological characteristics inherent in the memories of the victims and the need for a direct verification of the persecutory system seen from within – through a reading of the documents produced by the bureaucrats who fuelled it – have been among the main interpretative keys of the monumental research of Raul Hilberg.[23] He waged a hard battle on this theme, which left him for a long time in an isolated position, because until very recent times the history of the persecution was made by and for the victims: in the reconstruction of the past, the State of Israel like Jewish institutions of the Diaspora naturally tried to establish their identity, rather than provide a cold, exact and detached knowledge of history.[24] Without entering into an international debate which has been long and not without controversial bitterness, it seems important to point out the links between Jewish memory and the development of the historiography of the anti-Jewish persecution.

In Italy, the delay in historical research has meant that judgements expressed by the victims in their diaries, or even by their representatives in ceremonies and speeches after the war, have constituted, for a long time, one of the main reference points on a very delicate question, contributing to the legitimization of the myth of an Italy which was intolerant of, and rebellious towards, the ideology and practice of anti-Semitism. Jewish memory was not however the only element at issue. We have already shown how, starting from the immediate post-war period, different forces had combined to reinforce that vision, which soon became consolidated in a real interpretative paradigm. The interweaving of Jewish self-representation with reflections and needs from other sources has thus led to the construction of a pervasive and substantially prevalent public attitude, at least until the end of the 1980s.

NOTES

1. For a well-grounded review of the attitudes of the Jewish press, see P. Bertilotti, 'Mémoires et représentations des persecutions antisémites en italie sous le fascisme et pendant l'occupation allemande dans la presse communautaire juive entre 1944 et 1961', supervisor Prof. Marc Lazar (Unpublished thesis, Institut d'Etudes Politiques de Paris, 2003); in particular see the first part; E. Mazzini, 'La memoria del 1938 nella stampa periodica ebraica. Come ricordare?', *XXI Secolo*, 17 (2010), pp.21–45.
2. See, for example, the discussion in the meeting of 12 December 1954, in Verb. Cons.
3. Ibid., Part 1, Chapter 3.
4. See *Israel*, 8, 23 October 1952. The event gave rise to controversies in the Council of the UCII; see Verb. Cons., meeting of 19 October 1952.
5. For a preliminary interpretation of the character of the celebrations of Liberation, see M. Ridolfi, *Le feste nazionali* (Bologna: Il Mulino, 2003), pp.105ff; Y. Guaiana, *Il tempo della Repubblica. Le feste civili in Italia* (Milan: Unicopli, 2007).
6. For an overall assesssment of the commemoration of the anti-fascist Resistance and its political implications in post-war Italy, see P. Cooke, *The Legacy of the Italian Resistance* (New York and Basingstoke: Palgrave Macmillan, 2011); F. Focardi, *La guerra della memoria. La Resistenza nel dibattito politico italiano dal 1945 ad oggi* (Bari: Laterza, 2005).
7. Regarding the political stance of that executive, see M.G. Rossi, 'Il governo Scelba tra crisi del centrismo e ritorno anticomunista', *Italia Contemporanea*, 46 (1994), pp.791–806. On the international context and the anti-Communist American pressure, see M. Del Pero, *L'alleato scomodo. Gli USA e la DC negli anni del centrismo (1948–1955)* (Rome: Carocci, 2001), pp.230ff.
8. The first and better known of the two volumes contained studies by important scholars: see *Il second Risorgimento. Nel decennale della Resistenza e del ritorno alla democrazia 1945–1955* (Rome: Istituto Poligrafico dello Stato, 1955). The second, instead, was an anthology of literary texts for schools: A. Marchetti and G. Tassinari (eds), *La Resistenza nella letteratura*, preface by G. Gronchi (Milan: Ass.ne Parigiani Alfredo di Dio, 1955), Verb. Cons. dei Ministri, meeting 29 January 1955.
9. G. Crainz, 'I programmi. Dalla Liberazione ai primi anni Settanta', in *La Resistenza italiana nei programmi della Rai* (Rome: Rai-Eri, 1996), p.44.
10. ACS, PCM, 1959–62, cat.3.3.3, f.8859, sf.7.2.
11. This issue was the first dealing with the Resistance; it originated from a proposal by the ANPI (Associazione Nazionale Partigiani d'Italia). See ACS, PCM, 1951–54, cat.3.3.3, f.8859, sf.7.3.
12. See the six reports sent to the prefects from 13 March to 15 April 1955. In ACS, PCM, 1951–54, cat.3.3.3, f.8859, sf.1.

13. See, in this regard, the 'Appunto', dated 3 March 1955, drawn up by the Cabinet of the Prime Minister's Office regarding the envisaged ceremonies, issue 8, ibid.
14. Ibid.
15. In a letter written on 15 May 1955 by Raffaele Cadorna, President of the FIVL (Federazione Italiana Volontari della Libertà), to Prime Minister Scelba, the General stated that 'The reactions of the circles of public opinion near to us have been excellent; finally this year we have been able, effectively, to oppose and in some zones even sink the communist organization of the ANPI'. ACS, PCM, 1951–54, cat.3.3.3, f.8859, sf.1.
16. See ACS, PCM, 1951–54, cat. 3.3.3, f.8859, sf.7.2b 'Decennale della Liberazione manifestazioni nelle varie città d'Italia': the bulky file contains the prefects' catalogues of all the evens (massacres, battles, etc.) worthy of note which had taken place between 1943 and 1945 in their respective provinces. Each prefect also proposed some evaluations regarding which events it would be most appropriate to commemorate, the commemorative policies of past years, who was contesting the guardianship of memory.
17. *Israel*, 28–29, 21 April 1955.
18. Regarding the difficult integration of the Jewish tragedy in the national and patriotic *epos* in the countries of Western Europe, see P. Lagrou, 'Victims of Genocide and National Memory: Belgium, France and the Netherlands', *Past & Present*, 154 (1997), pp.181–222. Regarding France, see A. Wieviorka, *Déportation et Génocide. Entre la mémoire et l'oubli* (Paris: Plon, 1992), in particular pp.391–431.
19. Regarding the whole ceremony, see *Israel*, 28–29, 21 April 1955. See also P. Bertilotti, 'Italian Jews and the Memory of Rescue (1944–1961)', in J. Semelin, C. Andrieu and S. Grensburger (eds), *Resisting Genocide. The Multiple Forms of Rescue* (New York: Columbia University Press, 2011), pp.127–43, but in particular see pp.139–43.
20. On the general climate of the age and the suppression of the anti-fascist message, see M. Flores, 'L'antifascismo all'opposizione', in *Fascismo e antifascismo negli anni della Repubblica*, monographic issue of *Problemi del Socialismo*, 28 (1986), pp.34–60, in particular pp.44–6.
21. See *Israel*, 16, 20 December 1956; see also 'Testimonianza italiana di fraternità durante le persecuzioni razziali', *RMI*, 1, XXXI (1957).
22. R. De Felice, *Storia degli ebrei italiani sotto il fascismo* (Turin: Einaudi, 1993 [1961]), p.472.
23. R. Hilberg, *The Destruction of European Jews* (New York and London: Holmes & Meier, 1985 [1961]).
24. Regarding Israeli memories see at least T. Segev, *The Seventh Million: The Israelis and the Holocaust* (New York: Hill and Wang, 1993); I. Zerthal, *Israel's Holocaust and the Politics of Nationhood* (Cambridge: Cambridge University Press, 2005).

9

The Union of Italian-Jewish Communities and the Historiography on Fascist Anti-Semitism

A COMMITMENT FOR THE HISTORY OF THE PERSECUTION

The representatives of Italian Judaism demonstrated, as we have shown so far, a scarce inclination for a truly historical analysis of the recent past, nevertheless they were undoubtedly interested in the preservation of memory and the drawing up of a history of the persecutions. From the Minutes of the Council of the Union it is possible to reconstruct the great commitment, between 1945 and 1961, of the leaders of Italian-Judaism in promoting essays and studies which would document the persecution undergone.

The need to see their own tragedy accurately documented was clearly perceived as early as the immediate post-war period, as can be seen from the resolution, dated 15 July 1945, with which the Union's temporary commissioner Giuseppe Nathan instituted a Centre for Jewish Documentation and Studies whose task should have been, among other things, to 'prepare the material for a history of Judaism in Italy in recent years, in particular in the period of the persecutions'. Gino Luzzatto, Anselmo Colombo, Guido de Angelis and Vittore Colorni should have been called to direct the above-mentioned Centre, but it does not appear that this actually happened. The first failures did not cancel the deep need to see their collective suffering reconstructed; the need to construct the history of the persecutions was re-proposed almost two years later during a meeting of the Union's Committee held on 2 December 1947: President Cantoni referred, at that time, to the 'problem of the publications to be drawn up by the Union and, in the first place, one which would recall the persecutions undergone by Italian Jews and another one which would cover the history of Zionism, from Hertzl to our times'. In the ensuing discussion, an attempt was made to identify the people to whom it would be possible to entrust this task; with this aim in mind, the following names were proposed: Luciano Morpurgo, Carlo Alberto Viterbo and Massimo Adolfo Vitale.[1] Also in this case it does not seem that, at least as regards the history of the persecution, that first hypothesis was subsequently realized. At least not in the short term.

Among the names indicated in the above-mentioned meeting of the Committee, the key figure to bear in mind in order to reconstruct the UCII's activities, or rather the activities indirectly supported by the Jewish leadership as regards the history of the persecutions, is Massimo Adolfo Vitale. He is among that category of people – in general few and isolated individuals in Europe, America or in Israel who, with the cessation of hostilities, set out with tenacious perseverance to gather data and testimonies, stimulating individuals and the communities to remember. The history of these figures has received scant attention: they were often marginal and isolated voices, yet this does not mean that they are not of great interest to scholars, who want to trace the tortuous paths of memory. In fact, the work conducted by such men, only rarely professional historians, suggests how, with greater attention, with the will to review the events critically, it would have been possible to arrive earlier at a problematic and historically valid vision of the tragedy: those who had the courage to look into the abyss could discover precious strands of truth.[2]

The obstinate seeker of documents and testimonies, whose activities we are about to describe, was a retired army Colonel, interested in history, particularly in military-colonial studies; a scarcely practicing Jew but deeply affected by State racism.[3] In the post-war period, he was primarily involved as the director of the CRDE (Comitato Ricerche Deportati Ebrei – Committee for the Search of Deported Jews). Created on 26 September 1944, under the aegis of the Union of Italian Jewish Communities, that Committee had to answer to the ever more pressing necessities of tracing and helping the deportees, but the activities, not without difficulties, gradually expanded to consider historical research on the persecutions.[4] From that standpoint and having been appointed by Raffaele Cantoni, Vitale tried to gather the data to reconstruct the history of the anti-Jewish persecution, and with this aim in view in December 1947 he sent a letter asking for information and testimonies from all the Jewish communities. Seeing the scant collaboration received, the first letter was followed by a second request, dated 24 June 1948, in which he complained about how his previous appeal had been received 'with almost general indifference'. The lack of success encountered also by this last attempt led him to turn (probably in 1949) to the President of the Union, asking for his intervention.[5]

We do not know what the outcome was of the request for a direct intervention by the President of the UCII in order to encourage the various communities to forward all the available information regarding the persecution. In any case, the difficulties and resistance encountered by Vitale suggest a very scant willingness on the part of Italian Jews to come to terms with the past. In those first ten years, there were few people who contributed to preserving the memory of past events and to interpreting what had happened and, as has been seen, many of those who did so seemed inclined to shelve it rather than analyse it rigorously. Vitale was, therefore, under many aspects, an exception: no one else, it appears, in that period, gave so much time and energy to studying the Italian aspect of the Shoah.

The main result of Vitale's efforts to reconstruct the recent past is a report of over twenty pages written in French and entitled 'Les persecutions contre les juifs en Italie 1938–1945',[6] an expanded and unpublished version of a report presented in Paris in 1947, at the First European Congress of the Contemporary Jewish Documentation Centres.[7] Vitale certainly did not have the training or the sensibility of a professional historian, despite this, although not without its limitations, that report is characterized by a high level of originality and a strong autonomy when compared to the interpretations of the phenomenon prevalent at the time.

In very concise terms, it could be said that the distinctive features of Vitale's reconstruction of events are his judgement on the reaction of the Italians to the racial campaign and on the Church's behaviour. He states that before the beginning of the racial campaign anti-Semitism had been virtually non-existent in Italy and that the people had reacted to the sudden *volte-face* displaying its own disapproval and sympathy for the victims;[8] and up to this point his observations essentially retrace the interpretative canon then dominant. However, he significantly adds: 'But the government's insistence in the campaign of denigration, the advantages which the campaign itself had brought to many, the threats against those who showed compassion towards the victims did not fail to bear fruit. Those who had the courage to show their disapproval of the atrocities which were being committed were fewer and fewer.'[9]

He proceeds along this line in reconstructing the events following 8 September 1943:

> After the Armistice, the courageous people who ignored the dangers to save some Jews were not lacking, but there were few of them, while the policemen together with the *Carabinieri*, in almost all the cases, carried out their activity of betrayal, house searches, arrest and transfer to the camps of internment and death.
>
> We have gathered vast documentation relating to this, regarding all the Italian regions.[10]

Vitale's patient and methodical in-depth research on the fate of individual deportees enabled him to find a documentation which overturned many of the theses commonly accepted about Italian innocence.[11] In the above-mentioned report, the Director of the CRDE showed a notable independence of judgement also in evaluating the activity of the Church: he condemned, in fact, the ambiguity of Vatican policy, without however denying the value of the activity carried out by individual members of the religious hierarchy, and stated that the Vatican could have significantly changed the course of events if it had committed itself in more explicit terms and had done so from the beginning of the persecutions.[12] In Vitale's work, the historical research was accompanied by a daily battle to monitor and fight the demonstrations of anti-Semitism; he was thus led to commit himself more and more to stimulate a more accurate understanding of the Jewish situation in post-fascist Italy,[13] undertaking, among other things, a campaign, conducted with insistence together with his brother Enrico starting in 1945, to induce the Church to modify the Catholic liturgy of Good Friday.[14]

His solitary efforts succeeded, on several occasions, in influencing – even if indirectly – the development of the historiographic debate. The documentation he gathered served as a basis for numerous important works, including the Italian edition of the book by Gerhart Reitlinger on the extermination of the European Jews.[15] Vitale's work marked, above all, the very first studies dealing with the history of fascist anti-Semitism, that is the contributions of Antonio Spinosa and – in different forms – also Renzo De Felice's book.

After the work by Eucardio Momigliano, with which we have already dealt, a second crucial passage in the analysis of fascist anti-Semitism was the publication of four essays written by the journalist Antonio Spinosa for *Il Ponte*, published between July 1952 and July 1953 and unexpectedly interrupted without the fifth and last article – which should have tackled the period 1943–1945 – ever being published.[16] Vitale and the UCII gave a significant contribution to the drawing up of those texts.

The idea of those articles came from the Editor of the periodical, Piero Calamandrei, who as early as August 1949 had expressed, in a letter to Carlo Galante Garrone, the desire to 'find someone who will conduct, for *Il Ponte*, a kind of investigation, to be published in one or more instalments, on racism in Italy… Those are events which everyone is about to forget: no one talks about them any more: and names and facts are forgotten'.[17] There were contacts with the UCII: Raffaele Cantoni spoke about it for the first time in the Union's Council meeting of 14 January 1951, adding that 'Col. Vitale has already presented a lot of the material previously gathered';[18] the CRDE directed by Vitale provided 'Antonio Spinosa with letters, articles, documents, books and photographs'.[19] Vitale, who had reached a precarious agreement of collaboration with Spinosa,[20] stated on various occasions that an expanded version of his above-mentioned report 'served as a basis' for Spinosa's work.[21] Spinosa never refers to the report and only mentions once documents indicated to him by Vitale;[22] there are also important discrepancies between the two texts, but from a careful reading it emerges clearly that he utilized, in his articles, not only concepts similar to those proposed by Vitale but, in some cases reproduced the same sentences, the very same paragraphs. This is particularly evident as regards the critical judgement on the Church's activities.[23] Excepting that passage, it should be noted that Spinosa did not know how to make the most of the critical elements, the most original and interesting ideas present in Vitale's work. His essays reproduced, in effect, the interpretative canon then prevalent; as regards the general interpretation of fascist anti-Semitism the text published in *Il Ponte* is closer to the theses of Eucardio Momigliano than to those of Vitale.

In any case, the UCII recognized, in Calamandrei's initiative, the long-awaited opportunity to draw up a systematic history of the persecutions. Probably, in view of that goal, on 27 January 1953, Vitale wrote a first 'Sommario per la storia delle persecuzioni nazi-fasciste contro gli ebrei in Italia

1938–1945' ('Outline for the History of the Nazi-Fascist Persecutions of the Jews in Italy, 1938–1945').[24] Shortly afterwards, in a meeting of the Council of the UCII of 4 March 1953, Vice-President Dante Lattes informed the meeting about 'ongoing negotiations with the periodical *Il Ponte* and Dr Spinosa for the publication of a book on the persecutions'. On that occasion, Cantoni also intervened, informing the meeting about contacts, with the same end in view, with Tristano Codignola, which suggests that an agreement was being sought with the Florentine publisher La Nuova Italia. Cantoni also made other interesting observations, the minutes summarize the gist of his intervention: '[Cantoni] underlines the possibility that the publication might not be drawn up by Jews, but assures that, in any case, Col. Vitale, the engineer Piperno and the representative of the FGEI Mr Liberovici will collaborate on the work'.[25]

The last two people mentioned are Fernando Piperno, Secretary of the FGEI, and Sergio Liberovici, a left-wing militant, who later made himself known for his research in popular songs and musical folklore,[26] who at that time was particularly active in a Jewish Youth Federation which – as we have already seen – was mobilizing itself, with conviction, to link itself with the anti-fascist *epos* of the Resistance.

The contact with Spinosa and La Nuova Italia did not come to anything. The voluntary commitment of the young Sergio Liberovici, who in the spring of 1953 took on the project, did not lead to the drawing up of the desired work. Although the FGEI and its federated Jewish Youth Centres had committed themselves to support the planned publication, and also despite a first allocation of 200,000 liras by the UCII,[27] the planned publication stalled as early as February 1954.[28] Among other things, the clashes between the FGEI and the UCII had an impact: at that time, the tension between the Jewish ruling class and the Youth Federation was very high, reflecting the intensity of the political confrontation which was dividing the country.[29]

On abandoning the project he had taken on, Liberovici passed all the papers he had accumulated to another activist of the FGEI, Roberto Bassi.[30] He worked for the establishment of the· Centro di Documentazione Ebraica Contemporanea (Contemporary Jewish Documentation Centre), to whose constitution the FGEI had already committed itself as early as 1953.[31] The Centre, which officially came into being in 1955, found a first, provisional seat in Venice, in Bassi's own home. It had a precarious beginning, being able to count on the determined impetus of the FGEI and also on the less enthusiastic, but economically more relevant support of the UCII since 1956.[32]

At the same time, the Jewish leadership continued to foster the plan for the drawing up of a monograph on the persecution and, in fact, in the meeting of the Council of 17 June 1956, in allocating funds for cultural activities, 500,000 liras were set aside for the 'completion of the work of A. Spinosa on the persecutions in Italy'.[33] Shortly afterwards, on 30 September, the Committee of the Union formally charged Massimo Adolfo Vitale to 'gather the material which will be needed for the composition of the publication, also consulting the writer Antonio Spinosa, who had already written four articles in Il Ponte'.[34] On 13 December of the same year, the Committee intervened again on this subject, confirming that it was up to Vitale to gather the documentary material, and allocating for that task 200,000 liras, but also laying down that the writing of the work would be entrusted to the writer Bravetta for which he would receive 800,000 liras, the method of payment to be decided upon. As regards the publication of the work, Mr Levi is charged with making contact with a publisher. The summaries prepared by Col. Vitale will be examined by various Councillors and the Committee reaffirms the principle that the Council will be the arbiter of the final text of the 'History of the Persecutions'.[35]

The leadership of the UCII had therefore defined a clear objective, the publication of a book on the history of the persecutions, and also delineated a precise methodology: *the text should have followed the approach of Vitale's research* – who at that time was writing a new and more detailed summary approved by the Committee[36] – *and subject to the careful monitoring by the Council, but the drawing up of the work should have been entrusted to a non-Jew.* The UCII scrupulously followed that plan of action, even if, for a few more years, the attempts to find a suitable author were unsuccessful.

The contact established with the journalist Vittorio Emanuele Bravetta did not produce the hoped-for results. The choice of that person was criticized from several quarters, also because he had become known as the author of paeans to Mussolini and Badoglio published between 1939 and 1941.[37] In December 1957, that hypothesis came to a standstill and the Council tried to retrieve – once again without a positive outcome – the Spinosa option.[38] The umpteenth failure led, in March 1958, to a decision to 'wait before entrusting the task to another person'.[39] Everything restarted at the beginning of the 1960s, the theme of anti-Semitism was suddenly once again of burning topicality and it was finally possible to find an author, seeing in the young Renzo De Felice 'the right man at the right time'.[40]

•

THE GENESIS OF RENZO DE FELICE'S BOOK ON FASCIM AND THE JEWS

Between January and February 1960 a wave of anti-Semitic demonstrations, which accompanied the emergence of a network of neo-Nazi movements, struck the whole of Europe and also Italy, provoking alarmed reactions in the Jewish world.[41] This stimulated in some people the natural desire to promote a better knowledge of the historical roots of the phenomenon,[42] reconfirming the urgency and the importance of a more effective preservation of memory: 'never as in these days has the necessity, even more than the usefulness, of a well-stocked and adequately organized documentation centre emerged more clearly', Roberto Bassi wrote, on 2 February, to Massimo Adolfo Vitale.[43] Bassi was inclined to yield to others the direction of the CDEC and this, together with the determination to supervise appropriately the growth of the Centre, led him – in collaboration with Guido Neppi Modona – to outline a farsighted development plan: first of all, the young historian Guido Valabrega was regarded as suitable to follow the development of the body born in 1955 thanks to the decision of the FGEI. Such a hypothesis envisaged the transfer of the accumulated records from Venice to Milan, where a new seat of the CDEC had been created in a building made available by the local Jewish community; at the same time, the outlines of a statute were drawn up and furthermore the setting up of a board of governors, which saw Massimo Adolfo Vitale as President, was planned.[44]

The outbursts of anti-Semitism at the beginning of 1960 also renewed, within the UCII, the desire to promote the drawing up of a detailed history of the persecution and gave rise to an increased interest in the fate of the CDEC: taking up again an idea which had been developed some years earlier, within the Council of the UCII,[45] President Piperno considered transferring the records to Rome in the offices of the Union itself, however, provoking some unease in the FGEI, which wanted to safeguard the autonomy of its Centre.[46] By April 1960, the distinct plans of the FGEI and the UCII emerged quite clearly; the question was resolved in a meeting of the UCII's Council on 25 April 25, when the future of the CDEC was separated from the plan of a history of fascist anti-Semitism: the Council, in fact, voted to entrust to the young scholar Renzo De Felice the task of writing the longed-for book on the persecutions, while it approved, with some reservations, the transfer of the CDEC from Venice to Milan.[47] Thus the development of two separate initiatives unfolded, the one of the Union which led to the publication of an important monograph by De Felice, and that of the CDEC, directed by Guido Valabrega, who, while collaborating in the UCII plan, would in the meantime have carried forward his own autonomous plan of historical analysis, which within a few years led to the publication of three important booklets containing significant research essays as well as original testimonies.[48]

De Felice's name was arrived at in successive stages. Desiring to give the work prestige and prominence, President Piperno tried to entrust the drawing up of the book on fascist anti-Semitism to a famous historian. With this aim in mind, at the beginning of 1960, the outline drawn up in 1956 by Vitale was submitted to Prof. Alberto Maria Ghisalberti, who however declined the project.[49] In the meantime, Vitale and some Councillors called the President's attention to the figure of Renzo De Felice. The latter, since 1953, had taken an interest in the study of Jewish history, coming into contact with the circles of the *Rassegna Mensile di Israel*, directed by Dante Lattes, where he published several articles dedicated to the history of the Jews and anti-Semitism before and after the unification of Italy.[50]

Piperno appreciated this suggestion and so, as early as 7 April, in a circular forwarded to all the Councillors in view of the meeting of 25 April, was able to write that he had 'already spoken in general terms with Dr De Felice, who would be willing to accept the task'.[51] The issue was however still undecided; apparently Piperno preferred to entrust the task to Ghisalberti and approached him again. The latter definitively rejected the offer in a letter dated 16 April. In the same letter, pressed by Piperno who was asking for information, Ghisalberti warmly recommended, for the task, the young De Felice.[52] Just five days later, the President of the UCII invited De Felice to 'begin the preparatory work'[53] and on 29 April a contract was signed between De Felice and the UCII: it stipulated the drawing up of a book 'understandable by the general public', provisionally entitled *Storia delle persecuzioni nazi-fasciste contro gli ebrei in Italia 1938/1945* (*History of the Nazi-Fascist Persecutions of the Jews in Italy 1938/1945*), to be completed by 31 March.[54]

Keeping to the plan of action already outlined in 1956, the UCII provided the appointed author with all the material at its disposal, facilitating as much as possible the work of the young historian. He was granted full and free access to the papers of the UCII itself, access to the Central State Archives was facilitated; furthermore Massimo Adolfo Vitale – charged by Piperno – closely followed the progress of the work,[55] and made available to De Felice all the documentary and bibliographical material he had gathered over the years[56] and finally acted as an intermediary between De Felice and the CDEC. The Milanese Centre sent, to Rome, the complete series of the fascist periodical *La Difesa della Razza*[57] and subsequently also the microfilms of a periodical of the pro-fascist and anti-Zionist Italian-Jewish movement La Nostra Bandiera.[58] To complete the picture of the assistance De Felice received, it should be added that, from November 1960 to June 1961, he corresponded with Dante Lattes. The young historian turned to the latter, at the suggestion of the Presidency of the UCII, to ask for clarification on certain issues, including the conflicts within the UCII in 1935 and the difficulties encountered in placing the figure of Enzo Sereni in the context of Italian Zionism. Through the UCII, De Felice submitted the first draft of the manuscript to Lattes, while the latter made some suggestions and a few minor criticisms.[59]

This does not mean that De Felice's work was not carried out autonomously, in fact it does not appear that he was subject to censure of any kind from Vitale and Lattes, President Piperno, the Council of the UCII or the Commission appointed by the latter in March 1961 for a necessary verification of the text prior to its publication.[60] The scholar enjoyed 'invaluable Jewish support',[61] which undoubtedly eased his task, facilitating the tracing of documents and publications, helping him in his contacts with witnesses and scholars, finally also assisting him after the work had been published. The UCII in fact guaranteed a widespread dissemination of the book, sending hundreds of complimentary copies to leading figures of Italian politics and culture, Italian and foreign academic and research institutions, ranging from France to Germany, from the United States to Israel.[62]

The exceptional support afforded to the author by the UCII, as well as the notable gifts as a researcher of the young De Felice, meant that the work could be drawn up in a very short time: from the first contacts, of 16 April 1960, until the handing over of the complete manuscript to the publisher Einaudi, at the beginning of June 1961, just over a year elapsed.[63] Thus *Storia degli ebrei italiani sotto il fascismo*, was published in the series Biblioteca di Cultura Storica Einaudi, with an important preface by an influential scholar such as Delio Cantimori.

Thus, the cultural project developed by the Jewish ruling class with tenacity and determination, since the end of the war, was crowned with success. The motivation for such a strong commitment, which lasted for over fifteen years, certainly included the desire to remember the victims of the tragedy, to repel the revival of racial hatred thanks to the preservation of memory, but – apart from all this – it is possible to perceive the desperate wish to see one's own drama recognized and respected. Although throughout the post-war period the leadership of the UCII had energetically stated over and over again its full confidence in the Italian people and the Republican institutions, it had to realize, with bitterness, how its requests were often not heeded by the government. The needs and the rights of the persecuted did not always receive full and immediate attention from State institutions, and this was also due to the fact that the weight of the injustices suffered by the Jews since July 1938 took a long time to be correctly assessed by the politicians and by public opinion.[64]

The problem of the lack of perception or understanding of the seriousness of the events which had taken place in the country after the beginning of the racist campaign would not have been resolved by producing a book, even though documented and exceptionally visible. The motivation for the lack of attention and interest, on the part of the authorities, for the problems of reintegration depended upon the practice of abdicating collective responsibility which had grown since the end of the war through historical representations which depicted the country as essentially innocent, the victim itself of a racial delirium considered decidedly foreign to its own sensibility and history. A myth fuelled for a long time by the Jewish ruling class itself and which Renzo De Felice's innovative and solid research would not have eradicated.

SILENCES AND CONTROVERSIES

Although presenting new elements, the result of the methodical investigation carried out, De Felice's interpretation of the racial persecution was strongly influenced by the cultural stereotypes which had consolidated in Italian society after Liberation. If, on the one hand, that work proved that fascist anti-Semitic policies were not the product of direct or indirect German pressure, on the other hand, it substantially confirmed the idea that anti-Semitism had been rejected by the nation and little or badly applied: taking up again a widely held prejudice, which was crystallized in a real historiographical paradigm, De Felice presented 1938 as the moment of the definitive split between the Italians and the regime.[65]

Inevitably, the interpretative tradition which had taken shape over more than fifteen years, and which found important confirmation between the end of the 1950s and the early 1960s, strongly influenced the reconstruction by the scholar from Rieti. We should remember that precisely in the phase immediately prior to the start of the young De Felice's important research (which, as we have seen, started at the beginning of April 1960), the innocence and honesty of the Italians were solemnly confirmed on two important occasions by two variously influential figures. In the first place, it is worth remembering how the weekly *Israel* commemorated the twentieth anniversary of the start of the persecutory campaign; in the issue of 17 July 1958 its editor, Carlo Alberto Viterbo, recalled the publication of the well-known 'Manifesto degli scienziati razzisti' ('Manifesto of Racist Scientists') and then the stages which had led to the deportations and the massacres, but a desperate desire for reconciliation prevailed over a detached evocation of the facts. Viterbo wrote, 'We want nevertheless to give credit to Italy and to the majority of Italians; to put those horrors down to the pressure which came from beyond the Alps, to the evil of a few followers. We want to celebrate a twentieth anniversary of reconciliation.'[66]

There was an even more sensational collective absolution of the Italians during the trial of Adolf Eichmann – the architect of the National Socialist system of extermination – which took place in Jerusalem between 1960 and 1961. In his opening statement in the trial, the Chief Appeal Court Prosecutor of the State of Israel, Gideon Hausner, made only a brief reference to Italy, concentrating exclusively on the events following 8 September 1943 and presenting the country as only a satellite state, occupied and therefore lacking autonomy. Taking care, however, to highlight the exceptional rescue operations carried out by the population.[67] Furthermore, on 11 May 1961, during the trial which was naturally followed by the main Italian dailies, as well as by the Italian-Jewish weekly *Israel*,[68] there was the testimony of an Italian citizen, which was significantly distorted by the press. The witness herself (Hulda Cassuto Campagnano) complained about this, she noted that her words had been totally misrepresented by the reports of the trial in the newspapers *La Nazione* and *Il Resto del Carlino*:[69]

> having received some Italian newspapers ... I was disagreeably surprised and hurt in seeing how my words had been badly interpreted, perhaps because of the translation from Hebrew ... I have never spoken of 'the

> unanimous help of the Italian people', but of help which came from all the strata of the population. If the help had really been unanimous how many fewer victims there would have been![70]

There is a notable discrepancy between the original testimony and the summary given by the Italian dailies.[71] This event uncovers issues which transcend the mere problem of bad translations; I think this case illustrates very well the spirit of the times and helps us to understand how deeply entrenched the Italian tendency to self-absolution was.

It is difficult to believe that the young Renzo De Felice could be completely indifferent to the moods which were permeating the general cultural climate. Perhaps he did not know of Viterbo's statements which we quoted above, but certainly he had followed the Eichmann trial, which he did not fail to mention on various occasions, also recalling the absolution of Italy which had been decreed by that court.[72]

It is precisely because of the inevitable cultural conditioning to which the historian must have been subjected, that the support which, in the first editions of the work (1961 and 1972), he gave to the historiographical myth of the split between the Italians and the regime following the racist turning point, is completely understandable and justifiable; the stubbornness with which the historian wanted to defend that approach, starting from the expanded edition of 1988, appears nevertheless decidedly less valid and legitimate. During the 1980s, the studies on the fascist regime during the 1930s had undergone an important development and it is strange that De Felice himself, who had contributed significantly to that progress, also raising the thorny issue of the consensus afforded to the regime, seemed determined to stop the development of the reflection on the specific problem of the consensus given to the anti-Jewish campaign. During the 1980s and the early 1990s, the scholar insisted more and more on the differences between Italian fascism and National Socialism.[73] The themes of anti-Semitism and racism were also placed in this historiographical scenario: they were part of De Felice's interpretation, regarded by some as having a political end in view, in which they were presented as key elements through which operate a radical separation of fascism and Nazism.[74]

The problem of the comparison with the German case naturally has its specific historiographical importance, but one cannot help noting that the terms in which the comparison was approached by De Felice, and earlier still – since the end of the war – by vast circles which included Italian diplomacy, wide sectors of the world of culture, Jewish memoirs, but also the foreign press, simply led to the establishment of the minor gravity of fascist (and Italian) crimes. Generally, this conclusion was followed by the tendency to discard the hypothesis that racism and fascist anti-Semitism deserved deeper study.

It is easy to recognize the important differences between the choices made by National Socialism and those of Italian fascism regarding racial persecution, and certainly in Italy anti-Semitism never played a role comparable to the one it assumed in the Nazi system. This, however, does not mean that Italian anti-Semitism was only a superficial operation, of no importance, without any roots and without any terrible and lasting consequences. The enormity, the exceptional and devastating nature of the genocide perpetrated by the Nazi regime has resulted in Nazi anti-Semitism being elevated to an abstract model, in relation to which other and different historical experiences came to be presented. The enormous tragedy of European Judaism has for a long time acted as a lightning conductor, drawing upon itself people's attention and distorting the perception of anti-Jewish persecutions different from that of Nazism: 'Auschwitz has ended up killing, together with the Jews, also the memory of the other chronological and geographical stages of their persecutions'.[75] Several decades had to elapse to clarify this misinterpretation and to recognize that 'not all the anti-Semitisms lead to Auschwitz', thus freeing them from 'the demon of analogy' and beginning the study of each phenomenon in its uniqueness.[76]

So much time has been necessary also because, far from representing a first step towards the beginning of a period of intense research, the book published by De Felice in 1961 remained – for many years – the only detailed contribution to the subject. In promoting the drawing up and the publication of De Felice's work, the UCII had made up for the lack of initiative on the part of the relevant institutions (universities and research institutes), but obviously those efforts were not sufficient to stimulate a real interest among historians. Also because the book came out at a time when research on fascism was still at an early stage (the investigations on the origins of, and the conquest of power by the fascist movement were just starting), while the overall climate, characterized by an interest in scandals and the political exploitation of the subject, certainly did not favour the harmonious development of research. The publication of the work was followed by lively controversies, above all with regard to the names – some cited and others not mentioned – of accomplices or collaborators of the racist campaign who in the post-war period had attained positions of great prestige and had become prominent in Italian politics and culture. The most sensational case was that of Leopoldo Piccardi, then secretary of the Radical Party, who was forced to resign as a result of the De Felice's allegations regarding his role in the fascist racist campaign, leading to a crisis in the party.[77] Overall the book did not trigger meaningful debate in the academic community, while it stimulated scandalistic campaigns and personal accusation.[78] Such dynamics testify of the spirit of the times and of the way in which Italian society, and above all the party system and the main dailies, tended to approach the problem of the relationship with the fascist past.

Various political and cultural factors, and perhaps also a generational turning point, such as emerges in the youth protests of July 1960,[79] undoubtedly stimulated in Italian society a greater interest in the past, and particularly in the issue of fascism/anti-fascism. This finds confirmation in the success of the repeated cycles of lectures and lessons – later published by important publishers – which took place between 1959 and 1961. The problem of the anti-Jewish persecution tended, however, to remain beyond the horizon: it is significant that on those occasions little or no space was given to the regime's racist and anti-Semitic policies, which were only dealt with in superficial and formal references.[80] It was obviously still too early; Italian historiography continued for many years to show its lack of interest in this question.[81] Only since the 1980s did different sensibility lead to a new season of research and in-depth analysis, both critical and documentary.[82] This led to a substantial historiographical revision,[83] which developed during the 1990s together with the crisis of the so-called 'anti-fascist paradigm' and of the system of memories on which the political system and the mechanisms of self-representation of the Italians had been founded since 1945,[84] but which has undoubtedly also felt the influence of the progress in the historiographical debate about the consensus to the regime, as well as the echo of the *Historikerstreit*. This and other factors have to be taken into account when considering the evolution of the self-image of the Jewish minority: since the 1980s it was possible, for some sectors of the Italian Jewish world, to begin to question themselves and to challenge the usual representations of the past.

NOTES

1. See Verb. Giunta.
2. For a historical contextualization of the efforts of those pioneers in different countries, see B. Cohen, 'Holocaust Survivors and the Genesis of Holocaust Research', in D. Johannes-Steinert and I. Weber-Newth (eds), *Beyond Camps and Forced Labour: Current International Research on Survivors of Nazi Persecution* (Osnabrück: Secolo Verlag, 2005), pp.290–300; L. Jockush, 'Khurban Forshung: Jewish Historical Commission in Europe 1945–1949', *Simon Dubnow Institute Yearbook*, 6 (2007), pp.441–73.
3. He had spent part of his career in the colonies and it should be pointed out that he was the author of some volumes of military history, documented but lacking historiographic depth, published for the series 'L'Italia in Africa. Serie storico-militare', *L'opera dell'esercito*, 3 vols (Rome: Istituto Poligrafico dello Stato, 1960–1964). During the fascist era, he had also written a novel (*Sotto le stelle lontane* (Milan: Alfieri e Lacroix, 1923)) in which there are many commonplaces and stereotypes typical of the depiction of life in the colonies. For some information about Vitale and his activity, see R. Bassi, *Ricordo di Massimo Adolfo Vitale*, *RMI*, 1–3 (1979), pp.8–21.
4. On the activity of the CRDE, see L. Picciotto Fargion, 'L'attività del comitato ricerche deportati ebrei. Storia di un lavoro pionieristico (1944–1953)', in Istituto Storico della Resistenza in Piemonte (ed.), *Una storia di tutti. Prigionieri, internati, deportati italiani nella seconda guerra mondiale* (Milan: Angeli, 1985), pp.75–96.
5. AUCII, b.74b, f. 'Vitale', 'Promemoria per il Presidente'. But see also AUCII, b.44c, f. 'Comitato Ricerche Deportati Ebrei', report entitled 'Attività del Comitato 1951–1956' presented on 21 March 1956 by Vitale to the President of the Union. There is a reference to this event in C. Forti, *Il caso Pardo Roques. Un eccidio del 1944 tra memoria e oblio* (Turin: Einaudi, 1998), pp.241ff.

6. AUCII, b.44c, f. 'Comitato Ricerche Deportati Ebrei', 'Attività del Comitato, p.1. The report entitled 'Les persécutions contre les juifs en Italie' is attached to a letter sent on 29 March 1954 by Vitale to the President of the Union Giorgio Zevi, ibid. A copy of the report is also in CAHJP, b.It 1213/1; as well as in the Archive of M.A. Vitale, in ACDEC, b.3, f. 'Conferenze, relazioni, interventi del Col. M.A. Vitale sulle persecuzioni contro gli ebrei sotto il nazi-fascismo', sf. 'Bozze di un sommario eindicazioni di M.A. Vitale per la compilazione di una storia delle persecuzioni contro gli ebrei in Italia dal 1938 al 1945'. At the CDEC there are two different versions: a first draft dated 16 January and a subsequent one, dated 16 November 1947, which coincides with those found in Rome and Jerusalem; it is the later version – henceforward called the '1947 version' – which will be referred to in the following pages.
7. See M.A. Vitale, 'Les persécutions contre les juifs en Italie', in Centre de Documentation Juive Contemporaine (ed.), *Les Juifs en Europe (1939–1945). Rapports présentés à la première conférence européene des commissions historiques et des centres de documentation juifs* (Paris: Edition du Centre, 1949), pp.43–5.
8. M.A. Vitale, 'Les persécutions contre les juifs en Italie', '1947 version', p.7, in AUCII, b.44C, f. 'Comitato Ricerche Deportati Ebrei'.
9. Ibid.
10. Ibid., p.8. My italics.
11. It should be noted that that work served as a basis for the completed investigation, several decades later, by Lilliana Picciotto Fargion, leading to the realization of *Libro della memoria. Gli ebrei deportati dall'Italia 1943-45* (Milan: Mursia, 2002).
12. M.A. Vitale, '1947 version', pp.10–11. He would not have failed, in the 1960s, to clash, on this point with the more cautious Raffaele Cantoni; see S.I. Minerbi, *Un ebreo fra D'Annunzio e il sionismo. Raffaele Cantoni*, preface by R. De Felice (Rome: Bonacci, 1992), pp.251–7.
13. In this regard, see 'The Jewish Situation in Italy after the Fall of the Nazi-Fascist Regime', report edited by M.A. Vitale and destined for the American public, in AHJP, b.1213/2. A copy of the report is also in ACDEC, M.A. Vitale Archive, b.3, f. 'Conferenze, relazioni, interventi del Col. M.A. Vitale sulle persecuzioni contro gli ebrei sotto il nazi-fascismo', sf. 'The Jewish Situation in Italy After the Fall of the Nazi-Fascist Regime'; the report is indicated as being of 1952.
14. See AUCII, b.44c, f. 'CRDE', the report entitled 'Attività del Comitato 1951–1956', dated 21 March 1956, in particular pp.4–5. The campaign conducted by the Vitale brothers and by others achieved success when, on 27 March 1959, Pope John XXIII decided on the removal from the Good Friday Catholic liturgy of the references to *perfidious Jews* and *Jewish perfidy*. Regarding the debates within the Catholic world after 1945 and the slow development of a liturgical reform, see M. Paiano, 'Il dibattito sui riflessi dell'antisemitismo nella liturgia cattolica', *Studi Storici*, 3 (2000), pp.647–710, in particular pp.675ff.
15. G. Reitlinger, *La soluzione finale. Il tentative di sterminio degli Ebrei d'Europa 1939–1945* (Milano: Il Saggiatore, 1962 [or. ed. *The Final Solution: The Attempt to Exterminate the Jews in Europe 1939–1945* (London: Vallentine Mitchell, 1953)]). See p.440 of the Italian edition: 'The Notes referring to the paragraph on *Italy* … are not, for the most part, included in the original English edition, inasmuch as they have been integrated or compiled by Prof. Massimo Adolfo Vitale'. The works influenced by Vitale include also the study by S. Jona, 'Contributo allo studio degli ebrei in Italia durante il fascism', in G. Valabrega (ed.), *Gli Ebrei in Italia durante il fascismo*, vol. II (Milan: CDEC, 1962), pp.20 and 23. I would like to thank Michele Sarfatti for his generosity in providing me with this information.
16. The reference is to A. Spinosa, 'Le persecuzioni razziali in Italia', *Il Ponte*, 7 (1952), pp.964–78; 8 (1952), pp.1078–96; 11 (1952), pp.1604–22; 7 (1953), pp.950–68. With slight changes, the texts were reprinted in the book: A. Spinosa, *Mussolini razzista riluttante*, preface by F. Perfetti (Milan: Mondadori, 1994). Some possible reasons for the brusque interruption, before the drawing up of the fifth article, are suggested in G. Mughini, *A Via della Mercede c'era un fascista* (Milan: Rizzoli, 1990), p.239, in note.
17. P. Calamandrei, *Lettere 1915–1956*, vol. II, edited by G. Agosti and A. Galante Garrone (Florence: La Nuova Italia, 1968), p.229.
18. Verb. Cons.
19. We are informed about this by L. Polese Remaggi, *'Il Ponte' di Calamandrei 1945–1956* (Florence: Olschki, 2001), p.387. Regarding the UCII's involvement in that operation, see UCII, *IV Congresso delle Comunità, Relazione del Consiglio (1956)* (Rome, 1956), p.31. In the reprint of his contributions (*Mussolini razzista riluttante*, pp.11–12), Spinosa stated that he wrote the articles at the request of Piero Calamandrei and consulting with Gaetano Salvemini.

20. Such an agreement did not prevent conflicts from emerging: Remaggi informs us that 'on 28 July 1952 Vitale wrote to Calamandrei that despite having reached a precautionary agreement with the author, the latter had not left the Committee the possibility of exercising any supervision prior to publication. Spinosa, in a letter of 9 September, explained to *Il Ponte* that he had no intention of submitting to the Committee's vetoes'. Remaggi suggests that the clash reflected Spinosa's treatment of the problem of the Aryanizations and of the 'market' of the discriminations, and hypothesizes that the CRDE 'was concerned that the image of the solidarity of the Jewish communities should not be tarnished'. L. Polese Remaggi, *'Il Ponte' di Calamandrei*, respectively pp.387 and 388.
21. See AUCII, b.44c, f. 'Comitato Ricerche Deportati Ebrei', M.A. Vitale's letter of 29 March 1954. See also the report entitled 'Attività del Comitato 1951–1956', p.1.
22. A. Spinosa, 'Le persecuzioni razziali in Italia', *Il Ponte*, 8 (1952), p.1086.
23. Compare, for example, the penultimate paragraph of p.11 of the report of M.A. Vitale, '1947 version', with the last paragraph of A. Spinosa, 'Le persecuzioni razziali in Italia', p.1089. The paragraph in question takes up again precisely Vitale's criticism of the Church's behaviour.
24. In ACDEC, M.A. Vitale Archive, b.3.
25. Verb. Cons.
26. In 1957, together with Michele Luciano Straniero, he set up 'Cantacronache'. He edited the book *Le canzoni della cattiva coscienza. La musica leggera in Italia* (Milan: Bompiani, 1964) with Michele Straniero, Emilio Jona and Giorgio De Maria. Among his works, dealing mainly with the recovery of songs of the popular struggle, we remember finally (with M. Straniero) *Canti della nuova Resistenza spagnola 1939–1961* (Turin: Einaudi, 1962).
27. Verb. Cons., meeting of 17 May 1953. During the meeting, Cantoni, among other things, 'points out that in the book there should be detailed accounts of the figures of the Resistance and that it should be thoroughly documented, through visits to the various concentration camps, the prisons, the countries where the Jews were interned, as well as collecting photographs of documents and of anything else which can be traced in police archives, which should be examined'.
28. Verb. Cons., meeting of 14 February 1954, during which Cantoni accused Liberovici of not having fulfilled his commitments. See also the different assessment of R. Bassi, *Ricordo di Massimo Adolfo Vitale*, pp.15–16.
29. Significantly, immediately after having informed those present of the end of the Liberovici plan, the discussion turned to a consideration of the excesses of the FGEI and the UCII President stated that the Youth Centres 'have to show moderation', threatening to send men from the Union 'for the appropriate propaganda'. Verb. Cons., meeting of 14 February 1954.
30. E. D'Angeli, who represents the FGEI in the UCII Council, communicates it officially in the meeting of the UCII Council of 27 March 1954. Cf. Verb. Cons.
31. See ibid., Part 1, Chapter 4, pp.95–6.
32. On 20–21 May 1956, there was the V UCII Congress. Motion n.8 calls upon the new Council to 'continue under its aegis to develop the initiative and to carry out the necessary procedures both in the communities and among private individuals to ensure that all the material regarding the recent tragic events of Italian Jews should be promptly entrusted to the Archive Centre; it calls upon the new Council of the Union to support by every means the above-mentioned Centre, and to set aside every year funds for the running of the Centre and the further development of its activities'. See *Verbali del Congresso* in Verb. Cons.
33. Verb. Cons.
34. Verb. Giunta.
35. Ibid.
36. 'Sommario degli argomenti da svolgere per la storia delle persecuzioni nazi-fasciste contro gli ebrei in Italia 1937/1945', in ACDEC, M.A. Vitale Archive, b.3. Dante Lattes was also involved in the plan; after having received a letter on 31 December 1956, the UCII President Sergio Piperno communicated the Committee's decision to publish as soon as possible a history of the persecution, and attached the 'Sommario' drawn up by Vitale, asking for his advice and opinion; in BARM, Dante Lattes Archive, b.556.
37. Among others, the attitude of the Councillor Eugenio Heiman was critical. See Verb. Cons., meeting of 31 March 1957.
38. Verb. Cons., meeting of 1 December 1957. 'The President reads a letter from Col. Vitale, President of the CRDE, which communicates that the writer Bravetta, for health reasons, will not be able to continue the work he had started about the history of the persecutions. The Council regrets this and charges Prof. Zevi to contact the journalist A. Spinosa so that he would see to the drawing up of the

history of the persecutions, in accordance with the indications already decided upon in the previous resolution.' That choice was also confirmed in the next meeting of the Committee: Verb. Giunta, 23 January 1958.

39. Verb. Cons., meeting of 18 March 1958.
40. Massimo Adolfo Vitale defined him like this in a letter of 30 April 1960 to Roberto Bassi, in ACDEC, Corrispondenza CDEC 1955–1960, f. 'Posta in arrivo 1960'.
41. Regarding the Italian-Jewish reactions see *Israel*, 12, 7 January 1960, and 13, 14 January 1960; see also Delibera della Giunta UCII in an urgent meeting of 5 January, in Verb. Giunta.
42. For example, Giorgio Romano wrote to Dante Lattes from Tel Aviv: 'I think that the Jewish press in Italy has treated inadequately and without an overall approach the anti-Semitic demonstrations (in what is their original aspect and in what is the result of an unconscious camouflage of irresponsible elements). There have been very ceremonious thanks for every gesture or word from the Italian authorities which signified disapproval of the anti-Semitic gestures, but not a word was uttered to stigmatize the silence of all these years which has meant the young know little or nothing of the Jewish tragedy of the twentieth century and of the horrors of the concentration camps and the deportations. It seems to me that the real argument to be dealt with, in a dignified way, and without going into an examination of the causes of, and the reaction to, the most recent events, which could also have appeared inappropriate'. Letter of 10 January 1960, in BARM, Dante Lattes Archive, b.559.
43. Letter sent to M.A. Vitale, the UCII and the Secretary of the FGEI, in ACDEC, Corrispondenza CDEC 1955–1960, f. 'Corrispondenza inviata 1960'.
44. The role of Valabrega, and the defining of a statute plan for the CDEC, are themes dealt with in a letter of 20 February 1960 sent by Roberto Bassito to M.A. Vitale. In ACDEC, Corrispondenza CDEC 1955–1960, f. 'Corrispondenza inviata'. But see, in more general terms, all Roberto Bassi's correspondence between February and April, ibid.
45. See Verb. Cons., meeting of 22 July 1956.
46. See Guido Neppi Modona's letter of 5 April 1960, in ACDEC, Corrispondenza CDEC 1955–1960, f. 'Corrispondenza in arrivo 1960'.
47. Verb. Cons. The Council decides 'to entrust Dr De Felice, who will avail himself of the collaboration of Col. Vitale and of the material of the Archive Centre, with the task of compiling the history of the persecutions, to be completed within a year with a remuneration of about 600/700 thousand liras'.
48. The reference is to the three short books edited by G. Valabrega which appeared with the title *Gli ebrei in Italia durante il fascismo*, the first appeared as *Quaderno della FGEI* (Milan: FGEI, 1961) and the last two with the title *Quaderno del CDEC* (Milan: CDEC, 1962–1963). The first included the proceedings of a conference entitled 'Gli ebrei durante il fascismo' (Turin, 23–24 April 1961), to which De Felice himself had been invited, although at the last moment he decided not to participate; see *Ha-Tikwà*, 3 (March 1961), and 4 (April 1961). Valabrega had originally thought of publishing the book as a special issue of the *RMI*, but the plan was rejected by Dante Lattes and by the UCII leadership; see BARM, Dante Lattes Archive, b.559.
49. In a letter sent to Dante Lattes on 8 April 1960, Piperno conveyed the difficulty encountered in finding a suitable person and pointed out that 'another attempt with Prof. [Alberto Maria] Ghisalberti had failed'. Attached to this letter there was another one, of 7 April, addressed to all the UCII Councillors, who were asked to consider discussing the advisability of entrusting the drawing up of the history of the persecutions to De Felice, informing them of 'having spoken in general terms to Dr De Felice, who was willing to accept the task immediately and who has made a very favourable impression on me, also because he could have the possibility of consulting Prof. Ghisalberti with whom he is already in contact for reasons of work', in BARM, Dante Lattes Archive, b.559. Alberto Maria Ghisalberti (1894–1986), has been a prominent scholar of the Italian Risorgimento. He began his carrier at the University of Rome in 1931, obtaining the title of full Professor in 1936. He distanced himself from the fascist regime since 1938 and the beginning of the anti-Semitic campaign, which hit severely his wife Marcella Minerbi (of Jewish origins). After the Armistice he went to Rome where he lived in hiding, actively collaborating with the Resistance movement. After the war he was director of the Istituto per la Storia del Risorgimento [Institute for the History of the Resurgence] and rapidly obtained recognition as a prominent scholar within the Faculty of Humanities of the University of Rome. For further information, see the entry dedicated to his figure by G. Talamo in *Dizionario Biografico degli Italiani*.
50. See P. Simoncelli, *Renzo De Felice. La formazione intellettuale* (Florence: Le Lettere, 2001), Chapters

5 and 6. See also M. Toscano, 'Renzo De Felice storico dell'ebraismo e dell'antisemitismo', in G. Alberti and G. Parlato (eds), *Renzo De Felice. Il lavoro dello storico tra ricerca e didattica* (Milan: LED, 1999), pp.191–202.

51. AUCII, b.74e, f. 'Centro documentazione storia persecuzioni', Sergio Piperno's circular of 7 April 1960 to all the UCII councillors.
52. Ghisalberti's letter of 16 April 1960 to Piperno: 'I have considerable regard for that young scholar who was also my student and I know that he is responsible and very capable. My friend and colleague Chabod, with whom he got his degree, shares my regard for him'. Ghisalberti was responding to a letter of Piperno of 6 April, in which the UCII President made a final attempt to involve the illustrious historian. In AUCII, b.74e, f. 'Centro documentazione storia persecuzioni'.
53. Ibid.
54. Ibid. Another copy of the contract is in ACS, Carte De Felice, b.4, f.14.
55. He forwarded to the President three reports on how the work was proceeding: on 27 June, on 2 September and on 22 October 1960. In AUCII, b.74e, f. 'Centro documentazione storia persecuzioni'.
56. In a letter to Roberto Bassi of 30 April 1960, Vitale informed his interlocutor of the UCII Council's recent choices: 'I have succeeded in having my proposal (which the President has warmly supported) approved: of entrusting to Dr Renzo De Felice the compilation of the History of the Persecutions in Italy (1938/1945) … He has already started working on this and I have already given him my personal bibliographical material (about thirty rare books – published by the Centre of Paris à etc. etc.)'. ACDEC, Corrispondenza CDEC 1955–1960, f. 'Lettere ricevute 1960'. In fact, in the introduction to the first edition of his *Storia degli ebrei in Italia sotto il fascism*, De Felice thanks Vitale for 'indications and documents' which the latter had given him, while in the 1972 edition he pays 'a grateful tribute to the memory of Massimo Adolfo Vitale', who had followed the updating of the work, but who had not lived to see it completed.
57. For an analysis of this key organ of the regime's racist and anti-Semitic propaganda campaign, see F. Cassata, *'La Difesa della Razza'. Politica, ideologia e immagine del razzismo fascista* (Turin: Einaudi, 2008).
58. ACDEC, Corrispondenza CDEC 1955–1960, f. 'Corrispondenza in arrivo 1960', M.A. Vitale's letter of 30 April 1960 to Roberto Bassi and then Renzo De Felice's letter of 21 December 1960 to Guido Valabrega.
59. The drafts of Lattes' replies to De Felice are in BARM, Dante Lattes Archive, bb.559 and 560.
60. In the above-mentioned Commission, Elio Toaff, Vittorio Valobra and Tullia Zevi were entrusted, by the UCII Council, with the following task: 'The commission will only have to give a historical-political judgement and work with the greatest discretion and promptness since the manuscript has to be handed to the publisher Einaudi by 31 May next month'. See Verb. Cons., meeting of 26 March 1961.
61. I take up again the formula used by Michele Sarfatti, to whose study I refer the reader for the appropriate setting of De Felice's work in its historiographical context. See Michele Sarfatti, 'La Storia della persecuzione antiebraica di Renzo De Felice. Contesto, dimensione cronologica e fonti', *Qualestoria*, 2 (2004), pp.11–28.
62. AUCII, b.74e, f. 'Commissione' and f. 'Presentazioni'.
63. It was De Felice himself, turning to Cantimori, who got in touch with the publisher Einaudi; after a preliminary agreement in November 1960, on 16 January 1961 a contract was drawn up between the interested parties: Einaudi, De Felice, UCII. In this regard, see M. Sarfatti, 'La Storia della persecuzione antiebraica di Renzo De Felice'. See also P. Chessa, 'Renzo De Felice e il volume sugli ebrei italiani sotto il fascismo. Genesi e sviluppo di una ricerca storiografica', *Nuova Storia Contemporanea*, 2 (2000), pp.113–32.
64. In this regard, see the exhaustive documentation in I. Pavan, *Tra indifferenza e oblio. Le conseguenze economiche delle leggi razziali in Italia (1938–1970)* (Florence: Le Monnier, 2004).
65. We must remember that Federico Chabod, in the famous lectures at the Sorbonne at the beginning of the 1950s, raised the question of the rejection of the racial campaign, together with concerns about the alliance with Germany, as determining factors in the regime's definitive crisis of consent. The reflections of the authoritative scholar, in part still very useful and precious, had a tremendous impact on Italian culture, contributing to the outlining of the formulae and interpretative models which have moulded Italian historiography regarding fascism and the war. The theme of fascist anti-Semitism was only touched on in some fleeting observations, and yet the author's standing and influence imbued, with exceptional energy and vitality, an analysis which – not being based on in-depth studies since there were none – reflected the mood and feelings which permeated the culture and mentality of the age. Chabod's text was printed in Italy in 1961 by Einaudi with the title

Lezioni sull'Italia contemporanea, but the original French edition had already been widely available (*L'Italie Contemporaine. Conférences faites à l'Institut d'Etude Politiques del'Université de Paris* (Paris: Domat-Montchrestien, 1950)).

66. C.A. Viterbo, 'Vent'anni', *Israel*, 42, 17 July 1958.
67. G. Hausner, *6,000,000 accusers; Israel's case against Eichmann*, translated and edited by S. Rosenne (Jerusalem: Jerusalem Post, 1961), pp.132–3. A relevant contribution to the celebration of the 'good Italians' in the context of that trial was produced by Hannah Arendt; in her very successful report she compares the protection awarded to Jews in Denmark and in Italy in these terms: 'What in Denmark was the result of an authentic political sense ... was in Italy the outcome of the almost automatic general humanity of an old and civilized people'. See H. Arendt, *Eichmann in Jerusalem: A Report on the Banality of Evil* (London: Penguin Books, 1992 [1964]), p.126. Needless to say that such superficial statements on Italian national character do not help in any way to discern the various elements that determined the peculiar situation of the Jews in Italy (before and after German occupation). Nonetheless Arendt's assertion is relevant to us as it testifies of the force of the 'myth of the good Italian' at the time. With her prestige she also contributed in disseminating such a simplistic and distorting view of events. In recent years her position vis-a-vis that momentous event has been put into context and attentively scrutinized by scholars. For a severe but documented and convincing critique of Arendt's approach to the trial and of her representation of the event, see D. Cesarani, *Eichmann: His Life and Crimes* (London: Heinemann, 2004), in particular see pp.324ff.; see also D. Diner, 'Hannah Arendt Reconsidered: On the Banal and the Evil in her Holocaust Narrative', *New German Critique*, 71 (1997), pp.177–90; see also the stimulating contributions container in the rich volume edited by S.E. Ashheim, *Hannah Arendt in Jerusalem* (Berkeley, CA: University of California Press, 2001).
68. We still lack in-depth research on the echoes of the Eichmann trial in Italy. Some preliminary contributions have been made by G. Valabrega, *Ebrei fascismo, sionismo* (Urbino: Argalia, 1974), pp.307–15; M. Consonni, 'The Impact of the Eichmann Event in Italy, 1961', *Journal of Israeli History*, 23 (2004), Special Edition: *After Eichmann: Collective Memory and the Holocaust since 1961*, edited by D. Cesarani and A. Shapira, pp. 90–9.
69. Issues of the 12 May 1961.
70. See H. Cassuto Campagnano, 'Parola ad una testimone', *Israel*, 34, 22 June 1961. For a more detailed reconstruction of the echoes of the Eichmann trial in the Italian-Jewish press, see E. Mazzini, *Ebrei dopo la Shoah. Politica e cultura nella stampa ebraica italiana 1945–1970*, Degree thesis, supervisor Prof. Marco Palla, University of Florence, Academic Year 2001–02.
71. Campagnano's deposition is reproduced in S.I. Minerbi, *La belva in gabbia. Eichmann* (Milan: Longanesi, 1962), pp.47–51.
72. See R. De Felice, *Storia degli ebrei in Italia*. The reference appears, albeit with slight modifications, from the 1961 edition up to the pocket edition of 1993.
73. For a detailed assessment of these positions, see E. Collotti, *Fascismo, fascismi* (Florence: Sansoni, 1989).
74. De Felice paid considerable attention to this theme in *Mussolini il duce*, vol. II, *Lo stato totalitario 1936–1940* (Turin: Einaudi, 1981). He also insisted upon this theme in the 1983 preface to the new edition of his *Le interpretazioni del fascism* (Bari: Laterza, 1995 [1969]). Starting from the 1988 edition of his *Storia degli ebrei sotto il fascismo*, De Felice removed Cantimori's preface, which was critical of his work, and replaced it with his own introduction, insisting particularly on the differences between fascism and Nazism, maintaining, in this regard, the insignificance and marginality of anti-Semitism in Italian history. See the observations of E. Collotti, 'Il razzismo negato', in *Fascismo e antifascismo. Rimozioni, revisioni, negazioni* (Rome-Bari: Laterza, 2000), pp.363 and 371–2.
75. M. Sarfatti, 'Il volume 1938 Le leggi razziali contro gli ebrei e alcune considerazioni sulla normativa persecutoria', in *La legislazione antiebraica in Italia e in Europa* (Rome: Camera dei Deputati, 1989), p.54. Analogous considerations were made, anticipating to a certain extent research developments, by E. Enriques Agnoletti, 'Indivisibile libertà', *Il Ponte*, 11–12 (1978), p.1503.
76. 'Precisely because not all the anti-Semitisms lead to Auschwitz, investigating anti-Semitism and the history of the Shoah in Italy means, first of all, freeing oneself of the "demon of analogy" and assessing the phenomenon in its specificity', D. Bidussa, *Il mito del bravo italiano* (Milan: Il Saggiatore, 1994), p.73.
77. A first review of the reactions and reviews of the work of the young De Felice is in P. Simoncelli, *Renzo De Felice. La formazione intellettuale*, pp.241ff. On the Picardi case, see G. Fiori, *Una*

storia italiana. Vita di Ernesto Rossi (Turin: Einaudi, 1997), pp.272–5; A. Cardini, *Tempi di ferro. 'Il Mondo' e l'Italia del dopoguerra* (Bologna: Il Mulino, 1992), pp.422–7.

78. No less bitter controversies than those produced for the 'Picardi case' developed in relation to the figure of the popular writer Guido Piovene. This happened because of the 'rediscovery' of some of his racist writings, brought to light by Guido Ludovico Luzzatto during the conference 'Gli ebrei in Italia durante il fascismo' ('The Jews in Italy during Fascism'), organized in Turin by the Jewish Youth Federation on 24 April 1961; see G.L. Luzzatto, 'La partecipazione all'antifascismo in Italia e all' estero dal 1918 al 1938', in G. Valabrega (ed.), *Gli ebrei in Italia durante il fascismo*, vol. II (Milan: CDEC, 1962), p.40; observations later developed in G. Valabrega, 'Il caso Piovene. Il fenomeno dell'oblio', *Israel*, 29, 3 May 1962. This rather complex case dragged on with ups and downs until 1963. See S. Gerbi, *Tempi di malafede. Una storia italiana tra fascismo e dopoguerra. Guido Piovene ed Eugenio Colorni* (Turin: Einaudi, 1999), in particular pp.231ff.
79. See P. Cooke, *Luglio '60. Tambroni e la repressione fallita* (Milan: Teti, 2000).
80. In this regard, see the pungent observations of Angelo Ventura, 'Renzo De Felice. Il fascismo e gli ebrei', in *Incontro di studio sull'opera di Renzo De Felice* (Rome: Giunta Centrale per gli Studi Storici, 2000), pp.47–9.
81. I think it is important to note that, after the publication of Renzo De Felice's work, the, in any case, very few works of some importance written or published in Italy on the theme do not certainly bear witness to a great research interest on the part of academic institutions. Mention should be made, first of all, of the three volumes edited by Guido Valabrega (see this chapter, note 49); reference should also be made to: L. Preti, *I miti dell'impero e della razza nell'Italia degli anni '30* (Rome: Opere Nuove, 1965); S. Gherardi Bon, *La persecuzione antiebraica a Trieste (1938–1945)*, preface by E. Collotti (Udine: Del Bianco, 1972) [an updated and expanded edition was printed by Lint of Trieste in 2000]; G. Mayda, *Ebrei sotto Salò. La persecuzione antisemita 1943–1945* (Milan: Feltrinelli, 1978); the special issue, entitled 'La difesa della razza', *Il Ponte*, 11–12 (1978), edited by Ugo Caffaz. Also the detailed analysis by Meir Michaelis (*Mussolini and the Jews: German-Italian Relations and the Jewish Question in Italy, 1922–1945* (London: Clarendon Press, 1978)), which however offered a reductive view of Mussolini's racist change, interpreting it prevalently in relation to the evolution of the international political scene, received scant attention in Italian academic circles.
82. In this regard, we have to remember the conference promoted and published by the Camera dei Deputati, 'La legislazione antiebraica in Italia e in Europa'; as well as the publication the following year of *Conseguenze culturali delle leggi razziali in Italia* (Rome: Accademia dei Lincei, 1989). In 1988, the Senate of the Republic also promoted and published an important book: M. Toscano (ed.), *L'abrogazione delle leggi razziali in Italia (1943–1987)*, preface by G. Spadolini (Rome: Servizio Studi del Senato, 1988). Among the important scientific and cultural initiatives which took place on that occasion we should finally remember the publication, edited by Michele Sarfatti, of a monographic issue of the *RMI* entitled *1938. Le leggi contro gli ebrei*, 1–2, XXXII (1988).
83. For a review of the recent trends in the study of fascist racism and anti-Semitism, see M. Toscano, *Ebraismo e antisemitismo in Italia. Dal 1848 alla Guerra dei sei giorni* (Milan: Angeli, 2003), pp.208–43; S. Luconi, 'Recent Trends in the Study of Italian Anti-Semitism under the Fascist Regime', *Patterns of Prejudice*, 1 (2004), pp.1–17.
84. On the crisis of the anti-fascist discourse and its connection with the rise of a new sensibility towards the fascist persecution of the Jews see the critical considerations made by S. Luzzatto, *La crisi dell'antifascismo* (Turin: Einaudi, 2004), in particular see pp.45–6.

10

For a Critique of Italian-Jewish Self-Representation

Observing the Italian cultural dynamics of the post-1945 period, it seems to me difficult not to believe that there was, in the immediate post-war years, in embryo, an interpretation of the events which could not only have been different, but opposed to the reassuring and simplistic one which has acritically been accepted for decades. It is therefore necessary to ask oneself what led to the prevalence of those interpretations of the anti-Jewish persecution in terms of a superficial repression of any guilt or responsibility. The contradictions highlighted so far, the worries, the doubts, the uncertainties and the critical elements which timidly, but not imperceptibly, emerge here and there in the reflections, even though different, of a Debenedetti or of a Vitale, have ended up being buried, both in the recollections of the victims and in many of the historical reconstructions, by the extolling of the virtues of the Italian people. As noted by the historian Michele Sarfatti, it is 'as if the unrealized collective commitment to remember … has driven the memories, which are too true, and their possessors in a dimension of partial unreality. It is "difficult" to remember what according to others has not happened (or whose possible verification is not worth determining).'[1]

The problem, it is worth remembering, is not so much (or only) the gauging of the discrepancy between certain memories and representations of the past and a presumed 'truth', sanctioned by the scientific rigour of the modern historical reconstructions. What is remembered and how it is remembered is of considerable historical interest inasmuch as it offers precious information about the formation of the awareness of the person (or group) who carries out that exercise of data selection which is remembering. It is necessary to confront the problem, in secular terms, keeping well in mind the therapeutic function, soothing or even curative, of certain approaches to the past; freeing oneself, therefore, both from the present *fetishism of the memory* and from the tendency to demonize every form of oblivion, almost as if it were a crime or a sin.[2] Italian Jews, and in general all Italians, who after the war did not remember – or badly remembered – were not sinners who should be struck by the historian's scathing judgement.

The absolutory and parenthetic interpretation of Fascist anti-Semitism developed by the victims should not be simplistically considered an act of hypocrisy: one can find, in its origins, the many threads which intertwine in the Italian Jewish collective identity which had been developing since the emancipation. Some of these threads had been cut by the persecution and it was precisely in the working through of that event that they were renewed or replaced. The persecution had to be explained, but the reworking of the past did not so much have the aim of achieving a scientifically correct reconstruction, but rather in re-establishing the relationship with Italian society, in refashioning a collective identity through the production of myths and the seeking of symbols with which to identify: Remo Bodei observed, 'As no one manages to live in a totally meaningless reality, when there are only scattered ruins of the recent past, identity is ready to renew itself by recomposing them in imaginary figures or myths.'[3]

Initially, trust and despair, hopes and fears are intertwined in the victims' attitude towards the faults of the Italian nation. In an overall examination of the components of the Italian-Jewish discussion of the persecution, it emerges clearly that doubts and worries about the future are extremely important; it could be said that the unease caused by observing the consequences of the persecution led many Italian Jews to seek equality with increased energy. As has been observed, 'by recalling the persecution undergone, and not only on the part of the Germans, there was the danger of evoking their own presumed diversity'.[4] This favoured the repression, which developed on various planes, ranging from the concealment of the trauma undergone to the development of simplistic, but reassuring, interpretations of the fascist persecutory campaign.

The absence of a real liberal sensibility – both in Italian society as a whole and among the Jews in particular – also probably played an important part; this naturally made it very difficult to assess correctly the seriousness and significance of the racial policy, which denied civil rights and stole properties, put into effect by the fascist regime between 1938 and 1943.[5] In more general terms, it is necessary to bear in mind the overall situation of the national community following the Liberation. In a context in which everyone was – to a certain extent – a survivor, who had miraculously escaped death, it is easy to understand that there should be scant interest in the specific Jewish experience. There was certainly no desire to see one's own guilt and wrongdoing thoroughly exposed. Everyone, or almost everyone, was involved in hiding collusions and compromises, of various types, with the dictatorship which for twenty years had enveloped and devastated the lives of the Italians. Political and cultural institutions shared with many Italian Jews – who had often been enthusiastic fascists – the need for a reconciliatory memory.

But the behaviour of the Jewish minority, or most of it, cannot be explained only in relation to the formation of 'a shared anti-fascist feeling' following the Second World War; the roots of this attitude can be traced back to a much older tradition. The fascist persecution and then the deportations did not lead to a radical rejection of the identity models which had arisen with the Risorgimento and the emancipation, on the contrary, it was precisely through the cultural instruments developed since the opening of the ghettoes that the Italian Jews came to terms with the regime's anti-Semitism. From the time of the emancipation, many Italian Jews had sincerely believed that the 'real Italy' was the liberal and secular country which had given them their freedom: the Italy of the Risorgimento. As often happens, elements actually present (the exceptional quality and speed of the Jewish integration in the Italian social fabric) were transformed to such an extent as to produce an absolutely unreal overall picture, presenting Italy as a kind of earthly paradise.

The enthusiasm for the attainment of equality and freedom, the desire to be fully and quickly integrated in the national community led Italian Judaism, or at least important parts of it, to hide, or to relegate almost exclusively to the family context, their own identity. There was also the consequent tendency to minimize, or at least not to recall, above all in the relationships with non-Jews, the persecutions undergone beforehand.[6] In this regard, it is interesting to consider the testimony of Enzo Levi, who remembered how there was, in the Italian-Jewish world at the beginning of the twentieth century, a notable reticence in remembering the persecutions and the oppression suffered until not very many years earlier:

> I have often asked myself what was the reason for the reluctance, in Jewish circles (even though not absolute), to talk about the past, life in the ghetto, the often dramatic persecutions, the inevitable dramatic political upheavals and the spontaneous popular persecutions or those started by the princes and the Church.
>
> Silence was almost a watchword … [there were some elderly people who] loved to remember the daily life of the ghetto, generally in a humorous way very far from a tragic one, which would often have been called for by the events being narrated.[7]

The author has identified the reason for this behaviour in what he has defined as a 'defensive necessity'. According to him 'the Jews were like freed prisoners, who had to forget their unjust and cruel imprisonment'.[8] Behaviour which can be explained by the desire to simplify the relationship with the surrounding society, but which also finds its ultimate origin in an obvious difficulty in coming to terms with the complexity of the social and cultural processes which the emancipation reflected. In Jewish autobiographies one can see the tendency to perceive the equality attained not as an inalienable right, but rather as a sort of prize or privilege which one had to do everything possible not to lose: by not reminding the others of the past, of one's diversity, and also trying to be worthy of citizenship, by showing one deserved it through total loyalty to the national cause.[9] Feelings and attitudes of this type soon turned into a habitual behaviour which reinforced a distorting interpretation of reality.

The impact of the Shoah led many to feel the *duty of remembering*, but attention was concentrated on the Nazi genocide, in comparison with which it was easy to highlight the relative mildness of the fascist measures. After the war, the commemoration of the persecutions became the foundation of a renewed Jewish identity profoundly marked by the extermination, nevertheless the development of a common memory, capable of uniting the persecuted, necessitated bringing the many, diversified and distant national and local series of events back to a single historical context, a single persecutory paradigm, that of Auschwitz. German anti-Semitism was raised to the level of an archetype and there was not much room left for what could not easily be traced back to it. Thus, the commemoration of the extermination did not cancel the pre-existing tendency to minimize Italian anti-Semitism, but was added to it: similarly to what also happened elsewhere in the West, a complex interweaving of repression and commemoration developed in the collective consciousness of Italian Judaism. The monumentalization of the memory of the genocide, with the condemnation of the German people, and the repression of Italian responsibility as regards anti-Semitism could coexist.[10]

Italian-Jewish self-representation, tending to extol, with excessive zeal, the wonders of integration, very soon favoured the structuring of a strong narration, also capable of influencing high-level reflection, that of the intellectuals and scholars, complicating – if not exactly obstructing – a serene examination of the problem of anti-Judaism in Italy. In this emblematic perspective, it is worth considering the extraordinary success of a concise review written by a very young scholar destined to have a brilliant career. The famous 1933 reflection of Arnaldo Momigliano concerning the integration of Jews in contemporary Italy, placed at the end of his review of Cecil Roth's *The Jews in Venice*, should be read today as an indication of the sensibility and of the imagination typical of important sectors of an Italian-Jewish intellectual bourgeoisie, which aimed at reinforcing the pact of citizenship established with the Risorgimento. Instead, as is known, that text – read in conjunction with Gramsci's remarks which moved from Momigliano's book review and then went on to theorize the absence of anti-Semitism in contemporary Italy – has, for a long time, been the reference point of a historiography which was lazy, acritical and, generally, showed scant interest in verifying empirically the actual validity of those theses.[11] The Italian debate and the self-image of the Jewish minority did not leave those tracks until a recent, and very welcome derailment.

Therefore, a very important part was played, in the inclination to minimize the role and significance of the racist persecutions, by a certain type of Jewish self-image, which modelled itself on the system of cultural representations coined with the emancipation: a network of signs which concealed the problem of anti-Semitism and obstructed an objective analysis of reality, permitting, however, the pursuit of the dream of a happy and aproblematic integration. The conventions and stereotypes upon which very many had modelled their own identity could not be set aside so easily and also on account of this, in the post-war period, many Italian Jews remained 'prisoners of hope'.[12] An irrational hope, a trust in Italy and the Italians, not always unfounded, but sometimes blind.

NOTES

1. M. Sarfatti, 'La persecuzione antiebraica nel periodo 1938–1943 e il suo difficile ricordo', in A.L. Carlotti (ed.), *Italia 1939–1945. Storia e memoria*, preface by F. Della Peruta (Milan: Edizioni Vita e Pensiero, 1995), p.84.
2. For a theoretical clarification cf. M. Bal, J. Crewe and L. Spitzer (eds), *Acts of Memory. Cultural Recall in the Present* (Hanover and London: University Press of New England, 1999); in particular on the theme of therapeutic memory cf. ibid., M. Sturken, 'Narratives of Recovery', pp.241–5.
3. R. Bodei, *Libro della memoria e della speranza* (Bologna: Il Mulino, 1995), p.35.
4. It was noted by Carla Forti: *Il caso Pardo Roques. Un eccidio del 1944 tra memoria e oblio* (Turin: Einaudi, 1998), p.245.
5. Ibid., pp.231ff.
6. In this regard, see the accurate observations of G. Luzzatto Voghera, *Il prezzo dell'eguaglianza. Il dibattito sull'emancipazione degli ebrei in Italia (1781–1848)* (Milan: Angeli, 1998), pp.166–7.
7. E. Levi, *Memorie di una vita* (Modena: STEM Mucchi, 1972), p.17.
8. Ibid., pp.19–20.
9. See, for example, the account by Augusto Segre: 'Even if in my days, when I was a boy, there were sporadic episodes which were unpleasant for us and we encountered an … anti-Semite … many of us were always ready to overlook these minor events, to minimize them maintaining that it was not wise … to quarrel with the Christians and that it was instead much more important and useful, for the good of all, to keep quiet, to act as if nothing had happened … In short, they taught us, that we should do everything possible not only 'not to be noticed', but to show more and more, through our work, charity, participation in the political life of the country, if possible, that the freedom conceded was amply justified by so much Italian patriotic fervour.' And a few pages later he observes that 'there was a constant preoccupation that our gratitude was never sufficiently expressed, almost as if we felt guilty for having been confined, for so many centuries, in the ghettoes, which we had left amnestied thanks to the magnanimity of the House of Savoy'. A. Segre, *Memorie di vita ebraica*, preface by R. De Felice (Rome: Bonacci, 1979), pp.24 and 31–2.
10. Something very similar happened in France; see A. Wieviorka, *Déportation et Génocide. Entre la mémoire et l'oubli* (Paris: Plon, 1992), in particular pp.391–431.
11. A. Momigliano, 'Recensione a C. Roth. Gli ebrei in Venezia', *La Nuova Italia*, 20 April 1933, now in A. Momigliano, *Essays on Ancient and Modern Judaism*, edited by S. Berti (Chicago, IL: University of Chicago Press, 1994), pp.225–7. A. Gramsci, *Quaderni del carcere* (Turin: Einaudi, 1975), pp.1801–2. During the 1990s, those theses were under discussion and perhaps definitively superseded: they have highlighted the distortions produced in the Italian historiographic debate by the reception of the theses of Momigliano and Gramsci: D. Bidussa, 'Gli ebrei in Italia in età moderna-contemporanea. Considerazioni per una storia ancora da scrivere', *Bailamme*, 15–16 (1994), pp.52ff., and G. Luzzatto Voghera, *Il prezzo dell'uguaglianza. Il dibattito sull'emancipazione degli ebrei in Italia (1781–1848)* (Milan: Angeli, 1998) pp.14–15.
12. The allusion is to the work of H. Stewart Hughes, *Prisoners of Hope: The Silver Age of Italian Jews 1924–1974* (Cambridge, MA: Harvard University Press, 1996).

Conclusion

Socio-territorial rootedness is one of the constituent elements of identity, both individual and collective. When it was put under strain, because of the persecution, compensatory processes were triggered which enabled people to deal with feelings of being out of place and the sense of disorientation.[1] The main compensatory mechanisms with which Italian Judaism tackled the difficulties were: a reassuring and distorted memory, seeking refuge in daily life and the reinforcing of eminently pre-political ties with the nation (the language, the culture, the familiar places and dear ones), the search for new means of identification with the national community (anti-fascism and Resistance) or the adherence to ideological paths which proposed a radical transformation of society (communism). To these should be added an accentuated cohesion: the persecution had very forcefully re-proposed the theme of belonging to the Jewish group; it was possible to find strength and safety in the group. A result of the renewed sense of brotherhood was also an unprecedented adherence to Zionism, which manifested itself mainly in philanthropy. These are the main elements which characterized Italian-Jewish life in the long post-war period.

The persecution gave a new form and consistency to the Judaism of many, drawing it out of the private and family sphere in which it had been jealously guarded since the time of the emancipation. During the nineteenth century and at the beginning of the twentieth, Jewishness had flowed back into the private domain. *Jews at home and citizens outside*, according to Mendelssohn's formula: this had been the behaviour of very many Jews, especially the well-integrated bourgeoisie. Reflecting on his identity, Arnaldo Momigliano recalled,

> It was a religion enclosed within the family … On account of this I cannot separate my domestic feelings from the religious ceremonies of every day and above all of the Sabbath when everything changed … we would often go and spend Saturday afternoons at 'Paniale', a house, half way between town and country surrounded by fields and chestnut groves, which had been bought measuring the distance permitted for an orthodox Jew to move away from his Sabbath home. My real experience of the Jewish religion is in this intense, austere, domestic piety. Children who are blessed by their father on Friday evening, a mother who embraces husband and children.[2]

It was only at the beginning of the twentieth century that the first timid signs of a revision of this identity model began to appear, reinforced by the emergence of modern anti-Semitism and the birth of political Zionism. The persecution accentuated this tendency but also altered its significance: everyone's Jewishness was abruptly cast outside the context of family intimacy and suddenly became a *public* fact, since relations with the external world were dramatically mutilated and Judaism could no longer only be a matter of individual conscience, but was raised to a matter of belonging to a separate, inferior and yet threatening, 'race'.

State racism catalyzed the evolutionary processes already under way in Italian Judaism: in the short term, it contributed to heightening tensions and conflicts between the opposing currents, but in the long term, it led to the structuring of a new Jewish solidarity and also, even though slowly and laboriously, to the development of a different way of living in society and of responding to current challenges and problems not only as individuals, but also as a collectivity.[3] The new esprit de corps which transpires from the vitality of the youth movements, the survival of the schools and more generally from the different forms which community life took on for the Jews of Europe are amidst the most enduring legacies of the persecution: 'Auschwitz', noted Isaac Deutscher, a lively Trotskyist intellectual of Polish extraction, 'has been the terrible cradle of the new Jewish consciousness and the new Jewish nation'.[4] Analogous considerations were made in the immediate post-war period by the young Roman Zionist Giorgio Piperno:

> The destruction of more than one third of our people is a phenomenon of such gravity that it transcends our powers of representation … It is something which has not only changed the number of Jews in the world, it has changed the structure of the people in the very depths of their collective consciousness … *In this immense communion of suffering there has certainly arisen among the Jews of the whole world a new tie of brotherhood*.[5]

The spread of reinforced community ties as a consequence of the persecution emerges in numerous memoirs and accounts,[6] even if one certainly should not think that there was unanimity in these reactions. In any case, it is important to stress that 'rediscovering themselves as Jews', meeting other members of the community much more often, did not mean, in the vast majority of cases, initiating a return to orthodoxy, which would have envisaged studying the Hebrew language and the sacred texts, as well as the observing of precepts which for many were by then outdated. Many maintained an instinctive attachment to the religious tradition, in a way very well illustrated by Natalia Ginzburg, who has recounted how her grandmother 'used to say her prayers, every day, in Hebrew without understanding anything, because she did not know Hebrew'.[7]

A return to religious practice would have been very difficult also because of a serious shortage of teachers: death and emigration had notably impoverished Italian Judaism leaving it bereft of its religious guides. After the Liberation, and for several years, the UCII was beset by the problem of filling rabbinical posts: perhaps this situation had an impact, obstructing, or at least not helping the rapprochement with religious culture.

Even after the Shoah, Italian Judaism preserved its particular characteristics: as regards the institutions and internal self-regulation it remained a formally orthodox community, while the majority of individuals continued to keep away from religious observance. This state of affairs depended upon the absence in Italy of the religious reformation movement, which elsewhere had developed beginning in the late eighteenth century;[8] only lately has the Italian-Jewish world begun, not without some reluctance, to open itself to the circles and experiences of Anglo-Saxon reformed Judaism.[9]

In Italian Judaism, only officially orthodox, there often remained the habit of carrying out some rituals and customs, expressions – as in many other integrated Jewish communities – of a group spirit, a manifestation of family unity rather than a consistent and fully conscious adherence to traditional culture. Having said this, it should be noted that also in the post-war period the occasions when the greatest number of the members of the communities gathered together were the religious ceremonies: Giorgio Piperno noted bitterly, 'while the participants at the meetings of the Zionist group were few and a small minority were deeply involved in the activities of the cultural circles, the Synagogue of Rome was full on holy days'.[10] Soon after the Liberation, the synagogues constituted the places in which to gather spontaneously and meet, to count the fallen and make a joint commitment for the future; above and beyond the faith of individuals, the places of worship represented, together with schools, the heart of community life.

But what did that massive attendance mean if the relationship with the authentic, primary sources of Jewish thought had, in effect, been interrupted? Was it only the expression of a habitual procedure to which was added a reinforced feeling of brotherhood? How did the renewed feeling of belonging to Judaism, of which we have found unmistakable traces, express itself? The persecution had produced new needs, stimulating a strong feeling of diversity which, however, appeared intangible and fleeting. Having regained equality, the diversity experienced seemed to many like an indelible mark, something which they did not want to, and could not, do without. After 1945, there were certainly some, ever fewer with the passage of time, who, like Giacomo Debenedetti, wanted to go back to being ordinary individuals, in every way just like the others.[11] Nevertheless, the trend of evolution was pushing Italian Jews, like those throughout the West, in a completely different direction: proclaiming their diversity, praising it, extolling it, this was the view reflected in the activities of the youth movements and the official institutions of Italian Judaism. But where was, and above all what was the authentic and vital heart of that otherness?

Perhaps it was lost forever. According to Yeshayahu Leibowitz, 'the historical crisis of Judaism and of the Jewish people in modern times' would manifest itself primarily as the 'loss of the significant essence of common values'; what would remain would be 'only a kind of abstract consciousness of being "Jews"'.[12] A judgement which is as perceptive as it is hard. However, we have to note that the crisis of 'traditional' Judaism left room for a different, vague and confused, but at the same time a strong and explicit declaration of belonging: the identity imposed in 1938 was in many cases like a tattoo displayed with pride, whose meaning, however, appeared difficult to decipher. This 'abstract consciousness' of belonging to Judaism is for the historian, who pays attention to the construction of the collective imagination, extremely curious and fascinating.

The essence and embodiment of that evasive and indeterminate Judaism was (and continues to be) *Memory*, to be understood 'no longer as a synthetic expression of a trace of oneself, but rather as the basis of oneself'.[13] In Italy, as elsewhere, during the post-war period, an inexplicable diversity was seen in absolute terms and celebrated through the commemoration of the persecution. As if one could provide an answer to the obscure questions raised by the tragedy simply by putting the tragedy itself on a pedestal. In fact, this is not unusual behaviour, in processing a trauma it is natural and common for human communities to respond through the commemoration and memory of the drama which comes to be incorporated in a broader history in which, according to its significance, it assumes a more or less important position. What is perhaps characteristic of the memory of the enormous catastrophe is that it soon assumed a dominant position in the mythical representation of the collective past: sometimes one has the feeling that in recalling the religious tradition, by juxtapositioning its stories and characters with the tragedy of the Second World War, there is not the wish to explain the more recent event in relation to the more remote ones, consecrated by time and the reflections of the masters, but rather the contrary.[14] For a Judaism which seems to have lost touch with the live sources of tradition, they only appear to have acquired meaning by modelling themselves on the latest drama, whose recollection transcends history and becomes a 'substitute religion'. This formula has been coined by Shmuel Trigano, who bitterly commented on the evolution of the Jewish condition in the post-war period, as follows: 'The Shoah tends to replace Judaism itself, with its ceremonies, its places of commemoration where the "Memory", raised to an absolute value, takes the place of faith. Very often it is only in this perspective that modern consciousness understands Jewish existence.'[15]

The commemorated trauma seems to have become the only, still intelligible, sign of one's own identity. One cannot help noting that such a memory runs the risk of being as intransitive as it is self-related, it is not a vehicle of critical reflection, nor, as far as I am concerned, does it appear to have the potentiality of leading to a process of self-regeneration and self-reinvention.

On a different, but in a way complementary, plane, *Memory* has certainly fuelled the subject of Zionism. The Shoah was soon taken up as a founding myth of the State of Israel: that memory was able to fuel a positive expression of identity giving unusual force and intensity to the call of the nation, which no one could any longer have pretended not to have heard.[16]After the persecutions, Zionism acquired a series of implications which gave that ideal a new significance and an unexpected consensus, but which at the same time, in a way, impoverished and weakened it. The woeful developments of European history altered the conditions in which, at the beginning of the century, Zionism had been able to represent, for some sectors of Italian Judaism and beyond, an exceptional opportunity to relaunch one's own identity, a 'challenge'.[17] Until 1938, approaching Zionist themes had involved an intense reworking and rediscovery of one's own culture, it had constituted a way of confronting the existential unease induced, in a restricted intellectual élite, by the process of integration which it had wanted to counter with a regenerative process. Things changed radically from the beginning of the fascist persecution: a spontaneous and instinctive approach to Zionism had then been one of the most obvious reactions, above all for the youngest.[18] Some suddenly chose to leave Italy which was marginalizing them, going to Palestine driven more by the rejection of a society which did not seem to offer them any hope, rather than by a mature and informed ideological choice: Zionism became 'a harsh necessity, imposed by human stupidity and cruelty'.[19] It became a refuge, perhaps momentary, to which one arrived fleeing from ostracism; it lost its significance of a 'challenge' and there was a sometimes superficial adherence to it, which deprived it of the breathtaking impetus and revolutionary force which, at the beginning of the century, someone like Enzo Sereni[20] had recognized in it.

The birth of the State of Israel fitted into that context, but it also had other and more wide-ranging implications. It was an event of the greatest significance which led to a radical transformation in the mechanisms of self-representation of the Jews, as well as the reinstatement of the figure of the Jew in the collective imagination. The new State rapidly became an element with which the Jews were forced to come to terms: the Diaspora Jews did not necessarily subscribe to its fundamental ideology, nor did they easily recognize themselves in its proposed identity model, but it is realistic to believe that almost all of them followed its fortunes with interest and also with a certain emotional involvement. In this regard, I think it is enlightening to consider Aldo Zargani's account of his father, who 'always remained Italian' and, after the war, with serene inconsistency associated 'the most convinced anti-Zionism with childish enthusiasm for the dazzling successes of Haganà'.[21] This testimony brings to mind the challenge posed by Alain Finkielkraut who, making an implicit reference to Max Weber's considerations that reading the daily is like modern man's prayer, observed:

> Without beliefs, community or a culture to call their own, Jews nonetheless salvage an identity from this triple catastrophe. They hold on to something imperishable: the news. Reading the newspaper takes up where religious observance left off, providing Diaspora Jewry with a daily feeling of attachment to the Israeli people as a whole. Now there are two types of practising Jew: the devout who attend synagogue, and the much more numerous group who produce a running (and delectable) commentary on the situation in the Middle East as their form of observance. What do the oil embargo, the Camp David Accords or the Islamic revival actually mean to assimilated Jews in Europe or America? Constant recognition, and a regular reminder of their condition.[22]

In effect, for a Judaism which is by now secularized, fundraising for Israel and the campaigns for accurate information about Middle Eastern tensions have in a way replaced (or come alongside) religious practice, taking on the character of a kind of secular religion.[23] We have already seen how Italian immigration to Israel has been relatively scant, nevertheless it has been sufficient to mean that almost every Italian-Jewish family has relatives and friends overseas. This has contributed to the building of a bond which can manifest itself in various forms, but which has undoubtedly had an impact on the Italian-Jewish community, like those of other Western countries, adding new implications to the old tension – characteristic of the post-emancipation Western Jewish world – between integration and ethnicity.[24] The spectrum of feelings and behaviours could be extremely broad; nevertheless, in observing the activities of the Jewish associations one can clearly see how the connection with Israel and Zionism has played a crucial role in stimulating intra-community cohesion: in Italy, analogously with what has been registered for French Judaism, one can see the formation of a kind of 'community Zionism': a Zionist impetus which does not imply a rejection of Italian society or of the Diaspora, nor a prelude to emigration, but constitutes the ideal and symbolic reference point which reinforces the very idea of 'community'.[25] In time, a kind of allegorical vision has developed: projecting itself through Zionism in an *elsewhere* which is the generative location of identity, the Italian-Jewish community has become aware of itself and also developed its own, metaphorical and uncertain, position in the context of the Italian political scene. During the last fifty years, a minority identity has slowly taken shape, which interacts with the Italian political reality being strongly influenced by an extra-systemic element: Israel. Apart from reacting to anti-Semitic demonstrations, it is, in fact, almost exclusively in relation to the link Zionism/Israel that the community expresses itself publicly and that its institutions enter the lists of the political and cultural clash.

Such public expressions, it should be noted, needed time to overcome a kind of reluctance and acquire particular visibility: in Italy there have not been demonstrations comparable, in intensity and scale, with those which broke out in France, when in 1967 the community reacted against some unfortunate pronouncements by De Gaulle about the Six Day War.[26] Nevertheless, also in Italy, even if with greater caution and slowness compared to the French situation, there have been instances when the Jewish groupings – or rather several Jewish communities – have made their presence felt publicly, mainly, even if not exclusively, with regard to the intricate Middle Eastern question. This has happened more forcefully starting from the 1980s, but rather than a series of unrelated episodes, it has been more a question of the slow building of an identity.

An identity, thus postulated, which rests largely on an extra-systemic relationship (Zionism/Israel), will inevitably appear fragile and dangerously unstable. Moreover, it is destined to trigger increasing difficulties in terms of animosity and prejudice, which derive from the re-emergence of the accusations of *double loyalty* and above all from the mounting anti-Semitism whose roots are not to be found so much in the traditional collection of stereotypes, as in a more frequent and intense hostility towards the State of Israel, which includes anti-Americanism and anti-modern drives together with ferments of a different nature.

These considerations lead us to reflect on the origins of the current situation. It could be said that the first post-war decade witnessed the re-semantization of the identity of the persecuted minority, which developed along two potentially contradictory lines: on the one hand, the re-proposition of the cultural paradigms worked out in the period of integration and before the persecution, on the other hand, the difficult emergence of different drives (Zionism, growing cohesion and reinforcement of community ties). Barely a decade after the Liberation, that synthesis, the difficult balance achieved by combining dated cultural models with new feelings triggered by the persecutions and the birth of the State of Israel, began to show its intrinsic fragility and the prospects of future crises soon became apparent.

The situation began to develop starting from the second half of the 1950s (the Suez Canal crisis of 1956), but it reached a crescendo in the 1960s and 1970s. The denunciation of Stalinist crimes and later the repression of dissent within the Soviet Block cast a shadow over the communist myth, ushering in a season of grave uncertainty among the forces of the Left; and this could not fail to have an impact on the many Jews of the peninsula who were spellbound by that dream. At the same time, the Suez crisis highlighted Israel's drawing closer to the Western Block, and in the short term caused an intense migration of Jews from Egypt: it was the beginning of a more extensive migration which, because of the events in the region following the birth of Israel, redrew the map of the centuries-old Jewish communities in the Mediterranean.

Starting from the 1960s, Italian Judaism welcomed massive influxes of Jewish refugees fleeing from Libya and later from Persia.[27] They were not always easy to integrate in the fragile fabric of the Italian-Jewish community, also because such Jewish groups came from very distant cultural contexts: for them, fascism and anti-fascism, fundamental phenomena for the Jews after 1945, were inevitably of little importance, representing foreign and perhaps incomprehensible experiences. While, for them, the observance of precepts and more generally the feeling of the unity of the community were very marked. More recently new arrivals have included orthodox Ashkenazy Jews, from the Lubavitch community of New York, who have settled in the places where the peninsula's major Jewish communities are to be found. All these groups, even though in different ways, have preserved a broadly autonomous social life and – particularly the last mentioned – maintain a notable independence and detachment from the Italian-Jewish community system, regulated by the agreements of 1930 and 1987. These new arrivals, together with various other changes, have led to a substantial metamorphosis in the Jewish community in Italy.[28]

The social transformations induced by the economic miracle, the internal and international political evolution, the slow transition – resulting in the Second Vatican Council – which led the Catholic Church to reformulate its relationship with Judaism, growing anti-Zionist tensions in the Left, the consolidation of the memory of the Shoah – which has increasingly taken on the character of a 'substitute religion' – and finally the arrival in Italy of Jewish groups difficult to assimilate, are all factors which, starting from the second half of the 1950s, contributed to radically changing the overall framework in which the Italian-Jewish minority lived.[29] The reactions to those events were diverse and anything but coordinated, nevertheless they stimulated a slow and difficult process of reappraisal of identity which, I think, underwent a fundamental leap forward starting in the 1980s. Those years and the war in Lebanon triggered an accelerated transformation in the Western perception of the Jew and pushed the Jews of Europe towards a clear-cut reassessment of their condition and their history.

Starting from 1980 (and for over two years), a wave of deadly terrorist attacks, mainly of Palestinian origin, struck the European continent, concentrating on Jewish objectives and reproducing – on a smaller scale – the violence of the Middle Eastern conflict. In January 1980, an explosion destroyed a Jewish restaurant in Berlin, killing a child, a little more than a year old, and injuring twenty-four people. In July, hand grenades were thrown at a Jewish nursery school in Antwerp, leaving one dead and several wounded. In October, a bomb exploded near the synagogue of Rue Copernic, in Paris, killing four people and wounding fifteen. The following year, in August 1981, an attack against the Central Synagogue of Vienna caused the death of two people and the wounding of another eighteen. In October of the same year, a car-bomb exploded in

Antwerp, in a zone densely populated by Jews, causing three deaths and 106 wounded. In 1982, a Jewish restaurant in Paris was the target – on 9 August, killing six people and wounding twenty-two – while on 9 October, Palestinian groups, supported by extreme left-wing Italian subversive groups, struck the main synagogue of Rome, killing little Stefano Taché, barely a year old, and wounding another thirty-five people. These tragedies had the effect of shaking public opinion in the continent and especially the Jewish communities.

In this regard, the French situation is particularly interesting: the bomb which exploded in October 1980 near the synagogue of Rue Copernic triggered a lively controversy when the French Prime Minister, Raymond Barre, commenting on what had happened on the television channel TF1, made a curious slip of the tongue, distinguishing, among the victims, between the 'Jews' and the 'innocent French'.[30] The attacks by the Palestinian groups were, in effect, succeeding, to a greater or lesser extent in the various countries, in isolating the Jewish communities of the old continent from the rest of society; the widespread tendency to *denationalize* the Jewish minorities had not been eliminated by post-Nazi Europe simply by abrogating the racist laws and was re-emerging with particular emphasis in that difficult situation, when the Jews were being schematically identified with the State of Israel whose policies were being severely condemned by a large part of public opinion. These developments had a profound impact on the Jewish communities, in some cases, encouraging a reinterpretation of their history and their relationship with the European nation-states; this was particularly evident in France, where, in the 1980s, an intense political-cultural ferment roused various sectors of the Jewish world. Taking his cue from the 1980 act of terrorism, Shmuel Trigano directly attacked the centralizing Republican system, criticizing the model of citizenship which emerged with the emancipation because, according to him, it stifled the minority, preventing it from living its own diversity serenely and freely.[31] As Bernard Wassertein noted,[32] something was changing in the minds of many Jewish intellectuals, even though very well integrated in the French social fabric; in the 1980s, a former Marxist like Bernard-Henry Lévy recovered his Jewishness and did not fail to launch a violent attack against the heritage of Vichy, against that racist and anti-Semitic 'idéologie française', with which, he maintained, the national spirit was still imbued.[33] With greater sobriety, a serious scholar like Pierre Birnbaum started an important investigation of the Dreyfus case, the historical roots of French anti-Semitism and the forms of Jewish integration.[34] The ferment which marked these and other intellectuals of Jewish extraction has to be seen in a particular context in which the post-war myths were falling to pieces and historiography was reconsidering the history of Vichy and particularly its anti-Semitic policies, which became very quickly the criterion with which to formulate a judgement, no longer historical but ethical on the regime itself.[35] In that particular context, which encouraged the revision of old and consolidated cultural paradigms, it was possible for some limited but important circles of the French-Jewish world – and European, to a lesser extent – to call into question the model of citizenship established after the emancipation.[36]

The unexpected echoes of the Israeli invasion of Lebanon in 1982 also contributed to rousing people's spirits, provoking heated debates and impassioned reflections. That war represented, in many ways, a definitive loss of innocence: the aggression against Lebanon seemed to compromise the purity of the Zionist dream and led to a grave crisis in the Israeli nation's mechanisms of self-representation.[37] It gave rise to dramatic clashes within Israeli society, which also found an echo, in various forms, in the communities of the Diaspora: Israel (or the Zionist reflection on Israel), which had been, in the post-war period, among the main resources/responses for facing the anxieties raised by the racist persecution, presented itself – more than ever – in a different way, much less engaging: it became one of the main problems in the life of the Diaspora communities. For the Jews, the very intensity of the affective tie with the State led to the exacerbation of the divisions already present in the Jewish communities since 1967, increasing the level of internal conflict. In Italy, while a group of left-wing intellectuals – which included Primo Levi and Natalia Ginzburg – condemned the military action of the Israeli Government led by Menachem Begin,[38] other sectors of the Italian-Jewish world expressed unconditional solidarity for Israel.[39] Naturally, such events became intertwined with the ferment which these events had provoked in Italian society and particularly in the world of politics and journalism.[40]

In the first half of the 1980s, there was a wave of anti-Semitic demonstrations throughout Italy: the aggression of Begin's government towards Lebanon unleashed a feeling of anger mainly directed against the Jewish communities.[41] A new phenomenon then took shape in Italy: while, after 1967, anti-Zionism – sometimes very close to purely anti-Semitic rhetoric – had been the prerogative of specific circles of the political and cultural Left, after 1982, wider social strata were involved, even including that middle class which had until then supported Israel;[42] a feeling, which was in many ways new, was then developing even though it could be traced back to older cultural roots, capable of transcending traditional political boundaries, involving groups and movements covering a broad ideological spectrum. Following the war in Lebanon, the issue took on a different and unprecedented aspect, and it would be inappropriate to interpret expressions of prejudice and hatred, following that event, simply as the umpteenth variation on a very old theme.[43] While the events following the Six Day War (June 1967) can be viewed in the context of the Cold War, the post-1982 events seem to anticipate uncertainties and instability of a new age, which was then looming on the horizon: after the Second World War, anti-Semitism and the Jews had been real taboos for Western society, the 1980s witnessed the end of the post-war period, or rather the collapse of the system of cultural representations on which was based the political-cultural system which had arisen from the ashes of the fascist regimes. The images of the Jew and of Israel, so closely tied to the memories of the Second World War, were also dramatically marked by it.[44]

From today's perspective, one can clearly see the reactivation and updating of a system of signs which had at its heart the image of the Jew: a 'new Judaeophobia', decidedly post-Nazi, took shape at that time. It was not so closely linked to the nineteenth-century racist stereotypes. It foreshadowed the unbridgeable diversity and contrast between 'Semites' and 'Aryans',[45] but rather to the perception of Israel – and of the Jews, simplistically linked to it – as embodying the worst qualities of the West.[46] Mirroring itself in the Israeli military operation, a meaningful portion of Western public opinion felt disgust, a rejection particularly intense maybe because it recognized a part of itself in it.[47]

In the face of the outbursts of intolerance of those years, there were reactions of sincere concern: many commentators were upset and sincerely shocked or unable to believe that even in Italy there could be anti-Semitism. In fact, the analysis undertaken then by the main newspapers tended to arrive at a rapid and superficial minimization of the phenomenon. But in the face of the increasing number of episodes, which were also serious, the attempts to provide reassurance – for themselves and for the minority in question – seemed weaker and weaker and less convincing.[48] That climate, the sad and tragic echoes, in Italy, of the 1982 conflict, inflicted deep wounds in the Italian-Jewish minority.

> It would be foolish – noted Arnaldo Momigliano in concluding a brief, but detailed, *excursus* on the history of the Jews in Italy given at Brandeis University in 1984 – to close on a note of optimism when a Jewish child can be assassinated in the synagogue of Rome, as one was in 1982, without an outcry of public opinion.[49]

That anxiety impacted the processes of identity revision already in progress. Since the end of the 1970s – and during the 1980s – the minority had been deeply involved in reconsidering its organization, not only in terms of its own internal set-up, but also, more generally, its own role in society: even if with great tardiness, the appropriate conditions were slowly developing for the definitive surmounting of the Royal Decree n.1731 of 1930 which established the UCII.[50] It is not difficult to see how the reflection which prepared the ground for the drawing up of the Agreement with the State, signed in 1987, could be clearly traced back to more wide-ranging developments and concerning the whole of society. At stake, among other things, were the reformulation of the concept of citizenship and the reorganization of the relationship between individuals, religious groups and the State, issues which were connected to the delicate and vital problem of the *right to be different*.[51]

That ferment, fusing with the new anxieties produced by the expressions of hatred of the early 1980s, gave rise, in some sectors of the Italian-Jewish world, even if with greater difficulty and more slowly than beyond the Alps, to a deep desire/need to reconsider the meaning of the pact of citizenship, beginning timidly to question a cultural and political model whose outlines had been drawn in the late eighteenth century, with the beginning of the process of integration.[52] The awareness of the 'new anti-Judaism' and the development of the reflection on its own condition as a minority implied a process of rediscovery/reformulation of oneself which could not fail to also constitute a need to reconsider and review the past, questioning the validity and effectiveness of the interpretative models in which the history of Jewish integration and of anti-Semitism in contemporary Italy had become enclosed. In that tendency one can recognize one of the factors which – combining with other forces, including the attempts made in the Left to revitalize the anti-fascist myth through anti-racism – have stimulated the intensification of scientific and journalistic debate about the racial persecutions over the last thirty years.

NOTES

1. Regarding the theme of disorientation, see T. Todorov, *L'homme dépaysé* (Paris: Seuil, 1997).
2. A. Momigliano, preface to *Essays on Ancient and Modern Judaism*, edited by S. Berti (Chicago, IL: University of Chicago Press, 1994), p.xxvi. For another example see the autobiography of V. Foa, *Il cavallo e la torre. Riflessioni su una vita* (Turin: Einaudi, 1991), p.5.
3. That trial had different periods of development and outcomes in the various countries, but in general terms the judgement of the sociologist S.N. Eisenstadt is reasonable. He noted that 'a new element developed in its fullest way in the period after the Second World War. This was the emergence of legitimate collective Jewish political activity within the political framework of the respective societies. For the first time in exilic history, Jewish communities throughout the world became politically active and conscious as Jews. The pinnacle of this development, of course, was the establishment of the state of Israel and the continuous relations between it and all the Jewish communities in the Diaspora.' S.N. Eisenstadt, *Jewish Civilization: The Jewish Historical Experience in Comparative Perspective* (Albany, NY: State University of New York, 1992), p.260.
4. Thus, his reflection continued: 'We, who have rejected the religious tradition, now belong to the negative community of those, who have, so many times in history, been singled out for persecution and extermination… It was from the ashes of six million Jews that the phoenix of Jewry has risen. What a resurrection!', *The Non-Jewish Jew and Other Essays*, edited and with an introduction by T. Deutscher (New York and London: Oxford University Press, 1968), p.5.
5. G. Piperno, *Ebraismo, Sionismo, Halutzismo* (Rome: Carucci, 1976), p.143, my italics.
6. See, for example, the account of L. Della Pergola: 'our new friends were mainly from the Jewish Community; before the racial laws we used to see above all non-Jews but, after what we had gone through, it was natural to bond mostly with our own co-religionists. After the war, we never forgot that we were Jews', in *Una gioventù offesa. Ebrei genovesi ricordano*, edited by C. Bricarelli (Florence: La Giuntina, 1995), p.52.
7. See N. Ginzburg, *Lessico famigliare* (Turin: Einaudi, 1963), p.16.
8. Regarding the causes, see A. Cavaglion, 'Qualche riflessione sulla "mancata Riforma"', in M. Toscano (ed.), *Integrazione e identità. L'esperienza ebraica in Germania e Italia dall'Illuminismo al fascismo* (Milan: Angeli, 1998), pp.152–66; see also G. Luzzatto Voghera, 'Cenni storici per una ricostruzione del dibattito sulla riforma religiosa nell'Italia ebraica', *RMI*, 1–2, LIX (1993), pp.47–70.

9. For an assertion of the need for, and the importance of, a modernizing reform, see the heartfelt reflection of A. Cavaglion, *Ebrei senza saperlo* (Naples: L'Ancora del Mediterraneo, 2001). Recently, in Milan, a Reformed synagogue has been opened and there has also been the affiliation of the Italian group with the World Union for Progressive Judaism.
10. G.J. Piperno, *Ebraismo, Sionismo, Halutzismo*, p.110.
11. In one of the most interesting and less quoted passages of his acute reflection following the Liberation of Rome he writes: 'But the living who did not understand and who do not understand the reason for the persecution, it is right that today they should be alarmed by an equally donated indulgence. This closing an eye, of making exceptions for the Jews, is not the way to make reparation for injustices. Reparation would be to put the Jews back in the midst of the life of others, in the cycle of human fate, and not to keep them separate, even if for good motives. This is an anti-persecution: therefore made of the same psychological and moral substance which motivated the persecution. If first in the Jews one punished the Jew, today, on seeing the situation, not exactly corrected, but simply overturned with such a perfect symmetry of antithesis, the doubt can arise that in the Jews one forgives the Jew', G. Debenedetti, *Otto ebrei* (Rome: Atlantica, 1944), pp.12–13.
12. Y. Leibowitz, letter to Assa Kasher, in *La fede ebraica* (Florence: La Giuntina, 2001 [1995]), p.107.
13. D. Bidussa, 'Introduzione. Gli ebrei moderni e gli uomini di mezzanotte', in *Ebrei moderni. Identità e stereotipi culturali* (Turin: Bollati Boringhieri, 1989), p.18.
14. For example, in a Jewish-Italian newspaper, after the Second World War, there was the translation of an imaginary dialogue between Hitler and Antiochus Epiphanes in which the two characters, having met in the hereafter, boasted of the evil deeds they had committed against the Jews. The Shoah and the persecution of Antiochus Epiphanes, which ended in the revolt of the Maccabees, were proposed as two aspects of the same question; see *L'eco dell'educazione ebraica. Bollettino di informazione professionale e didattica per gli insegnanti ebrei*, Milan, 2–3 (November–December 1949).
15. S. Trigano, 'Introduction' in *Pardès*, special issue edited by S. Trigano, *Pensèr Auschwitz*, 9–10 (1989). Regarding these themes, and in general on the fragile set-up of Western Judaism proposed in S. Trigano, *La nouvelle question juive* (Paris: Gallimard, 2002 [reprint of the first edition of 1979 with the addition of a postface]).
16. We have already touched on this question in the preceding chapters; apart from the texts already cited, see I. Zerthal, 'Du bon usage du souvenir', *Le Débat*, 58 (1990), pp.92–103, and A. Ofir, *La nuova religione di Israele, Il Mulino*, 1 (1989), pp.92–100.
17. See D. Bidussa, 'Radicalità e politica. Su Enzo Sereni', postface to E. Sereni, *Le origini del fascismo*, edited by Y. Viterbo and with an introduction by M.G. Meriggi (Florence: La Nuova Italia, 2000), p.266.
18. Emanuele Artom, for example, wrote in his diary on 3 September 1941: 'until then I had only felt a liking for Zionism, but in 1939 I became a Zionist'. It was only a question of a momentary adherence which, in the case of Artom, and probably also in many other cases, was not destined to have significant consequences. See E. Artom, *Diari di un partigiano ebreo. Gennaio 1940–febbraio 1944*, edited by G. Schwarz (Turin: Bollati Boringhieri, 2008), p.14.
19. It was thus that the writer Giorgio Voghera, who had fled from Trieste in 1938 and had then returned in 1948, wrote of himself. In the extraordinary memoirs, *Quaderno d'Israele* (Pordenone: Edizioni reflect on Italian Jews and their sudden 'discovery' of Zionism: see pp.127–33, for the quotation p.24. But on the spirit and feelings of those who then chose to go to Palestine see also A. Marzano, *Una terra per rinascere. Gli ebrei italiani e l'emigrazione in Palestina prima della guerra (1920–1940)*, preface by A. Cavaglion (Genoa and Milan: Marietti, 2003), pp.92–101.
20. Regarding Sereni, see the detailed observations of D. Bidussa: see the postface to E. Sereni, *Le origini del fascismo*, pp.265–347; D. Bidussa, 'La nostalgia del futuro', introduction to Enzo Sereni and Emilio Sereni, *Politica e utopia. Lettere 1926–1943*, edited by D. Bidussa and M.G. Meriggi (Florence: La Nuova Italia, 2000). For a biography, see R. Bondy, *The Emissary: Life of Enzo Sereni* (Boston, MA and Toronto: Little Brown, 1977).
21. A. Zargani, *Per violino solo. La mia infanzia nell'aldiquà* (Bologna: Il Mulino, 1997), p.84.
22. See A. Finkielkraut, *The Imaginary Jew* (Lincoln, NE: University of Nebraska Press, 1994 [1980]), p.132.
23. B. Wasserstein, *Vanishing Diaspora: The Jews in Europe since 1945* (Cambridge, MA: Harvard University Press, 1994), p.103.
24. See the considerations regarding the French situation, but easily applicable to Italy, of P. Cohen Albert, 'L'intégration et la persistence de l'ethnicité chez les juifs dans la France modern', in P. Birnbaum (ed.), *Histoire politique des juifs de France* (Paris: Presses de la Fondation Nationale des Sciences Politiques, 1990), pp.221–42.

25. I take up here the reflection of S. Trigano, 'From Individual to Collectivity: The Rebirth of the "Jewish Nation" in France', in F. Malino and B. Wasserstein (eds), *The Jews in Modern France* (Hanover, NH and London: Brandeis University Press, 1985), pp.244–81.
26. Lucid and stimulating observations were made, on the spot, by R. Aron, *De Gaulle, Israël et les Juifs* [1968], now in R. Aron, *Essais sur la condition juive contemporaine*, edited by P. Simon-Nahum (Paris: Edition de Fallois, 1989), pp.35–181.
27. On the expulsion of the Jews from Lybia, see R. De Felice, *Ebrei in un paese arabo. Gli ebrei nella Libia contemporanea tra colonialismo, nazionalismo arabo e sionismo (1835–1970)* (Bologna: Il Mulino, 1978), in particular see the last chapter. While the approximately 6,000 Lybians – for the most part from Tripoli – settled mainly in Rome, the Persians who arrived in the following decades formed a compact nucleus in Milan.
28. See D. Bidussa, 'Le società ebraiche contemporanee tra multiculturalismo e riscrittura dell'appartenenza', *Parolechiave*, 3 (1993), pp.76–84.
29. Some indications have been proposed by M. Toscano, 'Tra identità culturale e partecipazione politica. Aspetti e moment di vita ebraica italiana (1956–1976)', *Annuario di Studi Ebraici* (1985–1987), pp.293–325.
30. This is the exact wording: 'cet attentat odieux qui voulait frapper les Israélites qui se rendaient à la synagogue et qui a frappé des Français innocents qui traversaient la rue'. On the event and its controversial aftermath, see M. Szafran, *Les juifs dans la politique française. De 1945 à nos jours* (Paris: Flamarion, 1990), pp.231–3.
31. S. Trigano, *La République et les Juifs après Copernic* (Paris: Les Presses D'aujourd'hui, 1982).
32. B. Wasserstein, *Vanished Diaspora*, pp.113ff.
33. B.-H. Lévy, *L'idéologie française* (Paris: Grasset, 1981).
34. See works by Pierre Birnbaum: *Les fous de la République. Histoire politique des Juifs d'Etat de Gambetta à Vichy* (Paris: Fayard, 1992); *'La France aux Français'. Histoire des haines nationalists* (Paris: Seuil, 1993); *L'affaire Dreyfus. La République en peril* (Paris: Gallimard, 1994); *Destins juifs. De la Révolution française à Carpentras* (Paris: Calmann-Lévy ,1995); *Un mythe politique, la 'République juive'. De Léon Blum à Mendès France* (Paris: Gallimard, 1995); *Le moment anti-Semite. Un tour de la France en 1898* (Paris: Fayard, 1998); *Sur la corde raide. Parcours juifs entre exil et citoyenneté* (Paris: Flamarion, 2002).
35. For a critical outlook on the changes in the 1970s and 1980s and the affirmation of Jewish memories over the traditional anti-fascist canon, see H. Rousso, *La syndrome de Vichy de 1944 à nos jours* (Paris: Seuil, 1990), pp.270ff.
36. For a European perspective, which underlines how the 1980s (and then the 1990s) have constituted a fundamental moment for reviewing the Jewish condition, see J. Weber (ed.), *Jewish Identities in the New Europe* (London and Washington, DC: The Littman Library of Jewish Civilization, 1994). On the French situation see also the synthetic contextualization by M. Cohen, *Les juifs de France*, *Le Débat*, 75 (1993), pp.110–15.
37. For example, I think that this emerges clearly from the newspaper articles published during and shortly after that conflict (between 1982 and 1987) by the writer, and activist of the Peace Now movement, Amos Oz. See A. Oz, *The Slopes of Lebanon* (San Diego, CA, New York and London: Harcourt Brace Jovanovich, 1989 [1987]).
38. The appeal, entitled 'Perché Israele si ritiri', appeared in *La Repubblica*, 16 June 1982. The appeal collected over 1,500 signatures, not only of Jews.
39. See the account of Elio Toaff, who in his capacity as Chief Rabbi of Rome was at the centre of so many confrontations and controversies, and who maintained a line of committed support for Israel: *Perfidi giudei, fratelli maggiori* (Milan: Mondadori, 1987), Chapter 10.
40. For a synthetic but effective reconstruction of the echoes of the war in Lebanon in the Italian press, see R. Cipollini, 'Note su un dibattito incompiuto; analisi della stampa', in E. Campelli and R. Cipollini, *Contro il seme di Abramo. Indagine sull'antisemitismo a Roma* (Milan: Angeli, 1984), pp.101–46.
41. There was then a sharp increase in acts which were clearly anti-Semitic: graffiti, acts of vandalism against buildings of the Jewish community, threats and intimidation directed against its leaders or even ordinary citizens of Jewish extraction. For a documented review of such episodes in Italy, see A. Goldstaub (ed.), *La guerra nel Libano e l'opinione pubblica italiana* (Milan: CDEC, 1983).
42. This was noted by S. Levi della Torre, 'Fine del dopoguerra e sintomi antisemitici', *Rivista di Storia Contemporanea*, 3 (1984), p.445.
43. Without denying that there are common, even important, elements in traditional anti-Judaism,

nationalist and racist anti-Semitism and modern anti-Zionism/anti-Semitism, I think it is important to bear in mind the new and distinct elements which have come into being in the last decades. This appears very difficult, also because there is a consolidated historiographic paradigm – which, for example, finds one of its most important expressions in the work of Léon Poliakov – which favours the theme of continuity, strongly complicating however an understanding of the different interruptions produced in the evolution of anti-Semitic views. The reference is to L. Poliakov, *Storia dell' antisemitismo*, 5 vols (Florence: La Nuova Italia, 1974–1996).

44. S. Levi della Torre, 'Fine del dopoguerra e sintomi antisemitici', p.455.
45. I refer here to what I regard as one of the most convincing passages of the work of P.A. Taguieff, *La nouvelle judéophobie* (Paris: Mille et une nuits, 2002), p.26. It is stimulating, but not without strained interpretations and excesses. It is in relation to the particular French situation, where (apart from America) there is the largest Western Jewish community and where there is also the large and at times problematic presence of populations from North Africa, that this explicitly activist text should be interpreted.
46. S. Levi della Torre, 'Fine del dopoguerra e sintomi antisemitici', pp.445ff. In more general terms see also L. Picciotto Fargion (ed.), *L'immagine dell'ebreo nell'Italia degli anni Ottanta*, special issue of *RMI*, 3, LVI (1990).
47. And in this, in anti-Zionism as a rejection and a condemnation of what is perceived as the worst aspect of an aggressive and colonial West, one can perhaps recognize a structural similarity with the essence of anti-Semitism: 'The commonplace which defines anti-Semitism as "hostility towards diversity" captures its generic nature, which links it with racism and xenophobia, but not its specificity. Anti-Semitism is more precisely hostility towards fellow creatures, or rather, the small difference, the deviant contiguity'. See S. Levi della Torre, *Mosaico. Attualità e inattualità degli ebrei* (Turin: Rosenberg & Sellier, 1994), p.79.
48. A reading of the newspaper treatment, in the 1980s, shows difficulties and unpreparedness of the intelligentsia. In this regard see the critical contextualization of the debate which took place in the press, at that time, proposed by R. Cipollini, 'Note su un dibattito incompiuto', pp.126ff.
49. A. Momigliano, 'The Jews of Italy', in *Essays on Ancient and Modern Judaism*, p.133.
50. See S. Dazzetti, 'Un percorso di libertà. Il dibattito e le scelte dell'ebraismo italiano preliminari all'Intesa collo Stato (1977–1987)', *Diritto Ecclesiastico*, 2 (1998), pp.242–64.
51. Guido Fubini was the champion of the right to diversity in Italy and among the Jews. In this regard, it is worth noting the critical comparison with a defender of classical liberal ideals, such as Jemolo: see the considerations put forward by the latter in the 'Presentazione alla prima edizione e la Risposta dell'autore', now in G. Fubini, *La condizione giuridica dell'ebraismo italiano* (Turin: Rosenberg & Sellier, 1998 [2nd ed. revised and expanded]), respectively pp.7–17 and 19–22.
52. Regarding the problem of citizenship see the interesting considerations put forward by David Bidussa, also taking into consideration the statute granted to the Jews following the emancipation: 'Europa infelix. Le fragili radici della democrazia europea', *RMI*, 6 (2003), pp.59–79.

Bibliography

ARCHIVAL SOURCES

Archivio Centrale dello Stato (Rome):
1. Presidenza del Consiglio dei Ministri
2. Ministero degli Interni, Direzione Generale Pubblica Sicurezza
3. Segreteria Particolare De Gasperi
4. Archivio Renzo De Felice

Archivio Centro di Documentazione Ebraica Contemporanea (Milan):
1. Archivio Federazione Giovanile Ebraica d'Italia
2. Archivio Aldo Ascoli
3. Archivio Massimo Adolfo Vitale
4. Corrispondenza CDEC

Archivio della Comunità Ebraica di Milano (Milan)
Verbali del Consiglio della Comunità

Archivio Storico Ministero Affari Esteri:
1. Gabinetto 1943–1948
2. Segretariato Generale 1945–1949

Archivio Unione delle Comunità Israelitiche Italiane (Rome)
1. Verbali del Consiglio dell'Unione delle Comunità
2. Verbali della Giunta dell'Unione delle Comunità
3. Buste: 11, 30–34, 44, 74, 85

Biblioteca-Archivio Renato Maestro (Venice):
Archivio Dante Lattes

Central Archives for the History of the Jewish People:
F. Italy n.1925

Central Zionist Archives (Jerusalem)
1. Archives of the British Section of the World Jewish Congress

2. Archives of the Federazione Sionistica Italiana
3. Private Archive Leone Carpi
4. Private Archive Alfredo Sarano

CONTEMPORARY PERIODICALS

Bollettino della Comunità Ebraica di Milano (1945–61)
Bollettino Ebraico d'Informazioni (1944)
Ha-Tikwà (1949–61)
Hechalutz (1946–56)
Israel (1944–61)
La Rassegna Mensile di Israel (1948–61)
La Voce della Comunità Israelitica di Roma (1952–61)

AUTHORED WORKS, EDITED COLLECTIONS AND JOURNALS

Abrams, P., *Historical Sociology* (Ithaca, NY: Cornell University Press, 1982).

Actes et documents du Saint Siège relatives à la Seconde Guerre Mondiale, vol. IX, *Le Saint Siège et les victimes de la guerre* (Vatican City, 1975).

Agosti, A. (ed.), *La coerenza della ragione. Per una biografia politica di Umberto Terracini* (Rome: Carocci, 1998).

Angier, C., *The Double Bond. Primo Levi: A Biography* (New York: Farrar, Straus and Giroux, 2002).

Arendt, H., *Eichmann in Jerusalem: A Report on the Banality of Evil* (London: Penguin Books, 1992 [1964]).

Arian Levi, G. and Montagnana, M., *I Montagnana. Una famiglia ebraica piemontese e il movimento operaio (1914–1948)*, preface by A. Luzzatto (Florence: La Giuntina, 2000).

Aron, R., *Essais sur la condition juive contemporaine*, edited by P. Simon-Nahum (Paris: Edition de Fallois, 1989).

Artom, E., *Diari di un partigiano ebreo. Gennaio 1940–febbraio 1944*, edited by G. Schwarz (Turin: Bollati Boringhieri, 2008).

Ashheim, S.E. (ed.), *Hannah Arendt in Jerusalem* (Berkeley, CA: University of California Press, 2001).

Bal, M., Crewe, J. and Spitzer, L. (eds), *Acts of Memory: Cultural Recall in the Present* (Hanover, PA and London: University Press of New England, 1999).

Bankier, D. (ed.), *The Jews are Coming Back: The Return of the Jews to their Countries of Origin after WWII* (New York and Jerusalem: Berghahn Books/Yad Vashem, 2005).

Bassani, G., *Opere*, edited by R. Cotroneo (Milan: Mondadori, 2001).

Battini, M., *The Missing Italian Nuremberg: Cultural Amnesia and Post-War Politcs* (New York and Basingstoke: Palgrave Macmillan, 2007).

Bauer, Y., *Flight and Rescue: Bricah* (New York: Random House, 1970).

Bauer, Y., *Out of Ashes: The Impact of American Jews on Post-Holocaust European Jewry* (Oxford: Pergamon Press, 1989).

Bedarida, G., *Ebrei d'Italia* (Livorno: Tirrenia, 1950).

Bemporad, M., *La Macine. Storia di una famiglia israelita negli ultimi 60 anni di vita italiana* (Rome: Carucci, 1984).

Bertilotti, P., 'Riconoscimento, reintegrazione e risarcimento. Le vittime della persecuzione antisemita in Italia 1944–1965', *Italia Contemporanea*, 254 (2008), pp.115–37.

Bertilotti, P., 'La notion de déporté en Italie, de 1945 à nos jours. Droit, politiques de la mémoire et mémoires concurrentes', in T. Bruttmann, L. Joly and A. Wieviorka (eds), *Qu'est-ce qu'un déporté? Histoire et mémoires des déportations de la Seconde Guerre mondiale* (Paris: CNRS, 2009), pp.377–402.

Bidussa, D. (ed.), *Ebrei moderni. Identità e stereotipi culturali* (Turin: Bollati Boringhieri, 1989).

Bidussa, D., 'Le società ebraiche contemporanee tra multiculturalismo e riscrittura dell'appartenenza', *Parolechiave*, 3 (1993), pp.76–84.

Bidussa, D., 'Gli ebrei in Italia in età moderna-contemporanea. Considerazioni per una storia ancora da scrivere', *Bailamme*, 15–16 (1994), pp.52–67.

Bidussa, D., *Il mito del bravo italiano* (Milan: Il Saggiatore, 1994).

Bidussa, D., 'Europa infelix. Le fragili radici della democrazia europea', *RMI*, 6, LXVIII (2003), pp.59–78.

Bidussa, D., Luzzatto, A. and Luzzatto Voghera, G., *Oltre il ghetto. Momenti e figure dell'emancipazione ebraica* (Brescia: Morcelliana, 1987).

Bloch, M., *The Historian's Craft* (Manchester: Manchester University Press, 1992).

Bloxam, D., *The Holocaust on Trial: The War Crimes Trials and the Formation of History and Memory* (Oxford: Oxford University Press, 2001).

Bodei, R., *Libro della memoria e della speranza* (Bologna: Il Mulino, 1995).

Bodeman, Y.M. (ed.), *Jews, Germans, Memory: The Reconstruction of Jewish Life in Germany* (Ann Arbor, MI: University of Michigan Press, 1996).

Bondy, R., *The Emissary: Life of Enzo Sereni* (Boston, MA and Toronto: Little Brown, 1977).

Brazzo, L. and Schwarz, G. (eds), 'Jews in Europe after the Shoah: Studies and Research Perspectives', *Quest. Issues in Contemporary History*, 1 (April 2010), http://www.quest-cdecjournal.it/.

Breger, M.J. (ed.), *The Vatican–Israel Accord: Political, Legal and Theological Contexts* (Notre Dame, IN: Notre Dame University Press, 2004).

Brenner, M., *After the Holocaust: Rebuilding Jewish Lives in Post-War Germany* (Princeton, NJ: Princeton University Press, 1997 [1995]).

Briccarelli, C. (ed.), *Una gioventù offesa. Ebrei genovesi ricordano* (Florence: La Giuntina, 1995).

Calamandrei, P., *Lettere 1915–1956*, vol. II, edited by G. Agosti and A. Galante Garrone (Florence: La Nuova Italia, 1968).

Campelli, E. and Cipollini, R., *Contro il seme di Abramo. Indagine sull' antisemitismo a Roma* (Milan: Angeli, 1984).

Capristo, A., *L'espulsione degli ebrei dalle accademie italiane* (Turin: Zamorani, 2002).

Capuzzo, E., *Gli ebrei nella società italiana. Comunità e istituzioni tra Ottocento e Novecento* (Rome: Carocci, 1999).

Cardini, A., *Tempi di ferro. 'Il Mondo' e l'Italia del dopoguerra* (Bologna: Il Mulino, 1992).

Caredda, G., *Governo e opposizione nell'Italia del dopoguerra 1947–1960* (Bari: Laterza, 1995).

Carlotti, A.L. (ed.), *Italia 1939–1945. Storia e memoria*, preface by F. Della Peruta (Milan: Edizioni Vita e Pensiero, 1995).

Carpi, D., 'Il movimento sionistico', in *Gli ebrei in Italia, in Storia d'Italia, Annali*, edited by C. Vivanti, vol. XI/2 (Turin: Einaudi, 1997), pp.1338–69.

Cases, C., 'Cosa fai in giro?', *Il Ponte*, 11–12 (1978), pp.1331–9.

Cases, C., *Confessioni di un ottuagenario* (Rome: Donzelli, 2000).

Cassata, F., *Molti sani e forti. L'eugenetica in Italia* (Turin: Bollati Boringhieri, 2006).

Cassata, F., *'La Difesa della Razza'. Politica, ideologia e immagine del razzismo fascista* (Turin: Einaudi, 2008).

Catalan, T., *La comunità ebraica di Trieste (1781–1914). Politica, società e cultura* (Trieste: Lint, 2000).

Cavaglion, A., 'Qualche riflessione sulla "mancata Riforma"', in M. Toscano (ed.), *Integrazione e identità. L'esperienza ebraica in Germania e Italia dall'Illuminismo al fascismo* (Milan: Angeli, 1998).

Cavaglion, A., *Ebrei senza saperlo* (Naples: L'Ancora del Mediterraneo, 2001).

Cesarani, D., 'Le Jewish Chronicle et la Shoah', *Revue d'Histoire de la Shoah*, 163 (1998).

Cesarani, D., *Eichmann: His Life and Crimes* (London: Heinemann, 2004).

Chessa, P., 'Renzo De Felice e il volume sugli ebrei italiani sotto il fascismo. Genesi e sviluppo di una ricerca storiografica', *Nuova Storia Contemporanea*, 2 (2000).

Cohen, Albert P., 'L'intégration et la persistence de l'ethnicité chez les juifs dans la France modern', in P. Birnbaum (ed.), *Histoire politique des juifs de France* (Paris: Presses de la Fondation Nationale des Sciences Politiques, 1990), pp.221–42.

Cohen, B., 'Holocaust Survivors and the Genesis of Holocaust Research', in J.-D. Steinert and I. Weber-Newth, (eds), *Beyond Camps and Forced Labour: Current International Research on Survivors of Nazi Persecution* (Osnabrück: Secolo Verlag, 2005), pp.290–300.

Cohen, M., 'Les juifs de France', *Le Débat*, 75 (1993), pp.110–15.

Collotti, E., *Fascismo, fascismi* (Florence: Sansoni, 1989).

Collotti, E. (ed.), *Razza e fascismo. La persecuzione contro gli ebrei in Toscana (1938–1943)*, vol. I (Rome: Carocci, 1999).

Collotti, E. (ed.), *Fascismo e antifascismo. Rimozioni, revisioni, negazioni* (Bari: Laterza, 2000).

Commissione per la ricostruzione delle vicende che hanno caratterizzato le attività di acquisizione dei beni ebraici da parte di organismi pubblici e privati (Commission for the examination of the acquisition of Jewish property by public and private bodies), *Rapporto Generale* (Rome: Presidenza del Consiglio dei Ministri, Dipartimento per l'informazione e l'editoria, 2001); http://www.governo.it/Presidenza/DICA/beni_ebraici/index.html.

Connerton, P., *How Societies Remember* (Cambridge: Cambridge University Press, 1989).

Consonni, M., 'The Impact of the Eichmann Event in Italy, 1961', *Journal of Israeli History*, 23 (2004).

Cooke, P., *Luglio '60. Tambroni e la repressione fallita* (Milan: Teti, 2000).

Cooke, P., *The Legacy of the Italian Resistance* (New York and Basingstoke: Palgrave Macmillan, 2011).

Croce, B., *Scritti e discorsi politici 1943–1947*, vol. II, edited by A. Carrella (Naples: Biliopolis, 1993).

D'Amico, G., *Quando l'eccezione diventa norma. La reintegrazione degli ebrei nell'Italia postfascista* (Turin: Bollati Boringhieri, 2006).

Dalma, G., *La verità sugli ebrei* (Rome: OET, 1945).

Dazzetti, S., 'Un percorso di libertà. Il dibattito e le scelte dell'ebraismo italiano preliminary all'Intesa con lo Stato (1977–1987)', *Diritto Ecclesiastico*, 2 (1998), pp.242–64.

Dazzetti, S., 'Gli ebrei italiani e il fascismo. La formazione della legge del 1930 sulle comunità israelitiche', in S. Mazzacane (ed.), *Diritto economia e istituzioni nell'Italia fascista* (Baden: Nomos Verlagsgesellschaft, 2002), pp.219–54.

De Felice, R., *Storia degli ebrei in Italia sotto il fascismo* (Turin: Einaudi, 1961); revised editions appeared in 1974, 1988 and 1993; English edition (based on the last Italian edition of 1993): *The Jews in Fascist Italy: A History* (New York: Enigma Books, 2001).

De Felice, R., *Le interpretazioni del fascism* (Bari: Laterza, 1995 [1969]).

De Felice, R., *Ebrei in un paese arabo. Gli ebrei nella Libia contemporanea tra colonialismo, nazionalismo arabo e sionismo (1835–1970)* (Bologna: Il Mulino, 1978).

De Felice, R., *Mussolini il duce*, vol. II, *Lo stato totalitario 1936–1940* (Turin: Einaudi, 1981).

Deak, I., Gross, J.T. and Judt, T. (eds), *The Politics of Retribution in Europe:*

World War II and its Aftermath (Princeton, NJ: Princeton University Press, 2000).

Dean, M., *Robbing the Jews: The Confiscation of Jewish Property in the Holocaust 1933–1945* (Cambridge: Cambridge University Press, 2010).

Dean, M., Goshler, C. and Ther, P. (eds), *Robbery and Restitution: The Conflict over Jewish Property in Europe* (New York: Berghahn Books, 2007).

Debenedetti, C.I., *Anni di rabbia e di speranze 1938–1949* (Florence: La Giuntina, 2003).

Debenedetti, G., *Otto ebrei*, preface by C. Sforza (Rome: Atlantica, 1944).

Debenedetti, G., *16 Ottobre 1943* (Rome: OET, 1945).

Debenedetti, R., 'La tragedia degli ebrei d'Europa', in the appendix of A. Errera, *Vita del popolo ebraico* (Milan: Garzanti, 1947), pp.316–48.

Del Boca, A., 'Il mancato dibattito sul colonialismo', in *L'Africa nella coscienza degli italiani* (Bari: Laterza, 1992).

Del Boca, A., *I gas di Mussolini. Il fascismo e la guerra d'Etiopia* (Rome: Editori Riuniti, 1996).

Del Canuto, F., 'La ripresa delle attività sionistiche e delle organizzazioni ebraiche alla Liberazione (1944–1945)', *RMI*, 1–3, XLVII (1981), pp.174–200.

Del Pero, M., *L'alleato scomodo. Gli USA e la DC negli anni del centrismo (1948–1955)* (Rome: Carocci, 2001).

Del Regno, F., 'Tendenze politiche, religiose e culturali nella Comunità ebraica di Roma tra il 1936 e il 1941', in *Zakhor. Rivista di storia degli ebrei d'Italia*, 5 (2002), pp.87–108.

Del Vecchio, G., *Una nuova persecuzione contro un perseguitato. Documenti* (Rome: Tipografia artigiana, 1945).

Della Pergola, L., *Una gioventù offesa. Ebrei genovesi ricordano*, edited by C. Bricarelli (Florence: La Giuntina, 1995).

Della Pergola, S., *Anatomia dell'ebraismo italiano* (Assisi: Carucci, 1976).

Della Pergola, S. and Tagliacozzo, A., *Gli italiani in Israele. Risultati di un'indagine socio-demografica* (Milan: La Rassegna Mensile di Israel and Federazione Sionistica Italiana, 1978).

Della Seta, F., *L'incendio del Tevere* (Udine: Gaspari, 1996).

Della Seta, S., *Gli ebrei nel Mediterraneo nella strategia politica fascista sino al 1938. Il caso di Rodi, Storia Contemporanea*, 6 (1986), pp.997–1032.

Deutscher, I., *The Non-Jewish Jew and Other Essays*, edited with an introduction by T. Deutscher (New York and London: Oxford University Press, 1968).

Di Cori, P., 'Le leggi razziali', in M. Isnenghi (ed.), *I luoghi della memoria. Simboli e miti dell'Italia unita* (Bari: Laterza, 1996).

Di Nola, A.M., *Antisemitismo in Italia 1962/1972* (Florence: Vallechi, 1973).

Di Nolfo, E., *Le paure e le speranze degli italiani 1943–1945* (Milan: Mondadori, 1986).

Diner, D., 'Hannah Arendt Reconsidered: On the Banal and the Evil in her Holocaust Narrative', *New German Critique*, 71 (1997).

Eisenstadt, S.N., *Jewish Civilization: The Jewish Historical Experience in Comparative Perspective* (Albany, NY: State University of New York, 1992).

Fabre, G., *L'elenco. Censura fascista, editoria e autori ebrei* (Turin: Zamorani, 1998).

Fano, A., 'L'alijàh dall'Italia dal 1928 al 1955', *RMI*, 7, XXI (1955), pp.263–76.

Fantini, S., *Notizie dalla Shoah. La stampa italiana nel 1945* (Bologna: Pendragon, 2005).

Feldman, R.H. (ed.), *The Jew as Pariah: Jewish Identity and Politics in the Modern Age* (New York: Grove Press, 1978).

Ferrari, S., *Vaticano e Israele. Dal secondo conflitto mondiale alla guerra del Golfo* (Florence: Sansoni, 1991).

FGEI, *Quarant'anni 1948–1988* (Florence: La Giuntina, 1988).

Finkielkraut, A., *The Imaginary Jew* (Lincoln, NE: University of Nebraska Press, 1994 [1980]).

Finzi, R., *L'università italiana e le leggi antiebraiche* [2nd ed., reviewed and enlarged] (Rome: Editori Riuniti, 2003).

Fiori, G., *Una storia italiana. Vita di Ernesto Rossi* (Turin: Einaudi, 1997).

Fishman, D., 'Una risposta ebraica alle leggi. L'organizzazione delle scuole', *RMI*, 1–2, XIV (1988), pp.335–64.

Flores, M., 'L'antifascismo all'opposizione', *Fascismo e antifascismo negli anni della Repubblica*, monographic issue of *Problemi del Socialismo*, 28 (1986), pp.34–60.

Flores, M., Levis, Sullam S., Matard-Bonucci, M.-A. and Traverso, E. (eds), *Storia della Shoah in Italia. Vicende, memorie, rappresentazioni*, 2 vols (Turin: UTET, 2010).

Foa, V., *Il cavallo e la torre. Riflessioni su una vita* (Turin: Einaudi, 1991).

Foa, V., *Questo Novecento. Un secolo di passione civile. La politica come responsabilità* (Turin: Einaudi, 1996).

Focardi, F., 'Alle origini di una grande rimozione. La questione dell' antisemitismo fascista nell'Italia dell'immediato dopoguerra', *Horizonte*, 4 (1999), pp.135–69.

Focardi, F., 'La questione della punizione dei criminali di guerra in Italia dopo la fine del secondo conflitto mondiale', *Quellen und Forschungen* (2000), pp.543–624.

Focardi, F., *La guerra della memoria. La Resistenza nel dibattito politico italiano dal 1945 ad oggi* (Bari: Laterza, 2005).

Focardi, F., *Criminali di guerra in libertà. Un accordo segreto tra Italia e Germania Federale 1949–1954*, preface by L. Klinkhammer (Rome: Carocci, 2008).

Focardi, F. and Klinkhammer, L., 'La questione dei "criminali di guerra" italiani e una commissione di inchiesta dimenticata', *Contemporanea*, 3 (2001), pp.497–528.

Forti, C., *Il caso Pardo Roques. Un eccidio del 1944 tra memoria e oblio* (Turin: Einaudi, 1998).

Fortini, F., *I cani del Sinai* (Turin: Einaudi, 1979 [1967]).

Fraenkel, J., *The History of the British Section of the World Jewish Congress* (London: World Jewish Congress, 1977).

Friedländer, S., *When Memory Comes* (Madison, WI: University of Winsconsin Press, 1979).

Friedländer, S., 'Die Shoah als Element in der Konstruktion israealischer Erinnerung', *Babylon*, 2 (1987), pp.10–22.

Friedländer, S., *Nazi Germany and the Jews. Volume I. The Years of Persecution 1933–1939* (New York: HarperCollins, 1997).

Fubini, G., *La condizione giuridica dell'ebraismo italiano*, introduction by A.C. Jemolo (Turin: Rosenberg & Sellier, 1998).

Galimi, V. and Procacci, G. (eds), *Per la difesa della razza. L'applicazione delle leggi antiebraiche nelle universita italiane* (Milan: Unicopli, 2009).

Ganapini, L., *La Repubblica delle Camicie nere. I combattenti, i politici, gli amministratori, i socialiszzatori* (Milan: Garzanti, 1999).

Geller, J.H., *Jews in Post-Holocaust Germany 1945–1953* (Cambridge: Cambridge University Press, 2005).

Gentile, E., *La Grande Italia: The Myth of the Nation in the 20th Century* (Madison, WI: University of Winsconsin Press, 2009).

Gerbi, S., *Tempi di malafede. Una storia italiana tra fascismo e dopoguerra. Guido Piovene ed Eugenio Colorni* (Turin: Einaudi, 1999).

Germinario, F., *L'altra memoria. L'Estrema destra, Salò e la Resistenza* (Turin: Bollati Boringhieri, 1999).

Germinario, F., *Estranei alla democrazia. Negazionismo e antisemitismo nella destra radicale italiana* (Pisa: Biblioteca Franco Serantini, 2001).

Ghiles-Meilhac, S., *Le CRIF. De la Résistance juive à la tentation du lobby. De 1943 à nos jours* (Paris: Éditions Robert Laffont, 2011).

Gillette, A., *Racial Theories in Fascist Italy* (London and New York: Routledge, 2002).

Ginsborg, P., *Storia d'Italia dal dopoguerra a oggi. Società e politica 1943–1988* (Turin: Einaudi, 1989).

Ginzburg, N., *Lessico famigliare* (Turin: Einaudi, 1963).

Gli ebrei nell'Italia unita 1870–1945 (Rome: Ufficio Centrale per i Beni Archivistici, 1993).

Goldstaub, A. (ed.), *La guerra nel Libano e l'opinione pubblica italiana* (Milan: CDEC, 1983).

Goldstaub, A., *L'antisemitismo in Italia*, in L. Poliakov (ed.), *Storia dell'antisemitismo 1945–1993* (Florence: La Nuova Italia, 1996), pp.425–71.

Gramsci, A., *Quaderni del carcere* (Turin: Einaudi, 1975).

Grobman, A., *Rekindling the Flame: American Jewish Chaplains and the Survivors of European Jewry 1944–1948* (Detroit, IL: Wayne State University Press, 1993).

Gross, J.T., *Fear: Anti-Semitism in Poland after Auschwitz: An Essay in Historical Interpretation* (New York: Random House, 2006).

Grossmann, A., *Jews, German, Allies: Close Encounters in Occupied Germany* (Princeton, NJ: Princeton University Press, 2009).

Guaiana, Y., *Il tempo della Repubblica. Le feste civili in Italia* (Milan: Unicopli, 2007).

Hausner, G., *6,000,000 accusers; Israel's case against Eichmann*, translated and edited by S. Rosenne (Jerusalem: Jerusalem Post, 1961).

Hilberg, R., *The Destruction of European Jews* (New York and London: Holmes & Meier, 1985 [1961]).

Ignazi, P., *Il polo escluso. Profilo del Movimento Sociale Italiano* (Bologna: Il Mulino, 1989).

Institute of Jewish Affairs, *Unity in Dispersion: A History of the WJC*, introduction by A.L. Kubowitsky (New York: World Jewish Congress, 1948).

Irani, G.E., *The Papacy and the Middle East: The Role of the Holy See in the Arab–Israeli Conflict 1962–1984* (Notre Dame, IN: Notre Dame University Press, 1989).

Israel, G., *Il fascismo e la razza. La scienza italiana e le politiche razziali del regime* (Bologna: Il Mulino, 2010).

Israel, G. and Nastasi, P., *Scienza e razza nell'Italia fascista* (Bologna: Il Mulino, 1998).

Jaspers, K., *The Question of German Guilt* (New York: Capricorn Books, 1961 [1947]).

Jemolo, A.C., *Anni di prova*, preface by F. Margiotta Broglio (Florence: Passigli, 1991).

Jockush, L., 'Khurban Forshung: Jewish Historical Commission in Europe 1945–1949', *Simon Dubnow Institute Yearbook*, 6 (2007), pp.441–73.

Kauders, A.D., *Unmögliche Heimat: Eine deutsch-jüdische Geschichte der Bundesrepublik* (Munich: Deutsche Verlags-Anstalt, 2007).

Kertzer, D.I., *Ritual, Politics and Power* (New Haven, CT: Yale University Press, 1989).

Klinkhammer, L., *L'occupazione tedesca in Italia 1943–1945* (Turin: Bollati Boringhieri, 1993).

Klinkhammer, L., *Stragi naziste in Italia. La Guerra contro i civili (1943–1944)* (Rome: Donzelli, 1997).

Knox, M., 'Das faschistische Italien und die "Endlösung", 1942/43', *Viertel-jahrshefte für Zeitgeschichte*, 1 (2007), pp.53–92.

Kochavi, A.J., *Post-Holocaust Politics: Britain, the United States & Jewish*

Refugees, 1945–1948 (Chapel Hill, NC and London: University of North Carolina Press, 2001).

Kolinsky, E., *After the Holocaust: Jewish Survivors in Germany after 1945* (London: Pimlico, 2004).

Königseder, A. and Wetzel, J., *Waiting for Hope: Jewish Displaced Persons in post–World War II Germany* (Evanston, IL: Northwestern University Press, 2001).

La legislazione antiebraica in Italia e in Europa (Rome: Edizioni della Camera dei Deputati, 1989).

Lagrou, P., 'Victims of Genocide and National Memory: Belgium, France and the Netherlands', *Past & Present*, 154 (1997), pp.181–222.

Lagrou, P., *The Legacy of Nazi Occupation: Patriotic Memory and National Recovery in Western Europe (1945–1965)* (Cambridge: Cambridge University Press, 2000).

Lattes, D., 'Coloro che son partiti', *RMI*, 8–9, XXVI (1960), pp.347–50.

Lattes, D., 'Problemi e polemiche', *RMI*, 2, XXVII (1961), pp.51–5.

Lavsky, H., *New Beginnings: Holocaust Survivors in Bergen Belsen and the British Zone in Germany 1945–1950* (Detroit, MI: Wayne State University Press, 2002).

Le Goff, J., 'Les mentalités. Une histoire ambiguë', in J. Le Goff and P. Nora (eds), *Faire de l'histoire* (Paris: Gallimard, 1974), vol. III, p.78–94.

Leone, M., *Le organizzazioni di soccorso ebraiche in età fascista (1918–1945)* (Rome: Carucci, 1983).

Leuzzi, V.A. and Esposito, G. (eds), *Terra di frontiera. Profughi ed ex internati in Puglia 1943–1945* (Bari: Progedit, 2000).

Levi della Torre, S., 'Fine del dopoguerra e sintomi antisemitici', *Rivista di Storia Contemporanea*, 3 (1984), pp.437–544.

Levi della Torre, S., *Mosaico. Attualità e inattualità degli ebrei* (Turin: Rosenberg & Sellier, 1994).

Levi, E., *Memorie di una vita* (Modena: STEM Mucchi, 1972).

Levi, F. (ed.), *L'ebreo in oggetto. L'applicazione della normativa antiebraica a Torino, 1938–1943* (Turin: Zamorani, 1991).

Levi, F., *L'identità imposta. Un padre ebreo di fronte alle leggi razziali di Mussolini* (Turin: Zamorani, 1996).

Levi, F. (ed.), *Le case e le cose. Persecuzione degli ebrei torinesi nelle carte dell'EGELI, 1938–1945* (Turin: Compagnia San Paolo, 1998).

Levi, Le., *Contro i dinosauri. Scritti civili 1931–1972*, edited by Arturo Marzano (Naples: L'Ancora del Mediterraneo, 2011).

Levi, Li., *Se va via il re* (Rome: e/o, 1996).

Levi, P., *Se questo è un uomo* (Turin: Einaudi, 1958).

Levi, P., *Il sistema periodico* (Turin: Einaudi, 1975).

Lévy, B.-H., *L'idéologie française* (Paris: Grasset, 1981).

Levis Sullam, S., *Una comunità immaginata. Gli ebrei a Venezia (1900–1938)*, postface by A. Cavaglion (Milan: Unicopli, 2001).

Lombroso, S., *Diario di una madre (si può stampare). Pagine vissute* (Rome: Dalmatia, 1945).

Lorenzini, S., *L'Italia e il trattato di pace del 1947* (Bologna: Il Mulino, 2007).

Luconi, S., 'Recent Trends in the Study of Italian Anti-Semitism under the Fascist Regime', *Patterns of Prejudice*, 1 (2004), pp.1–17.

Luzzatto, A., 'Autocoscienza e identità ebraica', in C. Vivanti (ed.), *Gli ebrei in Italia*, in *Storia d'Italia, Annali,* vol. XI/2 (Torino: Einaudi, 1997), pp.1831–99.

Luzzatto, S., *Il corpo del duce. Un cadaver tra immaginazione, storia e memoria* (Turin: Einaudi, 1998).

Luzzatto, S., *La crisi dell'antifascismo* (Turin: Einaudi, 2004).

Luzzatto Voghera, G., 'Cenni storici per una ricostruzione del dibattito sulla riforma religiosa nell'Italia ebraica', *RMI*, 1–2, LIX (1993), pp.47–70.

Luzzatto Voghera, G., *Il prezzo dell'eguaglianza. Il dibattito sull'emancipazione degli ebrei in Italia (1781–1848)* (Milan: Angeli, 1998).

Maida, B. (ed.), *1938. I bambini e le leggi razziali* (Florence: La Giuntina, 2000).

Maifreda, G., 'La riaggregazione della comunità israelitica di Milano (1945–1953)', *Storia in Lombardia*, 2–3 (1998), pp.619–42.

Maiocchi, R., *Scienza e fascismo* (Rome: Carocci, 2004).

Malocchi, R., *Scienza italiana e razzismo fascista* (Florence: La Nuova Italia, 1999).

Mangoni, L., *Civiltà della crisi. Gli intellettuali tra fascismo e antifascismo*, in F. Barbagallo (ed.), *Storia dell'Italia repubblicana*, vol. I, *La costruzione della democrazia. Dalla caduta del fascismo agli anni cinquanta* (Turin: Einaudi, 1994).

Mangoni, L., *Pensare i libri. La casa editrice Einaudi dagli anni Trenta agli anni Sessanta* (Turin: Bollati Boringhieri, 1999).

Mankowitz, Z.W., *Life between Memory and Hope: The Survivors of the Holocaust in Occupied Germany* (Cambridge: Cambridge University Press, 2002).

Mannheim, K., 'The Problem of Generations', in *Essays on the Sociology of Knowledge* (London: Routledge, 1972).

Mantovani, C., *Rigenerare la società: L'eugenetica in Italia dalle origini ottocentesche agli anni Trenta* (Catanzaro: Rubettino, 2004).

Maria, E., *Before the Dawn: Autobiographical Reflections* (New York: Sheed and Ward, 1954).

Marzano, A., *Una terra per rinascere. Gli ebrei italiani e l'emigrazione in Palestina prima della guerra (1920–1940)*, preface by A. Cavaglion (Genoa and Milan: Marietti, 2003).

Marzano, A., '"Prisoners of Hope" or "Amnesia"? The Italian Holocaust Survivors and Their Aliyah to Israel', *Quest. Issues in Contemporary History*,

1 (April 2010), available at http://www.quest-cdecjournal.it/focus.php?id=194.

Marzano, A. and Simoni, M. (eds), *Roma e Gerusalemme. Israele nella vita politica e culturale italiana 1949–2009* (Genova: ECIG, 2010).

Matard-Bonucci, M.-A., *L'Italia fascista e la persecuzione degli ebrei* (Bologna: Il Mulino, 2008).

Mayda, G., *Ebrei sotto Salò. La persecuzione antisemita 1943–1945* (Milan: Feltrinelli, 1978).

Mazzini, E., 'La memoria del 1938 nella stampa periodica ebraica. Come ricordare?', *XXI Secolo*, 17 (2010).

Mazzini, E., 'The Presence of Anti-Semitism in the Catholic World. The Case of the "Enciclopedia Cattolica" (1948–1954)', *Quest. Issues in Contemporary History*, 1 (April 2010); available at http://www.quest-cdecjournal.it/focus.php?id=196.

Menici, S., 'L'opera del Joint in Italia. Un "piano Marshall" ebraico per la ricostruzione', *RMI*, a special issue edited by L. Picciotto Fargion, *Saggi sull'ebraismo italiano del Novecento in onore di Luisella Mortasa Ottolenghi*, 1, LXIX (2003), pp.593–618.

Meyers Feinstein, M., *Holocaust Survivors in Post-War Germany (1945–1957)*, (Cambridge: Cambridge University Press, 2009).

Miccoli, G., 'Tra memoria, rimozioni e manipolazioni. Aspetti dell'atteggiamento cattolico verso la "Shoah"', *Qualestoria*, 3 (1991), pp.161–88.

Miccoli, G., *Due nodi. La libertà religiosa e le relazioni con gli ebrei*, in G. Alberigo (ed.), *Storia del Concilio Vaticano II*, vol. 4 (Bologna: Peeters/Il Mulino, 1999), pp.199–219.

Michaelis, M., *Mussolini and the Jews: German-Italian Relations and the Jewish Question in Italy, 1922–1945* (London: Clarendon Press, 1978).

Milano, A., *Storia degli ebrei in Italia* (Turin: Einaudi, 1992 [1963]).

Minerbi, A., 'Tra nazionalizzazione e persecuzione. La scuola ebraica in Italia 1930–1943', *Contemporanea*, 4 (1998), pp.703–30.

Minerbi, S.I., *La belva in gabbia. Eichmann* (Milan: Longanesi, 1962).

Minerbi, S.I., *Un ebreo fra D'Annunzio e il sionismo. Raffaele Cantoni*, preface by R. De Felice (Rome: Bonacci, 1992).

Ministry of Foreign Affairs, *Relazione sull'opera svolta dal Ministero degli Affari Esteri per la tutela delle comunità ebraiche (1938–1941)* (Rome, no date [1946]).

Momigliano, A., *Essays on Ancient and Modern Judaism*, edited by S. Berti (Chicago, IL: University of Chicago Press, 1994).

Momigliano, E., *Storia tragica e grottesca del razzismo fascista* (Milan: Mondadori, 1946).

Momigliano Levi, P. (ed.), *Storia e memoria della deportazione. Modelli di ricerca e di comunicazione in Italia e in Francia* (Florence: La Giuntina, 1996).

Moos, C., *Ausgrenzung, Internierung, Deportation. Antisemitismus und Gewalt im spaten italienischen Faschismus, 1938–1945* (Zurich: Chronos, 2004).

Morpurgo, L., *Caccia all'uomo! Vita sofferenze e beffe. Pagine di diario 1938–1944* (Rome: Dalmatia, 1946).

Mortara, A., 'In attesa di miracoli. Gli ebrei in Italia dal 1938 al 1940', *RMI*, 1–2, LIV (1988), pp.37–47.

Musselli, I., *Chiesa e Stato dalla Resistenza alla Costituente* (Turin: Giappichelli, 1990).

Nathan, V., *Roma 1943–45. Una famiglia nella tempesta*, preface by F. Boesch, introduction by M.I. Macisti (Rome: SEAM, 1998).

Newman, L.I., *'Chief Rabbi' of Rome Becomes a Catholic: A Study in Fright and Spite* (New York: Renascence Press, 1945).

Nidam Orvieto, I., 'Lettere a Mussolini. Gli ebrei italiani e le leggi antiebraiche', *RMI*, 1, LXIX (2003), pp.321–46.

Nidam Orvieto, I., 'Fighting Oblivion: The CDEC and its Impact on Italian Holocaust Historiography', in D. Bankier and D. Michaman (eds), *Holocaust Historiography in Context: Emrgence, Challenges, Polemics and Achievements* (New York and Jerusalem: Berghahn Books/Yad Vashem, 2008), pp.293–304.

Ofir, A., 'La nuova religione di Israele', *Il Mulino*, 1 (1989), pp.92–100.

Orvieto, L., *Storia di Angiolo e Laura* (Florence: Olschki, 2001).

Ottani, G. (ed.), *Un popolo piange. La tragedia degli ebrei italiani* (Milan: Spartaco Giovene Editore, 1945).

Oz, A., *The Slopes of Lebanon* (San Diego, CA, New York and London: Harcourt Brace Jovanovich, 1989 [1987]).

Paiano, M., 'Il dibattito sui riflessi dell'antisemitismo nella liturgia cattolica', *Studi Storici*, 3 (2000), pp.647–710.

Pardo, F., *L'ebraismo secondo B. Croce e la filosofia crociana* (Florence: Tipografia Giuntina, 1948).

Passerini, L., 'La giovinezza metafora del cambiamento sociale. Due dibattiti sui giovani nell'Italia fascista e negli Stati Uniti degli anni Cinquanta', in G. Levi and G. Schmitt (eds), *Storia dei giovani. 2 L'età contemporanea* (Bari: Laterza, 1994).

Patt, A. and Berkowitz, M. (eds), *We Are Here: New Approaches to Jewish Displaced Persons in Post–War Germany* (Detroit, MI: Wayne State University Press, 2010).

Patt, A.J., *Finding Home and Homeland: Jewish Youth and Zionism in the Aftermath of the Holocaust* (Detroit, MI: Wayne State University Press, 2009).

Pavan, I., *Il Comandante. La vita di Federico Jarach e la memoria di un'epoca 1874–1951* (Milan: Proedi, 2001).

Pavan, I., *Tra indifferenza e oblio. Le conseguenze economiche delle leggi razziali in Italia (1938–1970)* (Florence: Le Monnier, 2004).

Pavan, I. and Pelini, F., *La doppia epurazione. L'Universita di Pisa e le leggi razziali tra guerra e dopoguerra* (Bologna: Il Mulino, 2009).

Pavan, I. and Schwarz, G. (eds), *Gli ebrei in Italia tra persecuzione fascista e reintegrazione postbellica* (Florence: La Giuntina, 2001).

Pavone, C., *Una guerra civile. Saggio storico sulla moralità nella Resistenza* (Turin: Bollati Boringhieri, 1994 [1991]), Chapter 1.

Peck, A.J. (ed.), *American Jewish Archives, Cincinnati. The papers of the World Jewish Congress 1945–1950: Liberation and the Saving Remnant* (New York and London: Garland, 1990).

Pezzana, A., *Quest'anno a Gerusalemme. Gli ebrei italiani in Israele*, with an essay by V.D. Segre (Milan: Il Corbaccio, 1997).

Picciotto Fargion, L., 'Eloisa e il CDEC', *RMI*, 1–3, XLVII (1983), pp.9–44.

Picciotto Fargion, L. (ed.), *L'immagine dell'ebreo nell'Italia degli anni Ottanta*, special issue of *RMI*, 3, LVI (1990).

Picciotto Fargion, L., *Il libro della memoria. Gli ebrei deportati dall'Italia 1943–45* (Milan: Mursia, 2002).

Pieraccini, P., *Gerusalemme, luoghi santi e comunità religiose nella politica internazionale* (Bologna: EDB, 1997).

Pinto, V., 'Sionismo e "movimento Ebraico". La percezione del nazionalismo ebraico nelle carte della Direzione Generale Pubblica Sicurezza conservate nell'Archivio Centrale dello Stato (1927–1939)', *RMI*, 3, LXVI (2000), pp.37–62.

Pinto, V. (ed.), 'L'Italia fascista e la "questione palestinese"', *Contemporanea*, 1 (2003), pp.102–25.

Piperno, G.J., 'Fermenti di vita giovanile ebraica a Roma durante il periodo delle leggi razziali e dopo la liberazione della città', in D. Carpi, A. Milano and U. Nahon (eds), *Scritti in memoria di Enzo Sereni* (Jerusalem: Sally Mayer Foundation, 1970), pp.293–313.

Piperno, G.J., 'I soldati di Eretz Israel e la riapertura della scuola di Roma', *RMI*, 7–9, XXXVI (1970), pp.327–42.

Piperno, G.J., *Ebraismo, Sionismo, Halutzismo* (Rome: Carucci, 1976).

Piussi, A.M., *E li insegnerai ai tuoi figli. Educazione ebraica dalle leggi razziali ad oggi* (Florence: La Giuntina, 1997).

Piussi, A.M. (ed.), *Presto apprendere, tardi dimenticar. L'educazione ebraica nell'Italia contemporanea* (Milan: Angeli, 1998).

Poggiolini, I., *Diplomazia della transizione. Gli Alleati e il problema del trattato di pace italiano (1945–1947)*, preface by E. di Nolfo (Florence: Ponte alle Grazie, 1990).

Polese Remaggi, L., *'Il Ponte' di Calamandrei 1945–1956* (Florence: Olschki, 2001).

Poliakov, L., *La condition des Juifs en France*, foreword by L. Schneersohn, preface by J. Godard (Paris: Édition du Centre, 1946).

Poliakov, L., *Breviaire de la haine: le III Reich et les Juifs* (Paris: Calman–Levy, 1951).

Poliakov, L. and Sabille, J., *Gli ebrei sotto l'occupazione italiana* (Milan: Comunità, 1956).

Prato, D., *Dal Pergamo della Comunità di Roma* (Rome, 1950).

Preti, L., *I miti dell'impero e della razza nell'Italia degli anni '30* (Rome: Opere Nuove, 1965).

Quartararo, R., *Italia e Stati Uniti, gli anni difficili (1945–1952)* (Naples: Edizioni Scientifiche Italiane, 1986).

Ranzato, G., *Il linciaggio di Carretta. Violenza politica e ordinaria violenza* (Milan: Il Saggiatore, 1997).

Reitlinger, G., *La soluzione finale. Il tentative di sterminio degli Ebrei d'Europa 1939–1945* (Milano: Il Saggiatore, 1962 [or. ed. *The Final Solution: The Attempt to Exterminate the Jews in Europe 1939–1945* (London: Vallentine Mitchell, 1953)]).

Riccardi, A., *Roma 'città sacra'? Dalla conciliazione all'operazione Sturzo* (Milan: Vita e Pensiero, 1978).

Riccardi, L., *Il problema Israele. Diplomazia italiana e PCI di fronte allo Stato ebraico* (Milan: Guerrini e Associati, 2006).

Ricci, A.G. (ed.), *Verbali del Consiglio dei Ministri (1943–1948)*, 10 vols (Rome: Presidenza del Consiglio dei Ministri, 1995).

Ridolfi, M., *Le feste nazionali* (Bologna: Il Mulino, 2003).

Rigano, G., *Il caso Zolli. L'itinerario di un intellettuale in bilico tra fedi, culture e nazioni* (Milan: Guerrini e Associati, 2006).

Rodogno, D., *Il nuovo ordine mediterraneo. Le politiche di occupazione dell'Italia fascista in Europa (1940–1943)* (Turin: Bollati Boringhieri, 2003); English edition: *Fascism's European Empire: Italian Occupation During the Second World War* (Cambridge: Cambridge University Press, 2006).

Romano, G., 'Via eroica. Gli olé d'Italia caduti per Erez Israel', *RMI*, 7–8, XVI (1950), pp.106–15.

Rossi, G.S., *La destra e gli ebrei. Una storia italiana* (Catanzaro: Rubettino, 2003).

Rossi, M.G., 'Il governo Scelba tra crisi del centrismo e ritorno anticomunista', *Italia Contemporanea*, 46 (1994), pp.791–806.

Rossi-Doria, A., *Memoria e storia. Il caso della deportazione*, preface by P. Jedlowski (Catanzaro: Rubettino, 1998).

Roth, C., 'Gino Luzzatto and Jewish History', *Nuova Rivista Storica*, 49 (1965).

Rousso, H., *La syndrome de Vichy de 1944 à nos jours* (Paris: Seuil, 1990).

Rubinstein, R.L., 'Alliance et divinité. L'Holocauste et la problematique de la foi', *Pardès*, special issue edited by S. Trigano, *Penser Auschwitz*, 9–10 (1989), pp.99–117.

Rusconi, G.E., *Possiamo fare a meno di una religion civile?* (Bari: Laterza, 1999).

Rusconi, G.E., *Germania Italia Europa. Dallo stato di potenza alla 'potenza civile'* (Turin: Einaudi, 2003).

Rusconi, G.E., 'Religione civile e identità italiana', *Il Mulino*, 4 (2003), pp.832–8.

Sabille, J., 'L'attitude des Italiens envers les Juifs persecuté en Croatie', *Le Monde Juif*, 46–7 (1951).

Sabille, J., 'L'attitude des Italiens à l'égard des Juifs en Grèce occupée', *Le Monde Juif*, 49 (1951).

Sacerdoti, Giorgio, *Ricordi di un ebreo Bolognese. Illusioni e delusioni 1929–1945*, preface by R. De Felice (Rome: Bonacci, 1983).

Sachar, H.M., *A History of the Jews in America* (New York: Knopf, 1992).

Santese, A., 'Il partito comunista italiano e la questione palestinese 1945–1956', *Mondo Contemporaneo*, 2 (2007), pp.63–104.

Sarfatti, M. (ed.), *1938. Le leggi contro gli ebrei*, *RMI*, 1–2, XXXII (1988).

Sarfatti, M., 'L'antisemitismo fascista e l'interruzione della stampa ebraica italiana nel 1938', *Bailamme*, 11–12 (1992), pp.165–213.

Sarfatti, M., *Mussolini contro gli ebrei. Cronaca dell'elaborazione delle leggi razziali* (Turin: Zamorani, 1993).

Sarfatti, M., 'Fascist Italy and German Jews in South-Eastern France in July 1943', *Journal of Modern Italian Studies*, 3 (1998), pp.318–27.

Sarfatti, M. (ed.), *Funzioni dei centri di storia e cultura ebraica nella società contemporanea* (Milan: Proedi, 1998).

Sarfatti, M. (ed.), *Il ritorno alla vita. Vicende e diritti degli ebrei in Italia dopo la seconda guerra mondiale* (Florence: La Giuntina, 1998).

Sarfatti, M., 'La Storia della persecuzione antiebraica di Renzo De Felice. Contesto, dimensione cronologica e fonti', *Qualestoria*, 2 (2004), pp.11–28.

Sarfatti, M., *Gli ebrei nell'Italia fascista. Vicende, identità, persecuzione* (Turin: Einaudi, 2000); English edition: *The Jews in Mussolini's Italy: From Equality to Persecution* (Madison, WI: University of Wisconsin Press, 2006).

Sarfatti, M. (ed.), *La Repubblica sociale italiana a Desenzano. Giovanni Preziosi e l'Ispettorato generale per la razza* (Florence: La Giuntina, 2008).

Sasso, G., *Per invigilare me stesso. I taccuini di lavoro di B. Croce* (Bologna: Il Mulino, 1989).

Savaldi, M., 'I campeggi ebraici (1931–1939)', *Storia Contemporanea*, 6 (1988), pp.1121–52.

Schächter, E., *The Jews of Italy, 1848–1915: Between Tradition and Transformation* (London and Portland, OR: Vallentine Mitchell, 2010).

Schwarz, G., *Tu mi devi seppellir. Riti funebri e culto nazionale alle origini della Repubblica* (Turin: UTET, 2010).

Scoppola, P., *La repubblica dei partiti. Evoluzione e crisi di un sistema politico 1945–1995* (Bologna: Il Mulino, 1997).

Segev, T., *The Seventh Million: The Israelis and the Holocaust* (New York: Hill & Wang, 1993).

Segre, A., *Memorie di vita ebraica*, preface by R. De Felice (Rome: Bonacci, 1979).
Segre Amar, S., *Il mio ghetto* (Milan: Garzanti, 1987).
Segre, C., *Per curiosità. Una specie di autobiografia* (Turin: Einaudi, 1999).
Segre, R., *Venti mesi*, preface by N. Tranfaglia (Palermo: Sellerio, 1995).
Segre, V.D., *Storia di un ebreo fortunato* (Milan: Garzanti, 1985).
Sereni, A., *I clandestini del mare. L'emigrazione ebraica in terra d'Israele dal 1945 al 1948* (Milan: Mursia, 1973).
Sereni, E., *Le origini del fascismo*, edited by Y. Viterbo and with an introduction by M.G. Meriggi (Florence: La Nuova Italia, 2000).
Sereni, En. and Sereni, Em., *Politica e utopia. Lettere 1926–1943*, edited by D. Bidussa and M.G. Meriggi (Florence: La Nuova Italia, 2000).
Shelah, M., *Un debito di gratitudine. Storia dei rapport tra l'Esercito Italiano e gli ebrei in Dalmazia (1941–1943)* (Rome: USSME, 1991 [1986]).
Simoncelli, P., *Renzo De Felice. La formazione intellettuale* (Florence: Le Lettere, 2001).
Smolensky, E.M. and Vigevani Jarach, V. (eds), *Tante voci, una storia. Italiani ebrei in Argentina 1938–1948* (Bolgna: Il Mulino, 1998).
Soddu, P., *L'Italia del dopoguerra 1947–1953. Una democrazia precaria* (Rome: Editori Riuniti, 1998).
Sorani, S., *L'assistenza ai profughi ebrei in Italia (1933–1947). Contributo alla storia della 'Delasem'* (Rome: Carucci, 1983).
Spinosa, A., 'Le persecuzioni razziali in Italia', *Il Ponte*, 7 (1952), pp.964–78; 8, pp.1078–96; 11, pp.1604–22; 9 (1953), 7, pp.950–68.
Spitzer, L., *Hotel Bolivia: The Culture of Memory in a Refuge from Nazism* (New York: Hill & Wang, 1999).
Steinberg, A.J., *All or Nothing: The Axis and the Holocaust 1941–1943* (London and New York: Routledge, 1990).
Stille, A., *Uno su mille. Cinque famiglie ebraiche durante il fascismo* (Milan: Mondadori, 1991).
Stuart Hughes, H., *Prisoners of Hope: The Silver Age of Italian Jews 1924–1974* (Cambridge, MA: Harvard University Press, 1996).
Szafran, M., *Les juifs dans la politique française. De 1945 à nos jours* (Paris: Flamarion, 1990).
Tabet, A., 'Venticinque anni di libertà costituzionale', *RMI*, 6, XXXVI (1970), pp.291–301.
Tagliacozzo, A. (ed.), *Sulle orme della rinascita. Cronaca e memorie del Movimento Hechaluz italiano dal '44 al '54* (Rome: Litos, 2004).
Tagliacozzo, M., 'Attività dei soldati di Eretz Israel in Italia (1943–1946). Il corpo ausiliario dei soldati palestinesi nell'armata di liberazione inglese', *RMI*, 1, LXIX (2003), pp.575–92.
Taglicozzo Di Castro, F. and Di Castro, F., 'La memoria della persecuzione antiebraica. Due generazioni a confronto', *Parolechiave*, 16 (1998), pp.159–72.

Taguieff, P.A., *La nouvelle judéophobie* (Paris: Mille et une nuits, 2002).
Tas, L., *Cartina rossa del Medio Oriente. La storia dello stato di Israele raccontata dall'Unità*, preface by A. Cavallari (Rome: La Voce, 1971).
Tempestini, A., *Laici e clericali nel sistema partitico italiano. La constituente e l'articolo 7* (Milan: Angeli, 1987).
Terracini, L., 'Cacciati dalla scuola. Carteggio ebraico '38', *Belfagor*, 4 (1990), pp.444–50.
Toaff, E., *Perfidi giudei fratelli maggiori* (Milan: Mondadori, 1987).
Todorov, T., *L'homme dépaysé* (Paris: Seuil, 1997).
Tonini, C., 'The Jews in Poland after the Second World War: Most Recent Contributions of Polish Historiography', *Quest. Issues in Contemporary History*, 1 (April 2010), available at http://www.quest–cdecjournal.it/focus.php?issue=1&id=211.
Toscano, M., 'Fermenti culturali ed esperienze organizzative della gioventù ebraica italiana (1911–1925)', *Storia Contemporanea*, 6, XII (1982), pp.915–61.
Toscano, M. (ed.), *L'abrogazione delle leggi razziali in Italia (1943–1987)*, preface by G. Spadolini (Rome: Servizio Studi del Senato, 1988).
Toscano, M., *La 'porta di Sion'. L'Italia e l'immigrazione clandestina ebraica in Palestina (1945–1948)* (Bologna: Il Mulino, 1990).
Toscano, M., 'Renzo De Felice storico dell'ebraismo e dell'antisemitismo', in G. Alberti and G. Parlato (eds), *Renzo De Felice. Il lavoro dello storico tra ricerca e didattica* (Milan: LED, 1999), pp.191–202.
Toscano, M., *Ebraismo e antisemitismo in Italia. Dal 1848 alla Guerra dei sei giorni* (Milan: Angeli, 2003).
Toscano, M., 'L'antisemitismo nell'Italia contemporanea: note, ipotesi e problemi di ricerca', *Zakhor*, VI (2003), pp.21–33.
Toscano, M. and Sofia, F. (eds), *Stato nazionale ed emancipazione ebraica* (Rome: Bonacci, 1992).
Treves, A., *Le nascite e la politica nell'Italia del Novecento* (Milan: LED, 2001).
Treves, B. (ed.), *Tre vite dall'ultimo '800 alla metà del '900. Studi e memorie di Emilio-Emanuele-Ennio Artom* (Florence: Casa Editrice Israel, 1954).
Treves, P., 'Antifascisti ebrei o antifascism ebraico?', *RMI*, 6, XLVII (1981), pp.138–49.
Treves Alcalay, L., *Con occhi di bambina* (Florence: La Giuntina, 1994).
Trigano, S., *La République et les Juifs après Copernic* (Paris: Les Presses D'aujourd'hui, 1982).
Trigano, S., 'From Individual to Collectivity: The Rebirth of the "Jewish Nation" in France', in F. Malino and B. Wasserstein (eds), *The Jews in Modern France* (Hanover, NH and London: Brandeis University Press, 1985).
Trimbur, D., *De la Shoah à la réconciliation? La question des relations RFA-*

Israël (1949–1956) (Paris: CNRS, 2000).

Turi, G., *Il mecenate, il filosofo, il gesuita. L''Enciclopedia Italiana' specchio della nazione* (Bologna: Il Mulino. 2002).

Turi, G., *Lo stato educatore: politica e intellettuali nell'Italia fascista* (Bari: Laterza, 2002).

Valabrega, G. (ed.), *Gli ebrei in Italia durante il fascismo*, vol. I (Milan: FGEI, 1961); vol. II (Milan: CDEC, 1962); vol. III (Milan: CDEC, 1963).

Valabrega, G., *Ebrei fascismo, sionismo* (Urbino: Argalia, 1974).

Valentina Di Palma, S., 'Storia e memoria di bambini e adolescent nella Shoà', *RMI*, 3, LXVII (2001), pp.57–84.

Vansant, J., *Reclaiming Heimat: Trauma and Mourning in Memoirs by Jewish Austrian Remigrés* (Detroit, IL: Wayne State University Press, 2001).

Ventrone, V., *La cittadinanza repubblicana. Forma-partito e identità nazionale alle origini della democrazia italiana (1943–1948)* (Bologna: Il Mulino, 1996).

Ventura, A., 'Renzo De Felice. Il fascismo e gli ebrei', in *Incontro di studio sull'opera di Renzo De Felice* (Rome: Giunta Centrale per gli Studi Storici, 2000).

Ventura, L., *Ebrei con il Duce. La Nostra Bandiera 1934–38* (Turin: Zamorani, 2001).

Vismara Missiroli, M., 'Caro Falco. Lettere di Francesco Ruffini a Mario Falco (1906–1932)', *Quaderni di diritto e politica ecclesiastica*, 1 (1993), pp.229–90.

Vitale, M.A., 'Les persécutions contre les juifs en Italie', in Centre de Documentation Juive Contemporaine (ed.), *Les Juifs en Europe (1939–1945). Rapports présentés à la première conférence européene des commissions historiques et des centres de documentation juifs* (Paris: Edition du Centre, 1949).

Vivanti, C. (ed.), *Gli ebrei in Italia*. Storia *d'Italia, Annali*, vol. XI/2 (Turin: Einaudi, 1997).

Voghera, G., *Quaderno d'Israele* (Pordenone: Edizioni Studio Tesi, 1986 [1967]).

Voigt, K., *Il rifugio precario. Gli esuli in Italia dal 1933 al 1945*, 2 vols (Florence: La Nuva Italia, 1993 and 1996).

Wasserstein, B., *Vanishing Diaspora: The Jews in Europe since 1945* (Cambridge, MA: Harvard University Press, 1996).

Weber, J. (ed.), *Jewish Identities in the New Europe* (London and Washington, DC: The Littman Library of Jewish Civilization, 1994).

Weillier, G., *La bufera. Una famiglia di ebrei milanesi con i partigiani dell'Ossola* (Florence: La Giuntina, 2002).

Wieviorka, A., *Déportation et Génocide. Entre la mémoire et l'oubli* (Paris: Plon, 1992).

Wieviorka, A. and Mouchard, C. (eds), *La Shoah: témoignages, saviors, oeuvres*

(Orléans: Cercil/PUV, 1999).

Winter, J. and Sivan, E., 'Setting the Framework', in J. Winter and E. Sivan (eds), *War and Remembrance in the Twentieth Century* (Cambridge: Cambridge University Press, 1999).

Wyman, M., *DPs: Europe's Displaced Persons 1945–1951* (London and Toronto: Associated University Presses, 1989).

Yerushalmy, Y.H., *Zakhor: Jewish History and Jewish Memory* (Seattle, WA: University of Washington Press, 1996).

Young, J.E., *The Texture of Memory: Holocaust Memorials and Meaning* (New Haven, CT and London: Yale University Press, 1993).

Young, J.E. (ed.), *The Art of Memory: Holocaust Memorials in History* (New York: The Jewish Museum, 1994).

Zargani, A., *Certe promesse d'amore* (Bologna: Il Mulino, 1997).

Zargani, A., *Per violino solo. La mia infanzia nell'aldiquà* (Bologna: Il Mulino, 1997).

Zerthal, I., 'Du bon usage du souvenir', *Le Débat*, 58 (1990), pp.92–103.

Zerthal, I., *From Catastrophe to Power: Holocaust Survivors and the Emergence of Israel* (Los Angeles and Berkeley, CA: University of California Press, 1998).

Zerthal, I., *Israel's Holocaust and the Politics of Nationhood* (Cambridge: Cambridge University Press, 2005).

Zerubavel, Y., *Recovered Roots: Collective Memory and the Making of Israeli National Tradition* (Chicago, IL and London, University of Chicago Press, 1995).

Zweig, R.W., *German Reparations and the Jewish World: A History of the Claims Conference*, 2nd ed. (London: Frank Cass, 2001).

Index

Please note that page numbers relating to Notes will have the letter 'n' following the page number.

M

N

O

P

Q

R